FEDERATION OF FLY FISHERS

FLY PATTERN ENCYCLOPEDIA

Edited by Al & Gretchen Beatty

Photographed by Jim Schollmeyer

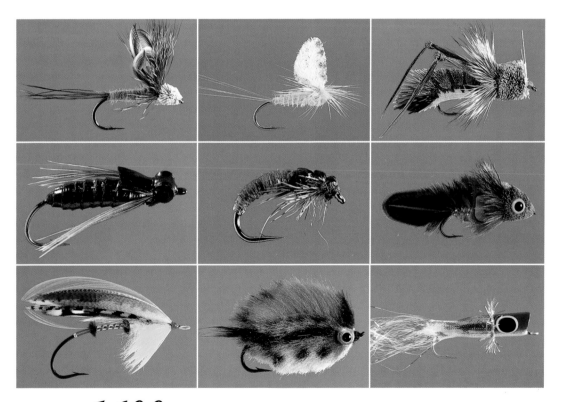

Over 1600 Of The Best Fly Patterns!

FEDERATION OF FLY FISHERS

FLY PATTERN ENCYCLOPEDIA

Edited by Al & Gretchen Beatty
Photographed by Jim Schollmeyer

Over 1600 Of The Best Fly Patterns!

Frank Amato
PORTLAND

ACKNOWLEDGEMENTS

Completing a book like this is always a combined effort with many different people participating. We want to recognize a few who stand above the rest. A very special recognition must go to Greg Pitts, Dave and Emily Whitlock, Bruce Staples (who started Al on his demonstration fly tying career), Gary Grant, Judy Lehmberg, Tom Broderidge, Tom Tripi, and Nick Amato and the staff at Frank Amato Publications. Each page herein is a tribute to the hundreds of Federation of Fly Fishers fly tiers who donated their time, effort, and flies to the success of this book. We could not have competed this book with out your help. Our thanks to all of you.

—Al & Gretchen Beatty
Delta, Colorado

Published in 2000 by Frank Amato Publications, Inc.
P.O. Box 82112, Portland, Oregon 97282
(503) 653-8108
www.amatobooks.com

Softbound ISBN: 1-57188-208-1
Softbound UPC: 0-66066-00422-2
Spiral Hardbound ISBN: 1-57188-209-X
Spiral Hardbound UPC: 0-66066-00423-9

Flies photographed by Jim Schollmeyer
Scenic Photographs:
Nick Amato, 97
Jeff Edvalds, 153
Ken Morrish, 48, 122, 186
Brian O'Keefe, 10
Scott Ripley, title page

Book design and layout: Tony Amato

Printed in Singapore by Star Standard Ind. Pte. Ltd

5 7 9 10 8 6 4

Contents

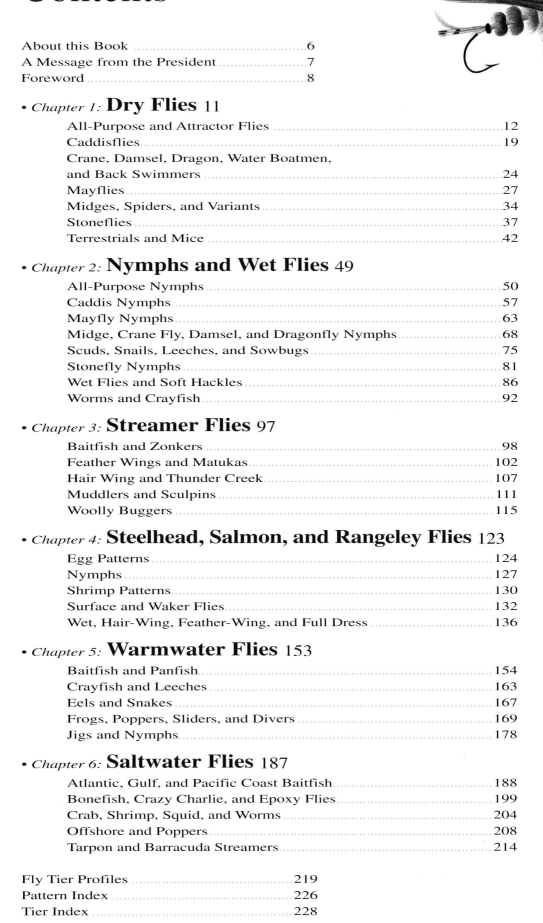

ABOUT THIS BOOK

By Al Beatty

Photographer Jim Schollmeyer and Frank Amato first discussed the idea behind this book after a Federation of Fly Fishers' regional conclave. At this FFF Conclave (as with almost all such expositions), demonstration fly tiers were an important part of the show and its success. They observed the simple formula of selfless sharing of ideas and techniques with fellow members that sets the Federation apart from other organizations focused on conservation or education issues. Recognizing the formula, their discussion led to the concept of a pattern book from the master demonstration fly tiers themselves.

Simply stated, this book is a Federation of Fly Fishers' Conclave taken to the next level, a level that allows the reader to enjoy the learning and sharing in the comfort of their own home. The flies, ideas, and techniques shared herein are from the "best of the best" demonstration fly tiers North America has to offer. The tiers are the famous as well as the unknown with one simple characteristic in common; they freely share their knowledge. Many of the unpublished patterns in these pages contain materials, tips, tricks, or gems of information never before seen.

As you leaf through these pages, you will get from them just what you would if you spent time in the fly tying area at any FFF function. At such a show, if you dedicate time observing the individual tiers, you can learn the information, tips, or tricks they are demonstrating. If instead you casually walk through the area without stopping to observe more closely you may not learn as much. This book is no different. The knowledge is here, you just need to take the time to bring each gem to the surface.

After many years of tying and observing fly tying all over the world, I assumed I had "seen it all" when it comes to "dressing the fly," to use the British vernacular. I was wrong. The flies we have received for this book have been a real education for me. I learned many new tips, ideas, and tricks; you can too. Enjoy!

—*Al Beatty*
Delta, Colorado

A Message from the President

By Greg Pitts

Fly tying is an interesting sport unto itself. It requires a certain manual dexterity (although not as much as the non-tier might think). It requires a sense of proportion and the discipline to replicate patterns. Once you have mastered the basics, it becomes creative. At the highest levels, it is an art form.

Bringing exceptionally talented fly tiers together at one location has always been a hallmark of the Federation of Fly Fishers. It began in 1965 when the FFF was formed. It continues today. Each year at shows all over the country dozens of the best tiers in the world can be seen. From Mountain Home, Arkansas to Eugene, Oregon; from Long Beach, California to Pensacola, Florida; and lots of places in between. One of the joys of the FFF shows is watching everyone freely sharing their skills, secrets, and techniques at the tying bench. Everyone benefits from the sharing. The sport is the better for it.

Randall Kaufmann may have said it best in the introductory chapter to his book, *Tying Dry Flies*: "The Federation of Fly Fishers Conclave presents the best array of tiers possible under one roof." Simply put, the best, most innovative fly tiers in the world share their skills at FFF events all over the country. This book is an effort to bring those tiers together to share their expertise.

Fly tying almost implores people to be innovative. In this collection of fly patterns you have a chance to see how some of the best tiers in the world have developed new patterns or applications for materials. What has always fascinated me in fly tying has been watching new solutions to old problems. You'll find plenty of new patterns and techniques in this book.

This book offers patterns for every type of fly fishing. It's only fair that it should. The Federation of Fly Fishers supports fly fishing efforts for all types of fish in all types of waters. We are not limited to cold waters, warm water or salt water. We embrace it all. We encourage fly fishing as the preferred method of angling no matter what the quarry. In addition, we encourage catch-and-release fishing, always have.

This book is a collaborative effort of the members of the FFF. A special thanks has to go to Al and Gretchen Beatty who volunteered their effort to edit these pages. The contributors and editors have all donated their time and expertise for this book. Thank you, one and all!

The royalties from the sale of this book will be used to support the ongoing efforts of the Federation of Fly Fishers. Our mission is to Conserve, Restore and Educate through Fly Fishing. As I said above, we focus on all fish in all waters. It is who we are. I encourage you to join us.

—Greg Pitts
President, FFF
Eugene, OR

FOREWORD

By Dave Whitlock

I've often wondered which came first, the fly or the fly rod. When I discovered fly fishing at the age of eight, it was first by tying a crude fly. A year later I got my first fly rod. Looking back now, more than fifty-seven years, it seems that fly tying has been the backbone of my personal progress as a successful fly fisher. I truly feel that the history, progress, and future of fly fishing evolves greatly around fly tying. In fact, I'll bet few fly tiers would not agree that fly tying is at least the other half of fly fishing.

Over the years, two fly tying landmarks have advanced this sport immensely. The first one, of which this book is a product, was the start of the Federation of Fly Fishers' tying program. Our FFF provides the ideal stage to showcase fly tying by discovering and bringing together the tying talents (amateur and professional) of the world to a stage where we can all learn by observing and contributing our ideas to other FFF members as well as new, prospective fly fishers at conclaves, club activities, and in publications.

I can vividly recall the wonderful elation I felt when I was first able to watch other fly tiers that I had idolized from afar. I was actually tying with and talking to my fly tying heroes about their backgrounds, ideas, and tying techniques. Just to sit between them and tie was such an honor! I would say that it was those opportunities that were most responsible for my position in the sport of fly tying today.

Each year at club, regional, and national conclave functions, FFF's fly tying programs encouraged (and continue to encourage) the advancement of fly tying, not just for trout, but also for cool, warm, and tropical fresh- and salt-water species. The completely open-minded approach stimulated us year after year to greatly expand fly fishing so that now we fish nearly every water in the world for nearly every species of fish!

The second landmark became possible after, and because of, the first. As the FFF's fly tying programs grew, the scope and popularity of fly tying grew by leaps and bounds and the demands from non-tiers for retail fly sales began to increase dramatically. However, domestic commercial fly tiers could not meet the demands and soon there was a great shortage of quality

flies. Our economy, cost of living, and the low resale prices of flies prevented the growth of domestic fly manufacturing. Most tiers just couldn't make a living at it and fly fishers could not find enough quality flies with which to fish.

About that time, an outstanding professional fly tier, Dennis Black, a product of FFF's fly tying program, formulated a revolutionary plan to produce a large amount of high-quality flies, at reasonable prices. To solve this handicapping fly shortage, Dennis' idea was to produce the flies in countries where skilled labor was abundant and less expensive (India, Shrilanka, Thailand, and Columbia). What really made it work was that Dennis asked our best-known, most innovative fly tiers to teach his staff of managers how to duplicate the precise materials and methods they used on their popular fly designs. For their assistance, he promised that our flies would be produced with the highest quality control and that we would be granted a royalty payment on every fly he sold of our design. This royalty was a revolutionary approach to fly tying that had never been done on a large scale.

Dennis' company, Umpqua Feather Merchants, created a new, professional fly tier or fly designer and encouraged the thousands of new fly designs they created. It also allowed the industry to expand in scope and sales growth. Today, in large part because of Dennis' ideas, a strong fly fishing retail service in this country is thriving. Now, with plenty of flies, fly fishing can grow as it needs to.

This book is a colorful and useful chronicle and example of the FFF's fly tying program and progress. It will serve all of us involved with fly tying and the Federation of Fly Fishers and our need to have an instructive reference for duplicating these many effective fly designs. Anyone from Buz Buszek Memorial Award recipients to beginner fly fishers will find much value in this book.

The historic and practical value far exceeds the price of it. That price, by the way, is funding future Federation of Fly Fishers fly tying programs. The tiers of the present and future will continue to benefit and improve our sport and the enjoyment of it.

Faithfully yours . . .

By Al Beatty

Although I have no proof, I suspect that at some point in time ancient man observed a fish take some type of a living creature from the water's surface. From this observation the sport of fly fishing and fly tying has blossomed into today's avid study of many species of insects, birds, and mammals that are prey to fish living within the water's confines. Yes, although early man probably first stalked fish with a spear, his hands, or natural bait, he eventually learned to construct rough imitations of the natural critters upon which fish feed. His pursuit of fish for food evolved in time into a sport in which keeping the food source was less important than as the reward in a game of hide and seek.

Photography changed many things in the daily life of the human species, and in time it helped to change some of our sporting attitudes. Although we began by taking photos of the harvest of nature's bounty we eventually learned the picture did not have to represent harvest; it could in fact represent success that did not include keeping the animal. Catch-and-release fly fishing is such a sport and one recommended by Lee Wulff, a founder of the Federation of Fly Fishers.

My evolution as a fly fisher is very much like man's angling history. I started fishing at a very young age for carp near my home in rural Iowa with my trusty bow and arrow. Very soon I was stalking fish with an old steel casting rod and whatever bait seemed appropriate at the time. On my fourteenth birthday I tied my first fly (a bucktail streamer) and soon after my first dry fly (a brown hackle peacock). Shortly thereafter I learned of the challenge and reward of catching fish on the dry fly. This knowledge started me down a path I've pursued now for more than forty years – the stalking of almost all species of fish with a dry fly, including those carp I pursued so many years ago with my bow and arrow. Yes, the dry fly, it is for me!

—*Al Beatty*
Delta, Colorado

All-Purpose and Attractor Flies . . .

Adams Variant

Hook: Dry fly #12 - #16
Thread: Black
Tail: Golden pheasant tippet
Back hackle: Grizzly slightly smaller than front
Body: Yellow ostrich herl
Wings: Grizzly hen
Front hackle: Grizzly slightly larger than back
Head: Thread
Fly Tier: Bruce Harang

Alder Fly Dry

Hook: Mustad 80000, #12 - #20
Thread: Black
Tail: Natural Coq de Leon saddle fibers
Body: Silver tinsel (back section) and peacock herl (thorax section)
Wings: Turkey tail quill segment, rolled and divided
Hackle: Black, palmered over the thorax
Head: Thread
Fly Tier: Al Beatty

The Alder Fly - Dry

Hook: Dry fly #12 - #24
Thread: Black
Body: Bronze peacock herl
Wings: Dark bronze mallard flank fibers
Hackle: Black
Head: Thread
Fly Tier: Jeff Hatton

Attractor Bug

Hook: Dry fly #10
Thread: Black
Body: Round foam & tape, green & black
Wings: Medallion sheeting
Under wing: Green calf tail & green crystal hair
Hackle: Hoffman grizzly dyed insect green
Head: Round foam
Legs: Round rubber
Fly Tier: Shane Stalcup

Attractor Trude

Hook: Dry fly #12
Thread: Color to match body
Tail: Deer hair, divided
Rib: Gold wire
Body: Midge tubing
Thorax: Possum dubbing
Wings: Medallion sheeting
Under wing: CDC & crystal hair
Hackle: Hoffman grizzly dyed insect green
Fly Tier: Shane Stalcup

Big Red Variant

Hook: MTC 531, #12
Thread: Red
Tail: Reddish brown microfibetts
Body: Red poly dubbing
Hackle: Two grizzly dyed red hackles, tied two sizes larger than the hook
Head: Thread
Fly Tier: Tom Broderidge

Black Coachman

Hook: Dry fly #12 - #14
Thread: Black 6/0
Tail: Golden pheasant tippets
Body: Peacock herl, black floss, peacock herl
Wings: Mallard quill sections
Hackle: Black dry fly
Head: Thread
Fly Tier: Cliff Stringer

Black Gnat

Hook: TMC 100, #10 - #18
Thread: Black
Tail: Dark Coq de Leon saddle fibers
Body: Black stripped hackle stem
Wings: Black hen hackle tips
Hackle: Black, tied dry fly style
Head: Thread
Fly Tier: Gale Doudy

Black Two Way

Hook: TMC 100, #12 - #20
Thread: Black
Tail: Dark Coq de Leon saddle fibers
Body: Dyed black stripped hackle stem
Thorax: Black muskrat dubbing
Wings: White turkey flat, tied as a parachute post
First hackle: Grizzly, two turns tied traditional dry fly style in front of the wing post
Second hackle: Grizzly, tied parachute style
Head: Thread
Fly Tier: Gale Doudy

Borcher's Parachute

Hook: Dry fly #8 - #20
Thread: Black
Tail: Moose body hair, divided
Rib: Optional wire
Body: Turkey tail fibers
Wings: Dun sparkle yarn
Hackle: Grizzly brown mix
Head: Thread
Fly Tier: Bear Andrews

Brook Trude

Hook: TMC 100 #14
Thread: Black
Tail: Golden pheasant crest, long
Rib: Copper wire
Body: Peacock herl
Wings: Calf tail
Hackle: Mix of grizzly dyed orange and Coachman
Head: Thread
Fly Tier: Gale Doudy

The Bubba

Hook: Dry fly #12 - #20
Thread: Gray
Tail: Hackle fibers, divided
Body: Olive yarn, wrapped
Wings: Dun hen hackle tips
Hackle: Grizzly dyed olive
Head: Thread
Fly Tier: John Schaper

CW Humpy Parachute

Hook: Daiichi 1100, #8 - #18
Thread: Chartreuse (or color of choice)
Tail: Moose body or main hairs
Body: Chartreuse Flex Floss
Hump: Moose hair remaining from the tail
Thorax: Peacock herl
Wing post: Pearl Crystal Splash, tied parachute style
Hackle: Grizzly, tied parachute style (or color of choice)
Head: Thread
Fly Tier: Bill Black, Spirit River Inc.

CW Stimulator

Hook: Daiichi 1280, #6 - #16
Thread: Gray or color to match the body
Tail: Elk hair, tied short and flared
Rib: Fine gold wire
Body: Gray Fine & Dry dubbing (or color of choice)
Body hackle: Brown, palmered through the body
Thorax: Gray Fine & Dry dubbing
Wings: Elk hair, tied trude style
Parachute post: Pearl Crystal Splash
Hackle: Grizzly, tied parachute style
Head: Thread   **Legs:** Optional rubber leg material
Fly Tier: Bill Black, Spirit River Inc.

Cliff's Dun

Hook: Dry fly #12
Thread: Black 6/0
Tail: Red hackle fibers
Rib: Coachman hackle trimmed
Body: Yellow yarn
Wings: Deer hair fanned 180 degrees
Hackle: Ginger
Head: Thread
Fly Tier: Cliff Adams

Close Carpet

Hook: Mustad 94840, #12 - #18
Thread: Gray or color of choice
Tail: Natural deer hair
Rib: Thread
Body: Base of the tail hair, criss crossed with the tying thread
Wings: Deer hair, fanned into a single post
Hackle: Dubbed carpet yarn fibers
Head: Thread
Fly Tier: George Close

Coq 'n Hen

Hook: Dry fly #14 - #22
Thread: Color to match body
Tail: Coq de Leon hackle fibers
Rib: Optional
Body: Brown dubbing or color to match insect
Wings: Hen saddle hackle tips
Hackle: Badger champagne (Hebert)
Head: Thread
Fly Tier: Al Beatty

Dirty Rat

Hook: TMC 101 #12 - #20
Thread: Black
Rib: Copper wire, optional
Body: Peacock herl
Wings: White poly yarn post
Hackle: Grizzly
Head: Thread
Fly Tier: Bob Lay

Dorato Hare's Ear

Hook: Mustad 94840, #10 - #18
Thread: Brown
Tail: Mixed grizzly and brown hackle fibers
Body: Hare's ear dubbing, either light or dark
Wings: Wood duck flank, divided (mallard or teal as a substitute)
Hackle: Mixed grizzly/brown (dark) or ginger/brown mix (light), trimmed on the bottom
Head: Thread
Fly Tier: Joyce Westphal

Everything Emerger

Hook: Dry fly #12 - #20
Thread: Rust brown or to match body
Shuck: Brown Hi Vis Float
Rib: Doubled tying thread
Body: Tan dubbing
Wings: Dark elk or deer
Head: Thread
Legs: Butts of the wing
Fly Tier: Scott Sanchez

Flash Wing Royal

Hook: TMC 100 #12 - #16
Thread: Black
Tail: Elk hair
Body: Peacock herl, red floss
Wings: Pearlescent Crystal Flash
Hackle: Brown
Head: Thread
Fly Tier: Pat & Carol Oglesby

Flashback Drake

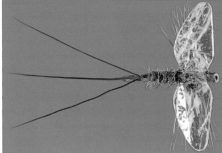

Hook: Dry fly #12 - #14
Thread: Olive
Tail: Three moose hair fibers
Body: Iridescent Dubbing, medium olive
Wings: Flashback cut wings, tied spent
Hackle: Grizzly dyed olive trimmed on bottom
Head: Thread
Fly Tier: Ronn Lucas

Gale's Bug

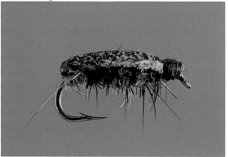

Hook: TMC 100 #18 - #20
Thread: Brown
Rib: Fine copper wire, optional
Body: Amber muskrat dubbing
Over body: Brown Bug Skin marked with a felt tip pen
Hackle: Brown, palmered over the body
Head: Thread
Fly Tier: Gale Doudy

Gale's Mosquito

Hook: TMC 100, #12 - #16
Thread: Black
Tail: Dark Coq de Leon saddle fibers
Rib: Light strand of moose main
Body: Thread
Wings: Laced Whiting hen hackle tips
Hackle: Grizzly, tied dry fly style, the bottom is trimmed even with the hook point
Head: Thread
Fly Tier: Gale Doudy

Gale's White Fly

Hook: TMC 100, #12 - #18
Thread: White
Tail: White hackle fibers
Body: White stripped hackle stem
Thorax: Peacock herl
Wings: White hen hackle tips
Hackle: White, tied dry fly style, the bottom is trimmed even with the hook point
Head: Thread
Fly Tier: Gale Doudy

Green Highlander

Hook: Partridge 01 #6, light weight single Wilson hook
Thread: Black 12/0
Tag 1: Lagartun varnished French tinsel, gold oval x-strong, small **Tag 2:** Japanese 100% pure silk floss, orange
Tail: Green dyed deer hair **Under Body:** Green dyed deer hair
Rib: Angler's Choice, orange flash ribbing
Over Body: Green dyed deer hair
Lateral line: Braided dyed orange buck tail
Wings: Green dyed deer hair
Epaulets: Matched barred lemon wood duck
Hackle: Dyed hackle, 1 green, 1 yellow, and 1 orange
Sled: Natural black moose hair **Eyes:** Natural jungle cock
Head: Revlon Top Speed
Fly Tier: Chuck Echer

Gunnison Humpy

Hook: Dry fly #8 - #22
Thread: Black
Tail: Moose hair
Body: Orange floss
Wings & over Body: Black poly yarn
Hackle: Grizzly dyed orange
Head: Thread
Fly Tier: Gretchen Beatty

Gunnison River Trude

Hook: Dry fly #12 - #20
Thread: Black
Tail: Moose hair
Rib: Optional
Body: Orange in back, peacock herl in front
Wings: Calf body hair
Hackle: Grizzly
Head: Thread
Legs: Orange rubber legs
Fly Tier: Gretchen Beatty

Hair Bare

Hook: Dry fly #8 - #20
Thread: Gray or to match the body
Tail: Moose hair
Rib: Optional
Body: Gray dubbing or to match insect
Hackle: Deer hair
Head: Gray dubbing
Fly Tier: Al Beatty

Hare's Ear Swimming Nymph

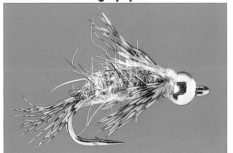

Hook: Daiichi 1150, #8 - #18
Thread: Gray
Tail: Partridge hackle fibers, tied equal to the body length
Rib: Flat gold tinsel
Body: Hare's ear dubbing
Wings: Two strands of pearl Crystal Splash, tied one half the length of the body
Head: Gold Brite Bead
Legs: Partridge hackle fibers, tied along the top and sides
Fly Tier: Bill Black, Spirit River Inc.

Hatching Renegade

Hook: Dry fly #10 - #16
Thread: Black
Tail: Rust antron yarn
Body: Back body, peacock herl - Front body orange thread
Wings: White calf tail (optional)
Hackle: Back hackle, brown - front hackle, grizzly
Head: Orange thread
Fly Tier: Vladimir Markov

Humpy Trude

Hook: Dry fly #10 - #14
Thread: Olive or color to match body
Tail: Moose hair
Body: Tying thread, deer over body
Wings: Gray calf tail, trude style
Hackle: Badger
Head: Thread
Fly Tier: Dave Borjas

Iridescent Black

Hook: TMC 200R #10
Thread: Black
Tail: Black stripped hackle stem
Rib: Thread
Body: Foam back #202 black
Wings: Dyed black turkey
Hackle: Black soft hackle trimmed short
Head: Iridescent Dubbing #2 black
Legs: Dyed black pheasant tail fibers
Fly Tier: Ronn Lucas

Iridescent Tan

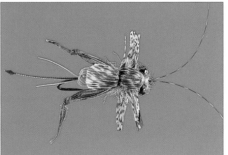

Hook: TMC 200R #10
Thread: Tan
Tail: Stripped hackle stem & pheasant back feather
Rib: Thread
Body: Bleached elk folded over
Wings: Mottled turkey
Hackle: Pheasant back feather
Head: Iridescent Dubbing #5 brown
Legs: Bleached pheasant tail fibers
Antenna: Grizzly hackle stems
Fly Tier: Ronn Lucas

Iron Blue Dry

Hook: Mustad 80000, #10 - #20
Thread: Gray
Tail: Dyed dun Coq de Leon cape fibers
Butt: Red floss or tying thread
Body: Sparse gray muskrat dubbing
Wings: Dyed dun Hebert hen cape feathers
Hackle: Dyed dun saddle
Head: Thread
Fly Tier: Al Beatty

SRI Irresistible Stimulator

Hook: Daiichi 1270, #4 - #14
Thread: Orange
Tail: Elk hair, tied short
Body: Orange dyed deer hair, spun and trimmed to shape
Body hackle: Brown, palmered
Wing: Elk hair, tied trude style
Eyes: Melted mono
Head: Tan Fine & Dry dubbing
Hackle: Grizzly, palmered over the head
Fly Tier: Bill Black, Spirit River Inc.

SRI Irresistible Wulff

Hook: Daiichi 1100, #12 - #18
Thread: Gray
Tail: Moose body hair
Body: Deer hair dyed light olive, spun and trimmed
Wings: White calf body hair, divided
Hackle: Grizzly dyed olive
Head: Thread
Fly Tier: Bill Black, Spirit River Inc.

The Laced Adams

Hook: Dry fly #12 - #20
Thread: Black
Tail: Deer body hair tied long
Rib: Optional
Body: Gray dubbing
Wings: Whiting silver laced hen tips
Hackle: Cree
Head: Thread
Fly Tier: Don Ordez

Laced Black Gnat

Hook: TMC 100 #12 - #20
Thread: Black
Tail: Coq de Leon hackle fibers
Body: Black Whiting turkey biot
Wings: Silver lace Whiting American hen hackle tips
Hackle: Black
Head: Thread
Fly Tier: Gale Doudy

Laced Light

Hook: TMC 100 #16
Thread: Pale yellow
Tail: Ginger hackle fibers
Body: Yellow Whiting turkey biot
Wings: Laced ginger Whiting American hen hackle tips
Hackle: Barred ginger
Head: Thread
Fly Tier: Gale Doudy

The Laced Royal

Hook: Dry fly #10 - #16
Thread: Black
Tail: Moose hair fibers tied long
Body: Peacock herl and red floss
Wings: Whiting silver laced hen tips
Hackle: Cree
Head: Thread
Fly Tier: Don Ordez

Light Green Trude

Hook: Dry fly #12 - #16
Thread: Gray
Tail: Golden pheasant tippets
Body: Light green dubbing
Wings: White calf
Hackle: Grizzly dyed brown
Head: Gray thread
Fly Tier: Pat & Carol Oglesby

Mattress Thrasher

Hook: Daiichi 1720 #10 - #16
Thread: Black
Body: Black dubbed abdomen, yellow antron thorax
Wings: Deer body hair
Hackle: Grizzly, clipped on the bottom
Head: Thread
Legs: Pumpkin silly legs
Fly Tier: Bear Andrews

Mottle Trude

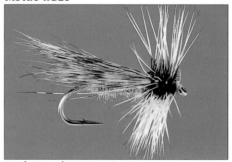

Hook: Mustad 80000, #12 - #22
Thread: Gray
Rib: Copper wire, optional
Body: Olive muskrat dubbing
Wings: Coq de Leon saddle fibers, stack and tied trude style
Hackle: Silver badger
Head: Thread
Fly Tier: Al Beatty

Mr. Bill's Flying Black Ant

Hook: Daiichi 1100, #14
Thread: Black
Body: Black Fine & Dry dubbing
Wings: Black Swiss straw coated with epoxy
Thorax: Black Fine & Dry dubbing
Head: Thread
Antenna: Black Mylar Motion
Legs: Black Mylar Motion, each strand is bent to shape
Fly Tier: Bill Black, Spirit River Inc.

Mr. Bill's Flying Red Ant

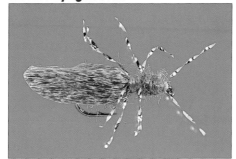

Hook: Daiichi 1100, #14
Thread: Amber
Body: Amber Fine & Dry dubbing
Wings: Amber Swiss straw coated with epoxy
Thorax: Amber Fine & Dry dubbing
Head: Thread
Antenna: Copper Mylar Motion
Legs: Copper Mylar Motion, each strand is bent to shape
Fly Tier: Bill Black, Spirit River Inc.

Ned's Fold Over

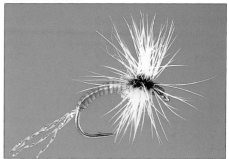

Hook: TMC 2487, #12 - #18
Thread: Brown
Tail: Pearl Krystal Flash, tied very sparse
Rib: Krystal Flash strand, optional
Body: Pale orange Super Floss
Wings: Badger saddle hackle, tied fold over style using a gallows tool
Thorax: Peacock herl under the fold over hackle
Fly Tier: Ned Long

PP Stimulator

Hook: TMC 200R, #8 - #18
Thread: Black
Tail: Elk hair, tied short and flared
Rib: Fine copper wire, optional
Body: Peacock herl
Wings: Elk hair, tied extending even with the end of the tail
Head: Peacock herl
Parachute post: White poly yarn
Hackle: Grizzly
Legs: Rubber leg material, optional
Fly Tier: Al Beatty

Para Glen (The Parachute That's Not)

Hook: Mustad 2487, #10 - #20 (the hook point rides straight down in the water)
Thread: Brown or color to match the body
Body: Furled poly yarn ninety-degrees to the hook shank, color to match the insect
Wings: Remaining ends of the body, tied straight out from the hook eye
Hackle: Color to match the body, tied around the hook but profiles as a parachute
Head: Thread
Fly Tier: Al Beatty

Pink Albert

Hook: TMC 100, #10 - #20
Thread: Brown
Tail: Coq de Leon saddle fibers
Rib: Copper wire, optional
Body: Pink dyed buck tail, wrapped
Thorax: Muskrat dubbing dyed brown
Wings: Large grizzly hackles swept back in a looped wonder wings, divided parachute style
Hackle: Brown saddle, parachute style
Head: Thread
Fly Tier: Bob Lay

Poly Royal

Hook: Dry fly #8 - #22
Thread: Black
Tail: Moose hair
Body: Gray poly hump over red floss
Wings: White poly yarn
Hackle: Brown
Head: Thread
Fly Tier: Gretchen Beatty

Provo Peacock

Hook: Dry fly #12 - #16
Thread: Color to match bead
Tail/Bead: Glass bead (pink, ruby, plum, orange, etc.)
Rib: Crystal Flash to match bead
Body: Peacock spun to chenille, thick
Hackle: Brown, front & back
Head: Thread to match bead
Fly Tier: Joyce Westphal

Queen of Waters

Hook: Dry fly #12 - #14
Thread: Dark olive
Tail: Mallard flank fibers
Rib: Brown hackle fibers shorter than gape, palmered
Body: Orange floss
Wings: Mallard flank in clump
Hackle: Brown
Head: Olive thread
Fly Tier: Cliff Stringer

Quick'n EZY

Hook: Dry fly #12 - #22
Thread: Color to match insect
Tail: Hackle fibers left over from the wings
Rib: Optional
Body: Dubbing to match the insect
Wings: Swept back hackle, Wonder Wings
Hackle: Ginger or color to match the insect
Head: Thread
Fly Tier: Gretchen Beatty

Roberts Yellow Drake

Hook: Dry fly #2 - #20
Thread: Yellow
Tail: Moose body hair
Rib: Crisscross tying thread
Body: Deer body hair
Wings: White sparkle yarn post
Hackle: Brown tied parachute
Head: Thread
Fly Tier: Bear Andrews

Royal Humpy

Hook: Dry Fly #14
Thread: 6/0 color of the body
Tail: Brown elk hock
Body: Dubbing - any color to suit the fisher
Wings: White calf hair
Hackle: Grizzly
Head: Thread
Fly Tier: Leonard Holt

Royal Lady

Hook: Dry fly #10 - #16
Thread: Black
Tail: Calf body hair
Body: Black ostrich & pink poly yarn
Hackle: White
Head: Thread
Fly Tier: Ruth Zinck

Rubber Legged Attractor

Hook: 4xlong fine wire
Thread: Orange
Tail: Golden pheasant tippets
Rib: Tying thread
Body: Closed cell foam, color with marker
Wings: Pre-formed stonefly wings
Hackle: Deer hair collar
Head: Deer hair bullet style
Legs: White rubber legs
Fly Tier: Eric Pettine

Simple Peacock

Hook: TMC 100 #12 - #20
Thread: Black
Tail: Elk
Rib: Copper wire, optional
Body: Peacock herl
Wings: White antron, parachute post
Hackle: Dun or grizzly
Head: Thread
Fly Tier: Don Richards

Squirrel May

Hook: Dry fly #10 - #20
Thread: Color to match body
Tail: Moose body hair
Rib: Optional
Body: Dubbing to match insect
Wings: Squirrel tail - fanned up
Head: Bullet - deer or elk
Legs: Optional
Fly Tier: Al Beatty

Stealth Adams

Hook: Long shank #12 - #16
Thread: Black
Tail: Deer hair, unstacked
Body: Gray dubbing
Wings: Laced hen hackle tips, delta style
Post: Unstacked calf hair
Hackle: Cree or grizzly, brown mix
Head: Thread
Fly Tier: Don Ordez

Synthetic Wulff

Hook: Dry fly #12 - #18
Thread: Black
Tail: Moose body hair
Body: Super Bright peacock dubbing and red floss
Wings: White poly post
Hackle: Brown tied parachute style
Head: Thread
Fly Tier: B. J. Lester

Variant Dorato

Hook: Mustad 94840, #10 - #18
Thread: Primrose
Tail: Coq de Leon saddle fibers
Body: Hare's ear dubbing, either light or dark
Wings: Tan (light) or gray (dark) Phentex poly yarn
Hackle: Mixed grizzly/brown (dark) or ginger/brown mix (light), trimmed on the bottom
Head: Thread
Fly Tier: Joyce Westphal

Yellow Hammer

Hook: Mustad 94840, #10 - #18
Thread: Yellow
Tail: Yellow hackle fibers
Body: Grizzly dyed yellow hackle, tightly palmered and trimmed to shape
Wings: Wood duck flank feather, tied divided
Hackle: White dyed yellow
Head: Thread
Fly Tier: Tom Logan

Yeller Hammer Variant

Hook: TMC 531, #12
Thread: Light yellow
Tail: Tan microfibetts
Body: Light yellow poly dubbing
Hackle: Two grizzly dyed yellow hackles, tied two sizes larger than the hook
Head: Thread
Fly Tier: Tom Broderidge

Caddis Flies . . .

Apple Caddis

Hook: TMC 2457 #14
Thread: Chartreuse
Body: Chartreuse CDC feather
Wings: Light tan deer hair mask fibers, unstacked
Head: Trimmed deer hair, thread
Fly Tier: Jerry Caruso

Black River Caddis

Hook: TMC 2457 #10
Thread: Chartreuse
Body: Mixed black and gray CDC feather
Wings: Black deer mask fibers, unstacked
Head: Trimmed deer hair, thread
Fly Tier: Jerry Caruso

Cajun Caddis

Hook: Daiichi 1720 #8 - #12
Thread: Rusty orange
Body: Iridescent Dubbing #7 Rust
Wings: Un-stacked deer or elk
Hackle: Black, palmered
Head: Trimmed hair
Antenna: Stripped black hackle stem
Fly Tier: Ronn Lucas

CDC & Elk Caddis

Hook: Daiichi 1100, #12 - #20
Thread: Brown or color of choice
Rib: Single strand of copper Krystal Flash
Body: Brown Fine & Dry dubbing over wrapped with brown CDC
Wings: Deer hair over excess CDC from the body
Head: Trimmed deer hair from the wing
Antenna: Ginger Fibetts
Fly Tier: Bill Black, Spirit River Inc.

CDC Caddis

Hook: TMC 100 #12 - #16
Thread: Gray
Rib: Fine copper wire
Body: Peacock herl
Wings: Deer hair over gray CDC
Head: Thread
Antenna: Monofilament (optional)
Fly Tiers: Pat & Carol Oglesby

CDC Caddis

Hook: Dry fly #14 - #20
Thread: Color to match fly
Tail: Z-lon, brown to match body
Rib: Brown hackle, palmered
Body: Wrapped brown CDC
Wings: Brown CDC
Hackle: Brown
Head: CDC pulled around bodkin for the wing
Fly Tier: Jerry Smalley

CDC Caddis - Light

Hook: TMC 9300, #12 - #20
Thread: Gray
Rib: Single strand of crystal flash
Body: Gray Fine and Dry dubbing
Wings: Elk hair over gray CDC under wing
Hackle: CDC palmered and trimmed on the bottom
Antenna: Stripped grizzly hackle stems
Head: Trimmed elk hair
Fly Tier: Bill Black

CDC Elk Caddis - Dark

Hook: TMC 9300, #12 - #20
Thread: Black
Rib: Clear extra fine thread
Body: Black dubbing
Wings: Elk hair over black CDC under wing
Hackle: CDC palmered and trimmed on the bottom
Antenna: Black marked mono
Head: Trimmed elk hair
Fly Tier: Bill Black

CDL Caddis - Peacock

Hook: Dry fly #12 - #20
Thread: Black
Body: Peacock herl, palmered dark dun hackle
  trimmed on top
Wings: Coq de Leon fibers
Hackle: Dark dun
Head: Thread
Fly Tier: John Schaper

CDL Caddis - Tan

Hook: Dry fly #12 - #20
Thread: Tan
Body: Stripped peacock herl stem
Wings: Coq de Leon fibers
Hackle: CDC in dubbing loop
Head: Thread
Fly Tier: John Schaper

Chickabou Caddis

Hook: Dry fly #12 - #20
Thread: Color to match insect
Tail: Chickabou, color to match insect
Body: Fine dubbing to match insect
Wings: Chickabou, color to match insect
Hackle: Color to match insect, wrapped tight
Head: Thread
Antenna: Two wood duck flank fibers (optional)
Fly Tier: Craig Jannsen

Clark's Deer Hair Caddis

Hook: Dry fly #12 - #18
Thread: Tan
First Body: Gold tinsel on shank
Second Body: Tan macramé yarn, combed, extended
  body
Wings: Deer hair
Hackle: Brown
Head: Thread
Fly Tier: Lee Clark

CW Caddis

Hook: Daiichi 1100, #12 - #20
Thread: Gray or color to match the body
Rib: Fine copper wire, optional
Body: Gray Fine & Dry dubbing (or color to match
  the insect)
Wings: Pearl Crystal Splash, tied as a parachute post
Hackle: Grizzly, tied parachute style
Head: Thread
Fly Tier: Bill Black, Spirit River Inc.

Donato's Hare's Ear

Hook: Dry fly #14 - #18
Thread: Tan
Tail: Grizzly brown mix, fanned
Body: Dark hare's ear dubbing
Wings: Wood duck, divided
Hackle: Grizzly brown mix, trimmed even with hook
  gape
Head: Thread
Fly Tier: Toby Richardson

Elk Caddis

Hook: TMC #200R, #18
Thread: Olive
Body: Cream dubbing
Wings: Elk hair
Hackle: Light ginger
Head: Very short elk hair butts
Fly Tier: Ray Radley

Goddard October Caddis

Hook: TMC 5212 #6 - #8
Thread: Brown
Body: Flared & trimmed natural and orange deer hair
Wings: Same as body
Hackle: Brown
Antenna: Horse tail
Legs: Peccary, splayed
Fly Tier: Mark Hoeser

Hammer Head Caddis

Hook: Dry fly #14 - #18
Thread: Black
Tail: Small tuft of chartreuse McFly Foam
Body: Black Holographic Mylar Motion
Wings: Deer hair over Black Mylar Motion
Head: Thread
Legs: Deer hair, splayed
Fly Tier: Steve Summerhill

Hi-Vis Para Caddis

Hook: Daiichi 1100, #14 - #20
Thread: Olive
Rib: Optional copper wire
Body: Light olive Fine & Dry dubbing
Wings: Spirit River Celo Z-Wing, colored with a felt tip marker
Parachute post: Spirit River Sparkle Yarn, white
Hackle: Dun, tied parachute style
Head: Thread
Fly Tier: Bill Black, Spirit River Inc.

Hi-Vis Parachute Caddis

Hook: Standard dry fly #12 - #20
Thread: Tan
Rib: Optional fine wire
Body: Tan Fine and Dry dubbing
Wings: Brown Wings and Thing, trimmed tent wing style
Post: Yellow poly wing
Hackle: Ginger parachute style
Head: Thread
Fly Tier: Bill Black

Hot Creek Caddis

Hook: Dry fly #12 - #22
Thread: Olive or color to match insect
Body: Olive dubbing or color to match insect
Wings: Deer hair, semi-Trude style and parachute post
Hackle: Grizzly, parachute
Head: Trimmed hair from the wings, parachute post
Fly Tier: John Schaper

J.C. Caddis

Hook: Dry fly #10
Thread: Cream
Rib: Palmered badger hackle
Body: Hairline Dubbing, cream/yellow mix
Wings: Bleached elk hair
Hackle: Badger
Head: Dubbed
Fly Tier: Randy Stonebraker

JN Caddis

Hook: Dry fly #14, up eye
Thread: Tan
Body: Tan poly dubbing
Wings: Elk shoulder, trimmed into small parachute post
Hackle: Brown
Head: Thread
Fly Tier: John Newbury

Kevin's Caddis

Hook: Dry fly #12 - #14
Thread: Black
Tail: Mallard flank fibers
Rib: Black thread
Body: Yellow foam sectioned by the rib
Wings: Mottled quill, glued flat along body
Head: Thread
Legs: Ginger hackle fibers
Fly Tier: Kevin McEnerney

Lacy's Caddis

Hook: Dry fly #12 - #20
Thread: Tan
Rib: Optional
Body: Two-thirds orange floss, one-third peacock herl
Wings: Deer body hair
Hackle: Brown palmered
Head: Trimmed deer hair
Fly Tier: Bear Andrews

Little Black Caddis

Hook: TMC 2457 #20
Thread: Black
Body: Black CDC feather
Wings: Black CDC feather
Head: Trimmed CDC feather
Fly Tier: Jerry Caruso

The Little Irishman

Hook: Dry fly #12 - #14
Thread: Orange
Rib: Orange or black
Body: Kelly green foam
Wings: Deer hair
Head: Deer hair trimmed short
Antenna: Bronze mallard
Fly Tier: Kevin McEnerney

Micro Caddis - Tan

Hook: Dry fly #18 - #24
Thread: Tan
Body: Tan tying thread
Wings: Brown hackle fibers
Hackle: Brown
Head: Thread
Fly Tier: John Schaper

Olive Caddis

Hook: Dry fly #12 - #22
Thread: Olive
Body: Olive dubbing
Wings: Deer hair
Hackle: Dark dun, palmered
Head: Trimmed deer hair
Fly Tier: John Schaper

Orange Sedge

Hook: TMC 100 #14
Thread: Orange
Rib: Copper wire
Body: Bleached peacock herl
Wings: Elk hair dyed orange
Hackle: Grizzly dyed orange & coachman, mixed
Head: Thread
Fly Tier: Gale Doudy

Patriot Caddis

Hook: Dry fly #12 - #18
Thread: Red
Tail: Optional
Body: Peacock fuzzy yarn, red floss in the center
Wings: Calf hair, Trude style
Hackle: Brown
Head: Thread
Fly Tier: Gretchen Beatty

Potters Pearl

Hook: Dry fly #12 - #20
Thread: Tan
Tail: None
Rib: Gold wire
Body: Pearl tinsel
Wings: Elk body hair
Hackle: Brown, palmered
Head: Trimmed elk hair
Fly Tier: Bear Andrews

Purple Sedge

Hook: Dry fly #12 - #18
Thread: Gray
Body: Peacock herl
Wings: Purple pheasant
Hackle: Blue dun
Head: Thread
Antenna: Mono mottled with marker
Fly Tier: Bruce Staples

Quill Body Caddis

Hook: Dry fly #14 - #18
Thread: Gray or color to match insect
Body: Two stripped quills, color to match insect
Wings: Deer hair
Hackle: Grizzly
Head: Thread
Fly Tier: B. J. Lester

Slick Water Caddis

Hook: Scud #12 - #20
Thread: Color to match insect
Body: Micro Chenille extended body, shaped with a flame
Wings: Gray or tan antron yarn
Hackle: Brown, ginger, or grizzly brown mix
Head: Thread
Antenna: Two strands of mono
Fly Tier: Adam Trina

Slow Water Caddis

Hook: Dry fly #14 - #22
Thread: Color to match insect
Tail: CDC tied one gape long
Body: Dubbing to match insect
Wings: CDC over clear Z-lon
Hackle: Two wraps of hen trimmed top and bottom
Head: Dubbing, same color as body
Antenna: Two wood duck flank fibers (optional)
Fly Tier: Craig Jannsen

Spanish Caddis

Hook: Dry fly #12 - #20
Thread: Color to match body
Rib: Optional
Body: Olive dubbing or color to match insect
Wings: Coq de Leon hackle fibers
Hackle: Badger champagne (Hebert)
Head: Thread
Fly Tier: Al Beatty

Sparkle Wing CDC Caddis

Hook: Mustad 539K
Thread: Tan or color to match insect
Body: CDC in dubbing loop, color to match insect
Wings: Zing wing, tent style
Hackle: Ginger
Head: Thread
Fly Tier: Kieran Frye

Spent Wing CDC Caddis

Hook: Mustad 539K
Thread: Tan or color to match insect
Body: CDC in dubbing loop, color to match insect
Wings: Two mottled hen saddle feathers
Hackle: Ginger
Head: Thread
Fly Tier: Kieran Frye

Squirrel Para-Caddis

Hook: Dry fly #8 - #20
Thread: Color to match body
Rib: Optional
Body: Dubbing to match insect
Wings: Squirrel hair tied Trude style
Hackle: Grizzly tied parachute
Head: Dubbing
Fly Tier: Al Beatty

Squirrel Tail Caddis

Hook: Dry fly #12 - #18
Thread: Color to match body
Rib: Ginger or color to match insect
Body: Dubbing to match insect
Wings: Turkey flat burnt to shape
Hackle: Ginger or color to match insect
Head: Black dubbing
Antenna: Moose body hair
Fly Tier: Jim Shearer

SS Caddis

Hook: Dry fly #12 - #20
Thread: Color to match body
Body: Turkey biot
Wings: Medallion sheeting
Under wing: CDC
Hackle: Hoffman saddle
Head: Superfine dubbing
Antenna: Lemon wood duck
Fly Tier: Shane Stalcup

Tyvek Caddis

Hook: Standard dry fly #12 - #20
Thread: Color to match the fly
Rib: Optional
Body: Dubbing to match the insect
Wings: Tent style Tyvek, colored with felt tip marker
Hackle: Ginger or color to match insect
Head: Thread
Fly Tier: Jay Buchner

Wissahickon Caddis

Hook: TMC 2457 #14
Thread: Black
Body: Gray CDC feather
Wings: Light tan deer hair mask fibers, unstacked
Head: Trimmed deer hair, thread
Fly Tier: Jerry Caruso

Woven Caddis

Hook: TMC 100, #12 - #20
Thread: Black
Tail: Pearl Krystal Flash, tied very short
Body: Light and dark antron, woven extended body style
Body coloring: Red felt tip marker on the end of the body
Wings: Turkey tied tent style under an elk over wing
Hackle: Pale dun, tied dry fly style
Head: Thread
Fly Tier: Gale Doudy

Crane, Damsel, Dragon, Water Boatmen, and Back Swimmers . . .

Adult Crane Fly

Hook: Dry fly #16
Thread: Color to match the body
Body: Stalcup's adult damsel body
Wings: Medallion sheeting
Hackle: Hoffman saddle
Eyes: Burnt mono
Legs: 2 lb. Maxima
Fly Tier: Shane Stalcup

Adult Dragon Fly

Hook: DaiRiki 270 or equivalent
Thread: 3/0 white
Tail: 50 lb. braided mono with blue poly inside
Rib: Felt tip marker
Body: Furry foam color with marker
Wings: Krystal Flash
Head & Over Body: Single piece of Evasote
Legs: 40 lb. dacron colored with blue marker
Fly Tier: Paul L. Maurer

Bailey's Dragon Fly

Hook: Long shank #6 - #10
Thread: Blue
Tail: Elk hair extended from the body
Rib: Thread
Body: Elk hair
Wings: Grizzly hackle tips
Hackle: Grizzly
Head: Clipped elk hair
Fly Tier: Bob Lay

Bob's Bug

Hook: Standard dry fly #10 - #14
Thread: Black
Tail: Two strands of crystal flash
Rib: Fine copper wire
Body: Peacock herl
Shell back: Several strands of peacock herl coated with AquaFlex
Head: Thread
Legs: One strand of black Silli-Con Legs
Fly Tier: Bob Lay

Bogus Adult Damsel

Hook: TMC 100 #16
Thread: Blue damsel to match body
Extended Body: Blue Z Lon furled & segmented with marker
Body: Natures Spirit blue damsel dubbing
Wings: White Z Lon with black Z Lon accents
Head: Dubbing
Eyes: Melted 25 lb. mono painted black
Fly Tier: Tim Witsman

BT's Boatman

Hook: Standard dry fly #14
Thread: Black
Body: Peacock herl
Shell back: Black closed cell foam
Hackle: Black
Head: Peacock herl
Eyes: Burnt mono
Legs: Coachman brown turkey biots
Fly Tier: Al Beatty

Bud's Double "X" Damsel

Hook: Dry fly #4 - #10
Thread: Black
Tail: Blue braided mono extended body
Body: Wrapped braided mono, color to match insect
Wings: Krystal Flash extend to end of tail
Hackle: Deer hair collar
Head: Blue deer hair, bullet style
Legs: Black round rubber, double "x"
Fly Tier: Bud Heintz

Chain-Stitched Damsel Adult

Hook: TMC 900BL #14
Thread: Black
Rib: Black felt tip markings
Body: Chain-stitched blue poly string, dubbed blue thorax
Wings: Light-Brite fibers
Head: Blue closed cell foam
Fly Tier: Robert Williamson

Chuck's Adult Damsel Fly

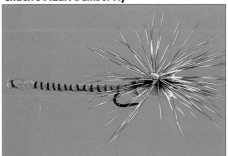

Hook: TMC 102Y Size 15
Thread: Benecchi 12/0 black **Rib:** Thin Thread
Body: Extended body, thorax and eyes - blue food tray foam
Wings: Hackle
Hackle: Grizzly hackle wings tied parachute
Head: Blue foam
Special Instructions: Hackle stem reinforced extended body with "v" loop for parachute post. Use Aqua Seal for internal and external coating. Normal head cements will dissolve foam.
Fly Tier: Chuck Echer

Convertible Damselfly

Hook: DaiRiki 270 #8 - #14
Thread: Blue
Tail: Blue buck tail, shank length
Body: Blue dubbing
Rear Wings: Gray calf tail, one & one-fourth shank length
Front Wings: Butts of rear wing tie Wulff style
Thorax: Blue dubbing
Hackle: Grizzly palmered over thorax
Legs: Blue rubber
Fly Tier: Scott Sanchez

Deer Hair Damsel

Hook: Dry fly #10
Thread: Black
Rib: Tying thread
Body: Extended - dyed deer
Wings: Light blue dun hackle
Hackle: Parachute for wings
Head: Dyed deer
Fly Tier: Al Beatty

Elk Dragon

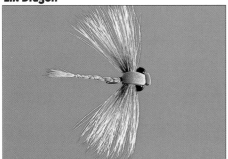

Hook: Standard dry fly #8
Thread: Blue
Tail: Elk tied extended body style
Body: Blue closed cell foam
Wings: Elk hair, tied spent style
Eyes: Black plastic bead chain
Head: Trimmed foam
Fly Tier: Gretchen Beatty

Flashback Boatman

Hook: Daiichi 1560 #12 - #14
Thread: Brown
Body: Iridescent Dubbing #5 brown
Shell back: Thin Ice Flashback
Head: Iridescent Dubbing #5 brown
Legs: Brown turkey biots
Fly Tier: Ronn Lucas

Foam-Back Boatman

Hook: Dry fly #12
Thread: Black
Body: Peacock herl over closed cell foam
Over-Body: Gray closed cell foam
Head: Trimmed closed cell foam
Legs: Black Super Floss
Fly Tier: Jim Cramer

Foam Damsel

Hook: Dry fly #12 - #14
Thread: White
Body: Blue closed cell foam
Thorax: Blue dubbing
Wings: Pearl Krystal Flash
Post: Pearl Krystal Flash
Hackle: Grizzly dyed blue, parachute style
Head: Thread
Fly Tier: Dave Borjas

Ian's Crane Fly

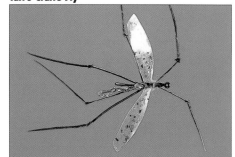

Hook: Partridge L3B #12
Thread: Black
Rib: Krystal Flash
Body: Olive dubbing, furled plastic bag with Krystal Flash
Wings: Cut plastic bag
Head: Thread
Legs: Knotted pheasant tail fibers
Fly Tier: Ian Russel

JC Crane Fly

Hook: TMC 2457 #10 - #14
Thread: Tan
Rib: Fine copper wire
Body: Tan poly yarn
Parachute post: Tan poly yarn, melted
Wings: Cream hackle tips, delta style
Hackle: Cream parachute
Thorax: Tan CDC feather
Head: Thread
Fly Tier: Jerry Caruso

Jeff's Furled Damsel

Hook: Dry fly #10 - #14
Thread: Black
Body: Blue poly yarn furled abdomen, blue poly wrapped as thorax
Wings: Light dun hackle tips, four
Hackle: Light dun
Head: Thread
Eyes: Melted Maxima
Fly Tier: Jeff Hatton

JS Damsel

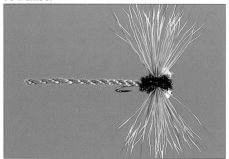

Hook: Dry fly #14
Thread: Blue
Body: Furled blue poly yarn, peacock herl thorax
Wings: Deer hair divided by several peacock herl strands
Head: Thread
Eyes: Looped clear crystal flash
Fly Tier: John Schaper

J.u.t.s. Damsel

Hook: Dry fly #12
Thread: Brown
Tail: Brown braided line
Rib: Felt tip marks on tail/extended body
Body: Brown dubbing, poly wing case
Hackle: Over sized webby grizzly collar, divided by wing case
Head: Trimmed poly yearn
Legs: Optional
Fly Tier: Thomas Leow

Parachute Crane Fly

Hook: DaiRiki 270 #6 - #10
Thread: Rusty brown
Rib: Orange thread
Body: Tying thread
Wings: Light elk, one & one-half shank length
Hackle: Grizzly brown mix
Fly Tier: Scott Sanchez

Parachute Damsel

Hook: TMC 5212 or Mustad 94831, #12
Thread: Black 6/0
Abdomen: Braided mono dyed blue (BCS 133/136)
Rib: None but ringed with black felt tip marker
Body/thorax: Blue dubbing
Wings: Blue dun or grizzly tied parachute style
Hackle: Parachute for the wings
Head: Tufted end of blue poly yarn
Fly Tier: Bob Pelzl

Rainy's Damselfly

Hook: Dry fly #12
Thread: Blue
Tail: Rainy's Damselfly Body Foam
Rib: Marker on foam
Body: Damselfly Body Foam over blue Sparkle Dub
Wings: Krystal Flash
Head: Foam
Eyes: Rainy's Bug Eyes
Fly Tier: Rainy Riding

Ronn's Cripple Crane

Hook: Dry fly #12
Thread: Brown
Body: Tan latex over yarn under body
Wings: Brown hackle tips
Hackle: Ginger tied sparse
Head: Thread
Legs: Knotted single pheasant tail fiber, six
Fly Tier: Ronn Lucas

Spent Crane Fly

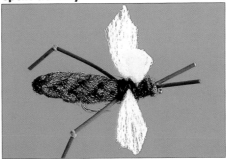

Hook: Dry fly #8 - #10
Thread: Brown
Body: Brown macramé cord abdomen, dubbed thorax
Wings & post: Beige poly yarn
Hackle: Optional
Head: Thread
Legs: Knotted brown rubber legs
Fly Tier: Dave Borjas

SS Adult Damselfly

Hook: Dry fly #14
Thread: Blue
Body: Stalcup's adult damsel body
Thorax: Possum dubbing
Wings: Medallion sheeting
Hackle: Hoffman saddle dyed blue
Head: Thread
Eyes: Burnt mono
Fly Tier: Shane Stalcup

Tak's Back Swimmer

Hook: TMC 101 #10
Thread: Black
Body: Spun and trimmed olive deer hair
Shell back: Speckled turkey
Head: Spun and trimmed olive deer hair
Legs: Brown rubber
Fly Tier: Tak Shimizu

Water Boatman

Hook: Daiichi 1560 #16
Thread: Green
Body: Midge tubing, green
Wings: Medallion sheeting
Head: Thread
Legs: Emu & Stalcup's damsel legs
Eyes: Burnt mono
Fly Tier: Shane Stalcup

Water Walker Crane Fly

Hook: Dry fly #12
Thread: Black or brown
Body: Furled brown poly yarn
Wings: White poly yarn, divided
Hackle: Grizzly tied water walker style
Head: Thread
Legs: Brown Flexi Floss, knotted
Fly Tier: Craig Jannsen

Water Walker Damsel

Hook: Dry fly #12
Thread: Black
Body: Furled blue poly yarn
Wings: White poly yarn, divided
Hackle: Grizzly tied water walker style
Head: Thread
Fly Tier: Steve Summerhill

Mayflies . . .

Baetis Dun

Hook: Dry fly #16 - #22
Thread: Color to match body
Tail: Microfibbets
Body: Turkey biots, olive
Wings: Medallion sheeting
Hackle: Hoffman dun saddle
Head: Thread
Fly Tier: Eric Pettine

Bear's Cala Baetis

Hook: Dry fly #14
Thread: Tan
Tail: Microfibetts, divided
Body: Gray dubbing
Wings: Dun sparkle yarn
Hackle: Badger dyed olive
Head: Thread
Fly Tier: Bear Andrews

Bear's Para Baetis

Hook: Dry fly #16 - #20
Thread: Tan
Tail: Moose body hair (supports extended body)
Body: Olive dubbed over moose
Wings: Dun sparkle yarn
Hackle: Badger dyed olive
Head: Thread
Fly Tier: Bear Andrews

Bob's CDL

Hook: TMC 100, #12 - #22
Thread: Tan
Tail: Coq de Leon saddle fibers, natural light
Rib: Fine copper wire, optional
Body: Bleached cream muskrat dubbing, tied sparse
Wings: Larger ginger hackles swept into looped
  wonder wings, divided parachute style
Hackle: Silver badger, tied parachute style
Head: Thread
Fly Tier: Bob Lay

Bowen Cut Wing

Hook: Daiichi 1100, #12 - #18
Thread: Black
Tail: Ginger Fibetts, divided
Body: Dark and light green Flex Floss, woven as an
  extended body fly
Wings: Perfect Cut Mayfly wings
Hackle Grizzly dyed yellow, trimmed Bing Lempke
  style
Head: Thread
Fly Tier: Bill Black, Spirit River Inc.

BT's Beauty

Hook: Mustad 2487, #12 - #20
Thread: Olive or color to match the insect
Body: Olive (or choice) Brazilian Velour, shaped with
  a flame, tied extended body style
Wings: Perfect Cut mayfly wings, parachute style
Hackle: Dun or color to match the insect, parachute
  style
Head: Thread
Fly Tier: Al Beatty

Bud's Dark Cahill

Hook: Dry fly #14 - #18
Thread: Black
Tail: Brown microfibetts
Body: Gray stripped hackle stem, gray dubbed thorax
Wings: Wood duck or dyed mallard
Hackle: Brown
Head: Thread
Fly Tier: Bud Heintz

Bud's Krystal Mayfly

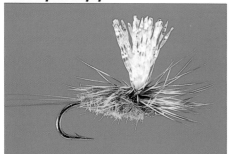

Hook: Dry fly #14 - #22
Thread: Color to match insect
Tail: Microfibetts, divided
Body: Dubbing to match insect
Wings: Pearl Krystal Flash
Hackle: Parachute style, color to match insect
Head: Thread
Fly Tier: Bud Heintz

Bud's Light Cahill

Hook: Dry fly #14 - #18
Thread: Tan
Tail: Tan microfibetts
Body: Stripped ginger hackle stem, tan dubbed
  thorax
Wings: Wood duck or dyed mallard
Hackle: Light ginger
Head: Thread
Fly Tier: Bud Heintz

Bud's Spinner

Hook: Dry fly #14 - #22
Thread: Color to match insect
Tail: Microfibetts, divided
Body: Stripped hackle stem, dubbed thorax with biot
  over
Wings: White Zelon
Head: Thread
Fly Tier: Bud Heintz

CW Light Cahill

Hook: Daiichi 1100, #14 - #20
Thread: Yellow
Tail: Ginger Spirit River Fibetts, divided
Body: Ginger goose biot, wrapped
Thorax: Light cahill Fine & Dry dubbing
Wings: Ginger Perfect Cut Wings, marked with a felt tip marker
Hackle: Ginger, tied parachute style
Head: Thread
Fly Tier: Bill Black, Spirit River Inc.

Callibaetis Dun (EXB)

Hook: Mustad 94840, #12 - #16
Thread: White
Tail: Two moose body hairs, divided
Rib: Tying thread, criss cross over the body
Body: Very light elk hair, tied extended body style
Wings: Dark speckled mallard flank, tied divided
Hackle: White saddle hackle
Head: Thread
Fly Tier: Craig Hull

CDC May

Hook: Dry fly #12 - #20
Thread: Color to match fly
Tail: Lower, moose - upper CDC
Rib: Thread
Body: Twisted CDC remaining from tail
Wings: Hackle tip
Hackle: Grizzly
Head: Thread
Fly Tier: Jim Shearer

CDC Rusty Spinner

Hook: Mustad 94840
Thread: Brown
Tail: Four moose fibers evenly split
Body: Pheasant tail fibers
Wings: CDC feathers tied spent
Head: Thread
Fly Tier: Kieran Frye

Chain-Stitched Mayfly

Hook: TMC 900Bl #14
Thread: Gray
Tail: End fibers of the body
Body: Chain-stitched gray poly string, gray dubbed thorax
Wings: Deer hair, comparadun style
Head: Black closed cell foam
Fly Tier: Robert Williamson

Chuck's Hexagenia

Hook: TMC 100 #8
Thread: Yellow Danville 3/0 monocord
Tail: Elk hair dyed yellow - split tails - 2 hairs per tail bonded with Qua Seal
Rib: Tying thread
Body: Deer hair dyed olive/yellow extended
Wings: Deer hair dyed olive/yellow
Hackle: One olive/yellow and one natural grizzly wrapped parachute
Head: Bullet head - deer hair dyed olive/yellow
Fly Tier: Chuck Echer

Clark's Big Yellow Mayfly

Hook: TMC 5212 #10
Thread: Yellow
First Body: Gold tinsel on hook shank
Extended Body: Combed & furled yellow macramé yarn
Wings: Yellow macramé yarn
Hackle: Grizzly dyed yellow tied parachute style
Head: Thread
Fly Tier: Lee Clark

Coffin Fly

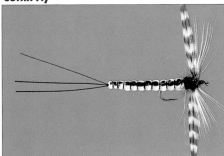

Hook: Dry fly #12
Thread: Black 10/0
Tail: Black paint brush fibers
Rib: Black thread
Body: White foam touched with a black marker
Wings: Grizzly hackle tips, tied spent
Hackle: Coq de Leon or badger tied spent
Thorax: Black fuzzy dubbing
Fly Tier: Chuck Moxley

Coffin Fly

Hook: Mustad 94840, #14
Thread: White
Tail: Moose body hair, tied very sparse to the tip of the extended body material
Body: Poly yarn, twisted into a very tight strand, extended body style
Body coating: Aqua Tuff over the twisted strand, allowed to dry while still tightly twisted
Wings: Grizzly hackle tips
Hackle: Silver badger
Head: Thread
Fly Tier: Toby Richardson

Cook's Dun

Hook: Dry fly #10 - #12
Thread: Color to match body
Tail: Deer hair fiber, long
Rib: Optional
Body: Dubbing to match insect
Wings: Deer hair spread using mono
Head: Thread
Fly Tier: LeRoy Cook

Craig's Coffin

Hook: Mustad 94840, #10 - #16
Thread: Yellow
Tail: Two bleached moose hairs, divided
Rib: Tying thread, criss cross over the body
Body: Dyed light yellow deer hair, tied extended body style
Wings: Wood duck flank feather, tied divided
Hackle: Light ginger saddle hackle
Head: Thread
Fly Tier: Craig Hull

Dan's Mayfly

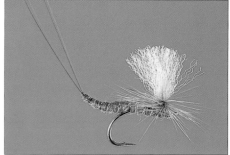

Hook: Two Daiichi 1150 hooks sizes #12 - #24
Thread: Color to match the body
Tail: Microfibbets
Rib: Extra fine oval gold tinsel
Body: Fine poly dubbing to match insect, olive
Wings: Poly tied as a parachute post
Hackle: Dun Hoffman saddle
Head: Thread
Fly Tier: Dan Curtis

Eastern Green Drake

Hook: TMC 100, #8 - #12
Thread: Olive
Tail: Three peccary fibers
Rib: Thread
Body: White buck tail, tied on a needle then tied on the hook extended body style
Thorax: Gray and olive mixed muskrat dubbing
Wings: Mallard flank fibers dyed olive, divided
Hackle: Silver badger, "V" trim from the bottom
Head: Thread
Fly Tier: Dave Schmezer

Extended Quill Gordon

Hook: Partridge GRS3A, #14
Thread: Gray
Tail: Two dun Microfibbets, divided, tied to the extended body with the rib material
Rib: Stripped peacock herl stem
Body: Light section of a porcupine quill
Wings: Wood duck fibers, divided
Hackle: Medium dun
Head: Thread
Fly Tier: Dave Schmezer

Fan Tail Cahill

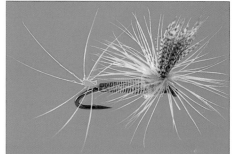

Hook: TMC 102Y #15
Thread: Black Benecchi 12/0 thread
Tail: Barbs stripped from one side of hackle stem then bent into a fan tail
Body: Barb stripped from hackle stem, tied in tip first ad wrapped quill style forward
Wings: Lemon wood duck flank
Hackle: Ginger hackle wrapped parachute style
Head: Black thread
Fly Tier: Chuck Echer

Foam Wing Parachute

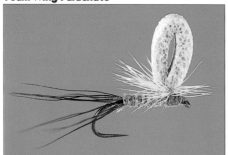

Hook: TMC 900BL #16 - #20
Thread: Olive
Tail: Moose, divided
Rib: Olive Krystal Flash
Body: BWO Super Fine dubbing
Wings: Gray closed cell foam, looped
Hackle: Light dun
Head: Same as body
Fly Tier: Morgan Thalken

Gale's BWO

Hook: TMC 100, #14 - #22
Thread: Olive
Tail: Dun hackle fibers
Body: Olive dyed stripped hackle stem
Wings: Dun hen hackle tips
Hackle: Medium dun, tied dry fly style, the bottom is trimmed even with the hook point
Head: Threat
Fly Tier: Gale Doudy

Gale's PMD

Hook: TMC 100, #12 - #20
Thread: Tan
Tail: Light Coq de Leon saddle fibers
Abdomen: Dyed pale yellow stripped hackle stem
Body: Tan muskrat dubbing
Wings: Ginger hen hackle tips
Hackle: Ginger, tied dry fly style
Head: Thread
Fly Tier: Gale Doudy

GD Baetis

Hook: TMC 100 #16
Thread: Olive
Tail: Coq de Leon spade fibers
Body: Olive Whiting turkey biot
Wings: Dun Whiting American hen hackle tips
Hackle: Grizzly dyed olive
Head: Thread
Fly Tier: Gale Doudy

GD Blue Winged Olive

Hook: TMC 100 #16
Thread: Olive
Tail: Coq de Leon spade fibers
Body: Pale green stripped hackle quill
Wings: Dun Whiting American hen hackle tips
Hackle: Grizzly dyed olive
Head: Thread
Fly Tier: Gale Doudy

Ginger Mayfly

Hook: TMC 100 #12 - #20
Thread: Tan
Tail: Barred ginger golden hackle barbs
Body: Stripped barred golden ginger hackle stem
Wings: Barred golden ginger hackle tips
Hackle: Barred golden ginger
Head: Thread
Fly Tier: Henry Hoffman

GM Emerger

Hook: Mustad 94840 #18
Thread: Tan
Tail: Antron trailing shuck
Body: Adams gray dubbing, furled tan sparkle organza
Wings: Antron post
Hackle: Hoffman dun, parachute style
Head: Thread
Fly Tier: Gordon Mankins

Green Drake (EXB)

Hook: Mustad 94840, #10 - #14
Thread: Yellow
Tail: Two bleached moose hair fibers, divided
Rib: Tying thread, criss cross over the body
Body: Yellow dyed deer hair, tied extended body style
Top of the body: Colored on top with a olive felt tip marker
Wings: Wood duck flank feather, tied divided
Hackle: Dark barred ginger or cree
Head: Thread
Fly Tier: Craig Hull

Green Drake Irresistible

Hook: TMC 5212 #10
Thread: Olive
Tail: Moose hair
Body: Flared & trimmed olive and pale yellow deer hair
Wings: Grizzly hen hackle dyed olive
Hackle: Yellow dyed grizzly & olive dyed grizzly
Head: Thread
Fly Tier: Mark Hoeser

Hoffman Mayfly

Hook: TMC 100 #12 - #16
Thread: Tan
Tail: Barred golden ginger hackle barbs
Body: Stripped barred golden ginger hackle stem
Wings: Barred golden ginger, reverse hackle
Hackle: Barred golden ginger
Head: Thread
Fly Tier: Henry Hoffman

Laura's Snowshoe Wulff

Hook: Dry fly #12 or 13
Thread: Tan 8/0
Tail: Moose or black bear fibers
Body: Fox or tan beaver
Wings: Snowshoe rabbit foot
Hackle: Natural ginger
Head: Tying thread
Special Instructions: Tie the snowshoe as a clump, undivided.
Fly Tier: Michael Hogue

Mahogany Dun

Hook: Mustad 94840, #10 - #14
Thread: Brown
Tail: Two moose hairs, divided
Rib: Tying thread, criss cross over the body
Body: Dyed dark brown deer hair, tied extended body style
Wings: Dark mallard flank feather, divided
Hackle: Coachman brown
Head: Thread
Fly Tier: Craig Hull

The Muddle May

Hook: Dry fly #12 - #22
Thread: Color to match body
Tail: Moose hair fibers
Rib: Optional
Body: Dubbing to match insect
Wings: Looped wonder wings
Hackle: Deer hair
Head: Spun deer hair
Fly Tier: Al Beatty

Olive Two Way

Hook: TMC 100, #12 - #20
Thread: Black
Tail: Coq de Leon saddle hackle fibers
Body: Stripped dyed green hackle stem
Wings: White turkey flat, tied as a parachute post
First hackle: Black, two turns tied directly in front of the wing post in the traditional manner around the hook shank
Second hackle: Grizzly, tied parachute style around the wing post
Head: Thread
Fly Tier: Gale Doudy

Pale Morning Dun

Hook: Dry Fly #16 - #20
Thread: Color to match body
Tail: Microfibbet
Rib: Optional
Body: Turkey biot, PMD color
Wings: Z-lon post
Hackle: Hoffman ginger saddle
Head: Thread
Fly Tier: Eric Pettine

Pheasant Tail Dry

Hook: TMC 100, #12 - #22
Thread: Brown
Tail: Pheasant tail fibers
Rib: Fine copper wire
Body: Pheasant tail fibers, wrapped
Thorax: Peacock herl
Wings: Calf body, tied as a parachute post
Hackle: Brown saddle, parachute style
Head: Thread
Fly Tier: Bob Lay

PMD (James)

Hook: Dry fly #12
Thread: Light olive
Tail: 3 porcupine guard hairs
Body: SealTex, pressed around tail & welded to itself
Wings: Pre-made nylon with vein design
Hackle: Honey dun
Head: Pre-formed mono
Fly Tier: Gerald M. James

PW Green Drake

Hook: Dry fly #10 - #14
Thread: Olive
Tail: Moose mane
Rib: Brown button hole thread
Body: Blend of Ligas olive and pale sulpher
Wings: Poly yarn, divided
Hackle: Grizzly
Head: Thread
Fly Tier: Dan Turner

Quill Adams

Hook: Dry fly #12 - #22
Thread: Gray
Tail: Moose body hair
Body: Stripped peacock herl
Wings: Two hen hackle tips
Hackle: Cree or grizzly
Head: Thread
Fly Tier: B. J. Lester

Realistic Brown Drake

Hook: Dry fly #12
Thread: Brown
Tail: Two black Fishair fibers
Rib: Black floss
Body: Brown & yellow floss woven over athletic pretape under body
Wings: Foust wing material, cut
Eyes: Melted 6x tippet
Legs: Tan ultra chenille
Fly Tier: James Bowen

Realistic Green Drake

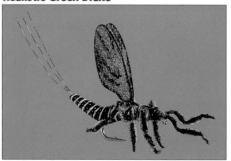

Hook: Dry fly #12
Thread: Olive
Tail: Three gray Fishair fiber
Rib: One strand of yellow floss
Body: One each green & olive "v" rib
Wings: Foust wing material, cut
Eyes: Melted 7x tippet
Legs: Ultra chenille
Fly Tier: James Bowen

Red Quill (Modified Traditional Catskill)

Hook: TMC #102Y Size 15
Thread: 12/0 black
Tail: Barred ginger hackle barbs
Body: Furnace brown hackle stem, barbs striped tied in tip first
Wings: Barred ginger hackle tips
Hackle: Barred ginger
Head: Black thread head with Loon hard head fly finish - black
Fly Tier: Chuck Echer

Sandfly Buck (Hex Mayfly)

Hook: Dry fly #6
Thread: Tan
Tail: Light elk
Rib: Brown floss coated with nail polish, apply after drying
Body: Light poly over elk tail to form extended body
Wings: Light elk
Hackle: Brown
Head: Thread
Fly Tier: John Newbury

Slate Drake

Hook: Dry fly #10
Thread: Dark brown
Tail: Dun hackle
Body: Brown floss, #16 palmered dun hackle
Wings: Dun hen hackle tips
Hackle: Dark dun grizzly mix
Head: Thread
Fly Tier: Toby Richardson

Spongilla Fly Spinner

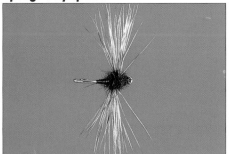

Hook: TMC 101 #20 or Mustad 94859 #18
Thread: Black 8/0
Body: Thread abdomen & mole fur dubbed thorax
Wings: Brown dun (BCS 29) hackle tied spent wing
Hackle: To form spent wings
Head: Thread
Fly Tier: Bob Pelzl

SS Mayfly

Hook: Dry fly #12 - #14
Thread: Color to match body
Tail: Lemon wood duck, divided
Body: Goose biot, color to match insect
Thorax: Superfine dubbing
Wings: Medallion sheeting
Hackle: Hoffman saddle to match body
Head: Thread
Fly Tier: Shane Stalcup

Tiny BWO Parachute

Hook: TMC 101, #18 - #22
Thread: Olive
Tail: Three Microfibbets, inserted through the body and splayed
Rib: Thread
Body: Trimmed dark end of a porcupine quill, tied extended body style
Thorax: Kreinik olive silk dubbing
Wings: Dun Antron yarn fibers
Hackle: Medium dun saddle hackle
Head: Thread
Fly Tier: Dave Schmezer

Toby's Light Fox

Hook: Dry Fly #12 - #18
Thread: Cream
Tail: Golden badger guard hair
Body: Light tan fox fur dubbing
Wings: Wood duck
Hackle: Golden badger
Head: Thread
Fly Tier: Toby Richardson

U.S.D. Callibaetis

Hook: Partridge L1A #12 - #14
Thread: Gray
Tail: Dun Microfibetts
Rib: Cream thread
Body: Fine and Dry hares ear over raffia under body
Wings: Teal flank wonder wings
Hackle: Grizzly tied on mono post
Head: Thread
Fly Tier: Ian Russel

The Whitcraft

Hook: Dry fly #12 - #18
Thread: Black
Tail: Brown hackle fibers
Body: Yellow quill
Wings: Grizzly hackle point
Hackle: Grizzly brown mix
Head: Thread
Fly Tier: Bruce Staples

Z-Ion Parachute Dun

Hook: TMC 100, #14 - #24
Thread: Color to match the insect
Tail: Z-Ion, tied sparse
Body: Dubbing to match the insect, tied sparse
Wings: Z-long, tied as a parachute post
Hackle: Grizzly or color to match the insect
Fly Tier: Charles Vestal

Zelon Wing Comparadun

Hook: Dry fly #14 - #22
Thread: Color to match insect
Tail: Microfibetts, divided
Body: Stripped hackle stem and dubbing
Wings: Fanned Zelon
Head: Thread
Fly Tier: Bub Heintz

Midges, Spiders, and Variants . . .

Adult Midge

Hook: Dry fly #16 - #22
Thread: Color to match the body
Rib: Fishair
Body: Micro tubing,
Wings: Medallion sheeting
Hackle: Hoffman saddle
Head: Thread
Shell back: Medallion sheeting
Fly Tier: Shane Stalcup

Black Midge

Hook: TMC 16 - #22
Thread: Black
Body: Thread
Wings: Strip of clear freezer bag, cut to shape
Hackle: Black, tied dry fly style
Head: Thread
Fly Tier: Gale Doudy

Black Variant

Hook: Dry fly #12 - #18
Thread: Black
Tail: Moose hair
Rib: Optional
Body: Peacock herl, stripped in the back, natural in front
Wings: Moose hair, divided
Hackle: Black, variant style
Head: Thread
Fly Tier: Al Beatty

Bloody Midge

Hook: Dry fly #18 - #24
Thread: Black
Body: Thread abdomen, red dubbed thorax
Wings: Krystal Flash post
Hackle: Black, tied parachute style
Head: Thread
Fly Tier: John Schaper

Brooks Midge

Hook: TMC 2487 #16 - #22
Thread: Black
Body: Black tying thread
Wings: Rainey's foam parachute post
Hackle: Black
Head: Thread
Fly Tiers: Pat & Carol Oglesby

Bud's Midge

Hook: TMC 2587 #16 - #22
Thread: Black or color to match insect
Body: Black ultra chenille or color to match insect
Wings: Turkey biot over body
Hackle: Black or color to match insect
Head: Thread
Fly Tier: Bud Heintz

Carrot Variant

Hook: Dry fly #12 - #16
Thread: Orange
Tail: Moose hair
Rib: One strand of DMC silver thread
Body: Orange tying thread
Hackle: Brown, variant style
Head: Thread
Fly Tier: Al Beatty

Copper King - Spider

Hook: Dry fly #10 - #18
Thread: Copper brown
Tail: Bleached moose hair
Body: Copper wire back, brown dubbing front under hackle
Wings: Bleached moose hair
Hackle: Brown, over sized
Head: Thread
Fly Tier: Al Beatty

Coq de Leon Skater

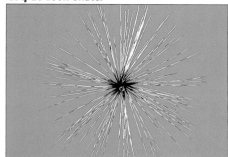

Hook: Short shank dry fly
Thread: Black 6/0
Hackle: Two Coq de Leon feathers tied concave sides together
Head: Thread
Fly Tier: Marvin Nolte

Deer Hair Adult Midge

Hook: TMC 100 #18-24   **Thread:** Sandy dun or gray 12/0
Rib: Tying thread or fine copper wire
Body: Fine texture deer hair light tan/ gray
Wings: Small white or dun gray hackle tips
Hackle: Same as legs   **Head & Thorax:** Gray dubbing
Legs: One turn of small partridge feather (from top of head)
To make the abdomen portion of the body: attach rib material first, above the hook barb, tie in & flare deer hair with fine tips pointing rearward. Advance the thread forward to a position 1/3 shank length behind the eye. Pull hair forward & tie down.
Fly Tier: Mike Jocobs

Green Weenie

Hook: Long shank #8
Thread: Olive
Tail: Ginger hackle fibers
Body: Spun and trimmed olive deer hair
Wings: Ginger hackle points
Hackle: Ginger
Head: Spun and trimmed olive deer
Eyes: Melted mono
Fly Tier: Thomas Leow

Gunnison Variant - Lime

Hook: Dry fly #12 - #20
Thread: Lime green
Tail: Moose hair
Rib: Grizzly dyed orange hackle, under sized
Body: Lime green thread
Wings: Moose hair, divided
Hackle: Cree or grizzly, variant style
Head: Thread
Fly Tier: Al Beatty

Gunnison Variant - Orange

Hook: Dry fly #12 - #20
Thread: Hot orange
Tail: Moose hair
Rib: Grizzly dyed orange hackle, under sized
Body: Orange tying thread
Wings: Moose hair, divided
Hackle: Cree or grizzly, variant style
Head: Thread
Fly Tier: Al Beatty

Hair Bare - Spider

Hook: Scud #8 - #16
Thread: Lime green or color of choice
Tail: Moose hair, tied long
Body: Tying Thread
Hackle: Stacked and spin deer hair
Head: Thread
Fly Tier: Al Beatty

Hatton's Gnat

Hook: Dry fly #16 - #22
Thread: Black
Body: Bleached peacock herl
Hackle: Dark ginger or brown
Head: Thread
Fly Tier: Jeff Hatton

Hot Spot Midge

Hook: Long shank #18 - #22
Thread: Black
Body: Peacock herl and hot color in center
Hackle: Black hackle front and back
Head: Thread
Fly Tier: Gretchen Beatty

Javallina Variant

Hook: Dry fly #14 - #18
Thread: Brown
Tail: Brown hackle fibers
Body: Two javallina fibers
Hackle: Brown oversize one hook size
Head: thread
Fly Tier: B. J. Lester

JJ Midge

Hook: Standard dry fly #20 - #24
Thread: Black
Tail: Coq de Leon fibers
Rib: Optional fine wire
Body: Tying thread
Hackle: Grizzly
Head: Thread
Fly Tier: Jerry Toft

K.C.'s Crystal

Hook: Mustad 80100
Thread: Black
Body: Holographic silver tinsel, black dubbing
Wings: CDC tuft
Head: Thread
Fly Tier: Kieran Frye

Lady McConnel

Hook: Dry fly #14 - #16
Thread: Gray, tan, olive
Tail: Moose hair, shuck - grizzly hackle tip
Body: Thread body with elk hair tied humpy style
Wings: Elk, single post
Hackle: Grizzly brown mix
Head: Thread
Fly Tier: John Newbury

Midge Cluster

Hook: Dry fly #16 - #24
Thread: Black
Rib: Optional fine wire
Body: Peacock herl front and back, black thread center
Hackle: Grizzly
Head: Thread
Fly Tier: Gretchen Beatty

Parachute Midge Cluster

Hook: Dry fly #14 - #16
Thread: Black
Body: Thread and a clump of Antron yarn
Wings: Antron body yarn in a very short post, pressed flat after wrapping hackle
Hackle: Grizzly
Head: Thread
Fly Tier: Jim Cramer

Peacock Midge

Hook: Standard dry fly #20 - #24
Thread: Black
Thorax: Stripped peacock herl stem
Abdomen: Peacock herl
Wings: Gray CDC
Head: Thread
Fly Tier: Jeff Hatton

Posted Midge Cluster

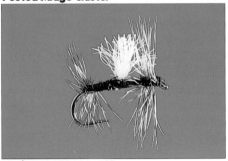

Hook: TMC 100 #16 - #22
Thread: Black
Body: Black thread
Wings: White synthetic post
Hackle: Grizzly, tied front and back
Head: Thread
Fly Tiers: Pat & Carol Oglesby

Quill Midge

Hook: Standard dry fly #20 - #24
Thread: Brown
Body: Stripped ginger hackle stem
Wings: Ginger CDC
Head: Thread
Fly Tier: Jeff Hatton

San Juan Midge

Hook: Dry fly #18 - #24
Thread: Brown
Rib: Optional fine wire
Body: Tying thread
Hackle: Brown, tied sparse
Head: Thread
Fly Tier: Al Beatty

Silver King - Variant

Hook: Dry fly #10 - #18
Thread: Gray
Tail: Moose hair
Body: Silver DMC thread, one strand
Wings: Moose hair, divided
Hackle: Grizzly
Head: Thread
Fly Tier: Al Beatty

Spent Midge

Hook: Mustad 94840 #24
Thread: Black
Tail: Microfibbets, split
Body: Black thread, peacock herl thorax
Wings: Spectra Flash cut to shape
Head: Thread
Fly Tier: Gordon Mankins

White's Midge

Hook: Dry fly #16 - #22
Thread: Black
Body: Black thread back, peacock herl front
Wings: Peacock herl delta style
Hackle: Black palmered
Head: Thread
Fly Tier: Gretchen Beatty

Wissahickon Midge

Hook: TMC 2457 #20 - #24
Thread: Black
Body: Black and brown CDC feather
Wings: White CDC
Head: Thread
Fly Tier: Jerry Caruso

Woven Hair Hackle Spider

Hook: Dry fly #10
Thread: Black
Body: Spun and trimmed black deer hair
Hackle: Woven long hair (badger or skunk), George Grant style
Head: Thread
Fly Tier: Jim Cramer

Stoneflies . . .

Air-Filled O2 Stonefly

Hook: TMC 5212 #6
Thread: Orange
Body: Stonefly imprint O2 Body Material
Wings: Blonde bull elk hair
Hackle: Natural or black deer hair collar
Head: Deer hair bullet style
Legs: Black rubber leg material
Fly Tier: Robert Williamson

Bird's Rubber Leg

Hook: Long shank #4
Thread: Orange
Butt: Orange tying thread
Tail: Brown rubber leg, short tuft of black poly yarn
Rib: Trimmed brown hackle, fine wire counter wrapped
Body: Orange floss over black poly yarn
Wings: Bull elk, brown bear over wing
Hackle: Brown, trimmed top and bottom
Head: Thread
Legs: Brown rubber legs
Fly Tier: Dave Borjas

Bubba's Yellow Sally

Hook: TMC 200R #16
Thread: Yellow
Butt: Small ball of orange dubbing
Body: Yellow dubbing
Wings: Swept back wonder wings, tent style
Hackle: Ginger, trimmed on top
Head: Thread
Fly Tier: John Schaper

Chartreuse Stimulator

Hook: TMC 200R #8 - #18
Thread: Olive
Tail: Deer hair, flared and short
Body: Peacock and chartreuse dubbing, tied royal Wulff style
Wings: Deer hair
Hackle: Grizzly palmered the length of the fly
Head: Chartreuse dubbing
Fly Tier: John Schaper

Clark's Parachute Stonefly

Hook: Dry fly #8 - #10
Thread: Orange
Body: Gold tinsel
Under Wings: Orange macramé yarn, combed
Wings: Deer hair
Parachute post: Pink macramé yarn
Hackle: Brown, parachute style
Head: Thread
Fly Tier: Lee Clark

Clark's Stonefly

Hook: Dry fly #8 - #10
Thread: Orange
Body: Gold tinsel
Under wing: Orange macramé yarn, combed
Wings: Deer hair
Hackle: Brown
Head: Thread
Fly Tier: Lee Clark

DB Stonefly

Hook: Long shank #4
Thread: Orange
Butt: Orange tying thread
Tail: Brown rubber legs
Rib: Trimmed brown hackle, fine wire counter wrapped
Body: Orange floss
Wings: Bull elk, brown bear over wing
Head: Moose hair, bullet style
Legs: Brown rubber legs, tied low for support
Fly Tier: Dave Borjas

Egg Sack Stone

Hook: TMC 200R #6 - #14
Thread: Color to match body
Body: Dubbing to match the insect
Egg sack: closed cell foam
Wings: Elk hair
Hackle: Grizzly brown mix
Head: Elk hair
Legs: Optional
Fly Tier: Adam Trina

Extended Foam Stone

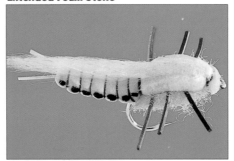

Hook: Mustad 80250G #8
Thread: Brown
Tail: Fine yellow living rubber
Rib: Thread
Abdomen: Yellow craft foam, felt tip markings
Thorax: Yellow craft foam, top - yellow wool, bottom
Wings: White craft fur
Head: Foam
Legs: Brown living rubber
Fly Tier: Floyd Franke

Fluttering Stone

Hook: TMC 200R, #4 - #12
Thread: Gray or to match the fly
Tail: Coachman brown turkey biots
Abdomen: Orange and brown embroidery yarn, woven
Thorax: Black closed cell foam
Wings: Deer hair, tied spent
Head: Trimmed foam
Legs: Optional
Fly Tier: Joe Ayre

Fluttering Stone

Hook: Dry fly #8 - #10
Thread: Orange
Body: Gold tinsel, orange macramé yarn dubbed
Under wing: Orange macramé yarn
Wings: Deer hair
Hackle: Brown
Head: Dubbed orange macramé yarn
Fly Tier: Lee Clark

Foam Stone-Legs

Hook: Dry fly #8
Thread: Hot orange
Tail: Coachman turkey biots
Rib: Thread in bands
Body: Black closed cell foam, tied on needle, removed and tied on hook
Wings: Elk hair
Hackle: Moose hair collar
Head: Moose
Legs: Optional rubber legs
Fly Tier: Al Beatty

Foam Stone

Hook: Dry fly #8
Thread: Orange
Tail: Two black turkey biots
Body: Black closed cell foam, extended body over needle then removed & tied to hook
Wings: Elk main hair
Hackle: Black deer hair collar
Head: Black deer hair bullet style
Fly Tier: Al Beatty

Golden Foam

Hook: Dry fly #12
Thread: Dark brown
Tail: Coachman turkey biots
Rib: Thread in bands
Body: Yellow closed cell foam, tied on needle, removed and tied on hook
Wings: Perfect Cut stone fly wings
Hackle: Elk hair collar
Head: Elk hair
Legs: Optional rubber legs
Fly Tier: Al Beatty

Golden Stone

Hook: Long shank dry fly
Thread: Yellow
Rib: Fine copper wire, counter wound
Body: Gold Antron yarn
Hackle 1: Brown, hook gape long barbs, palmered
Hackle 2: Yellow at the shoulder twice as long as brown
Hackle 3: Lemon wood duck at the head, barbs extending to the bend
Fly Tier: Marvin Nolte

Henry's Fork Salmon Fly

Hook: TMC 2302 #6 - #8
Thread: Fire orange
Tail: Black moose
Body: Black & orange molon yarn woven over .025 leader material
Wings: Dark elk over iridescent flat ribbon cut to shape
Hackle: Brown, palmered & trimmed
Head: Black elk tied bullet style
Legs: Black round rubber (optional)
Fly Tier: Mark Hoeser

Hoffman Stonefly

Hook: TMC #6
Thread: Light gray
Body: Orange poly yarn, twisted before wrapping
Wings: Deer or elk hair
Hackle: Grizzly dyed brown, tied reverse parachute
Head: Thread
Fly Tier: Henry Hoffman

Hole-In-One Stonefly

Hook: TMC 300 #4
Thread: Body orange, head hot fluorescent orange
Tail: Black biots
Body: Hot orange golf tee
Caseback: Black latex top back
Wings: Pre-made from vain marked material
Hackle: Deer hair collar
Head: Deer hair bullet style
Eyes: Mono, medium size
Legs: Black rubber leg
Fly Tier: Gerald M. James

Hot Spot Sally

Hook: Dry fly #12 - #18
Thread: Lime green
Tag & hot spot: Thread
Tail: Elk hair, flared
Rib: Optional
Body: Pale yellow dubbing
Wings: Elk hair
Hackle: Ginger, palmered and trimmed even with hook gape
Head: Trimmed elk
Legs: Optional rubber legs
Fly Tier: Gretchen Beatty

Iridescent Golden Stone

Hook: Daiichi 2220 #4 - #8
Thread: Rusty orange
Tail: Stripped hackle stems, divided
Body: Iridescent Dubbing #38 gold stone
Wings: Gray & brown Swiss straw glued together and trimmed
Hackle: Over sized ginger palmered over thorax
Head: Iridescent Dubbing #38 gold stone
Eyes: Small black glass beads
Antenna: Stripped hackle stems
Fly Tier: Ronn Lucas

Irres. Stimulator

Hook: Daiichi 1270 #6 - #16
Thread: Color to match body
Tail: Elk tied short
Rib: Extra fine clear nylon thread
Body: Orange spun deer, palmered brown hackle
Wings: Elk hair to end of the tail
Hackle: Grizzly
Head: Yellow dubbing
Eyes: Extra fine black mono
Legs: Optional
Fly Tier: Bill Black

SRI Irresistible Temptation

Hook: Daiichi 1270, #8 - #10
Thread: Orange
Tail: Elk hair, tied short
Body: Deer dyed orange, spun and trimmed to shape
Wings: Epoxied brown Swiss straw cut to shape under an elk hair over wing
Legs: Brown rubber leg material, three per side
Head: Orange Lite Brite dubbing
Eyes: Melted mono
Hackle: Grizzly dyed orange, palmered over the head
Antenna: Orange dyed mono
Fly Tier: Bill Black, Spirit River Inc.

Jeff's Furled Sally

Hook: Dry fly #14 - #18
Thread: Tan
Body: Furled yellow poly yarn,
Egg sack: Red marker
Wings: Medium gray CDC
Hackle: Honey dun or ginger
Head: Thread
Fly Tier: Jeff Hatton

Lime Green Seducer

Hook: TMC 200R #12 - #16
Thread: Red
Tail: Light elk
Rib: Fine copper wire
Body: Yellow dubbing, ginger palmered hackle
Thorax: Peacock herl
Wings: Elk over synthetic winging over Krystal Flash
Hackle: Grizzly
Head: Red thread
Fly Tier: Pat & Carol Oglesby

Little Yellowstone

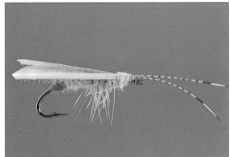

Hook: TMC 200R #14 - #20
Thread: Yellow
Butt: Red dubbing
Body: Cream dubbing
Wings: Two yellow turkey biots over wood duck fibers
Hackle: Ginger
Head: Thread
Antenna: Two wood duck fibers
Fly Tier: Gary Grant

Little Yellow Stonefly

Hook: TMC 921 #12 - #14
Thread: Light Cahill
Tail/extended Body: Yellow vernile/ red fabric paint egg sack
Body: Yellow llama dubbing
Wings: Blacked coastal deer hair over iridescent ribbon cut to shape
Hackle: Light ginger
Head: Yellow llama dubbing
Antenna: Gold Flexi Floss split in half
Fly Tier: Mark Hoeser

LP Gas

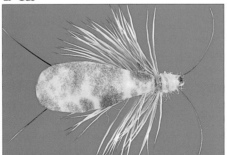

Hook: #10 Daiichi 1750 **Thread:** White tinted pale yellow
Tail: Two red pig hairs divided by small ball of pale yellow dubbing
Abdomen: Pale yellow dyed strip of Evasote, edged with Pantone 134-M
Legs: Three separated small bunches of elk spun to the sides and bottom
Thorax: Pale yellow dubbing around each of the three sets of legs
Wing: Tyvek dyed pale yellow marked with Pantone 464-M
Head: Pale yellow dubbing **Antenna:** Two red pig hairs
Fly Tier: Wayne Luallen

Parachute Simulator - Royal

Hook: TMC 200R #6 - #14
Thread: Black
Tail: Elk hair, tied short
Rib: Fine copper wire, optional
Body: Peacock herl and red floss
Wings: Elk hair with poly yarn post
Hackle: Brown parachute style
Head: Thread
Legs: Brown rubber legs, optional
Fly Tier: Adam Trina

Pteronarcys Dry

Hook: Long shank dry fly
Thread: Hot orange
Rib: Fine copper wire
Body: Hot orange Antron yarn
Hackle 1: Brown hook gape long barbs, palmered
Hackle 2: Hot orange at the shoulder twice as long as brown
Hackle 3: Teal flank at the head, barbs extending to hook bend
Fly Tier: Marvin Nolte

Rainy's Golden Stone

Hook: Dry fly #10 - #14
Thread: Yellow
Tail: Fine monofilament
Rib: Fine gold wire
Body: Yellow Cross Link foam, red glass bead
Wings: Mottled fly film
Hackle: Hoffman brown saddle
Head: Thread
Eyes: Rainy's Bug Eye Sticks
Antenna: Fine monofilament
Fly Tier: Rainy Riding

RL Stone

Hook: Daiichi 2220 #4 - #12
Thread: Color to match body
Body: Iridescent Dubbing to match insect
Wings: Elk hair
Hackle: Over sized to match insect
Head: Same as body
Eyes: Small glass beads
Antenna: Stripped hackle stems
Fly Tier: Ronn Lucas

Squirrel Stone

Hook: Dry fly #6 - #14
Thread: Color to match body
Body: Poly yarn to match insect
Wings: Squirrel tied Trude style
Head: Black deer tied bullet style
Legs: Black Silli-Con
Fly Tier: Al Beatty

SS Adult Stonefly

Hook: TMC 2312 #8
Thread: Black
Tail: Turkey biots
Body: Round foam & tape; coated with SofTex
Wings: Medallion sheeting
Head: Thread
Legs: Round rubber
Eyes: Burnt mono
Fly Tier: Shane Stalcup

SS Chuck's Little Yellow Sally

Hook: TMC 101 #14
Thread: Yellow Danville 3/0 monocord
Tail: Cream goose biots - egg sack - braided red floss
Rib: Tying thread
Body: Yellow food tray foam and yellow dubbing thorax
Wings: Lemon wood duck flank - reverse flank technique
Hackle: Ginger
Head: Eyes - yellow tying thread
Eyes: Burnt black crinkle hair
Fly Tier: Chuck Echer

Tom's Stonefly

Hook: Mustad 94831 #6 - #10
Thread: Black, hot orange
Tail: Gray goose biots
Body: Orange & brown antron yarn twisted and wrapped over closed cell foam
Wings: Black closed cell foam over a moose hair under wing
Over Wings: Elk hair
Head: Moose hair tied bullet style
Legs: Black round rubber
Fly Tier: Tom Hawley

Traveling Stonefly

Hook: Dry fly #8 - #10
Thread: Orange
Body: Gold tinsel
Under wing: Orange macramé yarn, combed
Wings: Deer hair
Hackle: Brown, sparse, trimmed on bottom
Head: Orange macramé yarn dubbed
Fly Tier: Lee Clark

Trout Candy

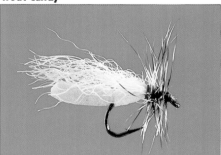

Hook: Eagle Claw LO55 #18
Thread: Brown 8/0
Abdomen: Green, yellow, or chartreuse craft foam
Thorax: Uni-Stretch color to match
Wings: Sparse light colored snowshoe hare's foot
Hackle: Grizzly
Head: Thread
Fly Tier: Floyd Franke

Wing Thing

Hook: Standard 3x long or TMC 200R, #6 - #16
Thread: Orange or to match the fly
Rib: Optional fine wire
Body: Peacock and orange floss
Wings: Gray closed cell foam, trimmed
Head: Trimmed foam from the wing
Legs: Black Silli-con
Fly Tier: Adam Trina

Wood Road #16 - Spent Stone

Hook: TMC 200R #4 - #16
Thread: Orange
Tail: Black turkey fibers
Body: Peacock herl butt, orange floss, grizzly body hackle
Wings: Russian squirrel and medium dun hackle tips
Hackle: Grizzly
Head: Thread
Antenna: Black turkey fibers
Fly Tier: Gary Grant

Woven Stonefly Adult

Hook: TMC 5212 #6
Thread: Rust
Body: Woven rust and brown poly yarn over cork board under body
Wings: Blonde bull elk
Hackle: Deer hair collar
Head: Deer hair bullet style
Legs: Black rubber leg material
Fly Tier: Robert Williamson

SRI Yellow Sally

Hook: TMC 200R, #14 - #18
Thread: Yellow
Tail: Mallard dyed wood duck fibers, tied short
Butt: Red Fine & Dry dubbing
Body: Yellow Fine & Dry dubbing
Wings: Yellow CDC with feather stems tied low along the hook shank
Topping: Gray turkey biot
Head: Thread
Antenna: Mallard dyed wood duck fibers
Fly Tier: Bill Black, Spirit River Inc.

Yellow Stimulator

Hook: TMC 200R #8 - #18
Thread: Yellow
Tail: Deer hair, flared and short
Body: Peacock and yellow dubbing, tied royal Wulff style
Wings: Deer hair
Hackle: Grizzly palmered the length of the fly
Head: Yellow dubbing
Fly Tier: John Schaper

Terrestrials & Mice . . .

Air-Filled O2 Cicada

Hook: TMC 5212 #8
Thread: Black
Body: Black O2 Body Material
Wings: Elk hair and Krystal Flash
Hackle: None
Head: Spun and trimmed black deer hair
Legs: Orange rubber legs with black marking
Fly Tier: Robert Williamson

Air-Filled O2 Hopper

Hook: TMC 5212 #10
Thread: Olive
Body: Light yellow O2 Body Material
Wings: Lacquered pheasant rump feather over elk hair under wing
Hackle: Deer hair collar
Head: Deer hair bullet style
Legs: Brown rubber leg material
Fly Tier: Robert Williamson

The Arctic Shrew

Hook: Wide gaped hook, #1/0 - 3/0
Thread: Black monocord
Tail: Elk mane
Body: Caribou hair spun and trimmed on the bottom
Head: Swept back caribou
Eyes: Black head needles
Fly Tier: Royce Dam

Bailey's Beetle

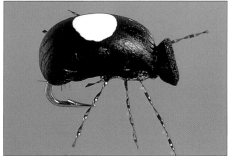

Hook: Dry fly #10 - #14
Thread: White for body & legs, black for rest
Body: Pearl mylar under black Rainey's foam
Head: Trimmed body foam
Legs: Black Krystal Flash
Fly Tier: Bill Murdich

Beamoc Beetle fr.

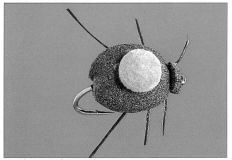

Hook: Mustad 80250BF #12
Thread: Black
Body: Craft Foam, black with orange dot
Head: Craft foam
Legs: Black mono coated with Flex-Cement
Fly Tier: Floyd Franke

Bill's Hopper

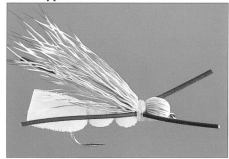

Hook: TMC 5212 #8 - #12
Thread: Yellow
Tail: Extension of foam body
Body: Yellow Evasote foam
Wings: Tips of deer hair from the head
Head: Deer hair bullet style
Legs: Brown rubber legs
Fly Tier: Bill Murdich

Bud's Cricket

Hook: Dry fly #4 - #10
Thread: Black or tan
Tail: Trimmed hackle center, hackle stem both sides
Body: Contrasting deer hair trimmed, black or tan
Hackle: Deer hair collar
Head: Trimmed deer hair
Legs: Knotted pheasant tail fibers
Antenna: Horse hair
Fly Tier: Bud Heintz

Bud's Hopper

Hook: Dry fly #4 - #14
Thread: Tan
Body: Trimmed deer hair, light top, dark bottom
Wings: None
Hackle: Deer hair collar
Head: Trimmed deer hair
Legs: Knotted pheasant tail fibers
Antenna: Horse hair (optional)
Fly Tier: Bud Heintz

CDC Foam Ant

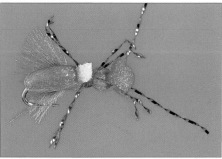

Hook: Daiichi 1100, #16 - #18
Thread: Red
Body: Red CDC
Over body: Red closed cell foam
Thorax: Red CDC under red closed cell foam
Indicator: Yellow closed cell foam tuft, tied between
the two body segments
Head: Thread
Legs: Red Crystal Splash, each leg is bent to shape
Antenna: Red Crystal Splash
Fly Tier: Bill Black, Spirit River Inc.

CDC Foam Beetle

Hook: Daiichi 1100, #12 - #16
Thread: Black
Body: Black CDC under and over body of black
closed cell foam
Legs: Black goose biots
Head: Trimmed foam remaining from the over body
Indicator: Yellow closed cell foam
Antenna: Black Crystal Splash
Fly Tier: Bill Black, Spirit River Inc.

Chernobyl Ant

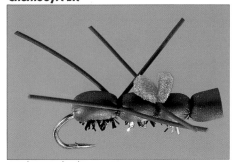

Hook: Long shank #6 - #10
Thread: Black
Body: Rainy's Float Foam over black crystal chenille
Head: Trimmed foam
Legs: Black Round Rubber Legs
Sight Indicator: Rainy's red Evasote
Fly Tier: Rainy Riding

Cook's Moth

Hook: Dry fly #12
Thread: Color to match body
Rib: Optional
Body: Dubbing to match insect
Wings: Deer hair fanned with mono
Head: Thread
Fly Tier: Leroy Cook

Copper Hopper

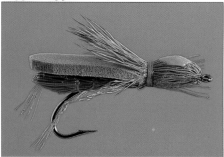

Hook: Dai-Riki 270 #4 - #12
Thread: Orange
Rib: Tying thread
Body: Gold dyed elk, extended body
Wings: Thin tan foam
Head: Gold elk bullet head
Legs: Orange super hair, knotted
Fly Tier: Scott Sanchez

CW Black Ant

Hook: Daiichi 1100, #14 - #20
Thread: Black
Body: Black dyed deer hair, spun and trimmed in two segments
Wing post: Pearl Crystal Splash, tied as a parachute post
Hackle: Black, tied parachute style
Head: Thread
Fly Tier: Bill Black, Spirit River Inc.

Deer Fly

Hook: Dry fly #14
Thread: Black
Tail: Moose body hair
Body: Peacock herl
Wings: Grizzly hen tips, delta style
Hackle: Grizzly brown mix
Head: Thread
Fly Tier: Bear Andrews

Flat Water Mosquito

Hook: Dry fly #18
Thread: Gray
Tail: Light dun hackle fibers
Body: Goose wing fibers with a gray dubbed thorax
Wings: Grizzly hackle tips, divided wide
Head: Thread
Fly Tier: John Schaper

Flopper

Hook: Dry fly #8
Thread: Red, black
Tail: Red yarn
Rib: Red thread
Body: Yellow yarn
Wings: Deer hair tied as a post
Hackle: Furnace or brown
Head: Black thread
Fly Tier: Carl E. Wolf

Flying Black Ant

Hook: TMC 5210, #12 - #16
Thread: Black
Body: Black muskrat dubbing, tied in two segments
Wings: Clear strip of freezer bag material
Hackle: Black, tied between the two body segments
Head: Thread
Fly Tier: Gale Doudy

Foam Cicada

Hook: TMC 9300 #8 - #12
Thread: Black
Body: Black foam over peacock herl
Wings: Light deer or elk over synthetic wing or Krystal Flash
Head: Trimmed foam
Legs: Black rubber
Fly Tiers: Pat & Carol Oglesby

Foam Post Hopper

Hook: Long shank #6 - #10
Thread: Brown
Rib: Brown thread
Body: Rainy's 1/16" tan Cross Link
Wings: Hoffman brown hen saddle over Krystal Flash, parachute post
Hackle: Hoffman bleached grizzly, parachute style
Head: Rainy's tan Sparkle Dub
Legs: Rainy's tan Round Rubber Legs
Fly Tier: Rainy Riding

GR Beetle - Orange

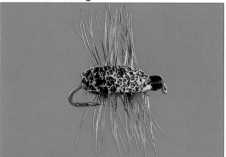

Hook: Dry fly #14 - #16
Thread: Black
Rib: Light copper wire (optional)
Body: Mix of brown and orange dubbing
Shell back: Mottled brown Bug Skin
Hackle: Grizzly dyed orange, palmered and trimmed top and bottom
Head: Thread
Fly Tier: Gale Doudy

Hi-Vis Hopper

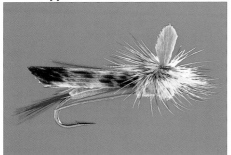

Hook: TMC 200R #8 - #10
Thread: Yellow
Tail: Red hackle
Body: Abdomen yellow closed cell foam
Thorax: Yellow dubbing
Wings: Turkey tent style over yellow elk hair
Post: Hi-Vis orange
Hackle: Grizzly and yellow, mixed
Legs: Orange biots
Fly Tier: Dave Borjas

Irresistible House Fly

Hook: Daiichi 1100, #12 - #16
Thread: Black
Body: Dyed black deer hair, spun and trimmed to shape
Wings: Black Swiss straw, coated with epoxy
Head: Spun dyed black deer, trimmed top and bottom for the head
Legs: The legs are dyed deer hair fibers left on the sides for the head
Fly Tier: Bill Black, Spirit River Inc.

Mini Mouse

Hook: 3xl #10
Thread: Black 6/0
Tail: Black Silli-Con
Body: Flared deer
Head: Spun deer, felt tip eyes
Fly Tier: Al Beatty

Ostrich/Pheasant Hopper

Hook: Stimulator type dry #8
Thread: Yellow
Tail: Black or red deer
Body: Yellow ostrich & copper wire
Under wing: Yellow or tan deer
Over Wing: Church window pheasant
Hackle: Brown
Head: Golden or tan dubbing
Legs: Knotted rubber legs
Fly Tier: Jim Shearer

Para Cricket

Hook: Daiichi 1720, #8 - #12
Thread: Black
Rib: Black hackle, trimmed and palmered
Body: Black yarn
Wings: Black Swiss straw, coated with epoxy
Poly post: Chartreuse Sparkle Yarn
Hackle: Black, tied parachute style
Fly Tier: Bill Black, Spirit River Inc.

Parachute Ant

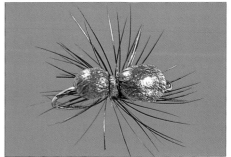

Hook: TMC 101 #10 - #18
Thread: Black
Body: Black foam
Post: White poly post, under body & pointed down
Hackle: Parachute under the hook
Head: Thread
Fly Tier: Bob Lay

Parachute Fly Ant

Hook: TMC 900BL #14 - #8
Thread: Black
Body: Black 1/8" closed cell foam
Wings: Cut to shape iridescent flat ribbon, yellow parachute post
Hackle: Black
Head: Thread
Legs: Black Krystal Flash
Fly Tier: Mark Hoeser

Parachute Grasshopper

Hook: TMC 200R #8 - #12
Thread: Tan
Rib: Gold wire
Body: Tan Soft Dub
Wings: White poly post & mottled turkey or peacock wing section
Hackle: Grizzly, tied parachute
Head: Thread
Legs: Two each, three strand pheasant tail fibers, knotted
Fly Tier: Bob Lay

Puff Ant (spent wing)

Hook: Mustad 3906 #14
Thread: Black
Body: Expanded Tulip Puffy black fabric paint
Wings: Black Hoffman hen
Hackle: Black Hoffman saddle, peacock herl under body
Head: Black Tulip Puffy fabric paint
Fly Tier: Gordon Mankins

Rainy's Bumble Bee

Hook: Dry fly #6
Thread: Yellow
Body: Rainy's 3/8" Bumble Bee popper
Wings: Two black goose biots
Hackle: Black Hoffman saddle
Head: Same as body
Legs: Yellow/black silly legs
Eyes: Rainy's large and small Bug-Eyes on a stick
Fly Tier: Rainy Riding

Rubber Legged Dave's Hopper

Hook: TMC 5212 #6 - 12
Thread: Tan 6/0
Tail: Red hackle fibers or red buck tail, extending past hook bend 1/3 shank length
Body: 1/16" yellow fly foam cut into a section 1/8" wide
Under wing: Dyed yellow deer hair
Wings: Mottled turkey
Hackle: Brown hackle palmered over yellow foam body
Collar: Coastal deer
Head: Tying thread
Legs: Yellow round rubber
Fly Tier: Mike Jacobs

Squirrel Hopper

Hook: 3xl #8
Thread: Yellow 6/0
Rib: Optional
Body: Yellow foam strip
Wings: Squirrel tail
Head: Deer hair tied bullet style
Legs: Knotted rubber
Fly Tier: Al Beatty

SS Cricket

Hook: TMC 2312 #10
Thread: Black
Tail: Turkey biot & Stalcup's damsel legs
Body: Round foam & tape
Wings: Medallion sheeting
Head: Round foam
Legs: Round rubber & Stalcup's cricket legs
Fly Tier: Shane Stalcup

Tom's Hopper

Hook: Mustad 94831 #6 - #12
Thread: Olive
Body: Brown & olive antron yarn twisted and wrapped over closed cell foam
Wings: Brown closed cell foam over a moose hair under wing
Over wing: Elk hair
Head: Olive deer hair tied bullet style
Legs: Brown round rubber
Fly Tier: Tom Hawley

Woven Cicada

Hook: TMC 5212 #8
Thread: Black
Body: Black and orange poly yarn woven over cork board under body
Wings: Elk hair and Krystal Flash
Hackle: Grizzly
Head: Black closed cell foam
Fly Tier: Robert Williamson

Chapter 2

NYMPHS AND WET FLIES

By Bruce Staples

Wet flies were probably the first flies to catch fish and they are inherently the most effective type of artificial flies. This is because they are surrogates for submerged food forms, which are the most available to fish. Fish also expend less energy in pursuit of submerged food forms. Wet flies simulate immature forms of aquatic insects (nymphs), a few terrestrial (aquatic wasps. certain crane flies) insects, and food forms that live submerged (shrimp, snails etc). That covers much ground for imitation potential and results in probably more wet-fly patterns, including nymphs, than any other pattern types.

Most tiers began in the art by constructing wet flies. And for most of these tiers, that quintessential wet fly, the Woolly Worm, was the first fly completed. Wet flies were reputedly first tied with cloth. These have appeared in southeast Europe early in the first millennium AD.

Quickly in time, natural materials including furs, feathers, and raffia were added in their construction. In the last few centuries synthetics appeared in wet-fly construction. Among the first used were glass beads and tinsels. Now the choice of natural and synthetic materials available for the construction of wet flies is endless.

Wet flies and nymphs are tied for the quest of all game fish, but their most developed use is for salmonoid. In this use they have traditional proportions. However the reader will see in the following chapter that these proportions are necessarily applied only in classic patterns. The result is a huge variety of wet flies, some very beautiful, some very effective, and some a combination of both. Wet flies will continue to dominate in variety because of the large number of submerged food forms. The only way to change this fact will be to outlaw the use of wet flies!

—Bruce Staples
Idaho Falls, Idaho

All-Purpose Nymphs . . .

Apache Lady

Hook: Mustad 59580, #10 - #16
Thread: Black
Tail: Golden pheasant tippets
Body: Peacock herl and glass bead, red or color of choice
Hackle: Brown, tied fore and aft
Head: Thread
Fly Tier: Gordon Mankins

Bead Head Prince

Hook: Mustad 9671, #8 - #18
Thread: Olive, black, or orange
Tail: Brown goose biots, divided
Rib: Fine copper wire or tinsel
Body: Peacock herl
Wings: White goose biots, divided
Hackle: Partridge or guinea, tied beard style
Head: Brass bead
Fly Tier: Cliff Stringer

Bear's Rump-Cock-Tail

Hook: Nymph hook, #8   **Thread:** Black
Tail: A tuft of fluff from the base of a pheasant rump feather
Body: Peacock herl, tied as three sections, pheasant rump collar between each
Wing case: Pheasant tail fibers, tied in four section with the last over the head
Hackle: Pheasant rump tied three sections in the body and one behind the hook eye
Eyes: Black mono
Head: Peacock herl and thread
Fly Tier: Bear Andrews

BT's Emerger

Hook: TMC 200R, #12 - #22   **Thread:** Tan
Tail: Brown hackle fibers, tied very sparse
Rib: One strand of copper Krystal Flash
Body: Hare's ear dubbing
Thorax: Orange and natural hare's ear dubbing, mixed
Gills: One turn of white ostrich, pulled to the sides
Wing case: Dark turkey tail section, coated with Aqua Flex
Hackle: Partridge, tied divided
Head: Dubbing from the thorax, thread
Fly Tier: Al Beatty

Bubble Bug

Hook: Mustad 3906B, #16 - #18
Thread: Black
Tail: Three pheasant tail fibers
Body: Wrapped pheasant tail fibers
Loop: White antron
Thorax: Black dubbing
Head: Thread
Fly Tier: Gene Trump

Buffalo Crane

Hook: Mustad 94831, #6
Thread: Brown
Rib: Thin copper wire
Body: Firmly wrapped buffalo hair over lead covered shank
Head: Dark fuzzy yarn
Fly Tier: Carl E. Wolf

Cham-mo The Killer Leech

Hook: Streamer 3XL, #8
Thread: Red
Tail: Spatula shaped chamois, colored with a black felt tip marker
Body: Brown dubbing or brown Canadian mohair yarn
Eyes: Black non-lead dumb bell
Legs: Optional
Fly Tier: Chuck Collins

Cream Dream

Hook: Mustad 9671, #8 - #16
Thread: Tan
Tail: Short tuft of white down under mallard breast fibers
Rib: Silver tinsel
Body: Pearl Lite Brite dubbing
Thorax: Peacock herl
Wing case: Rayon floss
Head: Thread
Fly Tier: Tom Tripi

Crystal Wing PT

Hook: Daiichi 1130, #10 - #18
Thread: Brown
Tail: Pheasant tail fibers, tied short
Rib: Copper wire
Body: Pheasant tail fiber, wrapped around the hook
Thorax: Peacock herl
Wing post: Pearl Crystal Splash, tied as a parachute post
Hackle: Brown, tied parachute style
Head: Thread
Fly Tier: Bill Black, Spirit River Inc.

Dan's Mysis Shrimp

Hook: Standard dry fly, #16 - #18
Thread: White
Tail: Clear plastic strip
Rib: Optional fine wire
Body: White sparkle dub
Eyes: Ultra Dub, trimmed even with body
Fly Tier: Dan Turner

Double Bead PT

Hook: Mustad 9671, #14 - #18
Thread: Black
Tail: Pheasant tail fibers
Rib: Fine gold wire
Body: Pheasant tail fibers, wrapped
Thorax: Brass bead behind peacock herl
Wing case: Pheasant tail fibers, pulled over the two part thorax
Head: Second brass bead
Fly Tier: Buzz Moss

Double Shell Back Nymph

Hook: Mustad 9672, #8 - #14, hook point rides up
Thread: Brown   **Tail:** Goose biots, divided
Body: Brown Larva Lace, adjust the size of Lace according to the hook size
Wing cases: Mottled turkey quill sections, one on top and bottom
Hackle & Thorax: Peacock and grizzly dyed brown hackle
Application: After wrapped the hackle, fold and tie the wing cases, lacquer each well
Head: Brown bead
Fly Tier: Mike Butler

Emu Nymph

Hook: TMC 3761, #10 - #14
Thread: Black
Tail: Emu fibers
Rib: Optional copper wire
Weight: Several wraps of lead in the thorax area
Body: Single emu feather, trimmed to shape
Wing case: Dark gray emu feather treated with thinned Aqua Seal
Head: Thread
Legs: Untrimmed emu feather left on the sides of the thorax
Fly Tier: Jerry Caruso

EZY Prince

Hook: Mustad 9671, #10 - #18
Thread: Black
Tail: Brown antron yarn
Rib: Fine copper wire
Body: Peacock herl
Wing: White antron yarn
Hackle: Brown, tied as a collar
Head: Brass bead, thread
Fly Tier: Al Beatty

Fat Tellico

Hook: Mustad 9672, #4 - #8
Thread: Brown
Rib: One strand of peacock herl
Body: Yellow chenille
Shell back: Several strand of peacock herl
Hackle: Brown or furnace, tied as a collar
Head: Thread or optional gold bead
Fly Tier: Craig Hull

Foam Biot Emerger

Hook: Daiichi 1100, #14 - #22
Thread: Gray
Tail: Gray Sparkle Yarn
Rib: Thread
Body: Gray goose biot
Thorax: Gray Fine & Dry dubbing
Wing case: Gray closed cell foam
Legs: Partridge
Head: Thread and trimmed foam from the wing case
Fly Tier: Bill Black, Spirit River Inc.

4th of July Nymph

Hook: Mustad 3906, #12 - #16
Thread: Black
Tail: Olive Krystal Flash, trimmed to length of hook shank
Body: Tan dubbing
Wing case: Olive Krystal Flash remaining from the tail
Legs: Olive Krystal Flash remaining from the wing case
Head: Pearl glass bead
Fly Tier: Derek Harryman

Full Motion Prince

Hook: Nymph, #12 - #18
Thread: Black
Tail: Brown CDC
Rib: Fine gold wire
Body: Peacock herl
Wings: White CDC
Hackle: Brown CDC, tied as a beard
Head: Thread
Fly Tier: David Curneal

Gimp

Hook: Mustad 94840, #10
Thread: Black
Tail: Dun hackle fibers
Body: Peacock herl
Wings: Two after shaft feathers tied on top of each other
Hackle: Dun hen hackle, tied as a collar
Head: Thread
Fly Tier: Dean Elder, Jr.

Ginger Bead Peacock

Hook: Mustad 3906, #10 - #14
Thread: Black
Tail: Ginger hackle fibers
Rib: Yellow thread
Body: Peacock herl
Hackle: Ginger, tied as a collar
Head: Spirit River #165 glass bead
Fly Tier: Bruce Staples

Golden Boy

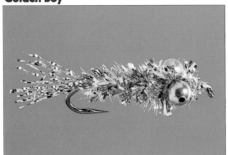

Hook: Mustad 9672, #10
Thread: Yellow
Tail: Gold Krystal Flash
Body: Small gold crystal chenille
Eyes: Gold bead chain
Head: Thread
Fly Tier: Tom Broderidge

The Gramper

Hook: Mustad 80050BR, #8
Thread: Black
Tail: Black goose biots
Body: Blackish/brown wool
Wing case: Black crow wing segment
Head: Blackish/brown wool
Legs: Black goose biots
Pinchers: Black goose biots
Fly Tier: Jim Childers

Gray Bunny

Hook: TMC 3761, #10 - #16
Thread: Black
Tail: Chinchilla guard hairs
Body: Gray rabbit dubbing
Hackle: Gray rabbit fur and guard hairs applied using a dubbing loop
Head: Black bead
Fly Tier: Lance Zook

Gray Fluff Nymph

Hook: Daiichi 1150, #12
Thread: White
Tail: Three teal fibers
Rib: Stripped quill
Body: Gray dubbing made from the fluff base of any duck feather
Wing case: Brown turkey tail fibers
Hackle: Teal fibers
Head: Thread
Fly Tier: Ted Patlin

Gray Goose

Hook: Standard nymph, #14
Thread: Black
Tail: Gray goose quill section, narrow
Rib: Thread
Body: Gray goose quill section, wrapped
Thorax: Gray glass bead and short segment of wrapped goose quill section
Wing case: Gray goose quill section
Head: Thread
Fly Tier: Buzz Moss

Gray Squirrel Nymph

Hook: TMC 200R, #10 - #20
Thread: Black
Tail: Wood duck
Rib: Gold oval tinsel
Body: Gray squirrel dubbing
Wing case: Gray duck quill section
Hackle: Wood duck, tied as a divided throat
Head: Thread
Fly Tier: Bill Chandler

GRHE Emerger

Hook: TMC 2487, #12 - #14
Thread: Tan
Tail: Partridge hackle fibers
Rib: Gold oval tinsel
Body: Hare's ear dubbing
Wings: Deer hair over CDC feather over 4 - 6 strands of Krystal Flash
Thorax: Hare's ear dubbing
Wing case: Deer hair
Fly Tier: David Hunter

H & L Emerger

Hook: Standard nymph, #12 - #20
Thread: Black
Tail: White poly
Rib: Optional
Abdomen: Stripped peacock herl quill
Thorax: Peacock herl
Wings: White poly, looped emerger style
Head: Thread and tuft of excess wing material
Fly Tier: Brett Clark

Hatton's Hare's Ear

Hook: TMC 2302, #10 - #20
Thread: Olive
Tail: Pine squirrel guard hairs and under fur
Rib: Yellow Krystal Flash
Hare's ear dubbing mix: Equal parts of dark brown otter and natural pine squirrel
Abdomen: Hare's ear dubbing, cigar shaped
Thorax: Hare's ear dubbing, loosely applied in a loop
Hackle: Picked out dubbing
Head: Thread
Fly Tier: Jeff Hatton

Hellgrammite

Hook: Mustad 9674, #6
Thread: White dyed black with a felt tip marker
Tail: Dark brown goose biots
Rib: Fine copper wire
Gills: White ostrich herl, black horse hair tied short through the abdomen
Body: Fine black chenille
Thorax: Black furry foam
Wing case & over Body: Black tyvek
Eyes: Melted 30 pound mono
Legs: Black New Dub
Fly Tier: Kent Bulfinch

Hump's Cress Bug

Hook: TMC 921, #12
Thread: Black
Rib: Fine brass or copper wire
Body: Mix of fox and gray squirrel dubbing
Hackle: Grizzly, palmered
Head: Thread
Fly Tier: Joe Humphreys

Hump's Pheasant Tail

Hook: TMC 921, #12 - #18
Thread: Black
Tail: Pheasant tail fibers
Rib: Fine brass or copper wire
Body: Wrapped pheasant tail fibers
Thorax: Brown dubbed thorax
Wings case: Brown hen back
Hackle: Partridge
Head: Thread
Fly Tier: Joe Humphreys

Len's Fuzzy

Hook: Mustad 9671, #8
Thread: Tan
Tail: Light orange elk
Body: Grizzly Chickabou dyed light orange, covering the hook
Head: Thread
Fly Tier: Len Holt

Lord Gray

Hook: Nymph, #12 - #18
Thread: Gray
Tail: Partridge fibers
Rib: Silver wire
Body: Gray muskrat dubbing
Thorax: Gray muskrat dubbing, picked out
Wing case: Partridge folded forward, tips to become the legs
Legs: Tips of feather for the wing case
Head: Thread
Fly Tier: George Harmeling

Mouse Nymph

Hook: TMC 100, #18 - #20
Thread: Gray
Tail: Narrow (1/16") strip of mouse hide with hair attached
Body: Mouse dubbing
Thorax: Mouse guard hairs in a dubbing loop
Wing case: Peacock herl
Head: Thread
Fly Tier: Marvin Nolte

O. J. Nymph

Hook: Mustad 9671, #10 - #16
Thread: Brown
Tail: Wood duck fibers
Body: Blend of orange, pink, yellow & white rabbit dubbing; light orange juice color
Rib: Dark brown thread
Thorax: Brown rabbit fur dubbing
Wing case: Brown dyed duck quill section
Hackle: Brown palmered overthorax, trim top and bottom
Head: Thread
Antenna: Optional, use fibers from the wing case
Fly Tier: Dave Engerbretson

Orange Asher (BH)

Hook: Mustad 80000, #12 - #20
Thread: Orange
Body: Tying thread
Hackle: Light grizzly or silver badger
Head: Gold or brass bead, thread
Fly Tier: Al Beatty

Orange Half Back

Hook: Mustad 9672, #6 - #14
Thread: Black
Tail: Pheasant tail fibers
Rib: Optional
Body: Peacock herl with a pheasant tail shell back
Thorax: Peacock herl
Hackle: Orange palmered over the thorax
Head: Thread
Fly Tier: Len Holt

Peacock Creeper

Hook: Scud, #8 - #18
Thread: Black
Tail: Wood duck fibers, tied sparse and short
Rib: Black thread
Body: Peacock herl
Hackle: Partridge tied as a collar between the body and thorax
Thorax: Peacock herl
Head: Bead, silver or gold
Fly Tier: Chuck Collins

Peacock Pearly Fly

Hook: TMC 2457, #12 - #14
Thread: Black
Tail: Four strands of Peacock Pearly or Krystal Flash
Body: Peacock Pearly, twisted and wrapped
Thorax: Black squirrel dubbing
Hackle: Black, optional
Head: Gold bead
Fly Tier: Mike Hogue

Phantom

Hook: Partridge K2B, #16
Thread: Clear nylon
Tail: Nylon, divided
Body: Larva lace, burnt markings
Head: Clear nylon
Fly Tier: Ian Russell

Pheasant Tail, Dazzle Eye

Hook: TMC 100, #10 - #16
Thread: Black
Tail: Pheasant tail fibers
Rib: Fine copper wire
Body: Pheasant tail fibers
Thorax: Peacock herl
Eyes: Small silver dumb bell
Legs: Grouse feather
Fly Tier: Gale Doudy

Prince Swimming Nymph

Hook: Daiichi 1150, #8 - #18
Thread: Black
Tail: Partridge hackle fibers, tied short
Rib: Fine copper wire, optional
Body: Peacock herl
Wings: Two strands of pearl Crystal Splash, tied one half the length of the body
Head: Gold Brite Bead
Legs: Partridge hackle fibers, tied along the top and sides
Fly Tier: Bill Black, Spirit River Inc.

PT 6-Pack

Hook: TMC 5263, #6 - #10
Thread: Green
Weight: Wrap copper wire on the first one-third of the hook, do not cut the excess
Rib: Spiral the excess copper wire to the bend of the hook and leave it there for the rib
Tail: Pheasant tail fibers
Body: Pheasant tail fibers dyed golden olive, wrapped
Hackle: Pheasant tail fibers as an under hackle and rump feather as a soft collar
Head: Thread
Fly Tier: Daniel Ferron

Puff's Hellgrammite

Hook: Mustad 94831, #6 - #10
Thread: Black
Tail: Black turkey biots
Body: Black ultra chenille
Thorax: Red ultra chenille
Wing case: Black ultra chenille
Hackle: Black
Head: Thread
Fly Tier: Gordon Mankins

Puffy Nymph

Hook: Mustad 94845, #10
Thread: Olive
Tail: Brown hackle fibers
Rib: Fine copper wire
Body: Brown thread
Wings: Dyed green partridge
Hackle: Olive marabou, tied as a collar
Head: Thread
Fly Tier: Eric Schubert

Quick Trip Nymph

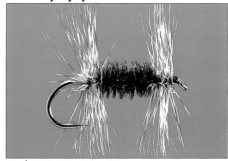

Hook: TMC 100, #12 - #22
Thread: Black
Tag: Fire orange floss
Weight: Optional
Rib: Fine gold or copper wire
Body: Peacock herl
Hackle: Grizzly tied front and back
Head: Thread
Fly Tier: Eric Pettine

Reed's Gunnison Coachman

Hook: TMC 2302, #12 - #16
Thread: Black
Tail: Golden pheasant crest fibers
Abdomen: Peacock herl
Thorax: Peacock herl, tied larger than the abdomen
Wings: White over brown calf tail fibers
Hackle: Furnace or coachman hen, tied as a collar
Head: Thread
Fly Tier: Carol Oglesby

RM Gray Bead

Hook: Mustad 9671, #12 - #16
Thread: Black
Tail: Gray marabou, tied short
Body: Gray rabbit dubbing
Hackle: Grizzly hen, tied as a collar
Head: Small black bead
Fly Tier: Robert Meuschke

Royal Coachman Nymph

Hook: Mustad 9674, #10 - #16
Thread: Brown
Tail: Golden pheasant tippets
Rib: Peacock herl
Body: Red floss
Thorax: Peacock herl
Wing case: Mallard flank
Legs: Fibers from a church window pheasant feather
Head: Thread
Fly Tier: Reginald Denny

Royal Lady Nymph

Hook: Mustad 9671, #10 - #16
Thread: Black
Tail: Three white ostrich herl tips
Rib: Black ostrich herl palmered over the body
Body: Fine black chenille
Wing case: Thin white plastic, folded
Head: Thread
Legs: Black hackle tied as a beard
Fly Tier: Ruth J. Zinck

Santa Fe Special

Hook: Mustad 3906B, #10
Thread: Brown
Tail: Pearlescent Fire Fly
Body: Burnt orange dubbing
Hackle: Brown hen, tied as a collar
Head: Thread
Fly Tier: Dana Griffin, III

Sheep Creek Special

Hook: Mustad 9672, #6 - #10
Thread: Black
Tail: Brown hackle wrapped at the hook bend
Rib: Fine gold, oval tinsel
Body: Peacock chenille
Wings: Mallard clump, tied trude style
Head: Thread
Fly Tier: Cliff Stringer

Soft & Dry Emerger

Hook: TMC 100, #10 - #20
Thread: Color to match the body
Rib: Orange Krystal Flash
Body: Olive dubbing or color of choice
Hackle one: Partridge tied as a soft hackle collar
Hackle two: Grizzly tied dry style - fish either wet, dry, or as an emerger
Head: Thread
Fly Tier: John Kimura

Still Water Creeper

Hook: Mustad 9671, #12 - #14
Thread: Black
Tail: Olive marabou, tied very sparse
Rib: Fine gold wire
Body: Olive angora goat dubbing
Over back: Olive marabou
Hackle: Grizzly dyed red or orange (optional)
Head: Thread
Fly Tier: George Nelson

Styx River Nymph

Hook: Mustad 9671, #8 - #16
Thread: Black
Tail: Black hackle fibers
Rib: Fine gold wire
Body: Black rabbit fur dubbing
Wing case: Wood duck fibers
Hackle: Black palmered over the thorax, trimmed top and bottom
Head: Thread
Fly Tier: Dave Engerbretson

Thorax Only Emerger

Hook: Mustad 94840, #16 - #22
Thread: Black
Tail: Long partridge coming directly from the thorax
Body: Brown dubbing in thorax only, no abdomen
Wing case: White antron yarn
Head: Thread
Fly Tier: Len Holt

Two Tone Series, Brown

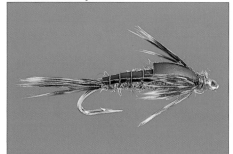

Hook: Mustad 9671, #12 - #18
Thread: Brown
Tail: Turkey tail fibers
Rib: Fine copper wire
Body: Light brown Fine & Dry dubbing
Back and wing case: Brown turkey biots
Head: Thread
Legs: Turkey tail fibers
Fly Tier: Duane Hada

Two Tone Series HE

Hook: Mustad 9671, #12 - #18
Thread: Brown
Tail: Turkey tail fibers
Rib: Fine copper wire
Body: Hare's ear dubbing
Back and wing case: Dark brown turkey biots
Head: Thread
Legs: Turkey tail fibers
Fly Tier: Duane Hada

Two Tone Series, Tan

Hook: Mustad 9671, #12 - #18
Thread: Tan
Tail: Pheasant tail fibers
Rib: Fine copper wire
Body: Tan Fine & Dry dubbing
Back and wing case: Tan turkey biots
Head: Thread
Legs: Pheasant tail fibers
Fly Tier: Duane Hada

Two Tone Series, Yellow

Hook: Mustad 9671, #12 - #18
Thread: Yellow
Tail: Pheasant tail fibers
Rib: Fine copper wire
Body: Yellow Fine & Dry dubbing
Back and wing case: Yellow turkey biots
Head: thread
Legs: Pheasant tail fibers
Fly Tier: Duane Hada

Ugly Bitch

Hook: Mustad 36890, #4 - #8
Thread: Black
Tail & antenna: Fine living rubber
Body: Medium peacock chenille
Hackle: Palmered furnace saddle hackle
Head: Thread
Fly Tier: Floyd Franke

Ultra Zug

Hook: Dai-Riki 075, #8 - #16
Thread: Dark brown
Tail: Guinea dyed green or olive
Rib: Pearl Krystal Flash
Body: Peacock Scintilla #46 dubbing
Hackle: Scintilla #46 tied as a clump at the front of the body
Head: Thread
Fly Tier: Scott Sanchez

Utility Nymph

Hook: TMC 200R, #10 - #22
Thread: color to match the body
Rib: Fine wire
Body: Dubbing on larger flies and biots on smaller, color of choice
Hackle: Optional
Head: Ostrich or peacock herl
Fly Tier: Bud Heintz

Water Boatman

Hook: Dai-Riki 070, #10 - #12
Thread: Black
Under Body: Black wool yarn
Body: Peacock herl
Shell back: Peacock wing fibers
Under belly: pearl ribbon strip to simulate an air bubble
Head: Peacock herl
Legs: Latex floss
Eyes: Burned mono
Fly Tier: John Newbury

Whispy

Hook: Mustad 94833, #6
Thread: Black
Tail: Orange marabou, tied sparse and short
Rib: Silver tinsel
Body: Medium black yarn
Hackle: Yellow, palmered
Head: Thread, tied extra large
Fly Tier: Carl E. Wolf

Caddis Nymphs . . .

B.B.H. Caddis Larva

Hook: TMC 200R, #10 - #18
Thread: Brown
Rib: Gray small ostrich herls
Body: Green ultra chenille
Thorax and Legs: Fox squirrel dubbing and guard hairs
Head: Gold bead
Fly Tier: Bill Chandler

Bead Head Caddis

Hook: TMC 2487, #14 - #18
Thread: Black
Rib: Fine gold wire
Body: Mix of olive and natural hare's ear dubbing
Hackle: Black ostrich
Head: Gold bead
Fly Tier: Matt Owens

Bead Head Caddis Pupa

Hook: Mustad 3906B, #12 - #18
Thread: Tan
Tail: Brown hen hackle fibers
Rib: Gold tinsel
Body: Natural Hare-Tron
Thorax: Dark natural Hare-Tron
Head: Gold bead
Legs: Brown hen hackle fibers, tied on both sides
Fly Tier: Jim Schollmeyer

Bead Pupa

Hook: TMC 3761, #12 - #18
Thread: Black
Body: Green glass beads, three or four depending on size
Head: Peacock herl
Fly Tier: Kurt Zelazny

Bead Thorax Peeking Caddis

Hook: Mustad 9671, #12 - #18
Thread: Black
Rib: Fine copper wire
Body: Turkey tail over dark dubbing
Thorax: Chartreuse bead
Legs: Black CDC, trimmed short
Head: Thread
Fly Tier: Paul Stimpson

Beamoc Caddis Emerger

Hook: Mustad 80200BR, #14 - #20
Thread: Olive
Body: Olive ultra chenille
Wings: Olive Krystal Flash
Head: Thread
Legs: Partridge
Fly Tier: Floyd Franke

Bill's Stick Caddis

Hook: TMC 200R, #6 - #10
Thread: Brown
Weight: 15 - 20 wraps of .015 non-lead wire
Tail: Dark brown marabou, tied very short
Body: Dark brown dubbing, orange antron, and copper Lite-Brite mixed
Sticks: Pheasant tail fibers, tied random along and around the body
Hackle: Black hen hackle, optional
Head: Bead
Fly Tier: Bill Carnazzo

Bonnet Carre Caddis

Hook: Mustad 80050, #10 - #14
Thread: Tan
Tail: Very small tuft of peacock herl
Body: Dark brown Larva Lace
Wings: Deer hair, tied very sparse
Head: Thread and ends of deer hair wing
Fly Tier: Tom Tripi

Bridge 99 Emerger

Hook: TMC 200R, #8 - #20
Thread: Brown
Rib: Fine copper wire
Body: Cream dubbing
Wing: Black squirrel under deer hair, the black under wing is longer than the over wing
Head: Trimmed fibers from the over wing, thread
Fly Tier: Gene Stutzman

Brook's Little Gray Caddis

Hook: Mustad 7957B, #10 - #14
Thread: Black
Tail: Yellow antron, trimmed short
Rib: Gold wire
Body: Gray hare's ear dubbing
Wing case: Gray ostrich
Hackle: Grouse, tied as a collar
Head: Thread
Fly Tier: Bruce Staples

Buckskin Caddis Larva

Hook: Daiichi 1270, #12 - #22
Thread: Brown
Under Body: Super Fine dubbing
Body: Buckskin midge tubing
Head: Brown SLF squirrel dubbing
Fly Tier: Shane Stalcup

Bud's Caddis Emerger

Hook: Mustad 37160
Thread: Black or color to match the body
Rib: Fine copper wire
Body: Dubbing or turkey biots
Wings: Duck quills, tied short and low, emerger style
Head: Black ostrich herl
Antenna: Wood duck fibers
Legs: Partridge, tied as a beard
Fly Tier: Bud Heintz

Caddis Larva

Hook: Daiichi 1120, #12 - #22
Thread: Brown
Under Body: Super Fine dubbing, color to match the insect
Body: Buckskin midge tubing
Shell back: Medallion Sheeting
Hackle: Partridge
Head: Brown SLF squirrel dubbing
Fly Tier: Shane Stalcup

Caddis Rock Worm

Hook: Mustad 80050, #16 - #22
Thread: Black
Rib: Very sparse Antron dubbing
Body: Fluorescent green Flexi-Floss
Thorax: Black Kreinik silk dubbing
Wing case: Black Bugskin
Legs: Starling hackle, fold over style
Head: Thread
Fly Tier: Dave Schmezer

Chickabou Caddis Pupa

Hook: TMC 200R, #8 - #10
Thread: Olive
Tail: Grizzly Chickabou
Rib: Fine gold wire
Body: Chickabou
Hackle: Grizzly rooster flank
Head: Dark gray Chickabou
Eyes: Dark brown melted mono
Fly Tier: Henry Hoffman

Dark Ovulating Caddis

Hook: Daiichi 1100, #10 - #14
Thread: Olive
Egg sack: Orange Fine & Dry dubbing
Body: Dark olive Fine & Dry dubbing
Thorax: Gold bead
Wings: Celo Z-Wing, colored with a green felt tip marker
Hackle: Dyed olive, tied as a collar
Antenna: Two moose body fibers
Head: Thread
Fly Tier: Bill Black, Spirit River Inc.

Dave's Muskrat

Hook: Dai-Riki 270, #14 - #18
Thread: Black
Tail: Black hackle fibers
Rib: Trimmed black hackle over fine gold tinsel
Body: Muskrat dubbing
Head: Black dubbing
Fly Tier: Eric Pettine

Echer's Wrecker

Hook: TMC 2487, #14
Thread: Black
Body: Micro Cable #25, peacock
Hackle: Black tip head feather from a Mearns quail
Head: Small glass bead, olive
Fly Tier: Chuck Echer

Edward's Emerger

Hook: TMC 200R, #14 - #22
Thread: Brown
Rib: Tying thread
Body: Olive brown Super Fine dubbing
Wings: Brown Swiss straw
Eyes: Melted mono
Head: Black Super Fine dubbing
Antenna: Two wood duck flank fibers
Fly Tier: Al Beatty

Emerging Traveling Sedge

Hook: Partridge K12ST, #8 - #14
Thread: Black
Rib: Krystal Flash
Body: Dark green seal fur dubbing
Wings: Gray duck quill section
Head: Foam tied on top of the fly to keep it in the surface film
Legs: Pheasant tail fibers
Fly Tier: Ian Russel

Flashy Caddis

Hook: Mustad 3906B, #14 - #16
Thread: Black
Body: Green Krystal Flash, twisted and wrapped
Thorax: Black ostrich herl
Head: Thread
Fly Tier: George Nelson

Free Swimming Caddis

Hook: Daiichi 1150, #16
Thread: White
Rib: Single strand of Krystal Flash
Body: Bright green dubbing
Thorax: Peacock herl
Head: Thread
Legs: Mottled brown soft hackle
Fly Tier: Ted Patlin

Glass House Caddis

Hook: Dai-Riki 060, #10 - #16
Thread: Black
Rib: Copper wire
Body: Scintilla peacock #46 dubbing
Thorax: Olive glass bead
Hackle: Grizzly or brown hen, tied as a collar
Head: Black metal bead
Fly Tier: Scott Sanchez

Golden Emerger

Hook: Kamasan 420, #12 - #16
Thread: Yellow
Body: Yellow micro Larva Lace
Thorax: Ginger rabbit dubbing
Hackle: Bob white quail, tied as a collar
Head: Thread or optional glass bead
Fly Tier: Mike Hogue

Green Rock Worm

Hook: Daiichi 1560, #12 - #16
Thread: Black
Rib: Fine gold wire
Body: A dubbing mix made from tan, green, brown, and black macramé yarn
Hackle: Optional
Head: A dubbing mix made from black and green macramé yarn
Fly Tier: Lee Clark

Hammer Caddis

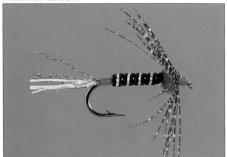

Hook: Mustad 9672, #10 - #14
Thread: Orange
Tail: Green Krystal Flash
Tag: Orange floss
Rib: One strand of yellow Krystal Flash
Body: Black body glass
Thorax: Orange micro chenille
Hackle: Partridge
Head: Thread
Fly Tier: Eric Schubert

Henry's Lake Pupa

Hook: Nymph 2xl, #8
Thread: Brown
Tail & body bubble: Wood duck flank fibers, tied on after dubbing the body
Rib: Fine gold wire
Body: Tan Antron dubbing
Hackle: Partridge, tied as a collar
Head: Brown dubbing
Fly Tier: Marvin Nolte

Hump's Caddis Pupa

Hook: TMC 921, #12 - #18
Thread: Black
Rib: Palmered brown hackle
Body: Gray squirrel or muskrat dubbing
Hackle: Palmered
Head & tag: Peacock herl
Fly Tier: Joe Humphreys

Hydropsyche Caddis Larva

Hook: Daiichi 1120, #14 - #20
Thread: Brown
Under Body: Mono
Body: Midge tubing
Thorax: Brown SLF squirrel dubbing
Wing case: Medallion Sheeting
Gills: White ostrich
Head: Thread
Fly Tier: Shane Stalcup

Hydy Dun Flymph

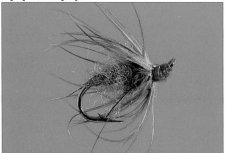

Hook: Mustad 94842, #14
Thread: Wine
Body: Mole hair dubbing, tapered
Hackle: Starling, two turns tied as a collar
Head: Thread
Fly Tier: Cliff Stringer

Kim's Cased Caddis

Hook: Mustad 80150BR, #14
Thread: Olive
Case: Gravel glued to thread base wrap
Body: Olive Larva Lace, woven
Head: Black dubbing
Legs: Black pheasant tail fibers
Fly Tier: Kim Jensen

Krystal Flash Rock Worm

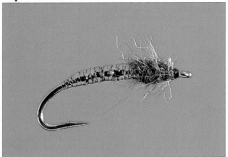

Hook: TMC 200R, #12 - #18
Thread: Brown
Body: Peacock or green color Krystal Flash, twisted and wrapped
Thorax: Brown Hare-Tron dubbing
Head: Thread
Fly Tier: Jim Schollmeyer

Light Ovulating Caddis

Hook: Daiichi 1100, #10 - #14
Thread: Gray
Egg sack: Light green Fine & Dry dubbing
Body: Gray Fine & Dry dubbing
Thorax: Gold bead
Wings: Celo Z-Wing, colored with a gray felt tip marker
Hackle: Dun soft hackle, tied as a collar
Antenna: Two moose body fibers
Head: Thread
Fly Tier: Bill Black, Spirit River Inc.

Lite Brite Caddis

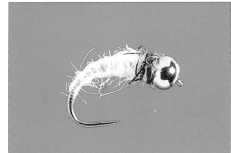

Hook: Daiichi 1130, #10 - #18
Thread: White
Body: White Lite Brite dubbing
Collar: Peacock Lite Brite dubbing
Head: Gold bead
Fly Tier: Bill Black, Spirit River Inc.

Missouri River Caddis

Hook: Scud, #14 - #22
Thread: Black
Back bubble: White Antron , pulled loosely over the top of the body
Body: Burnt orange yarn
Antenna: Wood duck flank fibers
Head: Peacock herl
Fly Tier: Bob Lay

Moss Rock Worm

Hook: Daiichi 1770, #12 - #18
Thread: Black
Tail: Brown goose biots, divided by a small ball of Fine & Dry dubbing
Abdomen: Kreinik thread, woven, colors of choice
Thorax: Two caddis green beads and one tan bead
Head: Olive bead
Legs: Span Flex between the bead segments, three each side
Fly Tier: Buzz Moss

Mustang Pupa

Hook: Standard dry fly hook, #16
Thread: Brown
Tail: Pheasant tail fibers, chenille and black glass bead
Rib: Fine gold wire
Body: Peacock herl
Head: Pheasant tail fibers
Fly Tier: T. D. Relihan

Olive Caddis Emerger

Hook: Kamasan 420, #12 - #16
Thread: Olive
Body: Olive micro Larva Lace
Thorax: Peacock herl
Hackle: Starling, tied as a collar
Head: Thread or optional glass bead
Fly Tier: Mike Hogue

Opal Emerger

Hook: TMC 2487, #14
Thread: Black
Weight: Two pieces of non-lead wire tied on each side of the shank
Body: Dubbing under braided pearl fly flash
Hackle: Quail soft hackle
Head: Thread
Fly Tier: Chuck Echer

Painted Caddis

Hook: Mustad 9672, #12 - #16
Thread: Black
Body: Non-lead wire wrapped then coated with Loon Hard Head
Body color: Fabric paint dabbed in colors to match the natural, brown, tan, white, etc.
Head: Black ostrich herl
Legs: Optional
Fly Tier: Tom Broderidge

P. M. Caddis

Hook: Dai-Riki 135, #8 - #16
Thread: Tan
Body: Chartreuse Larva Lace
Hackle: Brown hen saddle, tied as a collar
Head: Light hare's ear dubbing
Fly Tier: Bear Andrews

Q. T. Caddis

Hook: Scud, #14 - #18
Thread: Black
Body: Dubbing to match the natural insect
Wing: High Luster Flash
Head: Black Frost dubbing
Fly Tier: Brett Clark

Quick Tie Caddis

Hook: Scud, #14 - #18
Thread: Color to match the body
Rib: Optional
Body: Dubbing, color to match the insect
Wings: White Darlon
Head: Black dubbing
Fly Tier: Brett Clark

Rhychy

Hook: Mustad 94838, #10
Thread: Black
Tail: Pheasant tail fibers
Rib: Green copper wire
Body: Green yarn
Hackle: Long, soft brown saddle hackle
Head: Thread
Fly Tier: Carl E. Wolf

Robyn

Hook: TMC 2487, #12 - #18
Thread: Black
Body: Black (top) and yellow (bottom) floss, woven
Hackle: Deer leg hair attached before weaving the body, then stood up
Head: Thread wrapped against deer hair to stand it up
Fly Tier: Dean Elder, Jr.

Rock Worm

Hook: TMC 200R, #6 - #16
Thread: Brown
Tail: Deer hair, flared
Rib: Brown thread, criss cross style
Body: Light brown dubbing
Over Body: Deer hair from the tail
Collar: Light brown dubbing
Head: Brass bead
Fly Tier: Gene Stutzman

Rubber Legged Caddis

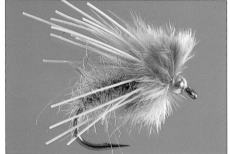

Hook: Dai-Riki 135, #8 - #14
Thread: Tan
Body: Green dubbing brush
Collar: Gray after shaft feather
Head: Gold bead
Legs: Gray fine rubber
Fly Tier: Bear Andrews

RW Pupa

Hook: TMC 2457, #10 - #16
Thread: Color to match the body
Rib: Fine copper wire
Abdomen: Light brown sparkle yarn cut and blended into dubbing
Thorax: Dark brown sparkle yarn dubbing, applied with Tacky Wax, dubbed loose
Wing: Loose, long thorax fibers to capture air bubbles, picked out
Hackle: Hungarian partridge
Head: Thread
Fly Tier: Ralph Woods

Sparkle Caddis Pupa

Hook: Mustad 3906B, #12 - #16
Thread: Green
Body: Caddis green antron yarn
Wing pad: Tan hen saddle feather, extending over part of the body
Antenna: Barred mallard fibers
Eyes: Melted mono
Head: Thread
Fly Tier: Chris Mihulka

Sparkle Pupa

Hook: TMC 109BL, #12 - #18
Thread: Red
Tail: Antron fibers
Body: Ginger dubbing in a silver tinsel dubbing loop
Over Body: Antron fibers
Wings: Gold CDC
Head: Thread
Fly Tier: David Hunter

Spotted Sedge Larva

Hook: Mustad 80200BR, #10 - #14
Thread: Brown
Tail: Short tuft of dark mink fur and guard hairs
Rib: Fine copper wire
Body: Cream, tan, or light brown dubbing
Thorax: Same as body
Thorax plates: Brown mink fur, two sections
Head: Brown mink dubbing
Fly Tier: Reginald Denny

III Rock Worm

Hook: Mustad 9671, #14
Thread: Black
Rib: Fine copper wire
Body: Green yarn dubbing, slightly picked out
Thorax: Peacock herl or black yarn dubbing
Head: Thread
Fly Tier: Dana Griffin, III

Twisted Caddis Nymph

Hook: Standard nymph, #12 - #20
Thread: Black
Body: Twisted and wrapped Darlon
Hackle: Peacock herl
Head: Brass bead
Fly Tier: David Curneal

Western Green Weenie

Hook: Mustad 9671, #8 - #12
Thread: Olive
Body: Olive rabbit dubbing, tied fat
Hackle: Ring-neck pheasant rump, tied as a collar
Head: Gold bead
Fly Tier: Dave Engerbretson

Woven Caddis Pupa

Hook: Mustad 80250BR, #14
Thread: Black
Body: Woven antron fibers, darker on the top and lighter on the bottom
Hackle: Optional
Head: Black rabbit dubbing
Legs: Rabbit guard hairs in the dubbing
Fly Tier: Kim Jensen

Mayfly Nymphs . . .

Baetis Krystal Flash Nymph

Hook: TMC 3761, #16 - #20
Thread: Black
Tail: Dark dun hen hackle fibers
Body: Black Krystal Flash, twisted and wrapped
Thorax: Brown or olive-brown Hare-Tron, picked out
Wing case: Black Krystal Flash, untwisted
Head: Thread
Fly Tier: Jim Schollmeyer

Baetis Nymph

Hook: Daiichi 1270, #16 - #22
Thread: Color to match the body
Tail: Partridge
Body: Micro Tubing, color to match the insect
Thorax: Super Fine dubbing
Wing case: Medallion Sheeting
Head: Thread
Legs: Partridge
Fly Tier: Shane Stalcup

Bear's Hex Nymph

Hook: Daiichi 1730, #8 **Thread:** Tan
Tail: Emu
Rib: Mono thread
Body: Sulpher squirrel blend
Gills: After shaft feather, pulled and covered by the next step
Back and Wing case: Pheasant tail fibers, pulled over and ribbed
Hackle: Tan hen saddle, palmered over the thorax
Eyes: Black mono
Head: Dubbed, same color as the body
Fly Tier: Bear Andrews

Biot Nymph

Hook: Daiichi 1270, #12 - #22
Thread: Color to match the body
Tail: Partridge
Body: Biot, color to match the insect
Thorax: Super Fine dubbing
Wing case: Medallion Sheeting
Head: Thread
Legs: Partridge
Fly Tier: Shane Stalcup

Black Thunder

Hook: Mustad 94840, #12 - #16
Thread: Black
Tail: Black hackle fibers
Body: Hairline peacock sparkle dubbing
Wing case: Black Swiss straw
Hackle: Black, tied as a beard
Fly Tier: Robert Meuschke

BT's Baetis

Hook: TMC 200R, #12 - #18
Thread: Olive
Tail: Two small black hen cape hackle feathers
Rib: One strand of copper Krystal Flash
Body: Olive gray muskrat dubbing
Gills: Tuff of gray feather fluff, tied behind the wing case
Wing case: Dark turkey tail quill section, coated with Aqua Tuff
Thorax: Olive gray muskrat dubbing
Legs: Partridge, tied divided
Fly Tier: Al Beatty

Callibaetis Nymph

Hook: Mustad 3906B, #10 - #14
Thread: Tan
Tail: Mallard flank fibers
Rib: Gray thread
Body: Creamy gray dubbing, tinted on top with a felt tip marker
Wing case: Brown turkey tail
Head: Thread
Legs: Picked out dubbing from the thorax
Fly Tier: George Nelson

Callibaetis Quill Nymph

Hook: Mustad 80000BR, #14
Thread: Black
Tail: Grizzly hackle fibers
Body: Stripped brown hackle quill
Thorax: Peacock herl
Wing case: Pheasant tail fibers
Hackle: Grizzly, two wraps palmered through the thorax
Head: Thread
Fly Tier: Gene Stutzman

CDC Isonychia

Hook: Mustad 9672, #12
Thread: Black
Tail: Dark brown CDC fibers
Rib: Fine copper wire
Body: One brown and one black CDC feather twisted together and wrapped
Wing case: Dark gray emu feather
Back stripe: White fiber or Krystal Flash
Hackle: One brown and one black CDC feather, palmered and trimmed top and bottom
Head: Thread
Fly Tier: Jerry Caruso

Ceramic May

Hook: Mustad9672, #14
Thread: Brown
Tail: Moose hair, tied sparse
Body: Dubbed rabbit, trimmed on all sides
Thorax: Ceramic bead
Wing case: Pheasant tail fibers
Head: Thread
Fly Tier: John Newbury

Chickabou Flash Back

Hook: TMC 3761, #10 - #18
Thread: Olive
Tail: Grizzly Chickabou
Rib: Fine gold wire
Body: Grizzly Chickabou, wrapped around the hook
Wing case: Green Rad's Ribbon floss
Hackle: Rooster flank fibers
Head: Thread
Fly Tier: Henry Hoffman

Crystal Biot Nymph

Hook: Mustad 9671, #12 - #16
Thread: Olive
Tail: Pale dun hackle fibers
Body: Dyed goose biot, color to match the insect
Thorax: Peacock herl
Wing case: Krystal Flash over pheasant tail fibers
Hackle: Grizzly, tied as a beard
Head: Thread
Fly Tier: Cliff Stringer

Darlon R. S. 2

Hook: Scud #14 - #20
Thread: Black
Tail: Pheasant tail fibers
Body: Olive dubbing
Wing: White Darlon
Head: Thread
Fly Tier: David Curneal

Dick's Hex

Hook: Mustad 9674 and Mustad 3906B, both #10
Thread: Gray
Tail: Partridge, tied short
Rib: Fine mono, dark brown
Abdomen: Tied on 9674, hook cut off, olive hairs ear dubbing
Connecting loop: Fifteen pound Maxima
Wing case and shell back: Mottled Bug Skin
Hackle: Partridge, tied as a throat
Head: Thread
Fly Tier: Toby Richardson

Emerger, Stage #1

Hook: TMC 3769, #10 - #20
Thread: To match dubbing
Tail: Barred wood duck
Body: Dubbing to match the insect
Wings: Folded and bundled nylon stocking, tied short
Hackle: Mottled brown partridge
Head: Dubbing to match the insect
Fly Tier: Ted Rogowski

Emerger, Stage #2

Hook: TMC 100, #10 - #20
Thread: To match dubbing
Tail: Barred wood duck
Body: Dubbing to match the insect
Wings: Folded and bundled nylon stocking, tied short
Hackle: Grizzly or brown/grizzly mix
Head: Dubbing under hackle, thread
Fly Tier: Ted Rogowski

Emerger, Stage #3

Hook: TMC 5212, #10 - #20
Thread: To match dubbing
Tail #1, the shuck: Mottled brown partridge
Tail #2, the emerging insect: Barred wood duck tied Darby "one fly" style
Rib: Optional
Body: Dubbing to match the insect
Wings: Folded and bundled nylon stock, tied short
Hackle: Grizzly or brown/grizzly mix
Head: Dubbing under the hackle, thread
Fly Tier: Ted Rogowski

Flash Loop PMD Emerger

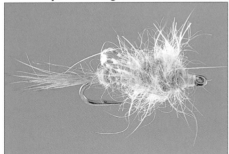

Hook: TMC 2302, #14 - #18
Thread: Pale yellow
Tail: Red squirrel tail
Rib: Fine gold wire
Body: Hare's ear dubbing
Wings: Looped pearl Krystal Flash
Head: Thread
Fly Tier: Matt Owens

Gem State Nymph

Hook: Mustad 3906B, #10
Thread: Black
Tail: Ginger hackle fibers
Rib: Gold wire
Abdomen: Peacock herl with a orange floss strip wrapped under the rib
Thorax: Peacock herl
Wing case: Pheasant tail fibers
Hackle: Ginger palmered over the thorax
Head: Thread
Fly Tier: Bruce Staples

Gill Weave Nymph

Hook: Nymph, #12 - #20
Thread: Brown
Tail: Partridge fibers
Under Body: Kreinik Blending Filament (095)
Abdomen: Larva Lace with a peacock herl weave on each fly side for gills
Thorax: Antron dubbing to match the abdomen
Wing case: Partridge folded and tips forming the legs
Legs: Partridge tips from the wing case
Head: Thread
Fly Tier: George Harmeling

Gilled Nymph

Hook: Daiichi 1270, #12 - #22
Thread: Color to match the body
Tail: Ostrich tips
Rib: Fine wire
Body: Ostrich, color to match the insect
Thorax: Opossum
Wing case: Medallion Sheeting
Head: Thread
Legs: Partridge
Fly Tier: Shane Stalcup

Gray Drake Nymph

Hook: Mustad 9672, #12
Thread: Dark olive
Tail: Squirrel guard hairs dyed olive
Rib: Brown button hole, twisted
Body: Dark olive dubbing
Thorax: Dark olive dubbing in dubbing loop with hackle
Wing case: Peacock herl strands
Hackle: Olive squirrel guard hairs prepared in a dubbing loop with thorax dubbing
Head: Thread
Fly Tier: Bob Pelzl

Green Drake Nymph

Hook: Mustad 9672, #14
Thread: Green
Tail: Peasant tail fibers, three, divided
Body: Brown yarn dubbing
Thorax: Rabbit guard hairs and body material in a dubbing loop
Wing case: Peacock herl
Head: Thread
Legs: Rabbit guard hairs tied with the thorax
Fly Tier: Dana Griffin, III

Hendrickson Nymph

Hook: Mustad 3906B, #12 - #18
Thread: Black
Tail: Speckled brown partridge fibers
Rib: Dark brown thread
Thorax: Tan beaver dubbing over .015 non-lead wire
Body: Tan beaver dubbing
Wing case: Mottled turkey quill section
Fly Tier: Mike Jacobs

Hump's Green Drake

Hook: TMC 5262, #10
Thread: Yellow
Tail: Ginger hackle fibers
Body: Mix of yellow and dark ginger dubbing
Wing case: Turkey quill, lacquered
Hackle: Ginger
Head: Thread
Gills: Gray marabou, trimmed short
Fly Tier: Joe Humphreys

Hump's Isonychia Nymph

Hook: TMC 5262, #12
Thread: Black
Tail: Brown hackle fibers
Body: Black dubbing
Wings case: Black turkey quill
Hackle: Brown
Head: Thread
Gills: Three clumps of black yarn trimmed short on sides
Fly Tier: Joe Humphreys

Hump's Sulphur Nymph

Hook: TMC 5210, #12
Thread: Rusty brown
Tail: Mottled hen back fibers
Rib: Fine brass or copper wire
Body: Tan Australian opossum dubbing
Thorax: Dark brown dubbing
Wing case: Mottled hen back
Hackle: Partridge
Head: Thread
Fly Tier: Joe Humphreys

Inovye Pheasant Tail USD

Hook: Dai-Riki 730, #16 - #18
Thread: Black
Tail: Pheasant tail fibers
Rib: Gold wire
Body: Pheasant tail fibers
Thorax: Peacock herl
Head: Brass bead
Legs: Pheasant tail fibers
Fly Tier: Eric Pettine

Lady Amherst Mayfly

Hook: Daiichi 1140, #18
Thread: White
Tail: Aftershaft feather from the base of a Lady Amherst tippet feather
Body: Cream dubbing
Wings: Mottle turkey tail, trimmed
Hackle: Mottled brown soft hackle
Head: Thread
Fly Tier: Ted Patlen

Leonard's Fur Nymph

Hook: Mustad 3906, #14 - #16
Thread: Brown
Tail: Wood duck fibers, tied sparse and tilted up
Body: Natural muskrat dubbing, trimmed on all sides
Thorax: Natural muskrat dubbing, picked out and trimmed on the bottom
Head: Thread
Fly Tier: John Newbury

Mahogany Drake Nymph

Hook: Streamer 4xl, ringed eye, #10
Thread: Black
Tail: Pheasant tail fiber (purple tips)
Stripe: Dorsal stripe of stripped grizzly hackle stem
Body: Peacock herl
Wings: Gray goose quill segment
Head: Brown wool, saturated with cement
Legs: Mottled brown partridge
Fly Tier: Reginald Denny

Marabou Ephemerella

Hook: Mustad 9672, #14
Thread: Tan
Tail: Tan marabou fibers, tied short
Rib: Optional copper wire
Body: Tan marabou wrapped around the shank
Wing case: Brown marabou fibers
Head: Thread
Legs: Tan marabou fibers
Fly Tier: Tom Broderidge

Marabou Nymph

Hook: Daiichi 1270, #12 - #22
Thread: Color to match the body
Tail: Marabou, tied short
Rib: Micro Tubing
Body: Marabou, color to match the insect
Thorax: Marabou
Wing case: Medallion Sheeting
Head: Thread
Legs: Partridge
Fly Tier: Shane Stalcup

Original Pheasant Tail

Hook: Nymph 2xl, #14 - #18
Thread: Fine copper wire
Tail: Pheasant tail fibers
Body: Pheasant tail
Thorax: Multiple wraps of copper wire
Wing case: Pheasant tail
Head: Copper wire
Fly Tier: Marvin Nolte

Pinot Gris

Hook: TMC 2312, #10 - #16
Thread: Black
Tail: Three pheasant tail fibers
Body: Stripped peacock herl stem
Thorax: Peacock herl
Head: Gold or black bead
Legs: Six pheasant tail fibers, beard style
Fly Tier: Gene Trump

P.T.O. Nymph

Hook: TMC 200R, #10 - #20
Thread: Brown
Tail: Pheasant tail, three fibers
Rib: Fine copper wire
Body: Pheasant tail fibers, wrapped
Thorax: Ostrich herl, black or olive
Wing case: Pheasant tail fibers
Head: Thread
Legs: Pheasant fibers pulled back, remaining from the wing case
Fly Tier: Bud Heintz

Simo Special

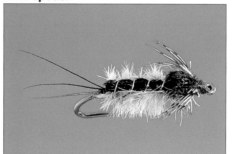

Hook: TMC 200R, #14 - #16
Thread: Tan or olive
Tail: Three moose fibers, splayed
Rib: Silver or copper wire
Body: Olive dun ostrich herl
Over Body: Dark mottle turkey fibers
Under Body: Light silver pheasant fibers
Wing case: Dark mottle turkey fibers
Thorax: Brown/olive dubbing
Legs: Partridge fibers
Fly Tier: John Simonson

Simple Nymph

Hook: Mustad 7957B, #10 - #16
Thread: Color to match the body
Tail: Tuft of dubbing
Rib: Copper wire
Body: Dubbing of choice
Thorax: Dubbing of choice
Legs: Tuft of dubbing
Head: Gold bead
Fly Tier: Buck Goodrich

Teal Nymph

Hook: Dai-Riki 060, #14 -#18
Thread: Gray
Tail: Teal flank fibers
Rib: Fine silver wire
Abdomen: Teal flank fibers, wrapped
Thorax: Gray dubbing
Hackle: Teal flank fibers, tied tips forward over the top of the hook and folded back
Neck: Gray dubbing to cover thread
Head: Black metal bead
Fly Tier: Scott Sanchez

Tom's Green

Hook: Mustad 37160, #10
Thread: Green
Tail: White ostrich herl
Rib: Fine gold wire
Abdomen: Olive Lite Brite dubbing
Thorax: Green Lite Brite dubbing
Wing case: Tan rayon
Hackle: Emu, palmered over the thorax
Head: Green Flashabou thread
Fly Tier: Tom Tripi

Tubing PT

Hook: Daiichi 1270, #12 - #22
Thread: Brown
Tail: Pheasant tail fibers
Body: Pheasant tail color Micro Tubing
Wing case: Medallion Sheeting
Head: Thread
Legs: Pheasant tail fibers
Fly Tier: Shane Stalcup

Wood Duck Callibaetis

Hook: TMC 2302, #10 - #16
Thread: Brown
Tail: Wood duck flank fibers
Rib: Copper wire
Body: Rusty dun Super Fine dubbing
Shell back: Wood duck flank fibers
Hackle: Grizzly, palmered
Head: Thread
Fly Tier: Larry Nicholas

Midge, Crane Fly, Damsel, and Dragonfly Nymphs . . .

B.C. Beady

Hook: TMC 200R, #18
Thread: Black
Body: Two strands of black Krystal Flash, wrapped
Thorax: Small black seed bead
Head: Two turns of hen, tied as a collar
Fly Tier: Roger Swengel

Bead Head Midge

Hook: TMC 200R, #14 - #22
Thread: Color of choice
Tail: Zelon, white, tied very sparse
Rib: Optional
Body: Fine copper wire or floss, color of choice
Wings: Turkey biots, white, trimmed short
Head: Bead head, black or other colored glass bead, white Zelon tuft tied forward
Fly Tier: Bud Heintz

Bead Head Midge Pupa

Hook: Daiichi 1120, #16 - #22
Thread: Color to match the body
Rear Gills: White CDC
Rib: White Fishair
Body: Micro tubing, color to match the insect
Thorax: Tying thread
Wing case: Medallion sheeting
Front Gills: White CDC
Head: Dark bead
Fly Tier: Shane Stalcup

Bear River Midge

Hook: Standard dry fly, #12 - #20
Thread: Black or to match the body
Tail: Midge Larva Lace, color to match the insect
Body: Thread
Hackle: Grizzly, palmered over the body
Head: Glass bead, color of choice
Fly Tier: Chuck Collins

Bear's Damsel

Hook: Streamer, #8
Thread: Olive
Tail: Grizzly dyed olive Chickabou
Rib: Green copper wire
Body: Olive ostrich herl
Over back: Pheasant tail fibers folded over the body and ribbed into place
Wing case: Pheasant tail fibers
Hackle: Grizzly dyed olive hen saddle feathers
Eyes: Melted mono
Head: Olive squirrel blend
Fly Tier: Bear Andrews

Bogus Damsel Nymph

Hook: TMC 2487, #14
Thread: Olive
Tail: Furled Z-lon, light olive
Body, head, & Wing case: Sparkle Blend, light olive
Legs: Picked out dubbing
Eyes: Melted 25 pound Mason mono, painted black
Fly Tier: Tim Witsman

Braided Midge Larva

Hook: Mustad 94840, #24
Thread: Black
Body: One strand of pearl and one strand of chartreuse Krystal Flash, braided
Thorax: Three wraps of peacock herl
Head: Thread
Fly Tier: Tom Broderidge

Bright Eyes

Hook: TMC 200R, #8 - #14
Thread: Olive
Tail: Olive Chickabou
Rib: Fine gold wire
Body: Olive Chickabou
Wings: Barred olive knee hackle
Hackle: Olive rooster flank
Head: Beaver dubbing
Eyes: Metallic green plastic
Fly Tier: Henry Hoffman

Brook's Green Damsel

Hook: Mustad 3906B, #8 - #10
Thread: Black
Tail: Three peacock herl tips
Rib: Gold oval tinsel
Body: Olive green yarn
Hackle: Grizzly dyed olive hen hackle
Head: Thread
Fly Tier: Bruce Staples

Bud's Damsel Nymph

Hook: Mustad 94840, #4 - #14
Thread: Olive
Tail: Olive ultra chenille with a tuft of marabou and a strip of tinsel, tied extended body
Rib: Fine tinsel
Body: Ostrich herl, olive
Wings and Wing case: Pheasant tail pulled over with the excess extending as short wings
Head: Ostrich herl
Legs: Fine rubber
Eyes: Melted mono
Fly Tier: Bud Heintz

Cheryl's Floating Nymph

Hook: Mustad 9671, #12
Thread: Black
Tail: Two peacock swords
Body: Blue Lite Brite dubbing
Hackle: Emu palmered over the thorax
Thorax: Blue Lite Brite dubbing
Shell back: Blue closed cell foam
Eyes: Trimmed blue closed cell foam remaining from the shell back
Head: Thread
Fly Tier: Tom Tripi

Chickabou Dragon

Hook: Mustad 9672, #4 - #8
Thread: Olive
Tail: Grizzly dyed olive Chickabou
Body: Olive Chickabou
Wings: Olive rooster flank
Hackle: Olive rooster flank, trimmed on the top and bottom
Head: Olive Chickabou
Eyes: Green plastic
Fly Tier: Henry Hoffman

Chicken Midge

Hook: Mustad 3906B, #10 - #16
Thread: Olive
Body: Red Rad Ribbon floss
Thorax: Peacock Rad Ribbon floss
Wings: Brown rooster biot
Gills: White Chickabou
Head: Thread
Fly Tier: Henry Hoffman

Cliff's Damsel

Hook: Mustad 9672, #10 - #12
Thread: Olive
Tail: Grizzly dyed olive feather fluff, tied short
Body: Small chartreuse chenille
Thorax: Peacock herl
Wing case: Turkey quill section
Hackle: Guinea feather folded over the thorax and under the wing case
Head: Thread
Fly Tier: Cliff Stringer

Cliff's Dragon

Hook: Mustad 9672, #6
Thread: Black
Tail: Pheasant rump fibers, tied short
Body: Dark olive chenille, tied in two sections
Hackle: Pheasant tail fibers, tied on the sides
Head: Black ostrich
Eyes: Black bead chain
Fly Tier: Cliff Stringer

Crane Fly Nymph

Hook: Daiichi 1730, #6
Thread: Black
Tail: Black goose biots divided by a small ball of black antron dubbing
Body: Black and white Kreinik, braided with the black on top
Thorax: Gray dubbing, two black and two white beads
Legs: Black Mylar Daddy Long Legs
Head: Thread
Fly Tier: Buzz Moss

Crystal Dragon

Hook: Mustad 9674, #8
Thread: Olive
Body: Peacock crystal chenille
Wing case: Squirrel tail dyed chartreuse
Head: Thread
Legs: Gray hen hackle
Eyes: Tarnished brass bead chain
Fly Tier: Tommy Marks

Crystal Midge

Hook: TMC 3761, #12 - #14
Thread: Black
Rib: Fine copper wire
Body: Peacock herl
Head: Green crystal chenille, one turn
Fly Tier: George Close

Damsel Nymph

Hook: Mustad 3906, #12
Thread: White dyed olive with felt tip marker
Tail: Three emu fiber tips, olive
Body: Strip of sports wrap foam, olive
Thorax: Olive dubbing
Wing case: Olive Swiss straw
Head: Olive dubbing
Eyes: Melted 50 pound mono
Legs: Olive dyed mallard, tied very sparse
Fly Tier: Kent Bulfinch

Deer Dragon

Hook: Mustad 9672, #8
Thread: Black
Tail: Brown turkey biots
Rib: Orange hackle, palmered and trimmed short
Body: Peacock herl with a strand of pearl Flashabou down each side
Hackle: Deer hair tied as a collar
Throat: Peacock herl between the hackle and the bead
Head: Brass bead
Fly Tier: Len Holt

Dolberg Dragon

Hook: Streamer 4xl, #6 - #10
Thread: Black
Tail: Bronze turkey flat fibers
Body: Mix of brown mink and olive seal, spin in a dubbing loop, trim top and bottom
Thorax: Same as body, trimmed to shape
Head: Thread
Legs: Turkey rump fibers, applied between the abdomen and thorax
Fly Tier: Reginald Denny

Doudy Damsel

Hook: Mustad 5862, #10 - #14
Thread: Olive
Tail: Marabou through clear larva lace, use beading needle to insert
Body: Olive after shaft feather behind dark after shaft, each tied in a dubbing loop
Head: Thread
Legs: Stalcup damsel legs
Eyes: Burned mono
Fly Tier: Gale Doudy

Dragon Booby Fly

Hook: Mustad 9674
Thread: Black
Tail: Two green turkey biots
Body: Peacock chenille over closed cell foam
Wing case: Peacock sword
Head: Peacock chenille
Eyes: Closed cell foam
Legs: Peacock sword
Fly Tier: Ian Russell

Drowned Crane Fly

Hook: Mustad 3906, #6 - #10
Thread: Black
Body: Banded wild boar hair
Wings: Grizzly hackle tips, tied spent style
Hackle: Ginger, tied as a collar
Head: Thread, tied extra large
Legs: Ten pheasant tail fibers
Fly Tier: Tom Tripi

Extended Marabou Damsel

Hook: Standard wet, #14
Thread: Black
Tail & abdomen: Olive marabou, tied extended body style
Rib: Thread
Thorax: Mix of Flashabou and olive dubbing
Wing case: Olive silk netting
Head: Dubbing from the thorax
Eyes: Melted black mono
Fly Tier: David Curneal

Floating Damsel Nymph

Hook: Mustad 94840, #12 - #16
Thread: Olive
Tail: Olive marabou as a tail and braided into an extended body
Thorax: Olive marabou dubbing
Head: Foam tied on top to keep the fly in the surface film
Eyes: Melted mono
Legs: Partridge
Fly Tier: Ian Russel

Foam Dragon Fly NAIAD

Hook: Partridge K2B, #12
Thread: Brown
Rib: Thread tied in segment on the foam abdomen
Body: Black craft foam, 1/16" folded
Thorax: Dark brown dubbing with black craft foam shell back
Legs: Hen back center stems, stripped and treated with Loon Soft Head for durability
Head: Thread
Eyes: Black bead chain, two millimeter
Fly Tier: Floyd Franke

Fur Damsel

Hook: Mustad 9674, #12 - #14
Thread: Olive
Tail: Three pale green ostrich herl tips, tied short
Rib: Fine gold wire
Body: Insect green rabbit fur dubbing
Wing case: Tuft of soft gray or olive fur
Head: Dark olive dubbing, saturated with cement
Legs: Mallard flank dyed olive
Fly Tier: Reginald Denny

GM Damsel Nymph

Hook: Mustad 79580, #14 - #18
Thread: Olive
Tail: Olive rabbit fur
Rib: Olive thread, counter wrapped
Body: Olive thread
Thorax: Olive rabbit dubbing
Wing case: Olive Swiss straw
Head: Thread
Legs: Olive rabbit dubbing, brushed out
Fly Tier: Gordon Mankins

Green Eyed Monster

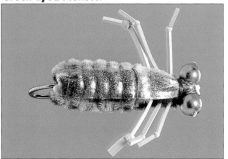

Hook: TMC 200R, #4 - #8
Thread: Gray
Rib: Very fine silver wire
Body: Dark gray and medium olive fine chenille, woven with gray on the top
Shell back & Wing case: Thin gray packing foam
Thorax: Gray chenille
Legs: Small green rubber bands, knotted
Eyes: Green plastic bead chain
Head: Chenille, thread, and foam
Fly Tier: Lance Zook

Green Damsel

Hook: Mustad 9672, #10
Thread: Green
Tail: Three peacock swords
Rib: Fine copper wire
Body: Green yarn dubbing
Hackle: Grizzly dyed green, wrapped as a very sparse collar
Eyes: Melted mono
Head: Green yarn dubbing, thread
Fly Tier: Dana Griffin, III

Holographic Chironomid

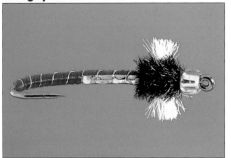

Hook: TMC 200R, #10 - #18
Thread: Color to match body
Rib: Silver or copper wire
Body: Flexi Floss to match insect
Gills: White antron
Thorax: Peacock herl
Head: Silver lined clear bead
Body bubble: Holographic tinsel, silver
Fly Tier: John Simonson

Holt's Midge

Hook: TMC 100, #18 - #22
Thread: Black
Rib: One strand of gray thread
Body: Black thread
Thorax: Peacock herl
Head: Thread
Fly Tier: Len Holt

John's Chironomid (BH)

Hook: Dai-Riki 270C, #12 - #14
Thread: Color to match the body
Body: Swannundaze, red, green, black, or brown
Thorax: Peacock herl
Gills: White ostrich
Head: Brass bead
Fly Tier: John Newbury

KC Midge

Hook: Mustad 3906B, #18 - #20
Thread: Black
Rib: Fine gold wire
Body: Tying thread
Thorax: Black Norwegian fox dubbing
Head: Small gold bead
Fly Tier: Kevin Cohenour

KJ's Dragon Nymph

Hook: Dai-Riki 700, #4
Thread: Olive
Tail: Goose biots, tied very short
Under Body: Lead wire and foam
Body: Dark and light chenille, woven with dark chenille on the top
Wing case: Pheasant rump
Head: Thread
Legs: Pheasant rump
Eyes: Melted mono
Fly Tier: Kim Jensen

KJ's Woven Damsel

Hook: Mustad 3906B, #14
Thread: Olive
Tail: Olive marabou
Abdomen: Light and dark olive antron woven on a needle, removed, and tied extended
Thorax: Olive antron dubbing
Wing case: Turkey quill section
Legs: Rubber hackle
Eyes: Melted mono
Fly Tier: Kim Jensen

The Lion

Hook: Mustad 9672, #8
Thread: Olive
Tail: Olive marabou, tied very sparse
Body: Olive chenille
Hackle: Olive emu
Eyes: Chartreuse bead chain
Head: Thread
Fly Tier: Kieran Frye

Lite Brite Dragonfly

Hook: Mustad 9672, #8
Thread: Olive
Body: Olive Lite Brite dubbing
Eyes: Dumb bell painted chartreuse
Head: Olive Lite Brite dubbing
Fly Tier: Chris Mihulka

Madison Midge

Hook: TMC 2487, #14 - #22
Thread: Black
Tag: Green antron yarn or color of choice
Rib: Fine copper wire (optional)
Body: Peacock herl
Wing: Green antron yarn remaining from the tag
Hackle: Brown, tied as a collar
Head: Brass bead, thread
Fly Tier: Al Beatty

Marabou Damsel (BP)

Hook: Mustad 94840, #12
Thread: Black
Tail: Brown marabou over olive marabou, tied sparse
Body: Olive dubbing
Thorax: Olive dubbing in a dubbing loop with the hackle
Wing case: Peacock herl strands
Hackle: Squirrel guard hairs dyed olive in a dubbing loop with the thorax
Head: Thread
Fly Tier: Bob Pelzl

SRI Marabou Dragon Nymph

Hook: Daiichi 2220, #4
Thread: Brown
Tail: Brown goose biots, divided
Body: Marabou tied in tufts, then trimmed to shape
Thorax: Brown Possum Plus dubbing
Wings case: Turkey tail
Eyes: Melted mono
Head: Thread and dubbing
Legs: Partridge dyed brown
Fly Tier: Bill Black, Spirit River Inc.

M & M Damsel Nymph

Hook: TMC 2487, #12 - #16
Thread: Olive
Tail: Marabou to match the natural, tied very sparse
Body: Marabou dubbing, same color as the tail
Wing case: Marabou ends remaining from the tail
Head: Thread
Legs: Picked out dubbing
Eyes: Black glass beads on melted mono
Fly Tier: Jeff Hatton

Matti's Midge

Hook: Dai-Riki 305, #16 - #22
Thread: Black
Tail: Gray antron
Hackle: Grizzly hackle palmered on the bare hook
Body: Black foam, tied on the top and bottom at the bend, pulled over and tied off at front
Head: Thread
Fly Tier: Eric Pettine

Mi. Andelle Dragon

Hook: Nymph 2xl, #6 - #10
Thread: Brown
Tail & body bubble: Wood duck fibers, tied on after dubbing the body
Body: Coarse dark olive dubbing
Hackle: Partridge
Head: Coarse brown dubbing
Fly Tier: Marvin Nolte

Midge Larva

Hook: Daiichi 1120, #16 - #22
Thread: Color to match the body
Rib: White Fishair
Body: Micro tubing, color to match the insect
Head: Thread and epoxy
Fly Tier: Shane Stalcup

Midge Pupa

Hook: Daiichi 1120, #16 - #22
Thread: Color to match the body
Rear Gills: White CDC
Rib: White Fishair
Body: Micro tubing, color to match the insect
Front Gills: White CDC, trimmed short
Head: Thread and epoxy
Fly Tier: Shane Stalcup

My Damsel

Hook: Scud, #12 - #14
Thread: Black or olive
Tail: Olive marabou, tied long and sparse
Body: Peacock herl
Head: Gold or black bead
Fly Tier: Dave Engerbretson

Olive Damsel

Hook: TMC 200R, #10 - #14
Thread: Olive
Tail: Golden olive marabou
Rib: Fine copper wire
Body: Marabou, wrapped very sparse
Thorax: Olive hare's ear dubbing
Wings: Olive Z-lon, clipped short
Eyes: Melted black mono
Head: Thread
Fly Tier: Larry Nicholas

Olive Midge Pupa

Hook: Mustad 80250, #12 - #16
Thread: Olive
Body: Green floss under stripped grizzly dyed olive quill
Head: Peacock herl
Fly Tier: Reginald Denny

Partridge Damsel

Hook: TMC 200R, #12
Thread: Olive
Tail: Olive marabou, tied short and sparse
Rib: Brown thread
Body: Hairline #34 olive hare's ear dubbing
Wing case: Pheasant tail fibers, trimmed at the one third point on the hook shank
Legs: Partridge, tied divided and positioned at the sides of the fly
Eyes: Small green barbell
Head: Thread
Fly Tier: George Nelson

Peacock Dragon

Hook: Partridge H3ST, #6
Thread: Black
Body: Peacock herl
Wing case: Peacock back feather
Head: Peacock
Legs: Golden pheasant tail fiber, tied on the sides
Eyes: Melted mono
Fly Tier: John Newbury

Pheasant Dragon

Hook: Mustad 5862, #10 - #14
Thread: Brown
Weight: .025 lead
Body: Pheasant rump after shaft feather, tied in dubbing loop
Hackle: Pheasant rump as hackle/over body
Head: Thread
Eyes: Burned mono
Fly Tier: Gale Doudy

Postman Midge

Hook: TMC 2487, #14 - #18
Thread: Orange or brown
Tail: Orange marabou
Rib: Optional
Body: Orange marabou wrapped from the tail excess
Wings: Gray CDC fibers
Head: Peacock herl
Fly Tier: Barry Glickman

Rubber Band Dragon

Hook: Partridge H3ST, #6
Thread: Black
Body: Size G4 rubber band, colored with felt tip marker
Wing case: Rubber band
Head: Rubber band
Legs: Pheasant tail fibers, tied on the sides
Eyes: Melted mono
Fly Tier: John Newbury

Scott's Fur Damsel

Hook: Dai-Riki 270, #8 - #14
Thread: Olive
Tail: Olive dyed fox fur
Body: Olive fox fur tied in by the tip, twisted and wrapped
Thorax: Olive fox fur, dubbing
Wing case: Olive dyed fox fur, tied on by the butts, excess to become legs
Legs: Olive dyed fox fur remaining from the wing case
Eyes: Black plastic bead chain
Head: Olive fox fur dubbing
Fly Tier: Scott Sanchez

Spring Creek Midge

Hook: TMC 200R, #16 - #22
Thread: Orange
Tail: Zelon, brown or olive, tied very sparse
Rib: Fine wire (optional)
Body: Zelon, brown or olive
Thorax: Orange dubbing
Wings: Zelon, white cut short
Head: Thread
Fly Tier: Bud Heintz

Suspender Chironomid

Hook: Partridge K2B, #12 - #18
Thread: Black
Rib: Krystal Flash, wrapped in a close palmer design
Body: Peacock herl (natural or bronzed)
Thorax: Black closed cell foam
Gills: White wool, tied short
Head: Thread
Fly Tier: Ian Russell

Suspender Midge Pupa

Hook: TMC 100, #10 - #20
Thread: Black
Tail: White Antron, tied very sparse
Rib: Silver wire
Body: Black tying thread
Thorax: Peacock herl
Wing: White closed cell foam, tied forward of the thorax
Head: Thread
Fly Tier: Larry Nicholas

Swanendaze Midge

Hook: TMC 200R, #10 - #16
Thread: Red
Body: Small red V Rib
Thorax: Peacock herl
Wing: White Antron, tied spent style, trimmed short
Head: Thread
Fly Tier: Larry Nicholas

TT Damsel

Hook: Mustad 80150, #10 - #12
Thread: Tan
Tail: Tan pheasant marabou
Rib: Fine gold wire
Body: Peacock herl
Hackle: Partridge, tied as a collar
Eyes: Gold bead chain
Head: Peacock herl around the eyes
Fly Tier: Tom Tripi

Tunkwannamid

Hook: TMC 100, #8 - #10
Thread: Red
Tag: Silver oval tinsel
Body: Peacock herl twisted with tinsel from the tag
Hackle: White ostrich herl
Head: Thread
Fly Tier: David Hunter

Tyler's Crystal Midge

Hook: Scud, #16 - #20
Thread: Color to match the insect
Rib: File silver wire
Body: Tying thread
Wing: High Luster Flash, trimmed short
Head: Pearl glass bead
Fly Tier: David Curneal

Ultra Damsel

Hook: Daiichi 1530, #14
Thread: Mono
Body: Damsel Nymph Body, colored with a felt tip marker
Thorax: Epoxy, colored with felt tip marker
Wing case: Medallion Sheeting
Legs: Sparkle Damsel Nymph Legs
Head: Thread
Eyes: Damsel Nymph Eyes
Fly Tier: Shane Stalcup

Water Bug

Hook: Mustad 90240, #8
Thread: Olive
Rib: Copper wire
Body: Olive SLF dubbing
Shell back: Olive Swiss straw, marked with a black felt tip marker
Wing case: Olive Swiss straw, marked with a black felt tip marker
Eyes: Melted mono
Head: Thread
Fly Tier: John Schaper

Scuds, Snails, Leeches, and Sowbugs . . .

B. B. Sowbug

Hook: Mustad 94840, #10 - #12
Thread: Gray
Rib: Gold oval tinsel
Body: Gray muskrat dubbing over flattened .015 non-lead wire
Hackle: Light dun, tied as a collar
Head: Thread
Fly Tier: Mike Jacobs

Bead Head Bunny Leech

Hook: Mustad 9672, #4 - #8
Thread: Brown
Tail: Rabbit fur strip, tied the length of the hook shank, brown, black, or olive
Body: Rabbit fur strip wrapped forward to the bead head
Throat: Rabbit fur dubbed over thread wraps behind the bead head
Head: Gold, black, or red bead
Fly Tier: Jim Schollmeyer

Bear's Claret Leech

Hook: Dai-Riki 710, #4 - #8
Thread: Black
Tail: Black marabou and Krystal Flash
Body: Black cactus chenille
Wings: Black rabbit strip, tied Zonker style
Hackle: Four black soft hackles, tied as a collar
Cheeks: Claret pheasant rump
Over Hackle: Claret pheasant rump, tied as a collar
Head: Thread
Fly Tier: Bear Andrews

B.S.M. Leech

Hook: Long shank streamer, #2 - #6
Thread: Black or color to match the body
Tail: Black SLF hank, or color of choice
Body: Black yarn and black SLF hanks in three sections plus the tail
Wings: SLF in sections tied with the body, color of choice
Head: Thread
Fly Tier: Bill Chandler

Chickabou Articulated Leech

Front Hook: Mustad 3399A #6 - #8, point cut off and attached to the eye of back hook
Back Hook: Mustad 3366A (ring eye), #8
Thread: Brown
Front & back bodies: Grizzly dyed brown Chickabou, wrapped around the hook shanks
Head: Grizzly dyed brown Chickabou
Eyes: Spirit River Real Eyes
Fly Tier: Henry Hoffman

Chuck's Water Boatman

Hook: TMC 102Y, #15
Thread: Black
Weight: Five wraps of non-lead wire in the middle of the shank
Body: Hare's ear dubbing
Shell back: Black moose hair
Hind Legs: Trimmed hackle stem
Front Legs: Black moose hair
Head: Thread
Fly Tier: Chuck Echer

Clark's Poly Scud

Hook: Daiichi 1130, #12 - #18
Thread: Orange
Rib: Fine gold wire
Body: Orange macramé yarn made into dubbing
Shell back: Dubbed body coated on top with Soft Body or Aqua Flex
Head: Thread
Fly Tier: Lee Clark

DG Scud

Hook: Mustad 3906B, #12
Thread: Tan
Tail: Wood duck flank fibers
Rib: Fine copper wire
Body: Light gray dubbing
Shell back: Craft wrapping
Head: Thread
Legs: Picked out dubbing
Fly Tier: Dana Griffin, III

Double Renegade

Hook: Mustad 9672, #2 - #12
Thread: Black
Rib: Optional fine wire
Body: Peacock herl in two sections
Hackle: Brown (back), grizzly (center), and white (front)
Head: Thread
Fly Tier: Bruce Staples

Elk Scud

Hook: Mustad 80250, #12 - #20
Thread: Color to match the body
Tail & feelers: Same clump of elk hair, feelers in front and trimmed elk for the tail
Rib: Tying thread
Body: Synthetic dubbing, color of choice
Shell back: Same clump of elk hair as the feelers and tail
Head: Thread
Fly Tier: Len Holt

Flash Back Scud

Hook: Standard wet, #14 - #20
Thread: Black
Body: Gray ostrich
Shell back: Red Flashabou
Head: Thread
Fly Tier: David Curneal

Hale-Bop Leech

Hook: Mustad 9672, #6 - #10
Thread: Black
Tail: Dark olive marabou, tied very sparse
Rib: Olive thread
Body: Olive African goat dubbing, picked out
Head: Thread
Fly Tier: George Nelson

Half & Half Shrimp

Hook: TMC 200R, #12 - #18
Thread: Tan
Tail: Brown hen pheasant fibers
Weight: Six wraps of .015 lead free wire
Rib: Thread
Body: Salmon dubbing in the rear and hare's ear dubbing in the front
Shell back: Clear plastic strip
Head: Thread
Legs: Picked out dubbing
Antenna: Brown hen pheasant fibers
Fly Tier: Mike Jacobs

Halo Leech

Hook: Mustad 9672, #6 - #10
Thread: Brown or color to match the body
Tail: Maroon Arctic fox fur
Body and Hackle: Maroon Arctic fox in a dubbing loop
Optional colors: Olive, brown, and black
Head: Thread
Fly Tier: Chris Mihulka

Henry's Leech

Hook: Dai-Riki 700, #4
Thread: Black
Tail: Black dyed rabbit strip
Body: Black Dan Bailey Body Fur tied flat on the top and bottom
Head: Thread
Fly Tier: Eric Pettine

Hot Scud

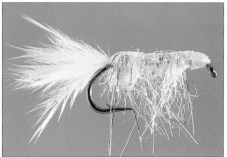

Hook: Mustad 3906B, #12 - #14
Thread: Color to match the body
Tail: Chartreuse marabou
Rib: Fine gold wire
Body: Lite Brite chartreuse dubbing
Shell back: Strip from a plastic bag
Head: Thread
Fly Tier: George Nelson

Larva Lace Scud

Hook: Nymph, #12 - #16
Thread: Color to match the body
Body: Larva Lace, color of choice
Gills: Two ostrich herls woven with each turn of the body, one on each side
Head: Thread
Fly Tier: George Harmeling

Lilly Lake Leech

Hook: TMC 100, #12 - #18
Thread: Olive
Tail: Several peacock herls, tied short
Rib: Fine copper wire
Body: Insect green dubbing
Head: Brass bead
Fly Tier: Gene Stutzman

Magic Mysis

Hook: TMC 2302, #14 - #18
Thread: White
Tail: Polar pearl Lite Brite
Abdomen: Clear tubing
Thorax: White ostrich herl
Shell back: Pearlescent Krystal Flash, tied over the thorax
Head: Thread
Eyes: Black mono melted to secure black glass beads
Antenna: Two strand of Krystal Flash from the shell back
Fly Tier: Pat Oglesby

Matt's Mysis

Hook: TMC 2487, #12 - #16
Thread: White
Tail: Pearl Krystal Flash
Body: White ostrich and clear V-Rib
Head: Thread
Eyes: Black brush bristles
Fly Tier: Matt Owens

Mini Leech

Hook: TMC 200R, #10
Thread: Red
Tail: Red marabou, four strands of Krystal Flash
Body: Red African goat in a Krystal Flash dubbing loop
Head: Thread or optional glass bead
Fly Tier: Kurt Zelazny

Mohair Leech

Hook: Mustad 9672, #2 - #6
Thread: Color to match the body
Tail: Sparse marabou, color to match the body
Body: Mohair leech yarn, brown, black purple, or olive
Head: Thread
Fly Tier: John Newbury

Mop-Top Leech

Hook: Streamer, #6
Thread: Black
Tail: Gray marabou and four strand of black Krystal Flash
Body: Brushed mohair
Wings: Natural wool
Head: Red glass bead
Fly Tier: Buzz Moss

Mysis Flasher

Hook: TMC 200R, #18
Thread: Yellow
Tail: White Z-lon
Abdomen: Thread
Thorax: White ostrich
Shell back: White Z-lon
Head: Thread
Eyes: Melted mono
Antenna: Pearl Krystal Flash
Fly Tier: Kurt Zelazny

Nymph Albertan

Hook: Mustad 9049, #8 - #12
Thread: Olive
Tail: Pheasant tail fibers
Rib: Medium ginger hackle, fibers stripped from one side
Body: Peacock herl
Wing case: Pheasant tail fibers
Head: Thread
Fly Tier: Reginald Denny

Olive Scud

Hook: Dai-Riki 135, #10 - #18
Thread: Olive
Tail: Olive Z-lon
Rib: Four-X tippet material
Body: Olive SLF dubbing, picket out and trimmed at an angle
Shell back: Pearl Flashabou
Antenna: Olive Z-lon
Head: Thread
Fly Tier: Larry Nicholas

Ostrich Scud

Hook: TMC 206BL, #12 - #18
Thread: Olive
Rib: Dark mono
Body: Two olive and two gray ostrich herls, wrapped
Shell back: Strip of plastic bag
Head: Thread
Fly Tier: Lance Zook

Ostrich Scud

Hook: Mustad 37160, #14 - #18
Thread: Color to match the body
Tail: Hackle fibers tied short, color of choice
Rib: Fine wire
Body: Ostrich herl
Shell back: Clear plastic strip
Head: Thread with short hackle fibers tied forward
Fly Tier: Bud Heintz

Parachute Snail

Hook: Dry fly, #10 - #18
Thread: Black
Body: Peacock herl, tied fat
Wing post: Orange Z-lon
Hackle: Brown, tied sparse
Head: Thread
Fly Tier: Marvin Nolte

Peacock Snail

Hook: Mustad 94840, #12
Thread: Black
Rib: Fine copper wire
Weight: Five wraps of lead wire in the middle of the shank
Body: Black yarn under body covered with peacock herl
Hackle: Brown or dark ginger tied fore and aft
Head: Thread
Fly Tier: Bob Pelzl

Pearl Peril

Hook: Mustad 94833, #14
Thread: Black
Rib: Wire wrapped with peacock herl
Body: Pearl sheathing
Hackle: Optional
Head: Thread
Fly Tier: Carl E. Wolf

Pearlescent Scud

Hook: Mustad 81001BR, #8
Thread: Yellow
Tail: Krystal Flash, chartreuse
Body: Chartreuse Krystal Flash under braided clear Vinyl Round Rib, medium size
Head: Thread
Legs: Krystal Flash
Antenna: Ends of Vinyl Round Rib
Fly Tier: Tom Broderidge

Polar Fiber Leech

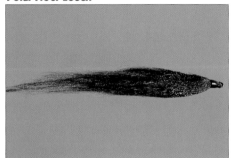

Hook: TMC 300, #8
Thread: Black
Tail: Sparse tuft of olive Polar Fiber
Rib: Krystal Flash
Body/wing: Olive Polar Fiber colored with a black felt tip, flatten the body with Softex
Head: Thread
Fly Tier: Jerry Caruso

Puff's Leech

Hook: Mustad 3665A, #6 - #10
Thread: Black
Tail: Red hackle fibers
Body: Black chenille
Body Hackle: Black, rear two thirds of the body
Hackle: Blue-eared pheasant, front one third of the body
Head: Thread
Fly Tier: Gordon Mankins

Red Leech

Hook: Dai-Riki 710, #8
Thread: Red
Tail: Red marabou
Rib: Fine copper wire
Body: Red marabou, wrapped and picked out
Head: Thread
Fly Tier: George Close

Ruddock Shrimp

Hook: Mustad 37160, #8 - #10
Thread: White silk
Tail: Two ostrich herls and a few fibers of ultra hair
Eyes: Silk flower stamens, tied at the hook bend
Under Body: Pearl Flashabou
Hackle: Ostrich herl, wrapped as a butt near the hook bend
Body: Tan Larva Lace or equivalent
Head: Thread
Fly Tier: Tom Tripi

Scud

Hook: Dai-Riki 135, #10
Thread: Color to match the body
Tail: Marabou tied short, gray, olive, or cream
Body: Rabbit dubbing, gray, olive, or cream
Hackle: Light dun, palmered and trimmed on the top
Shell back: Scud back
Head: Thread
Fly Tier: John Newbury

Seal Fur Leech

Hook: Mustad 9672, #4 - #8
Thread: Color of choice
Tail: Seal fur, color of choice
Body: Clumps of seal fur spaced along the hook shank
Head: Thread
Fly Tier: Cliff Stringer

Simple Scud

Hook: Standard wet #16
Thread: White
Rib: Fine gold wire
Body: Pale cream dubbing
Carapace: Pearl Krystal Flash
Head: Thread
Fly Tier: Ted Patlin

Slinky

Hook: DaiRiki 270, #6 - #8
Thread: Olive
Tail: Olive chamois cut to shape
Body: Olive zonker strip wrap from the back to the front of the hook
Head: Thread
Fly Tier: Robert Meuschke

Sluggo Leech

Hook: Mustad 3366, #4 - #8, the hook point rides up
Thread: Black
Body: Black rabbit strip, hide side treated with silicone caulking, sparkle flakes optional
Application: Treated rabbit strip impaled on the hook and tied behind the head
Head: Black cone head
Fly Tier: Scott Sanchez

Snail

Hook: Daiichi 1530, #14
Thread: Mono
Foot: Mono with Softex
Shell: Hot glue
Antenna: Melted mono
Color: Felt tip marker
Fly Tier: Shane Stalcup

Sow Bug

Hook: TMC 2302, #14 - #18
Thread: Mono
Feelers: Mallard flank, tied on at the bend of the hook
Eyes: Melted mono, tied on at the bend of the hook
Under Body: Softex
Legs: Emu
Shell back: Medallion Sheeting
Fly Tier: Shane Stalcup

Split Leech

Hook: Mustad 3906, #12 & #14 (one each)
Thread: Black
Tail fly: Burgundy marabou with strands of Krystal Flash, tied on a #14 hook
Front fly: Burgundy marabou with strands of Krystal Flash, tied on a #12 hook
Connection: Ten pound mono
Head: Thread and dubbed marabou on the front fly
Fly Tier: Eric Schubert

Tail Water Sowbug

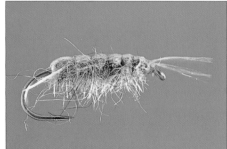

Hook: TMC 100, #12 - #16
Thread: Gray
Tail: Gray goose biots, tied very short
Rib: Fine copper wire
Body: Gray muskrat dubbing, picked out
Back: Clear plastic strip
Head: Thread
Antenna: Short tufts of tying thread
Fly Tier: Duane Hada

Taylor Snail

Hook: Mustad 37160, #10
Thread: Olive
Body: Dark olive chenille, tied larger in the center
Hackle: Dark olive hackle, one turn and over sized
Head: Thread
Fly Tier: Cliff Stringer

Turbo Leech

Hook: TMC 5262, #2 - #10
Thread: Color to match body
Tail: Blood quill marabou, any color
Rib: Gold or copper wire
Body: Wrapped marabou from tail
Head: Optional bead
Fly Tier: Gene Trump

Ultra Scud

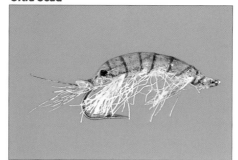

Hook: Daiichi 1120, #14 - #18
Thread: Mono
Feelers: Mallard flank fibers, tied on at the bend of the hook
Rib: Colored mono
Body: Mono under clear tubing, colored with a felt tip marker
Eyes: Melted mono, tied on at the bend of the hook
Legs: Z-lon
Shell back: Epoxy
Head: Thread
Fly Tier: Shane Stalcup

Ultra Suede Scud

Hook: TMC 2457, #14 - #16
Thread: Brown
Body: Dark Brown Ultra Suede
Thorax: Brown dubbing
Fly Tier: Dan Turner

Stonefly Nymphs . . .

Ayre's Woven Stone

Hook: TMC 200R, #4
Thread: Black
Tail: Optional
Body: Black and yellow embroidery yarn
Thorax: Black dubbing Ribbon that is lacquered and cut to shape
Head: Black dubbing
Eyes: Black beads on mono, mono melted to hold the beads in place
Fly Tier: Joe Ayre

Bead & Braid Stone

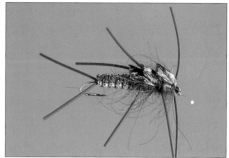

Hook: Streamer 3xl, #6
Thread: Black
Tail: Brown rubber leg material
Abdomen: Kreinik thread, braided
Thorax: Kaufmann's brown stonefly dubbing and two large root beer beads
Wing case: Brown Swiss straw
Head: Thread
Legs: Brown rubber leg material, three each side
Fly Tier: Buzz Moss

Black Hellgrammite

Hook: Mustad 38941, #8
Thread: Black
Tail: Two black turkey biots, divided
Rib: Ostrich herl
Body: Four strand floss
Thorax: Black chenille
Head: Thread
Fly Tier: Tom Broderidge

Black Mini-Stonefly

Hook: TMC 200R, #8 - #16
Thread: Black
Tail: Black turkey biots
Body: Black turkey biot
Thorax: Kaufmann's Black Stone dubbing mix
Wing case: Dark turkey tail
Head: Thread
Legs: Optional
Fly Tier: Gale Doudy

Black Rump Stone

Hook: Nymph, #6 - #14
Thread: Black
Tail: Black pheasant rump fibers
Abdomen: Black dubbing, tied in three sections, black after shaft collar dividing each
Thorax: Black dubbing
Over back & Wing case: Turkey tail, tied in four section, the last over the thorax
Hackle: Black pheasant rump, palmered over the thorax
Eyes: Black mono
Head: Black dubbing and thread
Fly Tier: Bear Andrews

Blackburn's Tellico

Hook: TMC 5262, #6 - #12
Thread: Brown
Tail: Mink guard hair fibers
Rib: Three peacock herls, twisted together and wrapped
Body: Golden yellow rabbit dubbing
Hackle: Brown palmered over the front one fourth of the body
Shell back: Turkey quill strip
Head: Thread
Fly Tier: Walter Babb

Bogus Brown Stone

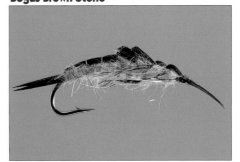

Hook: TMC 200R, #4 - #6
Thread: Dark olive
Tail: Black turkey biots
Rib: Fine gold wire
Top of abdomen, wing cases: Brown mottled, lacquered turkey tail
Body: Hot orange Seal EX and Haretron golden brown dubbing
Legs: Brown mottled grouse
Antenna: Black biots
Fly Tier: Tim Witsman

Bogus Yellow Stone

Hook: TMC 200R, #10
Thread: Tan
Tail: Ginger turkey biots
Rib: French wire tinsel, small gold
Top of abdomen, wing cases: Brown mottled, lacquered turkey tail quill section
Body: Haretron ginger dubbing
Legs: Picked out dubbing
Antenna: Ginger biots
Fly Tier: Tim Witsman

Bud's Black Stone

Hook: TMC 200R, #6 - #12
Thread: Black
Tail: Turkey biots, black
Rib: Fine copper wire
Body: Black ostrich herl
Over Body: Pheasant tail, dyed black
Wing case: Pheasant tail, dyed black
Head: Thread
Legs: Partridge, tied over the thorax and under the wing case
Fly Tier: Bud Heintz

Bud's Golden Stone

Hook: TMC 200R, #6 - #14
Thread: Brown
Tail: Turkey biots, brown
Rib: Fine brass wire
Body: Ostrich herl, yellow
Over Body: Pheasant tail fibers
Wing case: Pheasant tail fibers with brown marabou as a trailing wing case, tied short
Head: Thread
Legs: Partridge, tied over the thorax and under the wing case
Fly Tier: Bud Heintz

Burlap Stone

Hook: Mustad 9674, #6 - #10
Thread: Tan
Tail: Ginger goose biots, divided
Butt: Burlap dubbing
Rib: Gold floss
Abdomen: Burlap dubbing, tied tapered
Thorax: Burlap dubbing in loop, picked out, two segments
Wing cases: Fox squirrel back fur, one at the start of the thorax and one in the center
Head: Thread
Fly Tier: Reginald Denny

Canadian Stone

Hook: TMC 200R, #8
Thread: Brown
Tail: Brown goose biots
Body: Light and dark brown burlap, woven
Wing case: Turkey quill section
Abdomen & Legs: Canadian brown mohair leech yarn
Head: Thread
Legs: Picked out leech yarn
Fly Tier: Kim Jensen

Chickabou Stonefly

Hook: Dai-Riki 710, #6 - #8
Thread: Brown
Tail: Brown rooster biots, divided
Rib: Copper wire
Body: Brown Chickabou
Wing case: Grizzly dyed brown rooster soft hackle, lacquered and cut to shape
Hackle: Grizzly dyed brown soft hackle
Head: Brown dubbing
Eyes: Brown melted mono
Antenna: Brown rooster biots
Fly Tier: Henry Hoffman

Darlon Stone

Hook: Daiichi 1270, #6
Thread: Brown
Tail: Brown rubber leg material
Rib: Gold tinsel
Body: Brown Darlon, twisted and wrapped
Thorax: Bronze Flashabou dubbing
Wing cases: Thin Skin, three wing cases trimmed to shape
Legs: Brown rubber leg material
Antenna: Brown rubber leg material
Head: Bronze Flashabou dubbing and a gold bead
Fly Tier: Derek Harryman

Double Tungsten

Hook: Daiichi 1720, #6 - #10
Thread: Brown
Tail: Goose biots, divided
Rib: Fine copper wire
Body: Brown Possum Plus
Thorax: Two gold tungsten beads
Wings case: Turkey tail, folded once in the center
Legs: Brown hackle, trimmed top and bottom
Head: Thread
Fly Tier: Bill Black, Spirit River Inc.

Drifting Stonefly Nymph

Hook: Daiichi 1720, #4 - #10
Thread: Black
Tail: Black goose biots, divided
Body: Black Body Stretch
Thorax: Black Squirrel Brite dubbing
Wing cases: Black Swiss straw, cut to shape and coated with epoxy
Hackle: Black soft hackle, palmered over the thorax
Head: Gold Brite Bead
Antenna: Black goose biots, one on each side of the gold bead head
Fly Tier: Bill Black, Spirit River Inc.

Entwistle Creeper

Hook: Mustad 79580, #10
Thread: Brown
Tail: Fox squirrel tail fibers
Rib: Orange embroidery yarn
Body: Brown muskrat dubbing
Wings: Wood duck flank feather
Hackle: Brown, tied as a collar, under the wings
Head: Brown dubbing and thread
Fly Tier: George Harmeling

Furry Rubber Stone

Hook: Mustad 9672, #2
Thread: Brown
Tail: Brown turkey biots, divided
Rib: Brown Larva Lace, midge size
Body: Brown furry foam tied over a large Orvis Nymph Form
Wing case: Brown tyvek
Head: Thread
Eyes: Melted mono
Fly Tier: Robert Meuschke

Giant Stonefly Nymph

Hook: TMC 5263, #4 - #8
Thread: Black
Tail: Black rubber hackle
Body: Large black crystal chenille, trimmed top and bottom
Thorax: Black macramé yarn dubbing, picked out to simulate legs
Wing cases: Black macramé yarn coated with Soft Body and trimmed to shape
Head: Thread
Antenna: Black rubber hackle
Fly Tier: Lee Clark

Golden Prince Nymph

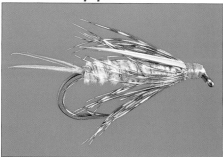

Hook: Mustad 9671, #8 - #16
Thread: Tan
Tail: Amber goose biots, divided
Weight: Lead free wire
Rib: Gold wire
Body: Turkey wing feather dyed golden orange, wrapped
Wings: Amber goose biots, divided
Hackle: Brown partridge, tied as a collar
Head: Thread
Fly Tier: Kevin Cohenour

Golden Princess

Hook: Mustad 9671, #10 - #18
Thread: Yellow
Tail: Ginger biots, divided
Rib: Embossed tinsel, gold
Body: Bleached peacock herl
Wings: White biots, divided
Hackle: Barred ginger, tied as a collar
Head: Yellow thread, larger than normal
Fly Tier: John Oppenlander

Golden Stone

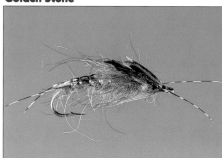

Hook: TMC 200R, #8 - #14   **Thread:** Brown
Tail: Peacock wing quill fibers, divided
Rib: Oval gold tinsel
Over Body: Peacock quill section, laced into place with the rib
Body: Bill's blend of Antron dubbing; yellow, buff fox, tan, fiery brown, claret, and black
Wing cases: Peacock shoulder feathers, trimmed to shape
Antenna: Peacock wing quill fibers, divided at the hook eye
Head: Thread   **Legs:** Dubbing picked out from the thorax
Fly Tier: Bill Chandler

Golden Stone

Hook: TMC 200R, #8 - #14
Thread: Yellow
Tail: Ginger goose biots
Abdomen: Yellow floss under clear larva lace
Thorax: Yellow Furry Foam
Wing case: Latex, shaped with stonefly burning tool
Hackle: Brown hen, last wrap over Furry Foam head
Head: Yellow Furry Foam
Eyes: Red Amnesia, melted
Fly Tier: *Gale Doudy*

NYMPHS AND WET FLIES | 83

Hair Leg Stonefly Nymph

Hook: Mustad 9672, #8 - #10
Thread: Black
Tail: Black calf tail
Rib: Silver oval tinsel
Body: Black dubbing
Thorax: Black dubbing in a dubbing loop with hackle
Hackle: Black calf tail prepared in a dubbing loop with thorax dubbing
Head: Thread
Legs: Optional
Fly Tier: Bob Pelzl

Harvey Stonefly Nymph

Hook: TMC 5262, #6 - #12
Thread: Black
Tail: Pheasant tail fibers
Rib: Fine gold or brass wire
Body: Yellow or gold wool
Wing case & back: Brown hen back feather
Hackle: Partridge
Head: Thread
Fly Tier: Joe Humphreys

Herl Stonefly Nymph

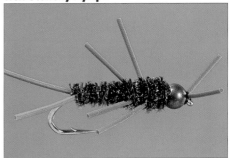

Hook: DaiRiki 710, #6 - #10
Thread: Black
Tail: Brown rubber legs
Body: Peacock herl in a dubbing loop
Legs: Brown rubber legs
Antenna: Brown rubber legs
Head: Thread
Fly Tier: Lance Zook

Isoperla Nymph

Hook: Nymph 2xl, #10 - #12
Thread: Yellow
Tail: Wood duck flank fibers serve both for the tail and the over body
Rib: Fine gold wire
Abdomen: Cream dubbing with a wood duck over body
Thorax: Light brown dubbing
Wing case: Peacock herl
Hackle: Partridge
Head: Thread
Fly Tier: Marvin Nolte

King's Golden Stone

Hook: DaiRiki 700, #4 - #12
Thread: Brown
Tail: Pumpkin color Silli-con Leg material
Body: Variegated brown and orange chenille
Wing case: Chenille from the body
Legs: Pumpkin color Silli-con Leg material
Eyes: Black bead chain
Head: Chenille, thread
Fly Tier: Al Beatty

Lite Brite Stonefly Nymph

Hook: Daiichi 1720, #4
Thread: Black
Tail: Black goose biots, divided
Rib: Black Jelly Rope
Body: Black Lite Brite dubbing
Legs: Black rubber leg material
Head: Gold Cone Head Bead
Antenna: Black goose biots
Fly Tier: Bill Black, Spirit River Inc.

Little Brown Stone

Hook: TMC 200R, #10
Thread: Brown
Tail: Brown goose biots
Weight: Fuse wire
Rib: Brown flat mono
Body: Hare's ear dubbing over fuse wire
Wing case: Turkey quill section
Hackle: Brown trimmed on the bottom
Head: Hare's ear dubbing
Antenna: Brown goose biots
Fly Tier: Eric Pettine

Little Yellow Stonefly

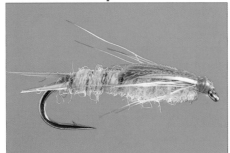

Hook: TMC 5263, #12
Thread: Tan
Tail: Golden tan goose biots, divided
Butt: Red ball of dubbing to divide the tail
Rib: Brown thread
Body: Golden yellow dubbing
Wing case: Turkey quill section
Hackle: Ginger, tied to the sides
Head: Thread
Fly Tier: Royce Dam

New Haven Golden Stone

Hook: TMC 200R, #6
Thread: White
Tail: Brown goose biots, divided
Rib: Fine black body glass and gold oval tinsel
Body: Golden antron, additional color from a felt tip marker
Wing cases: Pheasant feather, shaped in a wing burner
Head: Dubbing and melted mono eyes
Legs: Pheasant feather rolled
Antenna: Brown goose biots, divided
Fly Tier: Kevin McEnerney

Orange Stone

Hook: Mustad 9672, #6 - #10
Thread: Brown
Tail: Short brown marabou, tied sparse
Rib: Red wire
Body: Olive chenille
Wing case: Orange antron yarn
Hackle: Orange palmered over the thorax
Head: Thread and trimmed orange antron
Legs: Optional
Fly Tier: Len Holt

Ottauquechee Yellow

Hook: Mustad 79850, #8
Thread: Yellow
Tail: Emu fibers tinted yellow
Weight: Non-lead wire in the thorax area
Body: Emu fiber tinted yellow
Wings: Tan polar fibers
Hackle: Emu feather tinted yellow, trimmed on the bottom
Head: Thread with painted eyes, lacquered
Fly Tier: Jerry Caruso

Reversed Bitch Creek

Hook: Mustad 9672, #2 - #14
Thread: Black
Tail & antenna: White rubber hackle
Abdomen: Black chenille, last one-third of the hook shank
Thorax: Black and orange chenille, woven over front two-thirds of the hook shank
Hackle: Brown saddle, palmered over the thorax
Head: Thread
Legs: Optional rubber legs
Fly Tier: Bruce Staples

Rio Grande Golden Stone

Hook: Mustad 9672, #8
Thread: Tan
Tail: Yellow-dyed turkey tail, divided
Rib: Fine copper wire
Body: Gold yarn dubbing
Wing case: Yellow-dyed turkey tail
Hackle: Grizzly dyed brown
Fly Tier: Dana Griffin, III

Santiam Stone

Hook: Mustad 9671, #8 - #12
Thread: Black
Tail: Brown goose biots, divided
Body: Brown Larva Lace
Thorax: Hare's ear dubbing
Wing case: Brown turkey tail
Hackle: Brown palmered over the thorax
Head: Thread
Fly Tier: George Nelson

The Scorpion

Hook: TMC 200R, #4 - #12, hook point rides up
Thread: Black
Tail: Black goose biots, tied short and divided
Rib: Black mono
Body: Peacock herl
Wing case: Pheasant tail fibers
Hackle: Brown, palmered over the thorax
Eyes: Dumb bell, black with red pupils
Head: Black dubbing around the eyes
Fly Tier: Larry Nicholas

Simple Stonefly

Hook: Mustad 9671, #8
Thread: White
Tail: Teal fibers
Rib: Pale yellow thread
Body: Creamy yellow wool or dubbing
Over Body: Mottled brown turkey tail
Thorax: Creamy yellow wool or dubbing
Wing case: Mottled brown turkey tail
Head: Same as body
Legs: Mottled brown soft hackle
Fly Tier: Ted Patlin

Spandex Stone

Hook: Dai-Riki 270, #4 - #10
Thread: Yellow
Tail: Tan goose biots, divided
Rib: Yellow thread
Back: Six strands of brown Super Floss (spandex)
Abdomen: Golden brown dubbing
Thorax: Body dubbing and a brass bead
Wing case: Remainder of the brown spandex from back
Legs: The tips of the wing case, three per side
Head: Brass bead
Antenna: Tan goose biots
Fly Tier: Scott Sanchez

Sparkle Sam

Hook: Mustad 9672, #8 - #12
Thread: Black
Tail: Black rubber
Body: Woven diamond braid, black and orange
Thorax: Lite Brite dubbing, peacock color
Wing case: Glitter sheet strip
Hackle: Black
Head: Thread
Eyes: Melted mono
Antenna: Black rubber
Fly Tier: Eric Schubert

Stonefly Nymph

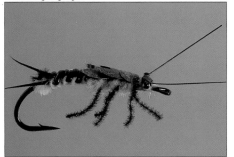

Hook: Daiichi 2151, #1
Thread: White colored orange with felt tip marker
Tail: Black goose biots
Body: Black Larva Lace and orange ultra chenille, woven
Thorax: Orange furry foam
Wing case: Tyvek dyed black and cut to shape
Head: Orange furry foam and black tyvek
Legs: Black New Dub
Eyes: Melted 80 pound mono
Antenna: Black horse hair
Fly Tier: Kent Bulfinch

Stripped Stone

Hook: Mustad 79580, #4 **Thread:** Orange
Tail: Black goose biots, divided
Weight: Several turns of .025 lead free wire
Under Body: Poly yarn **Body:** Stripped secondary wing quill soaked for five days in water/detergent, split
Thorax: Tan fur dubbing, tied in a dubbing loop and picked out
Wing case: Mottled turkey quill section
Hackle: Guinea or grouse folder over the thorax and under the wing case
Head: Black ostrich **Antenna:** Moose body hair
Fly Tier: Cliff Stringer

Wallow Mackinaw Stone

Hook: Mustad 80050BR, #4 - #8
Thread: Orange
Tail: Peccary fibers
Weighted: Several turns of .025 lead free wire
Rib: Fine copper wire
Body: Black wool yarn
Thorax: Black wool yarn, picked out
Hackle: Black, palmered over the thorax
Head: Thread
Fly Tier: Gene Stutzman

Yellow Stone

Hook: TMC 200R, #8 - #10
Thread: Red
Tail: Yellow dyed goose biots
Rib: Fine copper wire
Body: Golden stone dubbing
Wing case: Amber Krystal Flash
Hackle: Furnace
Thorax: Mix of brown and golden stone dubbing
Head: Thread
Fly Tier: David Hunter

Wet Flies and Soft Hackles . . .

A P Emerger

Hook: TMC 2302, #12 - #18
Thread: Brown
Tail: Wood duck flank fibers, tied as long as the hook
Rib: Fine copper wire
Body: Rusty dun Super Fine dubbing
Thorax: Peacock herl
Hackle: Partridge, tied as a collar
Head: Thread
Fly Tier: Larry Nicholas

AT&T Special

Hook: Mustad 3906B, #8 - #12
Thread: Black
Body: Color coded telephone wire
Hackle: Hen hackle tied as a collar
Head: Thread
Fly Tier: Tommy Marks

B. C. Red

Hook: TMC 200R, #8 - #22
Thread: Red
Body: Thread
Thorax: Red salmon steelhead dubbing
Hackle: Red hen feather
Head: Thread
Fly Tier: Roger Swengel

Bead Head Doc Spratley

Hook: Mustad 9671, #12 - #14
Thread: Black
Tail: Grizzly hackle fibers
Rib: Fine silver wire
Body: Black wool yarn
Wings: Pheasant tail fibers
Hackle: Grizzly, tied as a beard
Collar: Peacock herl
Head: Bead
Fly Tier: Jerry Smalley

Beaded Soft Hackle

Hook: Mustad 3906, #10 - #18
Thread: Black or color to match the body
Rib: Fine wire
Body: Dubbing, color of choice
Thorax: Copper, black, or brass bead
Hackle: Partridge, tied as a collar
Head: Thread
Fly Tier: Bub Heintz

Beaver & Knee

Hook: TMC 3761, #10 - #16
Thread: Brown
Tail: Grizzly dyed brown Chickabou
Rib: Fine gold wire
Body: Beaver dubbing dyed brown
Hackle: Grizzly dyed brown knee hackle
Head: Gold glass bead
Fly Tier: Henry Hoffman

Biot Soft Hackle

Hook: Daiichi 1140, #14 - #22
Thread: Color to match the body
Body: Goose biot, color of choice
Thorax: Super Fine dubbing, gray
Hackle: Partridge
Head: Thread
Fly Tier: Shane Stalcup

Bird's Eye Soft Hackle

Hook: Daiichi 1550, #16 - #18
Thread: Black
Body: Single barb from the eye of a peacock upper
  tail covert feather
Hackle: Starling, tied as a collar
Head: Thread
Fly Tier: Wayne Luallen

The Bloody Alder

Hook: Partridge L3A, #10 - #20
Thread: Fire orange
Tag: Fire orange tying thread
Rib: Thread
Body: Peacock herl, tied sparse
Wings: Pheasant tail fibers, rolled and tied trude style
Wing case: Pheasant tail fibers folder over from the
  wing
Hackle: Grizzly dyed orange
Head: Thread, tied extra large
Fly Tier: Al Beatty

Brassie Emerger

Hook: Standard nymph, #12 - #18
Thread: Black
Tail: Pheasant tail fibers
Body: Copper wire
Thorax: Peacock herl
Wings: White poly yarn
Head: Thread
Fly Tier: David Curneal

Buzzula

Hook: Wet fly, #14
Thread: Black
Tail: Red yarn
Body: Glass beads, color of choice
Hackle: Black hen hackle
Head: Thread
Fly Tier: Buzz Moss

Chukar and Copper

Hook: Standard wet, #10 - #14
Thread: Brown
Body: Soft copper wire, 28 to 30 gauge, oxidized
Hackle: Dun chukar body feather
Head: Thread
Fly Tier: Reginald Denny

Cliff's Lucky

Hook: Mustad 9671, #8
Thread: Black
Tail: Chukar flank, tied short
Body: Variegated black/tan chenille
Hackle: Grouse body feather, tied as a sparse collar
Head: Thread
Fly Tier: Cliff Stringer

Delaware Flymph

Hook: TMC 3761, #10 - #18
Thread: Hot orange
Body: Black dubbing, tied cigar shape
Hackle: Brown hen
Head: Thread
Fly Tier: Jerry Caruso

Dixie Tup

Hook: Mustad 3906B, #10 - #16
Thread: Brown
Tail: Gold Krystal Flash
Rib: Fine gold wire
Body: Gold four strand floss
Thorax: Pink dubbing
Hackle: Brown hen, tied as a collar
Head: Thread
Fly Tier: Dana Griffin, III

Double Hot Spot

Hook: Mustad 94840, #12 - #18
Thread: Hot orange
Tag: Hot orange
Body: Peacock herl
Hackle: Dun hen hackle, tied as a collar
Head: Hot orange thread
Fly Tier: Doug Farthing

Flash Loop Emerger

Hook: TMC 2487, #16 - #20
Thread: Brown
Tail/extended Body: Light olive New Dub
Thorax: Muskrat dubbing
Wings: Lime green Krystal Flash, looped short
Hackle: Grizzly hen
Head: Thread
Fly Tier: Matt Owens

Gold Bead Plastron Diver

Hook: TMC 34761, #10 - #14
Thread: Color to match the body
Tail: One strand of pearlescent Krystal Flash
Plastron: Thin, iridescent plastic sheet top and bottom
Body: Medium crystal chenille, color of choice
Legs: Silicone rubber
Head: Thread
Fly Tier: Deke Meyer

Golden Fever

Hook: Daiichi 1270, #12 - #18
Thread: Brown
Tail: Brown hackle fibers
Rib: Flat gold tinsel, small
Body: Golden brown dubbing
Under Hackle: Pheasant breast feather
Over Hackle: Gold Flashabou dubbing in a dubbing loop
Head: Gold bead
Fly Tier: Derek Harryman

Gray Hackle Yellow

Hook: Mustad 3906, #12 - #16
Thread: Black
Tail: Red hackle fibers
Rib: Gold tinsel
Body: Yellow yarn, dubbing, or floss
Hackle: Grizzly hen or gray partridge, tied as a collar
Head: Thread
Fly Tier: Kevin Cohenour

Green Drake

Hook: Mustad 94840, #8
Thread: Cream
Tail: Bright green hackle fibers
Rib: Twisted brown silk
Body: Pale cream floss
Wings: Bright green dyed mallard flank, tied wet style
Hackle: Dyed bright green
Head: Thread
Fly Tier: Ted Patlin

The Hatch Back

Hook: Mustad 3906B, #12 - #18
Thread: Brown
Rib: Fine gold tinsel
Body: Dark brown dubbing or peacock herl
Shell back: Dark turkey tail quill section, tied in two steps with a fold over in the center
Hackle: Light dun, tied as a collar divided by the shell back
Head: Thread
Fly Tier: Al Beatty

Hot Spot

Hook: Mustad 3399, #10
Thread: Black
Hackle: Five hen hackles, tied wet style, from the rear, black, orange, black, yellow, black
Head: Thread
Fly Tier: Tom Broderidge

JC's Emerger

Hook: TMC 100, #10 - #16
Thread: Brown
Tail: Coastal deer hair, tied very sparse
Rib: Copper wire
Body: Rusty dun Super Fine dubbing
Wings: Coastal deer hair, tied very sparse and trude style
Head: Thread
Fly Tier: Larry Nicholas

Krystal Flash Soft Hackle

Hook: Mustad 3906B, #14 - #18
Thread: Black
Body: Black or green Krystal Flash, twisted and wrapped
Thorax: Brass bead or optional brown dubbing
Hackle: Brown partridge or hen hackle
Head: Thread
Fly Tier: Jim Schollmeyer

Laced Sister

Hook: Mustad 94840, #14
Thread: Black
Tail: Black hackle fibers, tied short
Body: Purple yarn dubbing
Wing case: Purple plastic strip
Hackle: American laced hen, tied as a beard
Eyes: Gold bead chain
Head: Thread
Fly Tier: Sister Carol Ann Corley

Larva Soft Hackle

Hook: Daiichi 1270, #12 - #22
Thread: Brown
Under Body: Mono
Body: Midge tubing, color of choice
Thorax: Brown SLF squirrel dubbing
Hackle: Partridge
Head: Thread
Fly Tier: Shane Stalcup

Lauren's Soft Hackle

Hook: Dai-Riki 270, #16 - #18
Thread: Black
Body: Polymorphic glitter
Hackle: Partridge
Head: Thread
Fly Tier: Eric Pettine

Lemon Hare's Ear

Hook: Mustad 80000Br, #12 - #16
Thread: Brown
Tail: Lemon dyed mallard flank
Body: Hare's ear dubbing
Wings: Lemon dyed mallard flank, tied wet style
Hackle: Brown, tied as a collar
Head: Thread
Fly Tier: Gene Stutzman

Lost Lake PT

Hook: TMC 200R, #8 - #14
Thread: Brown
Rib: Fine copper wire
Body: Insect green dubbing (color of choice)
Hackle: Several pheasant tail fiber, spun into a collar
Head: Thread (optional bead head)
Fly Tier: Gene Stutzman

Marabou Soft Hackle

Hook: Mustad 3906, #14
Thread: Black
Rib: Fine silver wire
Body: Black tying thread
Hackle: Marabou feather tip fibers in a dubbing loop, tied as a collar
Head: Thread
Fly Tier: David Curneal

Master Bright

Hook: DaiRiki 135, #12 - #16
Thread: Brown
Body: Peacock color Master Bright dubbing
Hackle: Brown hen, tied as a collar, extra long
Head: Thread
Fly Tier: Robert Meuschke

Mosquito

Hook: Mustad 3906, #12 - #14
Thread: Black
Tail: Grizzly hackle fibers
Body: One light and one dark moose main fibers, wrapped parallel
Hackle: Gray partridge
Head: Thread
Fly Tier: Kevin Cohenour

Orange Bead

Hook: Mustad 5861, #10 - #16
Thread: Orange
Rib: Optional
Body: Orange floss
Thorax: Brass bead
Hackle: Furnace soft hackle
Head: Black ostrich
Fly Tier: Gale Doudy

Partridge and Argus

Hook: Mustad 3906, #6 - #10
Thread: Black
Tail: Grouse hackle fibers
Rib: Fine silver tinsel
Body: Gray otter dubbing
Wings: Argus pheasant body feather sections
Hackle: Grouse, tied as a collar under the wings
Head: Thread
Fly Tier: Bruce Staples

Partridge & Gray

Hook: Mustad 94840, #10 - #20
Thread: Black
Rib: Fine copper wire
Body: Natural muskrat dubbing
Hackle: Partridge, tied as a collar
Head: Peacock herl and thread
Fly Tier: Len Holt

Partridge and Orange

Hook: TMC 2487, #14 - #18
Thread: Orange
Body: Orange Pearsall's silk floss
Hackle: Partridge, tied as a collar
Head: Thread
Fly Tier: David Hunter

R. A. F.

Hook: Partridge Z2, #14 - #18
Thread: Black
Tag: Red nylon
Rib: Gray goose quill fiber
Body: Thread abdomen and peacock herl thorax
Hackle: Grouse tied sparse
Head: Thread
Fly Tier: Ian Russel

Red Ass Partridge

Hook: Mustad 3906B, #12 - #16
Thread: Black
Body: Red tinsel (green and black are also good colors)
Thorax: Peacock herl
Hackle: Partridge
Head: Thread
Fly Tier: John Newbury

Red Tail

Hook: Nymph, #10 - #20
Thread: Fluorescent red
Rib: Thread
Tag: Thread
Body: Peacock herl
Hackle: Partridge
Head: Thread
Fly Tier: George Harmeling

Royal Lead Wing Coachman

Hook: Mustad 3906, #10 - #16
Thread: Black
Tail: Golden pheasant tippets
Rib: Fine gold wire
Body: Peacock herl and red floss
Wings: Mallard quills, tied wet style
Hackle: Brown, tied as a collar
Head: Black ostrich herl
Fly Tier: Bud Heintz

Scarlet Ibis

Hook: Wet fly, #6 - #14
Thread: Red
Tail: Scarlet hen hackle fibers
Rib: Fine gold, oval tinsel
Body: Scarlet floss
Wings: Scarlet goose quill section
Hackle: Scarlet hen hackle
Head: Thread
Fly Tier: Marvin Nolte

Soft Hackle Quill

Hook: Mustad 3906, #12 - #16
Thread: Olive
Rib: Fine gold wire
Body: Stripped brown hackle stem
Hackle: Coot body feather, tied as a collar
Head: Thread
Fly Tier: Floyd Franke

Tubing Soft Hackle

Hook: Daiichi 1140, #14 - #20
Thread: Color to match the body
Body: Goose biot, color of choice
Thorax: Super Fine dubbing, gray
Hackle: Partridge
Head: Thread
Fly Tier: Shane Stalcup

Washington Nymph

Hook: Mustad 3906B, #6 - #16
Thread: Black
Body: Peacock herl
Wings: Pheasant rump
Head: Thread
Fly Tier: Bear Andrews

Western Lead Wing Coachman

Hook: Mustad 3906, #10 - #16
Thread: Black
Tail: Gold pheasant tippets
Rib: Fine gold wire
Body: Peacock herl
Wings: Mallard quills, tied wet style
Hackle: Brown, tied as a collar
Head: Black ostrich herl
Fly Tier: Bud Heintz

Yellow Hammer

Hook: Mustad 9671, #12 - #18
Thread: Yellow
Rib: Black thread
Body: Yellow floss
Thorax: Peacock herl
Hackle: Grizzly dyed yellow hen saddle, tied as a collar
Head: Thread
Fly Tier: Tom H. Logan

Yellow Hammer Soft Hackle

Hook: Mustad 9671, #14 - #16
Thread: Yellow
Rib: Black thread
Body: Yellow floss
Thorax: Peacock herl
Hackle: Mottle hen saddle dyed yellow
Head: Thread
Fly Tier: Tom H. Logan

Yellow Sally Soft Hackle

Hook: Dai-Riki 270, #8 - #16
Thread: Rust brown
Tail: Brown biots, divided, also they form the body sides
Rib: Fine copper wire over the body and biot sides
Body: Yellow antron yarn, sides formed from excess biots remaining from the tail
Thorax: Brown dubbing
Hackle: Pheasant church window feather, tied as a collar
Head: Thread
Fly Tier: Scott Sanchez

Worms and Crayfish . . .

Chamois San Juan

Hook: Mustad 3906, #18
Thread: Red
Rib: Thread
Body: Chamois, color of choice type San Juan Worm style
Head: Thread
Fly Tier: Mike Latschar

Chickabou Crayfish

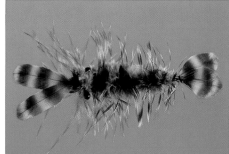

Hook: Mustad 79582, #6 - #8
Thread: Dark olive
Tail: Grizzly dyed brown hen saddle
Body: Mix of brown and tan Chickabou, wrapped and trimmed to shape
Hackle: Grizzly dyed brown
Head: Same as body
Eyes: Brown melded mono
Claws: Grizzly dyed brown hen saddle
Fly Tier: Henry Hoffman

Double Leather Worm

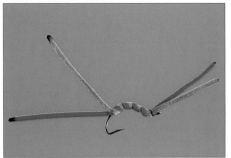

Hook: Mustad 37160, #8
Thread: Red
Tail: One red and one tan strip of leather
Body: Wrapped leather remaining from the tail
Front Body: Leather remaining from the body
Head: Thread
Fly Tier: David Curneal

EZY Crayfish

Hook: TMC 5263, #4 - #8
Thread: Brown
Claws/Tail: Four medium brown Chickabou feathers, divided
Rib: Copper wire
Body: Brown crystal chenille over non-lead wire
Shell back: Brown poly yarn
Hackle: Brown Hebert saddle, palmered
Head: Brown poly yarn, trimmed
Eyes: Brown Razzle Eyes
Fly Tier: Gretchen Beatty

Fire Tail Blood Worm

Hook: Eagle Claw 215FS, #8
Thread: Red
Tail: Hot pink Flurofibre
Body: Red and black yak hair wrapped over tinsel under body
Thorax: Peacock herl
Head: Thread
Fly Tier: Jerry Caruso

KJ's Woven Crayfish

Hook: Dai-Riki 700B, #2   **Thread:** Brown
Tail: Brown marabou
Abdomen: Woven Larva Lace
Under Body: Craft foam
Body: Brown leech yarn
Shell: Stretch Flex
Hackle: Brown soft hackle
Claws: Hen saddle hackle
Antenna: Moose hair
Mouth parts: Deer hair
Eyes: Melted mono
Fly Tier: Kim Jensen

Madam X Crawdad

Hook: Dai-Riki 270, #4 - #10
Thread: Orange
Eyes: Black plastic bead chain
Antenna: Tan Super Floss
Abdomen: Elk tied bullet head style over the front half of the hook
Rib: Thread
Thorax: Tips of the abdomen, trimmed flat on the bottom
Legs: Tan Super Floss, tied on the sides
Fly Tier: Scott Sanchez

Marabou Crayfish

Hook: TMC 200R, #8
Thread: White
Mouth parts: Mottled brown feather fibers
Body & Head: Fiery brown marabou, dubbed
Claws: Trimmed mottled brown feathers
Legs: Mottled brown soft hackle
Eyes: Gold bead chain, tied directly above the hook point
Fly Tier: Ted Patlin

Marabou Wiggler

Hook: TMC 2487, #12
Thread: Fire orange
Tail/Body: Red marabou, braided
Thorax: One turn of red marabou
Head: Brass bead
Fly Tier: Al Beatty

Mating Worms

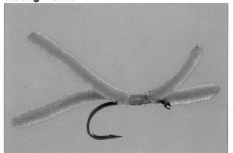

Hook: Mustad 3906, #14
Thread: Red
Body: Two orange pieces of ultra chenille
Fly Tier: Marvin Nolte

Preston's Crayfish

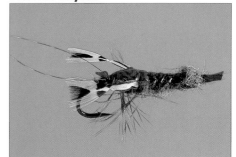

Hook: Heavy wire 4 X long, #2 - #8
Thread: Brown
Tail: Lead eyes tied at the hook eye
Rib: Eight pound mono
Body: Brown dubbing over closed cell foam under body
Carapace: Mottled sheet latex
Hackle: Brown palmered
Head: Elk hair and black mono eyes
Legs: Pheasant body feathers
Antenna: Brown hackle stems
Fly Tier: Eric Pettine

Red Angle Worm

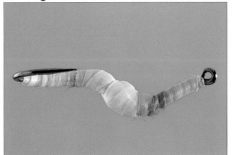

Hook: Mustad 9672, #6 (bent to shape, eye must line up with the hook point)
Thread: White dyed red with felt tip marker
Body: Red floss under body over wrapped with a latex strip
Egg sack: Orange glow bug yarn over wrapped with a latex strip
Head: Thread
Fly Tier: Kent Bulfinch

Royal Lady Worm

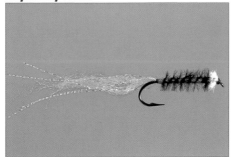

Hook: Mustad 79580, #6 - #12
Thread: Black
Tail: Brushed pink poly and four strands of Krystal Flash
Rib: Black ostrich palmered over the body
Body: Pink poly
Head: White ostrich collar, thread
Fly Tier: Ruth J. Zinck

San Antonio Wiggler

Hook: TMC 2457, #10 - #14
Thread: Black
Tail: Medium or large Ultra Chenille, any color
Body: Wrapped Ultra Chenille with excess from the tail
Head: Black bead
Front extension: Same as tail
Fly Tier: Tony Pagliei

San Juan Worm

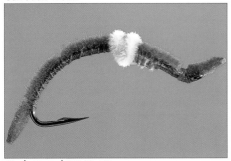

Hook: Mustad 37160, #8
Thread: Orange
Tail: Short piece of orange micro chenille, extended from the body
Body: Orange micro chenille tied from the eye to the bend
Center Body: Two turns of tan micro chenille
Head: Thread
Fly Tier: Len Holt

Sang Frog

Hook: Mustad 9672, #6 - #8
Thread: Olive
Kicker Legs: Knotted rubber hackle
Body: Light olive chenille
Head: Thread and body chenille
Eyes: Yellow plastic beads with black pupils
Fly Tier: Bruce Staples

Simple Crayfish

Hook: Mustad 9672, #6
Thread: Brown
Tail: Fox squirrel tail, divided to form claws
Rib: Black thread
Body: Brown or olive chenille, choice
Hackle: Furnace palmered on back half of the body
Shell back: Pheasant tail fibers
Head: Trimmed pheasant tail fibers to form the cray fish's tail
Legs: Optional rubber hackle
Fly Tier: Cliff Stringer

Sparkle Worm

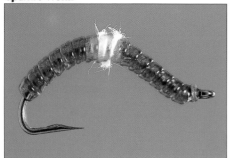

Hook: Mustad 37160, #12
Thread: Red
Body: Red Krystal Flash under clear Larva Lace, white dubbing in the middle
Head: Thread
Fly Tier: Derek Harryman

Squirrel Crawdad

Hook: Mustad 9672, #6
Thread: Brown
Pinchers: Fox squirrel tail, divided into two clumps to form the pinchers
Rib: Copper wire
Body: Brown and black variegated chenille
Shell back: Brown Swiss straw
Eyes: Melted mono, tied at the hook bend
Tail: Bronze turkey feather, tied at the hook eye
Fly Tier: Robert Meuschke

Suwannee River'dad

Hook: Mustad 9672, #8
Thread: Tan
Tail: Furry foam, tied at the eye
Rib: Copper wire
Body: Reddish-brown dubbing
Carapace: Tan furry foam
Hackle: Brown, tied palmered
Claws: Pheasant saddle feathers
Head: Foam and thread
Eyes: Felt tip marker
Fly Tier: Dana Griffin, III

Chapter 3

STREAMER FLIES

By Gary Grant

Since the turn of the century, using a fly as a method of catching fish has grown to be perhaps, the hallmark of sport fishing. The recent primary focus of fly fishing on coldwater species has resulted in almost exclusive attention to dry flies and nymphs while the streamer fly has gone practically unnoticed. Because insects represent the majority of a trout's diet, there is no argument that dry flies and nymphs can be very effective. However, the venerable streamer that imitates a baitfish can be equally effective in taking all types of game fish. In addition, for the larger trout in streams, rivers, and lakes, it can be the best choice for the fly fisher.

Of all the different types of flies used to catch fish, the streamer is the only fly that was originated in the Americas. The dry flies, nymphs, and wet flies that we use are primarily of European origin. Streamers, particularly the Rangeley Lakes style feather-wing streamers, which originated in the eastern United States, represent a history as rich as any in fly tying. Many of the time-honored patterns such as the Black Ghost, Gray Ghost, Muddler Minnow, and Mickey Finn were originated by such notable anglers as Herb Welch, Carrie Stevens, Don Gapen, and John Alden Knight.

The streamer fly patterns in this chapter, in a dazzling array of colors and styles, are the results of the efforts of many new and very talented fly tiers. In these inspired flies the tiers have used tinsel, hair, and feathers to create the next generation of time-honored patterns. These new streamer patterns will undoubtedly provide you with many flies with which to experiment in your favorite waters for all types of game fish.

—Gary Grant
Idaho Falls, Idaho

Baitfish and Zonkers . . .

Adam's Zonker

Hook: Mustad stinger, #4
Thread: Red
Tail: Fibers from the body
Body: Pearl mylar tubing
Wings: White rabbit strip, tied Zonker style
Throat: Red marabou under pearl Flashabou
Eyes: Doll eyes
Head: Thread
Fly Tier: Eric Pettine

The American Sandwich

Hook: DaiRiki 710, #2 - #6
Thread: Black
Tail: Olive marabou
Body: Olive chenille and three clumps of marabou, tied leech style
Wings: Two black sandwiched under two white Whiting American hen cape feathers
Hackle: Black American hen cape feather, tied as a collar
Head: Thread
Fly Tier: Al Beatty

Angle Hair Minnow

Hook: TMC 200R, #6 - #14
Thread: Chartreuse
Body: Chartreuse thread
Wings: Three separate, sparse clumps of holographic silver angel hair
Belly: Three separate, sparse clumps of pearl angel hair
Gills: Three strands of red Krystal Flash, tied short
Head: Thread
Fly Tier: Ted Patlin

Baby Blue

Hook: Mustad 36890, #2
Thread: Black
Tail: Kingfisher blue marabou
Fin: Blue body fur, tied matuka style
Body: White body fur trimmed flat, color with felt tip marker
Head: Trimmed body fur
Eyes: Glass taxidermy eyes on wire
Fly Tier: John Newbury

Baby Bluegill Streamer

Hook: Mustad 9672, #6
Thread: White dyed yellow with felt tip marker
Tail: Gray marabou
Body: Gold oval tinsel
Wings: Partridge SLF, yellow, orange, tan, gray and green tied matuka style
Belly: White SLF
Head: Tan wool colored with olive felt tip marker
Eyes: Stick on, gold with black pupil
Fly Tier: Kent Bulfinch

Bead Head Stayner's Duck Tail

Hook: Mustad 79580, #4
Thread: Black
Tail: Orange hackle fibers
Body: Black/yellow variegated chenille
Wings: Mallard flank dyed wood duck, tied tent style
Throat: Orange fluff from saddle hackle
Head: Orange plastic bead head
Fly Tier: Cliff Stringer

Bear's Olive Zonker

Hook: Streamer, #4 - #8
Thread: Olive
Rib: Green copper wire
Body: Dark olive crystal chenille
Wings: Olive rabbit strip, tied Zonker style
Under Hackle: Red soft hackle, tied as a collar
Cheeks: Pheasant rump
Over Hackle: Olive soft hackle, tied as a collar
Head: Thread
Fly Tier: Bear Andrews

Big Eye Bunny

Hook: DaiRiki 700, #4 - #8
Thread: Black
Under wing: White zonker strip, point through the strip and tied on the bottom
Over wing: Black zonker strip tied on top and crazy glued to the under wing
Eyes: Large black speckled Razzle Eyes
Head: Thread
Fly Tier: Al Beatty

Bill's Tooth Pick Zonker

Hook: Streamer, #4
Thread: White
Body: Pearlescent mylar tubing over a dental tooth pick trimmed to shape
Body color: Use felt tip markers in any color combination
Wings: Rabbit Zonker strip, color of choice
Eyes: Stick on, pearl with black pupils
Head: Thread
Fly Tier: Bill Chandler

Black Beauty

Hook: Mustad 9672, #2, hook point rides up
Thread: Black
Tail: Black marabou and pearl Flashabou
Body: Black rabbit dubbing
Wings: Black marabou with pearl Flashabou sides
Hackle: Black, tied as a collar
Head: Thread
Fly Tier: Craig Hull

Black Nosed Dace

Hook: Mustad 3366, #4
Thread: Black
Body: Silver tinsel
Wings: Olive over white Polar Fiber, top tinted with black and brown markers
Eyes: Plastic, chartreuse with a black pupil
Head: Front one third of the wing is coated with thinned Aqua Seal
Fly Tier: Jerry Caruso

Black Rabbit Night Fly

Hook: TMC 5263, #4 - #6
Thread: Black
Body: Black ice chenille
Wings: Black zonker strip
Hackle: Black tied as a collar
Head: Thread
Fly Tier: Joe Humphreys

Brook's Silverside

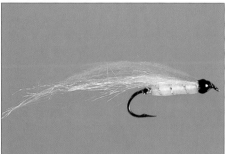

Hook: Mustad 9672, #6
Thread: Black
Rib: Silver oval tinsel
Body: White four strand floss, coated with five-minute epoxy
Wings: Green over silver craft fur
Head: Thread, coated with five-minute epoxy
Fly Tier: Dana Griffin, III

Brown Zonker

Hook: Daiichi 1720, #2 - #6
Thread: Brown
Tail: Brown zonker strip remaining from the zonker wing
Body: Copper Lite Brite dubbing
Thorax: Red Lite Brite dubbing behind a gold bead behind copper Lite Brite dubbing
Wings: Brown zonker strip
Head: Thread
Fly Tier: Bill Black, Spirit River Inc.

Chinchilla Killa

Hook: Mustad 94840, #12 - #14
Thread: Black
Tail: Gray chinchilla belly fur
Weight: Lead free wire
Rib: Fine oval tinsel
Body: Gray chinchilla dubbing
Hackle: Chinchilla fur, picked out
Head: Thread
Fly Tier: Bob Williams

Clark's Poly Fish

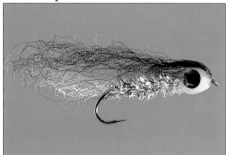

Hook: Daiichi 2340, #2 - #6
Thread: White
Tail: Light yellow macramé yarn, combed and trimmed
Body: Large silver crystal chenille
Wings: Green and black mixed over green macramé yarn, combed and trimmed
Head: White macramé yarn ball and over wing, coated with Soft Body or Aqua Flex
Eyes: Gold prismatic
Fly Tier: Lee Clark

Double Bunny

Hook: Dai-Riki 700, #1 - #2
Thread: Yellow
Weight: Several turns of .035 lead free wire
Body & Wings: Brown rabbit strip on top with yellow strip on the bottom
Application: Laminate the strips to themselves and around the hook with contact cement
Sides: Gold Krystal Flash
Eyes: Stick on, yellow with a black pupil
Head: Epoxy or Soft Body over the eyes and thread head
Fly Tier: Scott Sanchez

Double Hackle Rainbow

Hook: Long shank, #2
Thread: Black
Tail: Purple, green & yellow poly duster material
Rib: Small silver tinsel
Body: Peacock synthetic dubbing
Hackle: Large pink at the bend, small pink behind the eye
Head: Thread
Fly Tier: Tom Berry

Ed Zonker

Hook: Mustad 24039SS, #1/0 - #4, hook point rides up
Thread: Black and red
Body: EZ Body over lead foil, trimmed to shape, red thread at the hook bend
Wings: Zonker strip tied in at the head and impaled on the hook
Throat: Tuft of rabbit fur
Eyes: Plastic, clear with a black pupil
Head: Thread
Fly Tier: George Harmeling

Ever Green Streamer

Hook: Long shank, #6
Thread: Florescent green
Tail: Red, green, and yellow poly duster material
Rib: Green ostrich herl
Body: Pearlescent Flashabou
Eyes: Small silver bead chain
Fly Tier: Tom Berry

Fat Head Minnow

Hook: TMC 5262, #10
Thread: Black
Body: Flat gold tinsel
Wings: Art craft hair trimmed to shape, tan over black over white
Throat: Red art craft hair
Head: Thread
Fly Tier: Bob Pelzl

Foxy Fry

Hook: Streamer, #2 - #8
Thread: Olive
Body: Pearl body ribbon
Wings: Olive over white Arctic fox
Throat: Red hackle fibers
Head: Thread
Eggs: Stick on, pearl with a black pupil
Fly Tier: Bear Andrews

Hair Fry

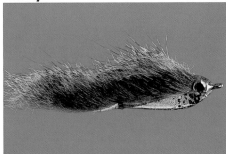

Hook: Daiichi 1750, #8, tied so the point rides up
Thread: Mono
Body: Mono and epoxy with glitter
Wings: Squirrel cut as a Zonker strip
Eyes: Yellow plastic with black pupil
Fly Tier: Shane Stalcup

Lake Shasta Smelt

Hook: Mustad 9672, #8
Thread: White
Tail: White marabou
Body: Pearl crystal chenille
Wings: Pearl Lure Flash under sky blue Fish Hair
Eyes: Painted black
Gills: Red thread
Head: Thread
Fly Tier: Robert Meuschke

Little Perch

Hook: Mustad stinger, #2   **Thread:** Brown
Tail: Grizzly dyed orange hackle tips   **Bodies:** Double (side by side) bodies, mylar tubing, tied Zonker style
Wings: Peacock sword under grizzly died brown hen saddle feathers
Hackle: "V" cut grizzly dyed brown hen saddle feather, tied as a beard
Cheeks: Silver pheasant under grizzly dyed brown hen saddle feathers, tied on the sides
Eyes: Stick on, yellow with black pupils
Head: Bronze Flashabou dubbing and gold bead
Fly Tier: Derek Harryman

Mini Toker USD

Hook: Long shank, #6
Thread: Black
Body: Crystal chenille
Wings: Olive over white zonker strip, glued together
Eyes: Weighted, fly tied up side down
Fly Tier: Chuck Moxley

Mist

Hook: Standard streamer or salmon, #4
Thread: Black
Rib: Broad gold, oval tinsel
Body: Flat silver tinsel
Wings: Two pintail flank feathers over two dyed blue hackle feathers
Throat: Red soft hackle
Hackle: Pintail flank feather, tied as a collar
Head: Thread
Fly Tier: Marvin Nolte

Mop Top Rainbow

Hook: Streamer 3xl, #6, the hook point rides up
Thread: Black
Tail: Coswold wool over black marabou
Under Body: Lead tape under vinyl tape colored with felt tip markers, cut to shape
Over Body: Pearl mylar tubing, tied in the back and the front
Wings: Coswold wool, to the end of the hook
Hackle: Black or red hackle fibers, tied as a beard
Head: Thread
Fly Tier: Buzz Moss

Mylar Red Fin Minnow

Hook: TMC 5263, #4 - #8
Thread: Black
Tail: Orange hackle fibers
Body: Gold tinsel with Mylar strips on the sides
Wings: Brown over white marabou
Hackle: Orange at throat and body (fins)
Head: Thread
Fly Tier: Joe Humphreys

Neutral Buoyancy Minnow

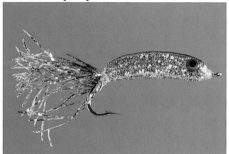

Hook: Mustad 34011, #1
Thread: Yellow
Tail: Ends of mylar body, picked apart
Body: Gold braided mylar, colored with brown and black felt tip markers
Under Body: Closed cell foam constructed to allow the fly to suspend six to twelve inches under the water's surface.
Eyes: Stick on, red with black pupil
Head: Thread
Fly Tier: Tom Broderidge

The Nightmare

Hook: DaiRiki 700, #4 - #8
Thread: Black
Tail: Black marabou
Body: One white and one black chenille, woven with the black on the top
Wings: Black marabou, tied short
Eyes: Medium black speckled Razzle Eyes
Hackle: Guinea, tied as a collar
Fly Tier: Gretchen Beatty

Prey Fish

Hook: Mustad 94831, #6
Thread: White for body, red for the head
Tail: End of the body yarn
Body: White yarn, tightly wrapped
Wings: Gray, cottontail rabbit fur strip, tied short
Head: Red thread
Fly Tier: Carl E. Wolf

Rainbow Minnow

Hook: VMC 9283, #4 - #6
Thread: White
Tail: Grizzly Chickabou
Body: Tinsel tubing, colored with felt tip marker
Hackle: Grizzly rooster flank
Head: Epoxy over thread, colored with felt tip marker
Eyes: Plastic stick on, yellow with black pupil
Fly Tier: Henry Hoffman

Reversed Glimmer Zonker

Hook: Stinger, #1/0 - #8, hook point rides up
Thread: Color of choice
Body: Estaz, color of choice
Wings: Rabbit strip, color of choice
Hackle: Red soft hackle fibers, tied as a beard
Head: Thread
Fly Tier: David Curneal

Seal Zonker

Hook: Partridge D7A, #2
Thread: Black
Tail: Brown marabou, tied sparse
Body: Black tying thread
Wings: Multiple tufts of brown seal tied along the top of the hook shank
Head: Thread
Fly Tier: David Barlow

Silver Shad

Hook: Mustad 79580, #2 - #10
Thread: Black
Tail: Clump of peacock sword herl
Body: Silver flexo tubing, red marking at the throat
Under Wings: Gray buck tail with pearl Krystal Flash
Side Wings: Grizzly hen hackle, one per side, shorter than the under wing
Topping: Flared gray deer hair placed at the start of the head, shorter than the side wings
Head: Thread
Fly Tier: Tom Tripi

Smelt Streamer

Hook: Mustad 9672, #4
Thread: White
Tail: Gray marabou veiled by gray Partridge SLF, sparse
Body: Silver embossed tinsel
Wings: Few strands of Krystal Flash over gray SLF over pink SLF over olive SLF
Gills: Tuft of red SLF
Belly: White SLF
Head: Light gray wool tinted with olive felt tip marker
Eyes: Stick on, gold with black pupil
Fly Tier: Kent Bulfinch

Soft Bead Shiner

Hook: Daiichi 1750, #4 - #6
Thread: Mono
Tail: Chartreuse Super Hair and six strands of red Metallic Mylar Motion
Body: Eight medium translucent red glass beads
Wing: Green Super Hair over bright green Super Hair over olive Krystal Flash
Head: Silver-lined gold glass beads, two medium and one large
Eyes: Silver Prizma tape, size 18
Coating: Thin Soft Body follow by thick Soft Body
Fly Tier: Joe Warren

Steroid Sculpin

Hook: Mustad 3366A, #1/0 - #4
Thread: Black
Tail: Black marabou
Body: Trimmed black body fur
Wings: Black rabbit strip tied Zonker style
Fins: Grouse feathers, two per side
Gills: Tuff of red marabou tied just in front of the fins
Head: Trimmed black body fur
Eyes: Glass taxidermy eyes on wire
Fly Tier: John Newbury

Swamp Darter

Hook: Mustad 36620, #2 - #10
Thread: White
Flank coloring: Silver Krystal Flash, 6 - 8 strands
Top of head and wing: Brown buck tail, reverse tied
Wings: Grizzly hackle feathers
   Bottom of head and wing: White buck tail, reverse tied
Head: Thin coat of lacquer over reversed tied buck tail
Gill coloring: Red lacquer on thread base
Eyes: White lacquer with black pupils
Fly Tier: Keith Fulsher

Toker

Hook: Long shank, #2 with #8 trailing hook
Thread: Black
Body: Crystal chenille
Wings: Black zonker strips, top and bottom, glued together
Eyes: Weighted
Gills: Ring neck pheasant dyed red
Fly Tier: Chuck Moxley

Trout Candy

Hook: Mustad 34011, #1 - #6
Thread: Red
Tail: Brown buck tail, Krystal Flash, and white buck tail
Body: Chartreuse and pink ice chenille
Head: Thread
Eyes: Dumb bell lead eyes
Fly Tier: Kevin Cohenour

Zook's Foam Minnow

Hook: TMC 9394, #4 - #8
Thread: White
Tail: White marabou
Body: Pearl mylar tubing over white foam, colored with felt tip marker
Eyes: Red with black pupil, coated with epoxy
Fly Tier: Lance Zook

Feather Wings and Matukas . . .

Alevin fr.

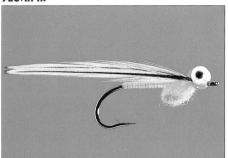

Hook: Mustad 80400BLN, #12
Thread: White
Body: Griffiths fluorescent white floss
Wings: Matched pair of Coq de Leon hackle feathers
Egg sack: Glow bug yarn
Head: Thread
Eyes: Two clear plastic bead strung on 50 pound mono
Fly Tier: Floyd Franke

Babe

Hook: Dai-Riki 975, #8, hook point rides up
Thread: Olive
Tail & Wings: Light olive marabou (tied sparse) under pearl Krystal Flash
Weight: Eight teen wraps of .015 lead free wire
Body: Olive crystal chenille
Head: Olive crystal chenille
Eyes: Bead chain
Fly Tier: Bill Murdich

The Back Water Smelt

Hook: Long shank streamer, #1
Thread: Black
Body: Flat silver tinsel
Wings: Peacock herl under blue under gray saddle hackle feathers
Throat: White buck tail
Shoulder: Lavender guinea fowl
Cheek: Jungle cock
Head: Thread
Fly Tier: Bill Chandler

Bear's Olive Matuka

Hook: Streamer, #4 - #8
Thread: Olive
Rib: Green wire
Body: Dark olive crystal chenille
Wings: Four grizzly dyed olive hen saddle feathers
Hackle: Olive soft hackle
Throat: Hot pink wool, combed
Cheeks: Pheasant church window feathers
Head: Thread
Fly Tier: Bear Andrews

Black and Pearl

Hook: Mustad 79580, #4
Thread: Red
Tail: Pearl strands from the body
Body: Pearl mylar tubing
Wings: Black marabou
Throat: Red marabou tuft
Head: Thread
Fly Tier: Cliff Stringer

Black Ghost Marabou

Hook: Mustad 9672, #2 - #12
Thread: Black
Tail: Yellow buck tail
Rib: Silver Tinsel
Body: Black floss
Wings: White marabou
Throat: Yellow marabou
Head: Thread
Eyes: Painted, yellow with a black pupil
Fly Tier: Paul Stimpson

Blue Shiner

Hook: TMC 9394, #6 - #10
Thread: Black
Rib: Fine silver mylar
Body: Light blue floss
Wings: Two slightly shorter grizzly hackle feathers under two light gray hackles
Hackle: Several turns of red ostrich
Head: Thread
Eyes: Jungle cock
Fly Tier: Lance Zook

Clark's Poly Matuka

Hook: Daiichi 1710, #2 - #12
Thread: Black
Tail: Green macramé yarn
Rib: Fine gold wire
Body: A dubbing mix made from tan, black, and green macramé yarn
Wings: The dubbed body is picked out to shape the wing
Head: Thread
Fly Tier: Lee Clark

Clear Lake FXDX

Hook: Orvis 0167, #6 - #8
Thread: Orange
Tail: Golden pheasant tippets
Body: Blue & red mixed crystal chenille
Wings: Pheasant tail
Hackle: Black, palmered
Head: Thread
Fly Tier: Gene Stutzman

Cree Spruce

Hook: Mustad 80400 BLN, #2 - #10
Thread: Black
Tail: Peacock sword fibers
Body: Yellow Flexi-floss behind, peacock herl
Wings: Four matched Cree hackle feathers
Head: Cree, tied as a collar
Fly Tier: Dave Schmezer

The Crown Royal

Hook: Mustad 79580, #2 - #10
Thread: Black
Tail: Golden pheasant tippets
Rib: Fine brass wire
Body: Peacock herl and red floss
Wings: Silver or golden badger, two pair tied matuka style
Hackle: Badger tied as a collar
Head: Black ostrich
Legs: Golden pheasant tippets tied as a beard
Fly Tier: Bud Heintz

Dark Spruce

Hook: Mustad 79580, #4
Thread: Black
Tail: Several peacock sword tips
Body: Red wool and peacock herl
Wings: Two furnace hackle feathers, tied flared
Hackle: Furnace, tied as a collar
Head: Thread
Fly Tier: Cliff Stringer

Dark Spruce

Hook: Daiichi 2051, E5
Thread: Black
Tail: Peacock sword fibers
Rib: Small silver oval tinsel
Body: Red floss and peacock herl
Wings: Pair of furnace saddle hackle feathers
Hackle: Furnace, tied as a collar
Head: Thread
Fly Tier: Mark Hoeser

The Dipper

Hook: Mustad 36890H, #1/0
Thread: Black
Body: Spun marabou
Wings: Jungle cock over turkey segments
Hackle: Soft hackle collar
Head: Thread
Fly Tier: Jim Childers

'84 Special

Hook: Mustad 9674, #8
Thread: Olive
Tail: Three peacock sword fibers
Rib: Peacock herl
Body: Golden olive burlap yarn
Wings: Four peacock sword fibers, extended to the end of the tail
Hackle: Pheasant rump, rust color, folded and wrapped
Head: Thread
Fly Tier: Reginald Denny

Fat Head Minnow

Hook: Mustad 9672, #6
Thread: Black
Rib: Fine copper wire
Body: Gray poly yarn
Wings: Four grizzly saddle feathers, tied matuka style
Hackle: Deer hair tied as a collar
Head: Spun and trimmed deer hair
Eyes: Plastic, white with black pupils
Fly Tier: Dana Griffin, III

Furnace Deceiver

Hook: TMC 9394, #8 - #10
Thread: White
Tail: Two orange hackle feathers covered by two furnace feathers
Body: White goat hair
Wings: Fox squirrel
Throat: Red dyed goat hair
Head: Black thread coated with high gloss head cement
Eyes: Stick on eyes
Fly Tier: David Hunter

Green Shiner

Hook: Mustad 24039SS, #1/0 - #4
Thread: White
Tail: Green and grizzly fibers, mixed
Body: Silver mylar tinsel
Rib: Gold tinsel
Wings: Two hackles dyed green between two grizzly hen hackles
Hackle: Throat of SLF with grizzly dyed green over, tied as a collar under the wings
Head: Thread
Fly Tier: George Harmeling

Hatton's Bend Back

Hook: Mustad 37187, #2 - #10, bent to shape
Thread: Black
Wings: Five to eight hackle feathers on each side, color of choice
Hackle: Soft hackle, color of choice, tied as a collar
Head: Thread
Eyes: Prismatic with black pupil, lacquered to the hackle collar
Fly Tier: Jeff Hatton

KC Special

Hook: Mustad 80400, #4 - #8
Thread: Black
Body: White thread and pearl tinsel
Thorax: Peacock herl
Wings: Six strands of Krystal Flash under olive marabou
Head: Thread
Fly Tier: Kieran Frye

Laced Lady

Hook: Partridge CS15, #4   **Thread:** Black
Tag: Flat silver tinsel   **Rib:** Gold oval tinsel
Body: Dark green floss
Under wing: Two orange rooster cape feathers, tied slightly longer than the hook bend
Over wing: Laced American hen cape feather, tied shorter than the under wing
Cheek: Black American hen saddle feather under laced American hen cape feather
Hackle: Laced white American hen cape feather, tied as a collar   **Head:** Thread
Fly Tier: Al Beatty

Marabou Fry

Hook: Daiichi 1750, #8, tied to ride with the point up
Thread: Mono
Tail: Marabou
Lateral line: Flashabou to the end of the tail
Body: Mono and epoxy with glitter
Wings: Marabou in clumps along the shank
Eyes: Yellow plastic with black pupil
Fly Tier: Shane Stalcup

Matuka Spruce Fly

Hook: Mustad 90240, #4 - #8
Thread: Black
Rib: Gold oval tinsel
Body: Red floss and peacock herl
Wings: Four badger saddle hackles, tied matuka style
Hackle: Badger, tied as a collar
Head: Thread
Fly Tier: Henry Hoffman

Mickey Gartside

Hook: TMC 8115, #2 - #8
Thread: Black
Wings & Hackle: Yellow over red over yellow marabou, tied as a collar
Sides: Wood duck flank strips and pearl sparkle flash
Head: Thread
Fly Tier: Bear Andrews

Mini Matuka

Hook: Mustad 80050, #14
Thread: Color to match the body
Rib: Fine wire
Body: Fine chenille, any color
Wings: Matched hen neck hackles, tied matuka style
Hackle: Hen hackle, tied as a collar
Head: Thread
Fly Tier: Ted Patlin

Montana White

Hook: TMC 5263, #6 - #10
Thread: Olive
Tail: Krystal Flash
Body: Pearl Mylar Cord
Wings: White marabou and six strands of Krystal Flash
Hackle: Olive, tied as a collar
Head: Thread
Fly Tier: Daniel Ferron

Olive Chickatuka Streamer

Hook: Mustad 9672, #2 - #6
Thread: Black
Rib: Silver or gold oval tinsel
Body: Flat silver or gold tinsel
Wings: Four matched Soft Hackle feathers curved away from each other, tied matuka
Hackle: Chickabou feather to match the wing color
Head: Thread
Eyes: Silver or gold bead chain
Fly Tier: Dave Engerbretson

Orange & Black

Hook: Mustad 79580, #2
Thread: Brown
Body: Thread formed from creating "Hy-ty" style of wings
Wings: Grizzly dyed orange, six pairs starting at the bend and progressing forward
Cheek: Tragopan body feather
Hackle: Tragopan rump fibers, tied as a beard
Head: Thread
Fly Tier: Tom Broderidge

Peacock Matuka

Hook: TMC 200R, #6 - #10
Thread: Red
Tag: Small gold oval tinsel
Rib: Small gold oval tinsel
Body: Peacock herl twisted over tinsel
Wings: Two grizzly died olive, tied matuka style
Hackle: Grizzly dyed olive, tied as a collar
Head: Thread
Fly Tier: David Hunter

Pheasant Matuka

Hook: Mustad 9672, #4 - #12
Thread: Brown
Rib: Gold wire
Body: Tan poly yarn
Wings: Ring neck pheasant breast feathers
Head: Thread
Fly Tier: Paul Stimpson

Platte River Variant

Hook: Dai-Riki 700, #4
Thread: Black
Body: Chartreuse Holographic Fly Flash
Wings: Coq de Leon over grizzly dyed green
Hackle: Coq de Leon, tied as a collar
Head: Thread
Fly Tier: Eric Pettine

Queen of Hearts Streamer

Hook: Low water salmon fly, #2 - #10
Thread: Black
Tail: Lady Amherst fibers
Rib: Oval tinsel, criss-cross wrapped
Butt: White chenille
Body: Red tinsel
Wings: White marabou with peacock sword feathers as a topping
Hackle: Yellow marabou, tied as a throat
Head: Thread
Fly Tier: Katie McEnerney

Red Fin

Hook: Partridge CS5, #1/0 - #10
Thread: Black
Tail: Red marabou, clipped short
Rib: Medium flat gold tinsel
Body: Tapered pink floss
Wings: Two golden badger feathers sandwiched over two black
Hackle: Red marabou throat, 2/3 the length of the body
Eyes: Jungle cock
Head: Lacquer on black thread base
Fly Tier: Keith Fulsher

Red Head

Hook: Streamer 4xl, #8
Thread: Red
Wings: Four hackle feathers, two brown over two yellow
Hackle: Red
Head: Thread
Fly Tier: Marvin Nolte

Ronn's Two Feather Matuka

Hook: Streamer 2xl, #2 - #10
Thread: Black
Rib: Fine gold wire
Body: Black thread
Wings: Two matched saddle hackle, color of choice
Application: Tie saddle hackles on the hook and bind the fuzzy parts to the shank with the ribbing wire, use a dubbing needle to pick out any trapped fuzzy fibers
Head: Thread
Fly Tier: Ronn Lucas

Royal Lady Streamer

Hook: Mustad 79580, #4 - #12
Thread: Black
Tail: White hackle fibers
Body: Fine black chenille and pink poly
Wings: White hackle tips
Hackle: Black, tied as a collar
Head: Black
Fly Tier: Ruth J. Zinck

Royal Matuka

Hook: Daiichi 2051, #5
Thread: Black
Rib: Small gold, oval tinsel
Body: Red floss and peacock herl
Wings: Two pair of white hen saddle feathers
Hackle: Mottled brown hen saddle, tied as a collar
Head: Thread
Fly Tier: Mark Hoeser

Silver Shiner

Hook: Mustad 3665 #6
Thread: White
Tail: Golden pheasant tippets
Body: Oval silver tinsel
Wings: Secondary covert feathers from Hoffman rooster, tied tent style
Shoulders: Small golden pheasant tippet feathers
Throat: Red wool yarn, combed out
Head: Pearl nail polish
Fly Tier: Ted Rogowski

Silver Streak

Hook: DaiRiki 270, #6 - #8
Thread: White
Tail: White marabou, tied short
Body: Pearl crystal chenille
Wings: Six white saddle hackle feathers
Head: Silver mylar tubing over one half of the body and the front part of the wings
Eyes: Doll eyes
Head covering: Softex or Aqua Flex over mylar and eyes, apply a second coat if needed
Fly Tier: Robert Meuschke

Spartan

Hook: TMC 300, #4 - #10
Thread: Black
Body: Fine silver tinsel
Under wing: Red under yellow dyed buck tail
Over wing: Mallard flank feather, tied tent style
Hackle: Grizzly hen
Head: Thread
Fly Tier: Gene Trump

Spruce Hen

Hook: Mustad 79580, #6 - #12
Thread: Black
Tail: Peacock herl
Body: Red floss and peacock herl
Wings: Four brown hen hackles
Hackle: Badger hen, tied as a collar
Head: Black
Fly Tier: Tom Tripi

The Sword

Hook: Mustad 33620, #4 - #8
Thread: Black
Tip: Medium flat gold tinsel
Rib: Medium flat gold tinsel
Body: Red floss
Wings: Tip section of peacock sword feather
Shirts: White polar bear hair, tied to the sides
Gills: Red dubbing
Head: Black rabbit dubbing, saturated with head cement
Fly Tier: Reginald Denny

Two Color Soft Hackle Streamer

Hook: Mustad 79580, #2 - #8
Thread: Black
Wings: Two different colors of marabou wrapped together as a collar
Hackle: One turn of a peacock body feather
Head: Thread
Fly Tier: Bruce Staples

Hair Wing and Thunder Creek . . .

Black Nose Dace (Flick)

Hook: Mustad 3908, #4 - #6
Thread: Black
Tail: Sparse tuft of red wool
Body: Flat silver tinsel
Wings: Three sparse layers of fine straight hair, brown over black over white
Head: Thread
Fly Tier: Ted Patlin

Buck Tail Royal Coachman

Hook: Mustad 36890, #2 - #4
Thread: Red
Tail: Golden pheasant tippets
Body: Red floss and peacock herl
Wings: White buck tail, tied very sparse
Hackle: Brown, tied as a throat
Head: Thread
Fly Tier: Cliff Stringer

Bud's Thunder

Hook: Mustad 79580, #2 - #10
Thread: Black
Body: Tinsel
Wings: Buck tail, three colors (white, chartreuse or purple, and black)
Head: Wing material pulled over Thunder Creek style
Eyes: Red plastic with black pupil
Fly Tier: Bud Heintz

Cascade Roach

Hook: TMC 5263, #4 - #8
Thread: Olive
Body: Pearl Lite Brite dubbing
Belly: White Arctic fox tail fibers
Wing: Chartreuse Arctic fox tail under olive Arctic fox tail fibers
Throat: Red hackle fibers
Head: Thread
Fly Tier: Chris Mihulka

Cheryl's Bead

Hook: Mustad 3906, #8 - #12
Thread: Olive
Tail: Golden olive marabou, tied very sparse
Body: Four green glass beads
Wings & Hackle: Olive zonker strip, tied as a collar
Head: Thread
Fly Tier: Tom Tripi

Clark's Red Side Shiner

Hook: Daiichi 2340, #4 - #12
Thread: Olive
Tail: Tan and white macramé yarn, combed and trimmed
Body: Frito Lay Doritos chip bag, cut into a thin strip and wrapped
Wings: Green and black mixed over green macramé yarn, combed and trimmed
Head: Black and green under white macramé yarn, coated with Soft Body or Aqua Flex
Eyes: White and black enamel
Fly Tier: Lee Clark

Conehead The Barbarian

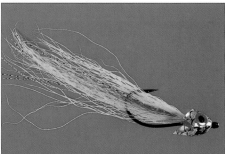

Hook: Mustad 3366, #1/0 - #8
Thread: Florescent red
Tail: Yellow buck tail over red buck tail over pearl Krystal Flash and yellow buck tail
Head: Silver cone head secured by thread and super glue
Head cover: Pearl prism tape wrapped over and trimmed to form gills
Eyes: Stick on, red with black pupil
Fly Tier: Scott Sanchez

CT's Shiner

Hook: Mustad 79580, #2 - #10
Thread: Black, red
Tail: Clump of peacock sword herl
Body: Silver mylar tubing with a red marking at the throat
Wings: Black over olive over green over chartreuse buck tail, several Krystal Flash fibers
Eyes: Jungle cock
Head: Thread, black with a red thread band
Fly Tier: Tom Tripi

Darlon Streamer

Hook: TMC 200R, #6 - #14
Thread: Black or brown
Body: Flat silver tinsel
Wings: Darlon, yellow over red over yellow or colors of choice
Head: Thread
Fly Tier: David Curneal

Edson Tiger

Hook: TMC 5263, #8
Thread: Black
Tail: Barred wood duck, folded
Tag: Flat silver tinsel, small
Body: Peacock herl twisted over oval tinsel
Wings: Dyed yellow squirrel tail over white squirrel tail
Topping: Red hen hackle
Head: Black with red stripe at the throat
Eyes: Jungle cock
Fly Tier: David Hunter

Emerald Shiner

Hook: Mustad 36620, #10 - #1/0
Thread: White
Flank coloring: Peacock color Krystal Flash, 6 - 8 strands
Top of head and wing: Brown part of green dyed buck tail, reverse tied
Bottom of head and wing: White buck tail, reverse tied
Head: Thin coat of epoxy over reversed tied buck tail
Gill coloring: Red lacquer on thread base
Eyes: White lacquer with a black pupil
Fly Tier: Keith Fulsher

49'er Rainbow

Hook: Mustad 36890, #6 - #8
Thread: Black
Tail: Red hackle fibers
Body: Pearl Lite Brite dubbing
Wings: Salmon pink Lite Brite under Rainbow Lite Brite
Throat: Red hackle fibers
Head: Thread
Fly Tier: Chris Mihulka

Hair Wing Night Stonefly

Hook: TMC 5263, #4 - #6
Thread: Black
Rib: Palmered black hackle
Body: Orange chenille
Wings: Brown buck or calf tail hair
Hackle: Furnace tied as a collar
Head: Thread
Fly Tier: Joe Humphreys

Kellen's Fox

Hook: Mustad 9672, #2 - #8
Thread: Yellow
Rib: Gold oval tinsel
Body: Gold mylar tinsel
Wings: Yellow Arctic fox under wing, cross fox as over wing
Throat: Red Arctic fox
Head: Thread
Fly Tier: Eric Pettine

Lake Erie Shiner

Hook: Mustad 36620, #4 - #8
Thread: Olive
Body: Griffiths fluorescent white floss over-wrapped with Pearlescent Mylar
Throat: White calf tail under blue calf tail, blue is tied shorter than the white
Wings: Olive Krystal Flash under light olive buck tail under dark olive buck tail
Head: Thread
Eyes: Yellow with a black pupil
Fly Tier: Floyd Franke

Light Edson Tiger

Hook: Mustad 79480, #4
Thread: Black
Tag: Gold flat tinsel
Tail: Wood duck flank fibers, tied short
Rib: Optional wire
Body: Peacock herl
Wings: Yellow buck tail
Hackle: Two short red hackle tips, tied on top of the wing
Eyes: Two jungle cock eyes, tied over the red hackle tips
Head: Thread
Fly Tier: Cliff Stringer

Little Rainbow Trout

Hook: Mustad 3665A, #2 - #8
Thread: Black
Body: Gold sparkle braid
Wings: Buck tail clumps, black over green over red over white
Head: Thread
Eggs: Painted eye, yellow with black pupil
Fly Tier: Bruce Staples

Llama

Hook: Mustad 249039SS, #1/0 - #4
Thread: Black
Tail: Grizzly hackle fibers
Rib: Gold tinsel
Body: Red floss
Wings: Tuft of badger guard hairs and under fur
Hackle: Grizzly, tied as a collar, under the wing
Head: Thread
Fly Tier: George Harmeling

Mylar Minnow

Hook: Mustad 79580, #2
Thread: Black
Tail: Teased out mylar tubing
Body: Pearl mylar tubing over duct tape under body
Wings: Dark blue over Silver Doctor blue over white buck tail
Head: Thread
Eyes: Painted yellow with black pupil
Fly Tier: John Newbury

Pinky

Hook: Mustad 9671, #2
Thread: Pink
Tail: Pink craft fur
Body: Pink Krystal Flash under clear 40 pound mono tied in a nail knot
Wings: Calf tail over Krystal Flash over craft fur, each material is pink
Throat: Pink craft fur
Head: Thread
Fly Tier: Tom Broderidge

Rainbow Minnow

Hook: TMC 9395, #6
Thread: Black
Weight: Eight wraps of .015 lead wire
Body: Clear Liqui Lace
Wings: Super hair green over gray over white
Head: Thread with painted eyes
Fly Tier: Dan Turner

Redfin Shiner

Hook: Mustad 36620, #10 - #1/0
Thread: White
Flank coloring: Silver Krystal Flash, 6 - 8 strands
Top of head and wing: Brown buck tail, reverse tied
Bottom of head and wing: Dyed red under white buck tail, white reversed tied
Head: Thin coat of epoxy over reversed tied buck tail
Gill coloring: Red lacquer on thread base
Eyes: White lacquer with a black pupil
Fly Tier: Keith Fulsher

Royal Lady Hair Wing

Hook: Mustad 79580, #4 - #12
Thread: Black
Tail: Silver pheasant breast feather, tied DeFoe style
Rib: Stripped white ostrich stem and pearl Krystal Flash, wrapped together
Body: Black crystal chenille and pink poly
Wings: White buck tail, tied sparse, extending to the end of the tail
Beard/Throat: Tuft of brushed pink poly
Head: Black crystal chenille
Fly Tier: Ruth J. Zinck

Salmon Seeker

Hook: Long shank streamer, #2
Thread: Black
Body: Flat silver tinsel
Wings: Blue over turquoise over chartreuse buck tail
Throat: White buck tail
Cheek: Jungle cock
Head: Black
Fly Tier: Bill Chandler

Silver Shiner

Hook: Mustad 36620, #10 - #1/0
Thread: White
Flank coloring: Silver Krystal Flash, 6 - 8 strands
Top of head and wing: Brown buck tail, reverse tied
Bottom of head and wing: White buck tail, reversed tied
Head: Thin coat of epoxy over reversed tied buck tail
Gill coloring: Red lacquer on thread base
Eyes: White lacquer with a black pupil
Fly Tier: Keith Fulsher

Silver Thunder

Hook: TMC 300, #4 - #8
Thread: White
Body: Pearl diamond braid
Wings: Blue, yellow, and white buck tail under peacock Krystal Flash
Head: Folded back buck tail, blue on the top and yellow/white on the bottom
Eyes: Silver prismatic with a black pupil
Fly Tier: Lance Zook

Squirrel Creek

Hook: Partridge CS5, #4 - #8
Thread: Red
Body: Flat silver tinsel
Wings & Head: Gray squirrel tail over white buck tail
Head: Folded over hair
Eyes: Yellow with black pupil
Fly Tier: Marvin Nolte

Squirrel Spruce BH

Hook: DaiRiki 700, #4 - #10
Thread: Black
Tail: Three peacock herls
Body: One half red floss and one half peacock herl
Wing: Fox squirrel tail, tied fan style to provide more action in the water
Head: Brass bead, thread
Fly Tier: Al Beatty

Squirrel Thunder

Hook: Mustad 79580, #2
Thread: 3/0 saddle repair thread, not waxed
Body: Tightly wrapped yellow yarn
Wings: Fox squirrel tail
Head: Thread
Fly Tier: Carl E. Wolf

Snake River Chub

Hook: Streamer 3XL, #6
Thread: Black
Body: Gold embossed medium tinsel
Wings: Three sparse clumps of buck tail, brown over orange over white
Over wing: Copper Krystal Flash
Hackle: White dyed orange, tied as a throat extending to the hook point
Head: Thread
Fly Tier: Chuck Collins

Spot Tail Minnow

Hook: Mustad 36620, #4 - #8
Thread: Black
Butt: Black ostrich herl
Rib: Silver mylar tinsel
Body: Medium gray floss
Under wing: White polar bear or substitute, tied sparse
Wings: Mallard flank
Over wing: Black bear hair
Gill: Red wool
Head: Black dubbing, saturated with head cement
Fly Tier: Reginald Denny

Spring Crappie Darter

Hook: Mustad 80050BR, #6 - #10
Thread: Black
Tail: White calf tail
Rib: Gold flat tinsel
Body: Black chenille
Wings: Yellow calf tail
Head: Thread
Fly Tier: Gene Stutzman

Tangerine Darter

Hook: Mustad 9575, #10
Thread: Brown
Tail: Orange marabou, trimmed short
Rib: Fine copper wire
Body: Dark orange yarn dubbing
Wings: Fox squirrel tail
Head: Thread
Fly Tier: Dana Griffin, III

Waldo Streamer

Hook: Mustad 36890, #4 - #10
Thread: Black
Tail: Green Krystal Flash
Rib: Working thread
Body: Green Krystal Flash
Wings: Buck tail, brown on top and white under the hook shank
Hackle: Red hackle, tied as a collar
Head: Thread
Fly Tier: Clifford Adams

Yak Hair Rainbow

Hook: Daiichi 2461, #1/0 - #6
Thread: White:
Body: Silver tinsel
Wings: Olive over pink over white yak hair, tied Thunder Creek style
Gills: Red felt tip marker
Head: Folded over wing material and covered with five-minute epoxy
Eyes: Plastic, chartreuse with a black pupil
Fly Tier: Jerry Caruso

Muddlers and Sculpins . . .

Baby Sculpin

Hook: DaiRiki 700, #10 - #14
Thread: Black
Rib: Silver oval tinsel
Body: Black muskrat dubbing
Wings: Four black hen cape feathers, tied matuka style
Fins: Two black hen cape feathers, tied to the sides behind the head
Head: Black wool, trimmed to shape
Eyes: Optional
Fly Tier: Al Beatty

Barred Ginger Muddler

Hook: DaiRiki 700, #4 - #12
Thread: Black
Tail: Turkey quill section
Body: Gold tinsel
Wings: Four barred ginger rooster cape feathers
Collar: Spun deer hair
Head: Spun and trimmed deer hair
Eyes: Optional
Fly Tier: Al Beatty

Bead Head Muddler

Hook: Mustad 9672, #8 - #10
Thread: Tan
Tail: Grizzly marabou dyed brown
Hackle: Both collars are tied from coastal deer
Head: Spun and trimmed deer hair
Fly Tier: Mike Jacobs

Big Eye Sculpin

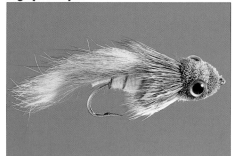

Hook: Mustad 24039SS, #1/0 - #4
Thread: Red
Rib: Copper wire
Weight: Lead free wire
Body: White knitting yarn
Wings: Gray zonker strip
Fins: Grouse feathers
Hackle: Deer hair tied as a collar
Head: Spun and trimmed deer hair
Eyes: Plastic, amber with a black pupil
Fly Tier: George Harmeling

Big Eyed Sculpin

Hook: Daiichi 2220, #4   **Thread:** Orange
Weight: Eighteen wraps of .030 lead wire
Rib: Gold braid
Body: Blend of SLF, natural seal, and copper Flashabou dubbing   **Wings:** Mottled hen saddle feathers, three pair dyed orange
Fins: Orange dyed pheasant backed with a red Lore parrot feather
Gills: Fiery orange SLF dubbing
Head: Spun and trimmed deer hair, orange, gold, dark brown and natural   **Eyes:** Yellow plastic, six millimeter
Fly Tier: Mark Hoeser

The Bugger Sculpin

Hook: DaiRiki 710, #2 - #8
Thread: Black
Tail: White under olive marabou
Rib: Grizzly hackle, tied palmered through the matuka wing
Body: White under olive marabou remaining from the tail, bound to the shank
Wings: Two Whiting American hen cape feathers
Hackle: Spun deer hair tied as a collar
Head: Spun and trimmed deer hair, trimmed flat and triangular in shape
Fly Tier: Al Beatty

Cardiac Kiwi

Hook: Dai-Riki 700, #1 - #4
Thread: Olive
Weight: Several turns of .035 lead free wire
Body: Cream yarn
Wings: Wide olive rabbit strip, tied Kiwi style
Hackle: Rabbit fur tied behind the head
Head: Peacock colored heart-shaped craft bead, super glued into place
Fly Tier: Scott Sanchez

Cher's Muddler

Hook: Mustad 79580, #2 - #10
Thread: Black
Tail: Olive and pearl Fire Fly, pheasant flank feathers
Body: Pearl crystal flash
Wings: Olive buck tail, tied sparse
Throat: Red marabou
Hackle: Olive deer hair, tied as a collar
Head: Olive deer hair, spun and trimmed to a triangle shape
Head covering: Clear nail polish and sparkle flakes
Fly Tier: Tom Tripi

Chickabou Sculpin

Hook: Mustad 79580, #2
Thread: Tan
Tail: Grizzly dyed tan Chickabou
Rib: Copper wire
Body: Tan chenille
Wings: Grizzly dyed tan rooster flank
Hackle: Grizzly dyed tan soft hackle
Head: Grizzly dyed tan Chickabou
Eyes: Spirit River Real Eyes (causes the hook point to ride up)
Fly Tier: Henry Hoffman

Cone Head Muddler

Hook: Dai-Riki 710, #6 - #8, hook point rides up
Thread: Brown
Tail: Grizzly dyed brown marabou
Body: Gold diamond braid
Hackle: Deer hair collar
Head: Spun and trimmed deer hair behind a gold cone head
Fly Tier: Lance Zook

Connor's YM

Hook: Mustad 9672, #2 - #14
Thread: Yellow
Tail: Mottled turkey quill section, dyed yellow
Body: Gold mylar tinsel
Wings: Red squirrel under mottle turkey quill section, dyed yellow
Hackle: Olive yellow dyed deer hair, tied as a collar
Head: Spun and trimmed olive yellow dyed deer hair
Fly Tier: Eric Pettine

Dusk to Dawn Sculpin

Hook: Daiichi 2220, #4
Thread: Black
Weight: Eighteen wraps of .030 lead free wire
Rib: Green braid
Body: Blend of black SLF dubbing and peacock Angel Hair
Wings: Black hen saddle feathers, three pair
Fins: Black pheasant feather backed with a red dyed ring neck pheasant feather
Head: Spun and trimmed deer hair, red, black, and chartreuse
Eyes: Green plastic, six millimeter
Fly Tier: Mark Hoeser

EZY Muddler

Hook: Mustad 33957, #4 - #10
Thread: Gray
Body: Several strands of Krystal Flash, color of choice
Under wing: Strands of Krystal Flash remaining from the body
Wings: American black laced, natural or dyed color of choice
Hackle: Coq de Leon cape, tied as a collar
Head: Gray chenille wrapped to muddler shape, trim lightly as needed
Eyes: Optional
Fly Tier: Al Beatty

Irish Wool Head

Hook: Streamer 4xl, #6 - #10
Thread: Black
Tail: Golden pheasant red breast feather, wound as a hackle collar at the hook bend
Body: Flat silver tinsel
Hackle: Grizzly
Head: Gray over white ram's wool
Fly Tier: Marvin Nolte

Mad Tom Matuka

Hook: Mustad 36620, #4 - #6
Thread: Black
Rib: Tying thread doubled for strength
Body: Dubbed black wool
Wings: Two or three pairs of matched hen saddle or body feathers
Throat: Black wool from the head
Head: Sculpin wool stacked and trimmed to shape
Eyes: Lead dumb bell, 5/32"
Fly Tier: Floyd Franke

Marabou Muddler

Hook: Mustad 36890, #4 - #8
Thread: Tan
Tail: Tan marabou
Body: Wrapped gold Krystal Flash
Wings: Mottled marabou, tied as a collar
Hackle: Deer hair tied as a collar, sparse
Head: Trimmed and spun deer hair
Fly Tier: Chris Mihulka

Marabou Muddler, Black

Hook: Mustad 9672, #2 - #6
Thread: Black
Tail: Black poly yarn
Rib: Fine copper wire
Body: Peacock herl
Wings: Black marabou under black Krystal Flash
Collar: Spun deer hair, black
Head: Spun and trimmed deer hair, black
Fly Tier: John Newbury

Marabou Muddler, Chartreuse

Hook: Mustad 9672, #2 - #6
Thread: Black
Tail: Red poly yarn
Body: Chartreuse diamond braid
Wings: Chartreuse marabou under chartreuse Krystal Flash
Collar: Spun deer hair, chartreuse
Head: Spun and trimmed deer hair, chartreuse, brown, and yellow bands
Fly Tier: John Newbury

Mini Pearl

Hook: Daiichi 1720, #8 - #14
Thread: Gray
Body: Pearl tinsel
Wings: White calf tail, tied sparse
Hackle: Deer hair, tied as a collar
Head: Spun and trimmed deer hair
Fly Tier: Bear Andrews

Mottled Matuka Sculpin

Hook: Eagle Claw D281, #6 **Thread:** Egg shell
Weight: Eighteen wraps of .030 lead free wire
Rib: Gold braid **Body:** Ginger SLF dubbing
Wings: Mottled black and gold hen saddle feathers, three pair
Fins: Brown dyed pheasant feather backed with a red Lore parrot feather
Gills: Red synthetic dubbing
Head: Spun and trimmed deer hair, gold, black, rust, and natural
Fly Tier: Mark Hoeser

Mottled Sculpin

Hook: Eagle Claw, 214EL, #1 - #4, hook point rides up
Thread: Black
Body: Silver tinsel
Weight: Real Eyes, black
Throat: White Polar Fiber
Wings: Olive over shrimp Polar Fiber, tinted by black, brown, and orange felt tip markers
Fins: Shrimp Polar Fiber, tinted with olive and brown felt tip markers
Eyes: Plastic, chartreuse with a black pupil
Head: Heavily coated with head cement
Fly Tier: Jerry Caruso

Muddler Minnow (Gapen Style)

Hook: Mustad 9672, #2 - #8
Thread: Black
Tail: Single section of turkey wing, folded
Body: Flat gold tinsel
Wings: Single section of turkey wing folded over gray squirrel under wing
Hackle: Deer hair collar, sparse
Head: Untrimmed butts from the collar
Fly Tier: Ted Patlin

Multicolor Sculpin

Hook: Mustad 9672, #2 - #6
Thread: Gray
Rib: Copper wire
Body: Yellow wool
Wings: Grizzly dyed olive cape feathers, tied matuka style
Head: Orange, lavender, brown, and gray wool, spun and trimmed to shape
Fly Tier: Bruce Staples

Pheasant Wing Sculpin

Hook: Partridge CS17, #2 - #4 **Thread:** Gray
Weight: Eighteen wraps of .035 lead free wire
Rib: Silver braid **Body:** SLF gray dubbing with min now blue Lite Brite side flash
Wings: Two matched pair of feathers from a ring-neck wing
Fins: Pheasant feather
Gills: SLF dubbing
Head & collar: Spun and trimmed deer hair, dyed dun, black and brown
Eyes: Orange plastic with black pupil
Fly Tier: Mark Hoeser

Poor Man's Muddler

Hook: Mustad 9672, #4 - #12
Thread: Yellow
Tail: Pheasant rump fibers
Body: Gold embossed tinsel
Wings: Pheasant rump feathers
Hackle: Deer hair, tied as a collar
Head: Spun and trimmed deer hair
Fly Tier: Buck Goodrich

Red Horse Muddler

Hook: Mustad 9672, #6
Thread: Red
Tail: Two grizzly hackle tips plus a collar of red ostrich
Body: Pearlescent mini-braid
Wings: Four red-dyed ostrich herls
Hackle: Deer hair tied as a collar
Head: Spun and trimmed deer hair
Fly Tier: Dana Griffin, III

Rock Sculpin

Hook: DaiRiki 710, #2 - #6 (the hook point rides up)
Thread: Olive
Tail: Grizzly dyed olive Chickabou
Rib: Fine copper wire
Body: Cream rabbit dubbing
Wings: Grizzly dyed olive Chickabou
Fins: Grizzly dyed olive Chickabou
Head: Olive and black mixed wool, spun and trimmed
Eyes: Spirit River Real Eyes
Fly Tier: Duane Hada

Standard Muddler

Hook: Mustad 79580, #2 - #12
Thread: Black
Tail: Two sections of mottled turkey quill
Body: Gold embossed tinsel
Wings: Brown/white buck tail under two section of mottled turkey quill
Hackle: Deer hair tied as a collar
Head: Spun and trimmed deer hair
Fly Tier: Cliff Stringer

Streaker Sculpin

Hook: Mustad 79580, #1   **Thread:** Brown
Weight: Eighteen wraps of .035 lead free wire
Rib: Gold braid   **Body:** SLF yellow dubbing with peacock Angel Hair side flash
Wings: Peacock sword feathers, one pair
Fins: Green dyed ring-neck pheasant feathers backed with a red dyed pheasant feathers
Gills: Orange SLF dubbing
Head: Spun and trimmed deer hair, red, yellow, green, orange, and blue
Eyes: Yellow plastic with black pupils
Fly Tier: Mark Hoeser

Struddler

Hook: Mustad 33957, #2
Thread: Black
Body: Flat gold tinsel
Wings: Four Coq de Leon neck feathers over Krystal Flash
Hackle: Deer hair collar
Head: Spun and trimmed deer hair
Eyes: Stick on, copper with black pupil
Fly Tier: Don Ordez

Tom's Sculpin

Hook: Mustad 3665A, #8
Thread: Tan
Tail: Barred wood duck flank feather, folded
Body: White died taupe medium chenille
Fins: Wood duck breast feathers
Head: Taupe dyed chenille
Eyes: Lead dumb bell, unpainted
Fly Tier: Tom Broderidge

Tricolor Marabou Muddler

Hook: Mustad 9672, #2 - #12
Thread: Gray
Tail: Red buck tail fibers
Body: Gold sparkle braid
Wings: Three colors of marabou clumps, colors are the tier's choice
Topping: Several peacock herl strands
Hackle: Deer hair spun as a collar
Head: Deer hair, spun and trimmed to shape
Fly Tier: Bruce Staples

White Miller

Hook: Mustad 9671, #10
Thread: White
Tail: White deer hair
Body: Silver mylar tinsel
Collar: Spun deer hair, white
Head: Spun and trimmed deer hair, white
Fly Tier: Tommy Marks

Woolly Buggers . . .

Annalideye

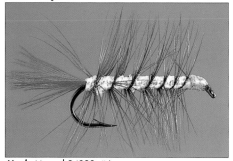

Hook: Mustad 94833, #6
Thread: White saddle repair thread, not waxed
Tail: Red marabou, very sparse and short
Body: Pearlescent sheathing
Hackle: Grizzly, palmered
Head: Thread tied full
Fly Tier: Carl E. Wulff

Baby Bugger

Hook: DaiRiki 700, #14 - #20
Thread: Black or color to match the body
Tail: Chartreuse marabou (or color of choice), several strands of Krystal Flash
Body: Chartreuse chenille or dubbing (or color of choice)
Hackle: Grizzly, tied palmered, sized even with the hook point
Head: Thread
Fly Tier: Al Beatty

Backward Bugger

Hook: DaiRiki 700, #4 - #10
Thread: Brown or color to match the fly
Tail: Brown marabou, several strands of Krystal Flash, tied on at the eye pointing forward
Rib: Fine copper wire
Weight: Non-lead wire (weighted body & forward tail creates wild action)
Body: Brown chenille or color of choice
Hackle: Brown, tied palmered
Head: Thread
Fly Tier: Al Beatty

Bass Masters

Hook: Daiichi 2220, #6
Thread: Olive
Tail: Chartreuse dyed marabou
Body: Chartreuse crystal chenille
Hackle: Silver Flashabou in a dubbing loop
Head: Thread
Fly Tier: Derek Harryman

Bead Head Peacock Leech

Hook: Mustad 9672, #4 - #10
Thread: Black
Tail: Rust marabou
Rib: Copper wire
Body: Peacock herl
Hackle: Ginger palmered over the body
Head: Gold bead, 5/32"
Fly Tier: Bruce Staples

Beady Eyed Crystal Bugger

Hook: Stinger, #10
Thread: Fluorescent orange
Tail: Chartreuse marabou
Body: Chartreuse crystal chenille
Hackle: Grizzly dyed chartreuse
Head: Thread
Eyes: Brass dumb bell
Fly Tier: Tommy Marks

BJ's Better Bugger

Hook: Dai-Riki 710, #4 - #12
Thread: Black
Tail: Black marabou
Body: Kreinik Braid #850 (peacock)
Hackle: Black, palmered
Head: Brass bead
Fly Tier: B. J. Lester

Black Devil Worm

Hook: Mustad 36890, #2 - #10
Thread: Black
Tail: Clump of peacock sword herl
Body: Black crystal chenille
Hackle: Grizzly dyed olive, palmered
Legs: Speckled olive latex legs
Head: Thread
Weed guard: Optional
Fly Tier: Tom Tripi

Black River Demon

Hook: Daiichi 2461, #1/0 - #12
Thread: Hot orange
Tail: Black marabou, tied sparse
Rib: Fine copper wire
Body: Black Kreinik thread
Hackle: Tapered black saddle hackle
Head: Black bead and orange thread collar
Eyes: Plastic, chartreuse with a black pupil
Head covering: Five-minute epoxy over the head,
eyes, and collar
Fly Tier: Jerry Caruso

Blue Eared Bugger

Hook: Nymph 2xl, #2 - #10
Thread: Olive
Tail: Olive marabou and olive Krystal Flash
Body: Olive chenille
Hackle: Blue eared pheasant, tied as a collar
Head: Thread
Fly Tier: Marvin Nolte

Blue Electric

Hook: Mustad 79580, #6 - #10
Thread: Black
Tail: Black marabou and peacock Krystal Flash
Rib: Blue Flashabou
Body: Black chenille
Hackle: Black, palmered
Head: Thread
Fly Tier: Kurt Zelazny

Brite-Butt Bugger

Hook: Mustad 9672, #8
Thread: Black
Tail: Black marabou and six strands of Krystal Flash,
tied very sparse
Butt: Chartreuse chenille
Body: Dark olive chenille
Hackle: Grizzly dyed yellow, tied palmered
Head: Thread
Fly Tier: Dana Griffin, III

Bronco Bugger

Hook: Mustad 79580, #4 - #12
Thread: Black
Tail: Blue over orange marabou
Rib: Fine copper or gold wire
Body: Blue chenille
Hackle: Orange
Head: Thread
Fly Tier: Jim Aubrey

Buck's Bugger

Hook: Mustad 9672, #4 - #14
Thread: Color to match the body
Tail: Olive marabou or color of choice, several strands of Krystal Flash
Rib: Copper wire, used to anchor the hackle and rib the fly
Body: Butt end of the tail marabou and the tying thread
Hackle: Grizzly dyed olive or color of choice, wrapped from the front to the back
Head: Thread
Fly Tier: Buck Goodrich

Chickabugger

Hook: Dai-Riki 710, #6 - #8
Thread: Maroon
Tail: Grizzly dyed maroon
Rib: Fine gold wire
Body: Maroon chenille
Hackle: Maroon rooster flank
Head: Fine maroon chenille
Eyes: Spirit River Real Eyes
Fly Tier: Henry Hoffman

Copper Killer

Hook: Mustad 9672, #8 - #12
Thread: Orange
Tail: Marabou dyed a copper brown, four strands of copper Krystal Flash
Body: Copper crystal chenille
Hackle: Brown, tied even with the hook point
Head: Brass bead, thread
Fly Tier: Tony Spezio

Crane Fly Streamer

Hook: Mustad 33620, #2 - #6
Thread: Olive
Tail: Golden olive marabou
Body: Golden olive chenille with a silver core
Rib: Grizzly dyed dark olive palmered hackle
Hackle: Golden olive marabou, tied as a collar
Head: Dark olive seal dubbing, saturated with cement
Fly Tier: Reginald Denny

Denny's Seal Bugger

Hook: TMC 300, #6 - #12
Thread: Brown
Tail: Cinnamon dyed marabou, 4 strands of Krystal Flash
Rib: Copper wire
Body: Dubbing, picked out
Dubbing mix: Amber, red, orange, and brown Angora goat with copper SLF
Hackle: Grizzly dyed cinnamon, tied palmered
Head: Thread
Fly Tier: Larry Nicholas

Emu Bugger

Hook: Long shank streamer, #2 - #6
Thread: Black
Tail: Black marabou
Rib: Optional wire
Body: Half black and half purple Lite Brite dubbing, mixed
Hackle: Black emu feather
Head: Thread
Fly Tier: Bill Chandler

Epoxy Bugger

Hook: DaiRiki 700, #6 - #12
Thread: White
Tail: Brown marabou (or color of choice), several strand of Krystal Flash
Body: Pearl tinsel
Hackle: Brown, tied palmered (or color of choice)
Eyes: Large dumb bell, yellow with black pupil
Head: White thread around the eyes, two coats of Aqua Tough
Fly Tier: Al Beatty

Fox's Bugger

Hook: Nymph, #6 - #10
Thread: Black
Tail: Black angora rabbit
Rib: Copper wire
Body: Black chenille
Hackle: Grizzly, palmered
Eyes: Brass bead chain
Head: Thread
Fly Tier: Larry Nicholas

George's Pregnant Shrimp

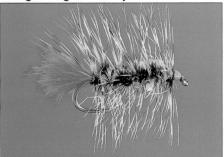

Hook: TMC 3761, #10 - 12
Thread: Yellow
Tail: Orange marabou, tied short
Rib: Fine copper wire
Body: Yellow/olive variegated chenille
Hackle: Grizzly tied yellow
Head: Thread
Fly Tier: George Close

Gold Bead Rubber Legs

Hook: TMC 5263, #6 - #10
Thread: Color to match the body
Tail: Marabou, color of choice
Body: Dubbing and Estaz, color of choice
Hackle: Soft hackle collar to match the body
Head: Thread
Legs: Round rubber, two per side
Fly Tier: Deke Meyer

Green Crystal Bugger

Hook: Dai-Riki 710, #8
Thread: Green
Tail: Olive marabou and four strands of Krystal Flash
Rib: Fine copper wire
Body: Green crystal chenille
Hackle: Grizzly dyed brown
Head: Thread
Fly Tier: George Close

Halloween

Hook: Mustad 9671, #8
Thread: Orange
Tail: Orange marabou, tied sparse
Rib: Optional copper wire
Body: Orange yarn
Hackle: Grizzly died orange
Head: Thread
Fly Tier: Tom Broderidge

Irish Red Side & Black

Hook: Mustad 3906B, #4 - #14
Thread: Black
Tail: Black marabou, tied sparse, red and black Krystal Flash
Rib: Red wire
Body: Black Seal-Ex dubbing
Body sides: Red and black Krystal Flash for the tail is tied as body sides
Hackle: Black hen, tied as a collar
Head: Thread
Fly Tier: Roger Swengel

Jacko's Bugger

Hook: Streamer 4xl, #2 - #8
Thread: Black
Tail: Black marabou and Krystal Flash
Body: Black crystal chenille
Wings: Black marabou topped with Wine Flashabou
Hackle: Palmered black saddle hackle
Head: Thread
Fly Tier: Eric Pettine

Lateral Peacock

Hook: TMC 5263, #6 - #12
Thread: Brown
Tail: Chocolate brown marabou, tied sparse
Flash: Gold Flashabou applied as a lateral line before wrapping the hackle
Body: Peacock herl twisted into a rope and wrapped
Hackle: Grizzly dyed chocolate brown, tied palmered
Head: Thread
Legs: Optional
Fly Tier: Larry Nicholas

Lite Brite Bugger

Hook: Daiichi 1720, #2 - #10
Thread: Black
Tail: Black marabou
Body: Red Lite Brite dubbing
Hackle: Black, palmered
Head: Black Brite Bead
Fly Tier: Bill Black, Spirit River Inc.

Lite Brite Woolly

Hook: Mustad 9672, #6 - #10
Thread: Brown
Tail: Bronze brown Lite Brite dubbing
Body: Dark brown crystal chenille
Hackle: Grizzly dyed dark brown
Head: Thread
Fly Tier: Robert Meuschke

Midnight Leech

Hook: Streamer 3XL, #2 - #12
Thread: Black
Tail: Black marabou and several strands of blue and red Krystal Flash, tied sparse
Rib: Red and blue Krystal Flash
Body: Black rayon chenille
Hackle: Black saddle hackle, palmered
Head: Thread or optional bead
Fly Tier: Chuck Collins

Mini Bead Head Bugger

Hook: Mustad 3906, #14
Thread: Chartreuse
Tail: Olive marabou, tied sparse
Body: Peacock herl
Hackle: Grizzly dyed olive hen neck feather, palmered
Head: Gold bead
Fly Tier: Ted Patlen

Minimum Flash

Hook: Mustad 9672, #10
Thread: Black
Tail: Black marabou
Body: Black ultra chenille
Over Body: Pearl tinsel strip
Hackle: Black ostrich, palmered
Head: Black bead
Fly Tier: Eric Schubert

Moose Mane Woolly

Hook: Mustad 9575, #6 - #10
Thread: Black
Tail: Brown goose biots, divided
Rib: Thread
Body: Peacock herl
Wing case: Moose mane
Hackle: Brown palmered
Head: Thread
Antenna: Brown goose biots, divided
Fly Tier: Kevin Cohenour

Mr. Right

Hook: TMC 207BL, #4 - #8, hook point rides up
Thread: Black
Tail: Black marabou
Body: Black chenille
Hackle: Black saddle, under sized
Legs: Black round rubber
Head: Painted dumb bell eyes, yellow with black pupils
Fly Tier: Chris Mihulka

Orange Belly

Hook: Mustad 9672, #6 - #12
Thread: Black
Tail: Black marabou, couple of strands of Krystal Flash
Body: Black chenille, orange antron strip on the belly
Hackle: Palmered grizzly over the body and belly
Head: Thread
Fly Tier: Len Holt

Orange Belly Woolly

Hook: Mustad 9672, #4 - #8
Thread: Olive
Tail: Orange hackle fibers
Rib: Copper wire counter wrapped
Body: Olive chenille with strip of orange wool yarn as a belly
Hackle: Olive hackle palmered over the body and belly
Head: Thread
Fly Tier: Cliff Stringer

Peacock Bugger

Hook: Long shank hook, #2 - #8
Thread: Black
Tail: Black marabou
Rib: Gold wire
Body: Five strands of peacock herl, spun
Hackle: Blue/green peacock body feather
Eyes: Weighted eyes
Fly Tier: Chuck Moxley

Persuader Bugger

Hook: Streamer 4xl, #2 - #8
Thread: Black
Tail: Marabou, color of choice
Body: Estaz, color of choice
Hackle: Daddy long legs synthetic hackle
Head: Thread
Fly Tier: David Curneal

Plain Brown Bugger

Hook: Mustad 79580, #4 - #8
Thread: Brown
Tail: Brown marabou, tied full
Rib: Copper wire, counter wrapped
Body: Dark brown chenille
Hackle: Furnace saddle hackle, tied from the front to the back, secured with the rib
Head: Thread
Fly Tier: Cliff Stringer

Purple Bugger

Hook: Mustad 79580, #2 - #8
Thread: Black
Tail: Purple marabou
Rib: Optional copper wire
Body: Purple diamond braid
Hackle: Purple, tied palmered
Head: Thread
Fly Tier: John Newbury

Purple Fish Eater

Hook: Mustad 94833, #6
Thread: Black
Tail: Gray rabbit strip
Rib: Silver wire
Body: Medium purple chenille
Hackle: Grizzly, palmered
Head: Thread, wrapped extra large
Fly Tier: Carl E. Wolf

River Witch

Hook: TMC 9394, #4 - #8
Thread: Black
Tail: Black marabou
Body: Black floss and pearl mylar under woven black and clear Larva Lace
Hackle: Black, wrapped as a collar
Head: Thread
Fly Tier: Lance Zook

Royal Lady Woolly Bugger

Hook: Mustad 79580, #2 - #12
Thread: Black
Tail: Black marabou and four strands of Krystal Flash
Body: Pink poly, twisted into a rope and wrapped
Hackle: White palmered over the body
Head: Thread
Fly Tier: Ruth J. Zinck

Sauk River Grub

Hook: TMC 5263, #4 - #10
Thread: Red
Tail: Red hack tips
Body: Black ostrich twisted with silver tinsel, tied in three sections
Hackle: Grizzly dyed olive, tied in four sections
Head: Red
Fly Tier: David Hunter

Seal Bugger

Hook: Mustad 9672, #6 - 310
Thread: Black
Tail: Wine marabou, tied sparse
Rib: Fine gold wire
Body: Black seal, Seal-Ex, or angora goat dubbing
Hackle: Picked out dubbing fibers
Head: Thread
Fly Tier: George Nelson

Skinny Woolly

Hook: Mustad 9672, #6 - #12
Thread: Brown
Tail: Brown marabou, couple strands of Krystal Flash, tied very sparse
Rib: Krystal Flash
Body: Brown marabou twisted and wrapped
Hackle: Palmered grizzly
Head: Thread (optional bead head)
Fly Tier: Len Holt

SRI Wooly Bomber

Hook: Daiichi 1720, #2 - #10
Thread: Black
Tail: Black marabou accented with pearl Fly Flash
Body: Black chenille accented with a pearl Fly Flash stripe down each side
Hackle: Black, palmered
Eyes: Real Eyes with stick on, green with black pupils
Head: Chartreuse Lite Brite dubbing around the eyes
Fly Tier: Bill Black, Spirit River Inc.

Thin Body Bugger

Hook: Swimming nymph, #8 - #14
Thread: Color to match the body
Tail: Marabou, color of choice
Abdomen: Tying thread over the marabou
Thorax: Estaz, color of choice
Head: Thread
Fly Tier: David Curneal

White Emu Woolly Bugger

Hook: Mustad 9672, #4 - #8
Thread: White
Tail: White marabou
Rib: Optional
Body: White chenille
Hackle: White emu body feather, palmered
Head: Thread
Eyes: Lead, 5/32"
Fly Tier: Floyd Franke

The Wiggler

Hook: Mustad 80500BL, #8
Thread: Black
Tail: Black marabou
Body: Spun marabou, any color
Head: Thread
Fly Tier: Jim Childers

Woolly Pup

Hook: Mustad 9672, #2 - #12
Thread: Color to match the body
Tail: Marabou, color of choice
Rib: Krystal Flash
Body: Ostrich herl (color of choice), Krystal Flash on both side to the end of the tail
Hackle: Color of choice, tied palmered over the body
Head: Ostrich herl
Eyes: Red dumb bell with black pupil
Fly Tier: Bud Heintz

Woolly Rainbow

Hook: Mustad 94833, #6
Thread: Black
Tail: Red marabou, tied short and sparse
Body: Multi-colored piping
Hackle: Black saddle, palmered
Head: Thread
Fly Tier: Carl E. Wolf

Wounded Woolly Worm

Hook: Orvis 0167, #8 - #10
Thread: Burnt orange
Tail: Florescent orange yarn, trimmed short, and four strands of red Flashabou
Body: Olive chenille
Hackle: Grizzly, palmered
Head: Thread
Fly Tier: Gene Stutzman

Chapter 4

Steelhead, Salmon, and Rangeley Flies

By Judy Lehmberg

In the early 1980s, during our annual trip to Yellowstone country, my husband Verne and I wandered into West Yellowstone, Montana and found the Federation of Fly Fishers annual conclave. With a minimum of forethought or planning we signed up for an Atlantic salmon fly class taught by Bill Blackstone. I had mixed feelings. Salmon flies were an attractive challenge, but they were gaudy and they didn't really imitate any living organism. Bill did an excellent job and I enjoyed the seminar but I tied only a few flies after that class. I wasn't really hooked. The following August we returned to the FFF conclave and attended a second Atlantic salmon fly class, this time taught by Wayne Luallen, John Van der Hoof, and Dave McNeese. The three instructors had a positive, synergistic effect on the class. The combination of Wayne's attention to detail and excellent technique, John's technique and versatility, and Dave's irreverence was a stimulating combination for the students. This time the lessons "took" and I began accumulating materials and practicing, practicing, practicing.

Some fly tiers avoid tying steelhead and Atlantic salmon flies because they believe them difficult to tie. Salmon flies do require a wide variety of materials, and they are time consuming, but they are not particularly difficult to tie. In fact, tying them can be quite therapeutic. After a long, tough day at the office, creating a pretty fly is relaxing.

And, you may not believe this if you have ever watched someone tie a salmon fly, but learning to tie them will actually make you a faster, more coordinated tier of other flies. As a salmon fly tier develops, his skills can be applied to other flies. He will find his trout dry flies begin to take on a more sophisticated look, with tapered, even bodies "without lumps and bumps" as Wayne Luallen stresses, and with precisely positioned wings.

Steelhead and Atlantic salmon flies were originally designed to attract fish that are moving upstream to spawn and are not supposed to be interested in feeding. The early salmon fly tiers designed multicolored flies with the materials available to them at the time, particularly those used in the millinery industry. Today, many of those materials are no longer available or are relatively rare. Part of the challenge of tying salmon flies today is finding suitable substitutes, due to the necessity of conserving rare species. The swan and bustard formerly used in married wings can be substituted with bleached peacock tail and wild turkey tail. The chatterer and Indian crow can be replaced with dyed neck feathers from the male ring-necked pheasant.

Used to catch fish or displayed on a wall, steelhead and Atlantic salmon flies are some of the most spectacular and colorful flies in existence.

—*Judy Lehmberg*
Dayton, Texas

Egg
Patterns . . .

Babine Special

Hook: Mustad 36890, #4 - #6
Thread: Red
Body: Fluorescent orange chenille, wrapped in two segments
Hackle: Red saddle in the middle and white saddle at the front
Head: Thread
Fly Tier: Cliff Stringer

Chickabou Cluster

Hook: Eagle Claw L193G, Red #2/0 - #4
Thread: Read
Tail: Short tuft of white Chickabou
Body: Four pink plastic bead propellers from a craft store
Hackle: White Chickabou tied as two sparse collars to represent spawn
Head: Thread
Fly Tier: Al Beatty

Chickabou Egg & Membrane

Hook: Daiichi X510, #8
Thread: White
Tail: White Chickabou, tied short and sparse
Body: Thread
Wing/egg: Orange Chickabou, tied short and full
Head: Thread
Fly Tier: Henry Hoffman

Chris' Phi Beta Kappa

Hook: Mustad 36890, #2/0 - #2
Thread: Clear mono
Tail: Two pink crystal eggs on #8 hooks, tied as trailers
Body: Pearl crystal chenille or Estaz
Hackle: Hot pink, palmered
Wing: Holographic fibers
Weed guard: Mono, optional
Head: Thread
Fly Tier: Tom Tripi

Crystal White

Hook: Mustad 3406, #6
Thread: White
Tail: White marabou, short and sparse
Body: Pink crystal chenille
Hackle: White marabou, tied as a sparse collar
Head: Thread
Fly Tier: Robert Meuschke

Dietz Doosy

Hook: Mustad 36890, #2 - #10
Thread: Orange
Body: Fluorescent orange chenille
Body Hackle: Orange, palmered
Wing: White marabou
Head: Thread
Fly Tier: Ilene Hirsh

Double Egg

Hook: TMC 7999, #4
Thread: Orange
Tail: Pearl angel hair
Body: Red and yellow chenille, tied in two egg-shaped segments
Over Body: Pearl mylar tubing over each body segment, coated with Softex or Aqua Flex
Head: Thread
Fly Tier: Lance Zook

Double Egg Sperm

Hook: Mustad 36890, #4 - #6
Thread: Red
Body: Fluorescent chartreuse chenille, wrapped in two segments
Body flash: Silver tinsel wrapped between the two body segments
Wing: White marabou, tied very sparse
Head: Thread
Fly Tier: Cliff Stringer

Egg Cluster

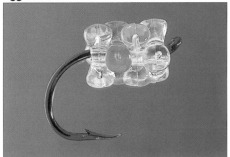

Hook: Eagle Claw L193G, Red #2/0 - #4
Thread: Clear mono
Body: Three pink and one orange plastic bead propellers from a craft store
Head: Thread
Fly Tier: Al Beatty

Egg EZY

Hook: Mustad 90240, #4 - #10
Thread: Fire orange
Tail: White Chickabou and pearl Flashabou, trimmed at various lengths
Body: Orange and pearl crystal chenille
Eyes: EZY Eyes, tied in the middle of the body
Head: Thread
Fly Tier: Al Beatty

Egg Sucking Streamer

Hook: Mustad 36890, #2 - #6
Thread: Black
Tail: Red buck tail
Body: Black Brazilian Velour
Wing: Black zonker strip, flanked with pearl Krystal Flash on the sides
Cheeks: Jungle cock nails
Head: Fluorescent orange chenille
Fly Tier: Al Beatty

Egg Over Easy

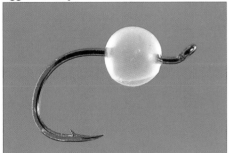

Hook: Gamakatsu Red Octopus, #2/0 - #8
Body: Fluorescent egg yarn body coated with hot glue from a glue gun
Fly Tier: Ilene Hirsh

Epoxy EZY Egg

Hook: Mustad 90240, #4 - #10
Thread: Fire orange
Tail: Peacock Krystal Flash mixed with pearl and black Flashabou topped with white Chickabou
Body: Pink and pearl crystal flash
Eyes: EZY Eyes, tied in the center of the body
Coating: Three coats of Aqua Flex over the body, eyes, and head
Head: Thread
Fly Tier: Al Beatty

Fluorescent EGGstravaganza

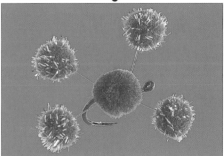

Hook: Mustad 92569FO, #6
Thread: Fluorescent orange
Body: Fluorescent orange Glo-Bug Yarn, trimmed to shape
Egg cluster: Four fluorescent orange Krystal Eggs, connected with eight-pound Fluorocarbon
Head: Thread
Fly Tier: Jeffrey Pierce

Foam Egg Sack Spawn

Hook: Jardine F114, #8 - #12
Thread: White
Body: Orange, yellow, and pink craft foam, tied as a series of small loops
Head: Thread
Fly Tier: Floyd Franke

Foam Fly Egg

Hook: TMC 200R, #12 - #18
Thread: Red
Body: Large crystal chenille, orange, red, or pink
Over Body: Closed cell foam, contrasting color
Head: Thread and trimmed closed cell foam from the over body
Fly Tier: Bill Chandler

Globug

Hook: Mustad 9174
Thread: Black
Body: Two purple and one chartreuse globug yarn, flared and trimmed to shape
Head: Thread
Fly Tier: Kieran Frye

Golden Globe

Hook: TMC 105, #4 - #6
Thread: Fluorescent fire orange
Tail: Krystal Flash, pearl & pink or colors of choice
Weight: Spirit River Dazl-Eyes, gold
Body: Glo Bug Yarn, orange, apricot, peach, or color of choice
Head: Thread
Fly Tier: Jack Schlotter

Jeff's Egg Cluster, Orange

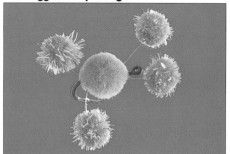

Hook: Mustad 92569FO, #6
Thread: Orange
Body: Steelhead orange Glo-Bug Yarn, trimmed to shape
Egg cluster: Four orange Krystal Eggs, connected by eight-pound Fluorocarbon
Head: Thread
Fly Tier: Jeffrey Pierce

Lucky Lisa

Hook: Mustad 92567R, #2 - #6
Thread: Red
Tail: Red Krystal Flash
Egg string: Two or more pink plastic 10mm beads
Attaching the beads: Heat the hook shank with a lighter, melt the plastic bead into place
Body: Red Estaz or crystal chenille
Head: Thread
Fly Tier: Steve Skrubis

Nushigak Special

Hook: Gamakatsu T10-6H, 34 - #10
Thread: Red
Tail: White zonker strip from the wing
Body: Large pink cactus chenille
Wing: White zonker strip
Legs: Fuschia super floss, three per side
Hackle: White saddle hackle, tied as a collar
Head: Thread
Fly Tier: Ilene Hirsh

Orange & Spawn

Hook: Eagle Claw L193G, Red #2/0 - #4
Thread: Red
Body: Four orange plastic bead propellers from a craft store
Throat: White Chickabou
Head: Thread
Fly Tier: Al Beatty

Pom Pom Cluster

Hook: Eagle Claw L193G, Red #2/0 - #4
Thread: Red
Tail: Sparse white Chickabou
Body: Red craft pom poms, strung on a thread and looped/tied around the hook
Hackle: White Chickabou, tied as two collars to represent spawn
Head: Thread
Fly Tier: Bob Lay

Regular Hot Spot

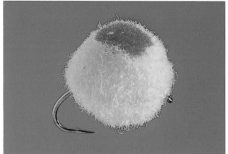

Hook: TMC 2487, #10
Thread: Chartreuse or color to match the body
Body: Four tufts of tow yarn, tied around the hook and trimmed to shape (color of choice)
Hot spot: Fluorescent orange paint spot on the top of the body
Head: Thread
Fly Tier: Al Beatty

Roe Fly

Hook: Daiichi 2055, #7
Thread: Yellow
Tail: Dyed yellow hackle fibers
Rib: Yellow crystal chenille, palmered
Body: Large fluorescent orange chenille
Hackle: Dyed yellow saddle hackle, palmered
Head: Thread
Fly Tier: Reginald Denny

Salmon River MVP

Hook: Gamakatsu L11S-#H, #2 - #6
Thread: Hot pink
Body: SLF fluorescent dubbing, rear two-thirds is pink and the front one-third is orange
Wing: White marabou under pink mylar tubing, picked out
Head: Thread
Fly Tier: Rich Youngers

Shaggy Egg

Hook: Mustad 9299, #1
Thread: Orange
Tail: Antron, tied sparse
Body: Body Basic Egg Dubbing
Eyes: Plastic bar bell
Head: Thread
Fly Tier: Dustin Harris

Taylor's Egg

Hook: Mustad Neon 92569, #8
Thread: Orange
Body: Orange Estaz, wrapped
Head: Thread
Fly Tier: Jeffrey Pierce

Two Tone Cluster

Hook: Mustad 9174, #4
Thread: Orange
Eggs: Orange and pink egg yarn tied on twenty-pound mono
Head: Eggs and mono attached as a cluster, thread
Fly Tier: Tom Broderidge

White Wiggle Tail

Hook: Mustad 7950, #4 - #6
Thread: Hot orange
Tail: White marabou with a few strands of silver Krystal Flash
Body: Medium fluorescent pink chenille
Hackle: Silver Flashabou, tied as a very sparse collar
Head: Thread
Fly Tier: Bruce Staples

Nymphs . . .

Black & White Nymph

Hook: Partridge N, #4
Thread: Black
Tag: Gold oval tinsel
Rear Hackle: Teal flank feather, tied collar style
Rib: Gold oval tinsel
Body: Black floss
Wing: Grizzly cape feathers
Front Hackle: Teal flank, tied as a collar
Head: Thread
Fly Tier: Tom Broderidge

Dave's Emerger

Hook: Mustad 90240, #4 - #12
Thread: Brown
Tail: Wood duck flank fibers
Body: Copper wire
Thorax: Peacock herl over dark olive chenille
Wing case: Wood duck flank fibers
Legs: Excess fiber tips from the wing case, pulled back and down
Head: Large brass bead, thread
Fly Tier: Al Beatty

Glimmer Stone

Hook: TMC 200R, #6
Thread: Black or brown to match the body
Weight: Bead head plus fifteen turns of .035 wire
Tail: Round rubber legs, brown or black
Rib: Copper wire
Back & wing case: Black or dark brown sparkle chenille
Body: Gold/brown sparkle chenille, lighter than the back
Legs: Round rubber legs, brown or black
Head: Bead & thread
Fly Tier: Jack Schlotter

Glitzie Nymph

Hook: TMC 200R, #4 - #10
Thread: Black
Tail and antenna: Black stripped hackle stems
Rib: Oval gold tinsel
Body: Black Brazilian Velour or vernile
Over Body: Blue or black metallic Glitzie Ribbon
Thorax: Black Lite Brite dubbing, picked out form the legs
Wing case: Blue or black metallic Glitzie Ribbon
Head: Thread
Fly Tier: Bill Chandler

Klamath Gold

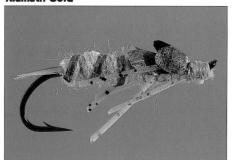

Hook: Mustad 36890, #4 - #6
Thread: Gold
Tail: Gold goose biots
Rib: Brown nylon
Body: Gold Antron yarn
Wing cases: Three shaped from brown Tyvek
Head: Thread
Legs: Sili-con leg material, gold with speckles
Fly Tier: Robert Meuschke

Lynx Terminator

Hook: Mustad 9672, #8
Thread: Black
Tail: Brown goose biots
Rib: Reddish brown hackle, trimmed and palmered
Side flash: Medium French tinsel on each side
Body: Peacock herl, wrapped
Hackle: Spun elk hair, tied as a collar
Head: Brass bead and peacock herl
Fly Tier: Len Holt

March Brown Bead Head

Hook: Daiichi 1530, #6
Thread: Camel
Tail: Brown Hungarian partridge
Rib: Medium copper wire
Body: Reddish brown rabbit/Antron dubbing mix
Weight: Five wraps of non-lead wire behind the bead head
Hackle: Brown Hungarian partridge, tied as a collar
Head: Gold tungsten bead
Fly Tier: Mark Hoeser

Mono Nymph

Hook: DaiRiki 135, #8
Thread: Purple
Tail: Pheasant tail fibers, dyed purple
Body: Body Basic Nymph Cord
Thorax: Peacock herl
Wing case: Pheasant tail, dyed purple
Legs: Tips of the wing case pulled back and to the sides
Head: Brass bead
Fly Tier: Dustin Harris

Neon Lion

Hook: Mustad 9672, #8 - #12
Thread: Chartreuse
Tail: Chartreuse marabou
Body: Chartreuse chenille
Hackle: Emu dyed olive, tied as a collar
Eyes: Chartreuse bead chain
Head: Thread
Fly Tier: Kieran Frye

Octo Caddis

Hook: Mustad 9049, #6 - #10
Thread: Brown
Rib: Orange thread
Body: Tan sparkle dubbing
Wing: A pair of mottle turkey wing slips, tied to the sides and slightly down
Hackle: Grizzly dyed brown saddle hackle, tied as a sparse collar
Head: Dark brown dubbing
Fly Tier: Reginald Denny

Orange Grizzly

Hook: Mustad 3906B, #4 - #8
Thread: Orange
Body: Orange Antron yarn
Hackle: Grizzly dyed orange, tied as a very sparse collar
Head: Thread
Fly Tier: Robert Meuschke

P. M. Midge

Hook: TMC 2457, #6 - #8
Thread: Brown
Body: Brown/orange speckled Sili Leg material, wrapped
Head/thorax: Natural fox squirrel dubbing
Fly Tier: Lance Zook

The Red Head

Hook: Mustad 9672, #4 - #10
Thread: Black
Tail: Black yarn, combed out
Body: Mix of copper Lite Brite and black yarn
Head: Red yarn mixed with red Angel Hair
Fly Tier: Lee Clark

Renegade Pheasant Tail

Hook: Partridge CS10/2, #6 - #12
Thread: Black
Tail: Pheasant tail fibers
Rib: Oval silver tinsel
Body: Pheasant tail fibers, wrapped
Body Hackle: Brown soft hackle, tied as a collar
Wing case: Pheasant tail fibers
Thorax: Peacock herl over a black wool under body
Front Hackle: White, tied as a collar
Head: Thread
Fly Tier: Al Beatty

Standard Tail Hook Leech

Hook: TMC 200R, #12, second hook is Mustad 94840 which is cut off
Thread: Black
Body: Olive zonker strip, impaled on the hook near the tail area
Wing: Same zonker strip, threaded on mono tippet from the body to hook to the head
Head: Tippet, body/wing strip tied to the cut off Mustad 94840
Fly Tier: Greg Peterka

Steel Head Nymph

Hook: Mustad 3366, #10
Thread: Brown
Rib: Copper wire
Body: Green Lite Brite dubbing
Head: Brown Lite Brite dubbing
Fly Tier: Bill Chandler

Steelhead Stonefly

Hook: Mustad 9672, #2
Thread: Black
Tail: Black round rubber leg material
Rib: Copper wire
Body: Black rabbit dubbing over several wraps of non-lead wire
Legs: Three sets of black rubber leg material
Wing case: Mottled turkey tail
Antenna: Black round rubber leg material
Head: Black dubbing
Fly Tier: Eric Pettine

Stew's Fly

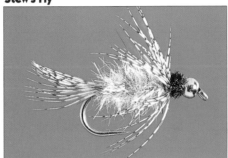

Hook: TMC 3761, #6 - #10
Thread: Olive
Tail: Hungarian partridge fibers
Body: Hare's ear dubbing brush
Hackle: Hungarian partridge, tied as a collar
Head: Brass bead, peacock herl, and thread
Fly Tier: Stew Stewart

Tail Hook Leech (BH)

Hook: TMC 200R, #12, second hook is Mustad 94840 which is cut off
Thread: Maroon
Body: Maroon zonker strip, impaled on the hook near the tail area
Wing: Same zonker strip, threaded on mono tippet from the body to hook to the head
Attaching the cut off Hook: Tippet, body/wing strip tied to the cut off Mustad 94840 with thread
Hackle: White dyed maroon, tied as a sparse collar
Head: Black tungsten bead head
Fly Tier: Greg Peterka

Ugly Bitch

Hook: Mustad 36890, #4 - #8
Thread: Black
Tail: Fine, black rubber leg material
Body: Dark olive chenille
Hackle: Dark ginger or furnace, palmered
Feelers: Fine, black rubber leg material
Head: Thread
Fly Tier: Floyd Franke

Wooly Bee

Hook: Partridge CS10/1, #6 - #12
Thread: Black
Tail: Red silk
Body: Three segments, two black and one yellow Brazilian Velour
Hackle: Dark dun sized small, palmered
Head: Thread
Fly Tier: Gretchen Beatty

X-File Pupa

Hook: Mustad Neon 92569GL, #8
Thread: Black
Rib: Thread over Mustad Neon (glow in the dark) hook
Body: Mustad hook, coated with Aqua Flex
Head: Peacock herl
Fly Tier: Jeffrey Pierce

Shrimp Patterns . . .

Blood Tail Shrimp

Hook: Mustad 37160, #6 - #10
Thread: Red
Tail: Dark red marabou
Body: Pearl Estaz
Eyes: Silver dumb bell, tied in the middle of the body
Head: Thread
Fly Tier: Kieran Frye

Brite Squirrel

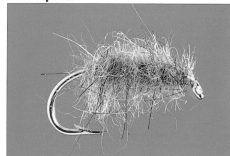

Hook: Mustad 3908C, #6
Thread: Gray
Body: Gray fox and bronze Lite Brite Dubbing, mixed
Legs: Picked out dubbing
Head: Thread
Fly Tier: Robert Meuschke

Buck Tail Shrimp (Chartreuse)

Hook: Mustad 36890, #4 - #8
Thread: Black
Tail: Chartreuse buck tail and green Krystal Flash
Rib: Fine, oval silver tinsel
Eyes: Melted mono, tied extended from the last body segment
Body: Chartreuse yarn, tied in four segments
Wings: Chartreuse buck tail, tied in three short segments
Hackle: Dyed chartreuse, tied collar style in three segments with the wings
Head: Thread
Fly Tier: Al Beatty

Chamy Shrimp

Hook: Partridge CS10/1, #2   **Thread:** Clear mono
Mouth parts: Gold Krystal Flash under a few deer hair fibers   **Antenna:** Two strands of gold Krystal Flash
Eyes: Melted mono, painted with black Aqua Head
Rib: Fine silver oval tinsel
Body: Tan Brazilian Velour
Carapace: Tan Chamois, trimmed to shape
Legs: Coq de Leon saddle feather, palmered
Tail: Chamois remaining from the carapace
Weight: Dumb bell eyes, tied on the under side of the hook
Head: Thread
Fly Tier: Al Beatty

Claret Shrimp

Hook: Partridge CS10/1, #6 - #12   **Thread:** Claret
Tag: Oval gold tinsel
Rear Hackle: Golden pheasant red breast feather, tied as a long collar
Rear Body: Medium claret Seal or Seal-Ex, ribbed with oval gold tinsel
Middle Hackle: Claret, tied collar style
Fore Body: Dark claret Seal or Seal-Ex, ribbed with oval gold tinsel
Fore Hackle: Hot orange under badger, tied as a collar
Cheeks: Jungle cock   **Head:** Thread
Fly Tier: Marvin Nolte

Fur Shrimp

Hook: TMC 7999, #1/0 - #4
Thread: Orange
Tail: Amber/gold speckled Sili Legs accented with orange Krystal Flash
Body: Fluorescent orange body fur, tied in two sections (each surrounding the hook)
Wing: Golden pheasant tippet feather over each body section
Topping: Small amount of fluorescent orange body fur, tied as a collar in a dubbing loop
Head: Thread
Fly Tier: Lance Zook

Golden Pheasant G. P.

Hook: Alec Jackson Spey, #1/0   **Thread:** Purple
Tag: Flat silver tinsel   **Tail/antenna:** Purple buck tail with one strand of red Krystal Flash on each side
Eyes: Golden pheasant dyed red, tied at the bend of the hook over the tail/antenna
Body: Purple dubbing, tied in three segments with a wing and hackle at each
Wing: Golden pheasant dyed purple, three, one at each body segment
Hackle: Golden pheasant dyed purple, three, tied as a collar at each body segment   **Head:** Thread
Fly Tier: Michael Rogers

Hank's Orange Shrimp

Hook: Mustad 80500BL, #2   **Thread:** Orange
Tail: Grizzly dyed orange knee hackle, tied at the hook eye
Claws: Grizzly dyed orange knee hackle, tied at the hook bend
Rib: Larva Lace   **Body:** Orange chenille
Shell back: Grizzly dyed orange flank feather coated with Aqua Flex or equivalent
Hackle: Orange schlappen, palmered
Eyes: Artificial flower stamens
Head: Thread
Fly Tier: Henry Hoffman

Hot Shrimp (Orange)

Hook: Mustad 36890, #4 - #8
Thread: Orange
Tail: Orange calf tail and gold Krystal Flash
Rib: Fine, oval silver tinsel
Eyes: Melted mono, tied extended from the last body
  segment
Body: Orange yarn, tied in four segments
Wings: Orange buck tail, tied in three short segments
Hackle: Dyed hot orange, tied collar style in three
  segments with the wings
Head: Thread
Fly Tier: Al Beatty

Mini Sand Shrimp

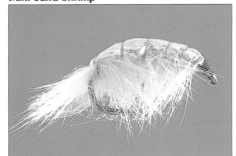

Hook: DaiRiki 135, #6
Thread: Orange
Tail: White rabbit hair, tied short
Rib: Orange Body Basic Nymph Cord
Body: Body Basic Shrimp Blend
Shell back: Plastic strip
Hackle: White saddle, palmered before the shell back
  is pulled over
Head: Thread
Fly Tier: Dustin Harris

Olive Crawfish

Hook: Gamakatsu T10-3H, #2
Thread: Black
Tail: Crawfish color rabbit zonker strip
Body: Tail material wrapped forward
Hackle: Olive marabou wrapped forward with the
  body material, extra turn at the front
Wing: Olive Flashabou, tied very sparse
Hackle: Wood duck flank feather, tied as a collar
Head: Thread
Fly Tier: Jon Harrang

Orange Shrimp

Hook: Partridge CS10/1, #2 - #10   **Thread:** Black
Tag: Silver wire
Tail: Ring neck pheasant, tied as a collar at the hook bend
Body: Flat silver tinsel
Body Hackle: Orange, tied as a collar in the center of
  the body
Body butt: Natural ostrich, tied directly
  in front of the body hackle
Wing: Natural fox squirrel tail fibers
Hackle: Orange, tied as a collar
Head: Natural ostrich and thread
Fly Tier: Gretchen Beatty

Polar Shrimp

Hook: Alec Jackson Spey, #3/0 - #2   **Thread:** Red
Tag: Flat silver tinsel
Tail: Golden pheasant crest dyed orange
Rib: Oval silver tinsel, fine
Body: One-third orange floss behind two-thirds
  orange Angora goat dubbing
Wing: Four white hackle tips, set low
Hackle: Orange soft hackle, palmered over the front
  two-thirds of the body
Throat: Golden pheasant flank feather
Head: Thread
Fly Tier: Larry Nicholas

Rebel Shrimp

Hook: TMC 200R, #6
Thread: Red
Tail: Pearl Krystal Flash
Tag: Red thread
Body: Chartreuse chenille
Hackle: Pink, palmered
Shell back: Krystal Flash from the tail
Throat: Krystal Flash from the tail/shell back
Eyes: White plastic bead chain
Head: Thread
Fly Tier: Gene Stutzman

Renegade Grub

Hook: Partridge CS10/1, #2 - #8
Thread: Black
Tail: Yellow golden pheasant body feathers, flanked
  by red golden pheasant body feathers
Body: Peacock color Brazilian Velour
Hackle: Tied as sections, collar style; brown (nearest
  the bend), grizzly, and white
Head: Thread
Fly Tier: Gretchen Beatty

Simple Steelhead Shrimp

Hook: Partridge CS10/1, #8
Thread: Tan
Mouth parts: Sparse tuft of BT's Dry Fly Poly Yarn
  accented with gold Krystal Flash
Antenna: Two strands of gold Krystal Flash
Eyes: Medium bronze Razzle Eyes
Rib: Flat gold tinsel
Body: Fluorescent orange chenille
Carapace: Tan BT's Dry Fly Poly Yarn and gold Krystal Flash
Tail: Short tuft of the carapace
Head: Thread
Fly Tier: Gretchen Beatty

Stop 'n Go Shrimp

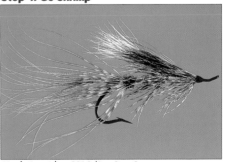

Hook: Partridge CS10/1, #2 - #8
Thread: Black
Tag: Silver wire
Tail: Pheasant rump feather, tied as a collar at the hook bend
Butt: Peacock herl, wrapped tight against the tail
Rib: Fine oval tinsel
Body: Red floss (back) and green floss (front)
Hackle: Mottled hen saddle feathers, tied as collars at
  the start of the two body segments
Wing: Gray squirrel tail fibers
Head: Thread
Fly Tier: Al Beatty

Tiger Prawn

Surface and Waker Flies . . .

Hook: Curved bait hook, #4/0 - #2 **Thread:** Orange
Tail: Grizzly Chickabou dyed orange
Body: Three or four clear glass Killer Caddis beads
Rib: Orange sparkle dubbing between the bead,
brushed ventrally **Thorax:** Peach ice chenille
Legs: Grizzly Soft Hackle dyed orange
Carapace: Orange Glo Bug yarn, coated with Soft
Body or Aqua Flex
Eyes: Large ruby red glass beads
Antenna: Hot orange Glitter Legs with two shorter
fibers of rainbow Krystal Flash **Head:** Thread
Fly Tier: Joe Warren

Adams Skipper

Hook: Mustad 90240, #6 - #12
Thread: Gray or brown
Tail: Fox squirrel tail fiber under grizzly hackle fibers
Body: Muskrat dubbing
Wing: Squirrel tail fibers, divided and tilted slightly
forward
Hackle: Brown and grizzly mixed
Head: Thread
Fly Tier: Al Beatty

Amherst Lady

Hook: Mustad 90240, #4 - #10
Thread: Black
Tail: Amherst pheasant tippets
Topping: Very short tuft of Amherst pheasant tippets
Body: Black floss (rear) and peacock herl (front)
Wing: Amherst pheasant tippets, divided and tilted
slight forward
Hackle: Black
Head: Thread
Fly Tier: Al Beatty

Badger Stimulator

Hook: Mustad 80050BR, #8 - #16
Thread: Yellow
Tail: Amber antron yarn, trimmed to length
Rib: Gold wire
Body: Yellow antron with a palmered ginger body
hackle
Wing: Bleached elk
Hackle: Silver badger
Head: Thread
Fly Tier: Tom Logan

Clark's Waker Stone

Hook: TMC 7989, #4 - #10
Thread: Orange
Body: Gold, flat tinsel
Wing: Deer hair over combed orange yarn
Hackle: Brown
Head: Thread
Fly Tier: Lee Clark

Copper Skater

Hook: Mustad 90240, #4 - #10
Thread: Brown
Tail: Fox squirrel tail fibers
Body: Fine copper wire (back) and mottled turkey tail
fibers (front)
Wing: Squirrel tail fibers, divided and tilted slightly
forward
Hackle: Brown
Head: Thread
Fly Tier: Al Beatty

Emu Bomber

Hook: Mustad 3366, #5/0 - #1/0
Thread: Black
Tail: Black marabou mixed with pearl Flashabou
Body: Spun and trimmed deer hair
Hackle: Grizzly palmered over the trimmed body
Collar: Tan emu feather, wrapped as a very sparse
collar
Wing: Tan ostrich herl
Head: Thread
Fly Tier: Tom Tripi

Floating Shrimp

Hook: Mustad 36890, #6
Thread: Gold
Mouth parts: Brown poly yarn tuft accented with
copper Krystal Flash
Antenna: Nylon strands, two longer than the rest
Body: Gold floss
Hackle: Medium ginger, palmered
Tail: Brown poly yarn tuft, tied at the hook eye
Head: Thread
Fly Tier: Al Beatty

Foam Skater

Hook: TMC 200R, #4
Thread: Orange
Body: One-eight inch closed cell foam, orange, segmented with the tying thread
Under Wing: Twenty strands of Krystal Flash, black & orange mixed, tied splay style
Wing: Moose body hair
Lip: Foam/moose hair from the body/wing, trimmed & stiffened with E-Z Shape Sparkle Body
Head: Thread
Fly Tier: Jack Schlotter

Golden Lady

Hook: Mustad 90240, #4 - #10
Thread: Orange
Tail: Golden pheasant tippets
Topping: Golden pheasant tippets, length to the center of the tail
Body: Orange floss (back) and peacock herl (front)
Wing: Golden pheasant tippets, divided and tilted slightly forward
Hackle: Silver badger
Head: Thread
Fly Tier: Al Beatty

Gray Macintosh

Hook: Mustad 90240, #2 - #10
Thread: Gray
Wings: Gray squirrel tail fibers
Hackle: Grizzly
Head: Thread
Fly Tier: Al Beatty

Green Sweeper

Hook: Partridge CS 10/1, #2 - #10
Thread: Fire orange
Tag: Fine silver tinsel and thread
Wing: Fox squirrel tail fibers under elk body hair
Head: Green Seal-Ex dubbing, thread
Hackle: Grizzly, palmered
Fly Tier: Al Beatty

Green Butt Bomber

Hook: TMC 7989, #4 - #10
Thread: Black
Tail: Red calf tail
Butt: Spun and trimmed fluorescent green deer hair
Body: Spun and trimmed black deer hair
Hackle: Grizzly, palmered
Wing: White calf tail, tied as a single post, tilted forward
Head: Thread
Fly Tier: Richard Raisler

H & L Waker

Hook: Mustad 90240, #4 - #10
Thread: Black
Tail: Calf
Body: Stripped peacock (back) and peacock herl (front)
Wing: Calf, divided and tilted slightly forward
Hackle: Brown
Head: Thread
Fly Tier: Al Beatty

Hot Spot Bomber

Hook: Partridge CS10/1, #2 - #10
Thread: Red
Tail: Calf tail hair
Body: Spun and trimmed deer hair
Wing: Single calf tail post, tilted forward
Hackle: Brown saddle, palmered after trimming the body
Hot spots: Thread, one in front and one at the rear of the fly
Head: Thread
Fly Tier: Al Beatty

Hot Spot Macintosh

Hook: Mustad 90240, #2 - #10
Thread: Fire orange
Butt: Thread coated with Aqua Flex
Wing: Fox squirrel tail fibers
Hackle: Brown
Head: Thread
Fly Tier: Al Beatty

Hunter's Stonefly

Hook: Mustad 36890, #2   **Thread:** Orange
Tail: Dyed brown goose biots   **Rib:** Thread, tied in segments
Body: Black and orange closed cell foam, epoxy together and trim to shape
Shaping the Body: Segment an extended body on a needle, then remove and tie it on the hook
Thorax: Dubbing mix of brown muskrat and orange Seal-Ex   **Wing:** Fox squirrel over two strand of white Antron, picked out
Antenna: Dyed brown goose biots
Head: Thread coated with epoxy
Fly Tier: David Hunter

Katmai Copper

Hook: Mustad 90240, #2 - #10
Thread: Dark brown
Tail: Dark brown deer hair
Body: Kreinik copper braid
Wing: Dark brown deer
Head: Trimmed deer hair from the wing
Fly Tier: Kieran Frye

Len's Skater

Hook: Mustad 36890, #8
Thread: Black
Tail: Yellow dyed elk
Rib: Peacock Krystal Flash
Body: Peacock herl, wrapped
Wing/skater: Yellow dyed elk, divided and tie under the hook, length equal to the hook gape
Hackle: Reddish brown, tied dry style
Head: Thread
Fly Tier: Len Holt

Newman's Waker

Hook: TMC 7999, #4
Thread: Red or color to match the body
Tail: Orange or color to match the body
Rib: Fine wire
Body: Orange closed cell foam (color of choice)
Under and over Wing case: Same as the body
Wings: Natural or dyed deer hair, tied spent style
Head: Tuft of foam from the over wing case, thread
Fly Tier: John Newbury

Octo Sedge

Hook: Mustad 9049, #4 - #8
Thread: Brown
Body: Orange and brown dubbing blend
Wing: Ringed neck pheasant tail fibers, tied in the tips and trimmed to shape
Hackle: Grizzly dyed brown
Head: Thread
Fly Tier: Reginald Denny

Orange Badger

Hook: Mustad 90240, #6 - #12
Thread: Hot orange
Tail: Moose body hair
Body: Thread, coated with Aqua Flex
Wing: Moose body hair, divided
Hackle: Dark silver badger
Head: Thread
Fly Tier: Al Beatty

Orange Slider

Hook: Mustad 36890, #4 - #6
Thread: Orange
Body: Orange deer hair, spun and trimmed
Wing: Orange deer hair, tied very sparse
Head: Spun and trimmed natural deer hair
Fly Tier: Robert Meuschke

Pheasant Caddis

Hook: TMC 905BL, #4 - #10
Thread: Brown
Body: Tan poly yarn, twisted into a tight rope like strand and wrapped
Wing: Ring neck pheasant feather tied tent style over a squirrel tail under wing
Head/collar: Spun and trimmed deer body hair
Fly Tier: Lance Zook

Purple Peril

Hook: TMC 7989, #8
Thread: Black
Tail: Purple dyed squirrel tail
Rib: Flat silver tinsel
Body: Purple SLF dubbing
Wing: Brown elk hair, divided and tilted forward
Hackle: Grizzly dyed purple
Head: Thread
Fly Tier: Mark Hoeser

Root Beer Float

Hook: Partridge 01 Wilson, #6
Thread: Black
Tail: Grizzly dyed ginger hackle tips
Hackle: Grizzly dyed ginger, palmer very tight
Head: Thread
Fly Tier: Henry Hoffman

Salt and Pepper Bomber

Hook: Partridge CS42, #2
Thread: Black
Tail: Fox guard hairs
Body: Black and white deer hair, spun and trimmed
Hackle: Grizzly, palmered over the trimmed body
Wing: Fox guard hairs, tied as a single post, tilted forward
Head: Thread
Fly Tier: Mark Hoeser

Schnauzer Waker

Hook: Mustad 9672, #2 - #10
Thread: DaiRiki 5x tippet material, wound on a spool
Tail: Zonker strip, tied hide side up
Rib: Tippet material
Under Body: Yarn, tied larger toward the front of the hook
Body: Stacked antelope hair, tied tips at the tail and butt end at the front
Coating: Black or clear silicone, trim the lip after drying
Flanks: Zonker strip, color of choice, attached at the eye and pulled tight to tie at the tail base
Head: Tippet material used as thread
Fly Tier: Harry Smith

Skipper Palmer

Hook: Mustad 90240, #4 - #10
Thread: Lime
Tail: Fox squirrel tail fibers
Body: Lime dubbing
Wing: Squirrel tail fibers, divided and tilted slightly forward
Hackle: Grizzly, palmered over the body and standard dry fly collar at the front
Head: Thread
Fly Tier: Al Beatty

Skipper Royal

Hook: Partridge CS10/1, #6 - #12
Thread: Red
Tail: Moose body hair
Body: Red floss, elk hump
Wing: White calf tail fibers
Hackle: Brown
Skipper: Tuft of moose body hair, tied like a throat (makes the fly skip on the surface)
Head: Thread
Fly Tier: Al Beatty

Skipping Sculpin

Hook: Partridge CS10/1, #2 - #4
Thread: Tan
Rib: Oval gold tinsel
Body: Tan Brazilian Velour
Wing: Ginger Whiting American hen cape feathers, tied matuka style
Fins: Two small ginger American hen cape feathers
Head and collar: Spun and trimmed deer hair
Fly Tier: Al Beatty

Squirrel Stimi

Hook: Mustad 90240, #4 - #14
Thread: Lime or color to match the body
Tail: Fox squirrel tail fibers, tied short
Body: Lime dubbing
Wing: Squirrel tail, tied trude style even with the end of the tail
Hackle: Grizzly, palmered
Head: Orange dubbing, thread
Fly Tier: Al Beatty

Swallow

Hook: Partridge Single Wilson, #6
Thread: Black
Tail: Moose body hair, divided
Body: Moose hair remaining from the tail
Wing: Deer hair, the end forms the back part of the head
Over Wing: Moose hair over the deer
Head: Spun and trimmed deer hair and trimmed moose, waker style
Fly Tier: Eric Pettine

Waker Wulff

Hook: Partridge CS10/1, #2 - #10
Thread: Red
Tail: Moose body hair
Body: Red floss
Wing: Calf tail fibers, divided and tilted forward
Hackle: Two clumps of stacked deer hair, spun in front and behind the wing
Head: Thread
Fly Tier: Al Beatty

Whipped Cream & Jello

Hook: Mustad 90240 #6 - #12
Thread: Lime or the color of your favorite Jello flavor
Tail: Moose body hair
Body: Thread, coated with Aqua Flex
Wing: Moose body hair, divided
Hackle: Creamy white
Head: Thread
Fly Tier: Al Beatty

Yellow Hammer

Hook: Mustad 80050BR, #8 - #16
Thread: Yellow
Tail: Amber antron yarn loop
Body: Grizzly dyed yellow, tightly wrapped and trimmed to shape
Wing: Deer hair, dyed yellow
Hackle: Dyed yellow
Head: Thread
Fly Tier: Tom Logan

Yellow Split Wing

Hook: Mustad 36890, #2 **Thread:** Black
Tail: Dyed yellow goose biots
Rib: Thread, tied in segments
Body: Black and yellow closed cell foam, epoxy together and trim to shape
Shaping the Body: Segment an extended body on a needle, then remove and tie it on the hook
Thorax: Yellow Seal-Ex
Wing: Dyed yellow squirrel, divided
Antenna: Dyed yellow goose biots
Head: Thread coated with epoxy
Fly Tier: David Hunter

Wet, Hair-Wing, Feather-Wing, and Full Dress . . .

Afognak Patriot (DB)

Hook: Mustad 3665A, #1 - #2
Thread: Black
Rib: Gold wire
Body: Gold sparkle braid
Wing: Blue over white Fishair
Throat: Red buck tail
Head: Thread coated with epoxy
Fly Tier: Bruce Staples

Annette

Hook: Partridge CS10/1, #2 **Thread:** Black
Tail: Golden pheasant crest feather, followed by silver oval tinsel
Butt: Black ostrich herl, wrapped **Rib:** Silver oval tinsel
Body: Claret Seal-EX
Spey Hackle: Blue eared pheasant, guinea
Wing: Bronze mallard feather
Topping: Black hen saddle feather, coated with head cement
Eyes: Jungle cock
Head: Thread
Fly Tier: Eric Pettine

Autumn Sunset

Hook: Daiichi 2052, #4 - #10   **Thread:** Orange
Tip: Oval gold tinsel
Tag: Orange floss
Tail: Golden pheasant crest feather, dyed orange
Rib: Oval gold tinsel
Body: Back one-third is red floss, the front two-thirds is red/orange mixed Seal-Ex
Wing: Red over orange poplar bear substitute
Hackle: Orange hackle, tied as a throat
Cheeks: Jungle cock nails
Head: Thread
Fly Tier: Gary Grant

Baby Cutthroat

Hook: Gamakatsu T10-6H, #1/0 **Thread:** Black
Tag: Fine silver tinsel
Tail: Teal fibers
Rib: Medium oval silver tinsel
Body: Silver diamond braid
Wing: Blue yak over yellow over white kid goat
Topping: Peacock herl, bronzed
Hackle: Dyed red hen hackle fiber, tied as a throat
Cheeks: Silver pheasant on each side under jungle cock nails
Head: Thread
Fly Tier: David Hunter

Belushi

Hook: Alec Jackson Bronze, #3 **Thread:** Tan
Tag: Fine, gold oval tinsel **Tail:** Golden pheasant red body feather, over dyed hot orange
Rib: Oval gold tinsel, counter wrapped
Body: Rear one-third is light orange and the front two-thirds is burgundy dubbing
Wing: Several strands of black Flashabou with two bronze mallard strips
Hackle: Blue eared pheasant, palmered over the front two-thirds of the body
Throat: Wood duck flank **Head:** Thread
Fly Tier: Jon Harrang

Black and Blue Spey

Hook: TMC 7999, #3/0 - #6
Thread: Black
Rib: Silver oval tinsel
Body: First one-half is gold embossed tinsel; the second one-half is black yarn
Hackle: Blue ear pheasant, palmered as a spey body hackle
Hackle: Dyed blue mallard flank over a blue peacock breast feather, tied as a collar
Head: Thread
Fly Tier: John Newbury

Black Dog

Hook: Partridge D7A, #2 **Thread:** Black **Tag:** Silver tinsel
Tail: Golden pheasant crest feather topped with red goose shoulder quill section **Butt:** Black ostrich herl, wrapped **Rib:** Yellow silk rib sandwiched by two silver oval tinsel ribs **Body:** Black silk **Throat:** Dyed black blue eared pheasant **First Wing:** Two red/orange hackle tips **Second Wing:** Two jungle cock feathers, tied long enough to reach the end of the tag
Third Wing: Married red and yellow goose shoulder with tail section from an Amherst pheasant
Topping: Golden pheasant crest feather **Head:** Thread
Fly Tier: David Barlow

Black Eagle

Hook: Partridge Code N, #1
Thread: Black
Rib: Gold and silver oval tinsel
Body: Back one-third is flat silver tinsel, the front two-thirds is black Seal-Ex
Wing: Amherst pheasant tail fibers, tied Dee wing style
Hackle: Black marabou, tied as a collar
Throat: Gadwall with a jungle cock drooping
Head: Thread
Fly Tier: Gary Grant

Black Ghost Variation

Hook: Daiichi 2340, #4 - #8
Thread: Black
Tail: Two golden pheasant crest feathers
Rib: Gold tinsel
Body: Black floss
Wing: Peacock herls, four white hackle feathers, & jungle cock
Hackle: Two yellow hackle feathers, tied as a collar
Head: Thread
Fly Tier: Gary Grant

Black Highland

Hook: Mustad 36890, #1
Thread: Red
Wing and Throat: Black marabou and green Krystal Flash, tied staggered on the top and bottom
Hackle: Yellow, tied as a collar over green Flashabou flanking
Head: Thread
Fly Tier: Bill Chandler

Black Hole

Hook: Mustad 36890, #1
Thread: Black
Tail: Black marabou, tied short
Rib: Oval gold tinsel
Body: Black wool yarn
Wing: Black over fluorescent green over black marabou, green Krystal Flash accent
Throat: Black marabou
Head: Thread
Fly Tier: Bill Chandler

Black Skunk

Hook: Partridge CS10/1, #4 - #12
Thread: Black
Tag: Oval silver tinsel
Tail: Black hackle fibers
Butt: Lime floss
Rib: Oval silver tinsel
Body: Black yarn
Wing: Black bear hair
Hackle: Dyed black, tied as a throat
Head: Thread
Fly Tier: Al Beatty

Black Spey

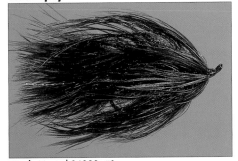

Hook: Mustad 36890, #1
Thread: Black
Tail: Black marabou with Krystal Flash
Body: Black Body Basic, coarse
Hackle: Black saddle, tied as a palmered spey
Head: Thread
Fly Tier: Dustin Harris

Blue Charm

Hook: Alec Jackson Spey, #3 - #7
Thread: Black
Tag: Oval silver tinsel and yellow floss
Tail: Golden pheasant crest feather
Butt: Black ostrich herl
Rib: Oval silver tinsel
Body: Black floss
Wing: Teal over matched turkey quill sections
Hackle: Blue, tied as a soft collar
Topping: Golden pheasant crest feather, tied to meet the tail
Head: Thread
Fly Tier: Larry Nicholas

Blue Fox

Hook: Partridge CS10/1, #6 - #12
Thread: Red
Tag: Thread
Rib: Fine gold wire
Body: Fine chamois strip, wrapped
Wing: Fox squirrel tail hair
Hackle: Dyed kingfisher blue, tied as a collar
Head: Thread
Fly Tier: Al Beatty

Blue Raven

Hook: Daiichi 2340, #4 - #8
Thread: Black
Tag: Silver tinsel
Rib: Silver tinsel
Body: Blue floss
Under Wing: Pink buck tail and a golden pheasant crest feather
Wing: Peacock herls, golden pheasant crest feather, & four grizzly feathers dyed blue
Shoulders: Wood duck under jungle cock
Head: Thread
Fly Tier: Gary Grant

Bridgette's Prince

Hook: Daiichi 2052, #4 - #10
Thread: Black
Tail: Golden pheasant crest feather
Rib: Gold oval tinsel over the front two-thirds of the body
Body: Back one-third is yellow floss, the front two-thirds is blue Seal-Ex
Wing: Polar bear substitute, flanked by blue turkey over Amherst pheasant tail fibers
Hackle: Kingfisher blue hackle, tied as a collar
Cheeks: Jungle cock nails
Head: Thread
Fly Tier: Gary Grant

Bright Black

Hook: Partridge CS10/1, #4 - #12
Thread: Black
Tail: Red hackle fibers
Butt: Marabou strand wrapped like ostrich, black
Body: Black/gold mixed mylar tubing
Wing: White mountain goat hair
Throat: Natural badger guards hairs
Head: Thread
Fly Tier: John Schaper

Bright Copper

Hook: Partridge CS10/1, #4 - #12
Thread: Black
Body: Copper mylar braid tubing
Wing: Orange badger fur under orange badger guards hairs
Throat: Orange badger fur
Head: Thread
Fly Tier: John Schaper

Bright Fuschia

Hook: Partridge CS10/1, #4 - #12
Thread: Black
Tail: Golden pheasant crest feather
Butt: Marabou strand wrapped like ostrich, fuschia
Body: Fuschia mylar braid tubing
Wing: Fuschia dyed badger fur under fuschia dyed badger guards hairs
Throat: Fuschia dyed badger fur
Head: Thread
Fly Tier: John Schaper

Bright Gold

Hook: Partridge CS10/1, #4 - #12
Thread: Black
Tail: Golden pheasant crest feather
Butt: Marabou strand wrapped like ostrich, black
Body: Gold mylar braid tubing
Wing: Orange dyed badger fur under orange dyed badger guard hairs
Throat: Orange dyed badger guard hairs
Head: Thread
Fly Tier: John Schaper

Bright Red

Hook: Partridge CS10/1, #4 - #12
Thread: Black
Tail: Golden pheasant crest feather-
Butt: Thread
Body: Red mylar braid tubing
Wing: Blue dyed badger fur under blue dyed badger guard hairs
Throat: Blue dyed badger fur
Head: Thread
Fly Tier: John Schaper

Brindle Bug

Hook: Mustad 36830, #4 - #10
Thread: Black
Tag: Copper wire
Tail: Brown hackle fibers
Rib: Copper wire
Body: Variegated chenille, black/yellow or brown/yellow
Hackle: Brown, tied as a collar
Head: Thread
Fly Tier: Kent Bulfinch

Burning Bright

Hook: Partridge N, #2
Thread: Hot pink
Tail: Pink Krystal Flash
Body: Yellow ice chenille
Wing: Pink calf tail
Hackle: Hot pink saddle hackle, tied as a collar
Head: Thread
Fly Tier: Tom Broderidge

Cascade Queen

Hook: Mustad 36890, #2 - #4
Thread: Black
Tail: Peacock sword herls, tied short
Body tuft: Peacock sword herls, tied short
Body: White chenille
Wing: One Amherst tippet feather
Hackle: Pale blue dun, tied as a collar
Head: Thread
Fly Tier: Cliff Stringer

CDC Steelhead Fly

Hook: Partridge CS10/2, #2 - #8
Thread: Black
Tail: Clump of spotted Guinea Fowl barbs
Body: Silver Diamond Braid
Body veiling: Purple dyed CDC
Hackle: Spotted Guinea Fowl
Head: Thread
Fly Tier: Marvin Nolte

Cerise Eagle

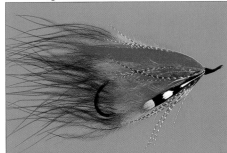

Hook: Partridge Code N, #1
Thread: Black
Rib: Gold and silver oval tinsel
Body: Back one-third is flat silver tinsel, the front two-thirds is cerise Seal-Ex
Wing: Cerise turkey tail fibers, tied Dee wing style
Hackle: Double dyed marabou, cerise center with black tips, tied as a collar
Throat: Gadwall with a jungle cock drooping
Head: Thread
Fly Tier: Gary Grant

Char & Dolly Fly

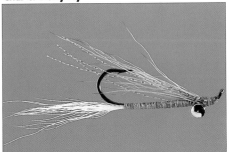

Hook: Mustad 9672, #4
Thread: Gray
Tail: White buck tail, twenty hairs
Body: Tying thread, gray
Wing: Gray buck tail, twenty hairs & four strands of Krystal Flash
Eyes: Silver dumb bell, one-eight of an inch
Head: Thread
Fly Tier: Howard Patterson

Chartreuse Flash Fly

Hook: Gamakatsu T10-6H, #4 - #10
Thread: Chartreuse
Tail: Chartreuse Flashabou
Body: Silver diamond braid
Weight: Non-lead wire, optional
Wing: Chartreuse Flashabou
Hackle: White dyed chartreuse, tied as a collar
Head: Thread
Fly Tier: Ilene Hirsh

Chickabou Rainlander

Hook: Mustad 80500BL, #2
Thread: Black
Tag: Flat gold tinsel a
Butt: Orange floss
Tail: Grizzly dyed orange saddle hackle tips
Rib: Flat gold tinsel
Body: Black chickabou, wrapped
Wing: Grizzly dyed orange saddle hackle tips
Hackle: Orange Chickabou, palmered
Collar: Black Chickabou
Head: Thread
Fly Tier: Henry Hoffman

Chuckar Smucker

Hook: TMC 7999, #2/0 - #2
Thread: Black
Tag: Gold embossed tinsel
Rib: Gold oval tinsel
Body: Black yarn
Wing: Chuckar breast feather under yellow marabou tips
Topping: Golden pheasant crest feather
Throat: Golden pheasant tippets
Head: Thread
Fly Tier: John Newbury

Claret Eagle

Hook: Partridge Code N, #1
Thread: Black
Rib: Gold and silver oval tinsel
Body: Back one-third is flat silver tinsel, the front two-thirds is claret Seal-Ex
Wing: Claret turkey tail fibers, tied Dee wing style
Hackle: Double dyed marabou, claret with black tips, tied as a collar
Throat: Gadwall with a jungle cock drooping
Head: Thread
Fly Tier: Gary Grant

Copper Head Spey

Hook: Daiichi Bronze, #1/0 - #3
Thread: Red
Tag: Fine copper wire
Body: Copper diamond braid
Spey Hackle: Peacock hackle tip
Hackle: Tragopan pheasant flank feather
Cheeks: Tragopan "eyes" from the back of the skin
Head: Thread
Fly Tier: David Hunter

Copper Herniator

Hook: TMC 200R, #4 - #10
Thread: Black
Rib: Optional oval silver tinsel
Body: Copper Krystal Flash behind a peacock herl thorax
Wing: Four peacock herls under copper Krystal Flash strands
Hackle: Spotted guinea hen, tied as a collar
Head: Thread
Fly Tier: Tim Paxton

Cummings Special

Hook: Alec Jackson Spey, #3 - #7
Thread: Black
Tag: Flat silver tinsel
Tail: Golden pheasant crest feather
Rib: Oval silver tinsel, fine
Body: Two sections, first one-third is yellow floss and second two-thirds is claret wool
Wing: Pine marten guard hairs
Hackle: Claret, tied as a soft collar
Cheeks: Jungle cock, optional
Head: Thread
Fly Tier: Larry Nicholas

Dark Wing Tiger

Hook: Mustad 80500BL, #2 - #8   *Thread:* Black
Tag: Flat gold tinsel
Tail: Golden pheasant crest feather
Butt: Red floss
Body: Yellow chenille
Body Hackle: Furnace, palmered
Under Wing: Two golden pheasant tippet feathers
Over Wing: Two mottle turkey quill sections
Topping: Root beet Krystal Flash, tied long
Hackle: Gray squirrel tail fibers, tied beard style
Head: Peacock herl and thread
Fly Tier: Jack Pangburn

Dave's Deschutes Purple

Hook: Eagle Claw L1197NFS, #2 - #4
Thread: Black
Tail: Red hackle fibers
Rib: Flat silver tinsel
Body: Purple chenille
Wing: White calf tail
Head: Thread
Fly Tier: Cliff Stringer

Dave's Orange & White

Hook: Mustad 36890, #4 - #6
Thread: Black
Tail: Mixed orange and white calf tail
Rib: Fine oval tinsel, gold
Body: Orange and black floss
Wing: Orange over white calf tail
Hackle: Black, tied as a throat
Head: Thread
Fly Tier: Cliff Stringer

D.H. Spey

Hook: Alec Jackson gold, #2
Thread: Red
Rib: Two ribs, fine oval silver tinsel and flat silver tinsel
Body: Pink rabbit dubbing
Wing: Teal dyed fluorescent pink, set high
Spey Hackle: Blue eared pheasant
Hackle: Dyed orange, tied as a collar
Head: Thread
Fly Tier: Bill Chandler

Dutot's Blue Charm

Hook: Atlantic salmon wet, #2 - #8
Thread: Black
Tag: Flat silver tinsel
Rib: Flat silver tinsel
Body: Black chenille or dubbing
Wing: Krystal Flash under squirrel tail, dyed dark red
Hackle: Teal blue, tied as a collar
Head: Thread
Fly Tier: Farrow Allen

Dun Raven

Hook: Daiichi 2340, #4 - #8
Thread: Black
Tag: Silver tinsel
Rib: Silver tinsel
Body: Black floss
Under Wing: White buck tail & golden pheasant crest feather
Wing: Peacock herls, golden pheasant crest feather, two black under four gray hackle feathers
Shoulders: Teal under jungle cock
Hackle: Black under red, tied as a throat
Head: Thread
Fly Tier: Gary Grant

Electric Skunk

Hook: Mustad 36890, #2 - #12
Thread: Black
Body: Fluorescent green Edge Bright and black dubbing
Wing: White fox tail with four strands of pearl Krystal Flash
Hackle: Black hen, tied as a collar
Head: Thread
Fly Tier: Roger Swengel

Espresso and Mint

Hook: Mustad 36890, #1
Thread: Red
Spey Hackle: Green Flashabou under fluorescent green marabou, tied as a spey collar
Hackle: Black, tied as a collar
Head: Thread
Fly Tier: Bill Chandler

Fallen Angel

Hook: Daiichi 2052, #4 - #10   **Thread:** Claret
Tail: Two golden pheasant crest feather, natural under dyed purple
Rib: Silver and gold oval tinsel over the front two-thirds of the body   **Body:** Back one-third is purple floss, the front two-thirds is black floss
Wing: Black bear over polar bear substitute, flanked by purple turkey over Amherst pheasant tail
Cheeks: Jungle cock nails
Hackle: Purple under black hackle, tied as a collar
Head: Thread
Fly Tier: Gary Grant

Fish Fry

Hook: Mustad 90240, #2 - #10
Thread: Pink
Tail: Black Flashabou, trimmed various lengths
Hackle: Ginger and white Chickabou, tied as a collar behind the head
Head: Pink and pearl crystal chenille
Eyes: EZY Eyes, tied in the middle of the body
Fly Tier: Al Beatty

Flame Fly

Hook: TMC 7989, #2 - #10
Thread: Red
Body: Flat, gold tinsel
Wing: Orange over yellow yarn, combed out
Throat: Red yarn, combed out
Head: Thread and ruby, red glass bead
Fly Tier: Lee Clark

Floodtide

Hook: Partridge D7A, #2   **Thread:** Black
Tail: Golden pheasant crest feather topped with a barred wood duck section
Butt: Black ostrich herl, wrapped   **Rib:** Flat silver tinsel
Body: From back; yellow silk, orange seal, and red seal
Throat: Golden pheasant rump feather
First Wing: Jungle cock   **Second Wing:** Married yellow and red goose shoulder with an Amherst tail section
Cheek: Two pair of jungle cock feathers, first pair tied longer than the second
Topping: Golden pheasant crest feather   **Head:** Thread
Fly Tier: David Barlow

Floydian Flip

Hook: Mustad 36890, #4 - #8
Thread: Red
Tail: Goat dyed orange
Rib: Copper wire
Body: Copper, flat tinsel
Wing: Gray squirrel tail over yellow dyed goat over pearlescent Krystal Flash
Hackle: Hen body feather, tied as a collar
Head: Thread
Fly Tier: Floyd Franke

Freight Train

Hook: Alec Jackson Spey, #3 - #7
Thread: Black
Tag: Flat silver tinsel
Tail: Purple hackle fibers
Rib: Oval silver tinsel, fine
Body: In three segments, orange then red stretch floss followed by fine black chenille
Wing: White Arctic fox guard hairs over blue calf tail
Hackle: Purple, tied as a soft collar
Head: Thread
Fly Tier: Larry Nicholas

Golden Demon

Hook: Alec Jackson Spey, #3 - #7
Thread: Black
Tag: Flat gold tinsel
Tail: Golden pheasant crest feather
Rib: Oval gold tinsel
Body: Flat silver tinsel
Wing: Bronze mallard
Hackle: Orange, tied as a soft collar
Cheeks: Jungle cock, optional
Head: Thread
Fly Tier: Larry Nicholas

Golden Girl

Hook: TMC 7999, #2/0 - #2
Thread: Black
Body: Gold diamond braid
Wing: Golden pheasant tippets
Topping: Yellow marabou tips
Throat: Golden pheasant tippets
Head: Thread
Fly Tier: John Newbury

Gray Ghost

Hook: Mustad 80500, #2 - #6
Thread: Black
Tag: Flat silver tinsel
Rib: Flat silver tinsel
Body: Orange floss
Wing: Four gray saddle hackles
Throat: Peacock herl and sparse white buck tail
Shoulder: Silver pheasant body feather
Cheek: Jungle cock nails
Head: Thread
Fly Tier: Jack Pangburn

Green & Gold

Hook: Alec Jackson black, #3
Thread: Black
Rib: Small, oval gold tinsel, counter wrapped
Body: Rear one-third is apple green floss and the front two-thirds is gold flat tinsel
Wing: Bronze mallard strips
Hackle: Blue eared pheasant, palmered over the front one-third of the body
Throat: Golden pheasant red color body feather
Head: Thread
Fly Tier: Jon Harrang

Green Butt Skunk

Hook: Alec Jackson Spey, #3 - #7
Thread: Black
Tag: Flat silver tinsel
Tail: Red hackle fibers
Rib: Oval silver tinsel, fine
Body: Black wool
Wing: White Arctic fox guard hairs
Hackle: Black, tied as a soft collar
Cheeks: Jungle cock, optional
Head: Thread
Fly Tier: Larry Nicholas

Green Butt Spider

Hook: Mustad 36890 (single) or 3582F, #4 - #10
Thread: Black
Tag: Fluorescent green Uni-Floss
Tail: Pearlescent Krystal Flash
Rib: Fine, silver oval tinsel
Body: Black wool
Hackle: Guinea body feather, tied as a collar
Head: Thread
Fly Tier: Floyd Franke

Green Rat

Hook: Atlantic salmon wet, #8 - #12
Thread: Chartreuse
Tag: Flat pearl Mylar tinsel or Flashabou
Tail: Peacock sword herls
Rib: Fine oval gold tinsel
Body: Fluorescent green floss behind peacock herl
Wing: Gray fox guard hairs
Hackle: Grizzly hen, tied as a collar
Head: Thread
Fly Tier: Farrow Allen

Halloween Matuka

Hook: Partridge CS10/1, #4
Thread: Black
Rib: Fine gold tinsel
Body: Black dubbing or chenille
Wing: Pair of orange hackle feathers, tied matuka style
Hackle: Orange, tied as a collar
Head: Thread
Fly Tier: Deke Meyer

Home Run

Hook: Daiichi 2151, #1 - #2
Thread: Hot pink
Tag: Flat, silver tinsel
Tail: Pink Krystal Flash
Body: Dubbing, rear two-thirds is fluorescent pink and the front one-third is orange Brite Blend
Wing: Hot orange Krystal Flash
Hackle: Hot pink hen hackle, tied as a collar
Head: Thread
Fly Tier: Rich Youngers

Hot Belly Bugger

Hook: Mustad 36890
Thread: Black
Tail: Black Chickabou with four strands of peacock Krystal Flash:
Body: Peacock herl with a pumpkin button yarn belly
Hackle: Grizzly, tied palmer style
Head: Thread
Fly Tier: Len Holt

Jock Scott (Hair Wing)

Hook: Gamakatsu T10-6H, #1/0   **Thread:** Black
Tip: Flat silver tinsel   **Tag:** Yellow floss
Tail: Golden pheasant crest with fluorescent orange veiling
Butt and body butt: Black ostrich herl, wrapped with a strand of small tinsel for strength   **Rib:** Small oval silver tinsel (rear) and medium oval silver tinsel (front)
Body: Yellow floss (rear) and black floss (front), yellow floss veiling (rear)   **Body Hackle:** Black saddle hackle, palmered over the front half of the body   **Wing:** Blue yak over red over yellow kid goat hair   **Hackle:** Natural guinea, tied as a throat   **Topping:** Golden pheasant crest feather   **Cheeks:** Jungle cock on each side veiled with a strand of blue floss   **Head:** Thread
Fly Tier: David Hunter

Jungled Skunk

Hook: Daiichi 2052, #4 - #10
Thread: Claret
Tail: Golden pheasant crest feather, dyed red
Rib: Silver oval tinsel over the front two-thirds of the body
Body: Back one-third is green floss, the front two-thirds is black Seal-Ex
Under Wings: Jungle cock, tied back to back
Wing: Polar bear substitute
Hackle: Claret and black hackle mixed, tied as a collar
Cheeks: Jungle cock nails
Head: Thread
Fly Tier: Gary Grant

Kennedy Red Ant

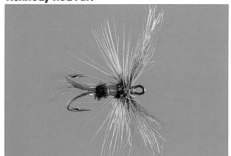

Hook: Partridge "P," #6 - #10
Thread: Black
Tag: Silver tinsel
Tail: Red hackle fibers
Rib: Fine silver wire
Body: Peacock & red floss
Wing: Brown buck tail, divided
Hackle: Brown, over sized & sparse
Head: Thread
Fly Tier: Kent Bulfinch

Klamath Bee

Hook: Mustad 36830, #4 - #10
Thread: Yellow
Tail: Brown hackle fibers
Body: Peacock herl & yellow chenille
Wing: Guinea hen
Hackle: Brown, tied sparse
Head: Thread
Fly Tier: Kent Bulfinch

Krystal Bear

Hook: Mustad 80500BL, #2 - #6
Thread: Black
Tag: Flat gold tinsel and green floss
Butt: Red floss
Rib: Flat gold tinsel
Body: Black chenille
Wing: Gray squirrel tail fibers under root beer Krystal Flash
Hackle: Brown, tied as a collar
Head: Thread
Fly Tier: Jack Pangburn

Lily

Hook: Bartleet Blind Eye, #1/0
Thread: Black
Rib: Flat and oval gold tinsel, wrapped in opposite directions
Body: Orange silk
Wing: Red and orange goose should, bronze mallard over the top
Hackle: Teal flank, tied as a beard
Head: Thread
Fly Tier: David Barlow

Lime Squeeze

Hook: TMC 7999, #2/0 - #2
Thread: Olive
Tail: Peacock swords herls
Body: Lime diamond braid
Hackle: Lime, tied as a collar
Head: Thread
Fly Tier: John Newbury

Little Sunrise

Hook: Partridge CS10/1, #2/0 - #6
Thread: Red
Tag: Copper wire
Body: Pink and orange yarn, braided
Wing: Orange Krystal Flash over a tuft of orange rabbit fur
Hackle: Red guinea over red and orange Chickabou, tied as a collar
Head: Thread
Fly Tier: Gretchen Beatty

Madison Sunrise

Hook: Partridge Ken Baker Streamer, #4 - #8
Thread: Black
Tail: Two golden pheasant crest feathers, dyed red
Body: Silver tinsel
Wing: Two yellow under two red hackle feathers
Shoulders: Amherst pheasant tail, dyed red
Hackle: One red and one yellow hackle feathers, tied as a collar
Head: Thread
Fly Tier: Gary Grant

Marabou Darter

Hook: Mustad 36890, #2 - #10
Thread: Black
Tail: Red hackle fibers
Rib: Fine copper wire, optional
Body: Variegated chenille, colors of choice
Wing: Peacock topping over dun marabou over pearl Krystal Flash
Head: Thread
Fly Tier: Kieran Frye

Max Canyon

Hook: Alec Jackson Spey, #3 - #7
Thread: Black
Tag: Flat gold tinsel
Tail: Orange hackle fibers
Rib: Oval gold tinsel, fine
Body: One-third orange wool and the front two-thirds is black wool
Wing: Orange white Arctic fox guard hairs
Hackle: Black, tied as a soft collar
Cheeks: Jungle cock, optional
Head: Thread
Fly Tier: Larry Nicholas

Meyer's Green Butt Skunk Spey

Hook: TMC 7999, #2 - #4
Thread: Black
Tail: Red hackle fibers accented with several strand of Krystal Flash
Butt: Fluorescent chartreuse chenille
Rib: Fine oval tinsel
Body: Black chenille or dubbing
Wing: White hackle tips
Hackle: Deke's Spey Hackle behind dark guinea
Head: Thread
Fly Tier: Deke Meyer

Mink Bunny

Hook: Mustad 80500BL, #4
Thread: Red
Tail: Zonker strip of bleached mink
Body & Wing: Zonker strip wrapped, stroked up & down, trimmed on the bottom
Head: Thread
Fly Tier: Mel Krieger

Mixed Drink

Hook: Mustad 36890, #1/0
Thread: Red
Wing: Fluorescent green marabou mixed with silver Flashabou accent
Topping: Pink marabou
Under Hackle: Orange marabou, tied spey style
Hackle: Black schlappen, tied as a collar
Head: Thread
Fly Tier: Bill Chandler

Moody Blue

Hook: Mustad 80500BL, #2 - #8
Thread: Black
Tag: Blue floss
Rib: Silver oval tinsel
Body: Black floss (back one-half) and blue SLF dubbing (front one-half)
Hackle: Blue and purple mixed, tied as a collar
Head: Thread
Fly Tier: Jack Pangburn

Nick's Night Mare

Hook: Alec Jackson Spey, #3 - #7
Thread: Black
Body: Flat gold tinsel
Thorax: Orange ram's wool dubbing
Wing: Black Arctic fox guard hairs over five strands of peacock Krystal Flash
Hackle: Purple, tied as a soft collar
Head: Thread
Fly Tier: Larry Nicholas

Nicole's Fancy

Hook: Daiichi 2052, #4 - #10
Thread: Black
Tail: Golden pheasant crest feather
Rib: Gold oval tinsel over the front two-thirds of the body
Body: Back one-third is yellow floss, the front two-thirds is cerise Seal-Ex
Wing: Poplar bear substitute, flanked by cerise turkey over Amherst pheasant tail fibers
Hackle: Cerise hackle, tied as a collar
Cheeks: Jungle cock nails
Head: Thread
Fly Tier: Gary Grant

Night Dancer

Hook: Alec Jackson Spey, #3 - #7
Thread: Black
Tag: Fine oval tinsel and red floss
Tail: Red hackle fibers
Rib: Flat silver tinsel, fine
Body: Black floss
Wing: Black Arctic fox guard hairs
Hackle: Black, tied as a soft collar
Cheeks: Jungle cock, optional
Head: Thread
Fly Tier: Larry Nicholas

No Name

Hook: Partridge D7A, #2
Thread: Red
Tail: Amherst Golden cross pheasant tail quill section
Butt: Black ostrich herl, wrapped
Rib: Silver oval tinsel
Body: Gold flat tinsel
Wing: Amherst Golden pheasant tail quill sections, a pair, flanked by two jungle cock feathers
Hackle: Badger, tied as a collar
Head: Thread
Fly Tier: David Barlow

October Orange

Hook: Mustad 36890, #4 - #8
Thread: Orange
Body: Orange Antron yarn
Wing: Orange Australian opossum fibers flanked by orange Krystal Flash
Hackle: Orange, tied as a collar
Head: Thread
Fly Tier: Robert Meuschke

Old Fashion Silver Ant

Hook: Mustad 3906, #8 - #12
Thread: Black
Butt: Peacock herl
Body: Embossed silver tinsel
Wing: Gray squirrel, divided & swept back
Hackle: Brown, tied sparse
Head: Thread
Fly Tier: Kent Bulfinch

O-N-B

Hook: TMC 7999, #2/0 - #2
Thread: Black
Tag: Gold embossed tinsel
Rib: Gold oval tinsel
Body: Black yarn
Throat: Golden pheasant tippets
Wing: Wood duck
Topping: Orange marabou tips
Head: Thread
Fly Tier: John Newbury

Orange Blossom

Hook: Alec Jackson Spey, #3 - #7   **Thread:** Black
Tag: Oval silver tinsel and orange floss
Tail: Golden pheasant crest topped with Red Bishop (Indian Crow substitute)
Rib: Oval silver tinsel
Body: Embossed silver tinsel
Body Hackle: Yellow, palmered
Wing: Pine marten guard hairs
Hackle: Orange, tied as a soft collar
Cheeks: Jungle cock, optional
Head: Thread
Fly Tier: Larry Nicholas

Orange Eagle

Hook: Partridge Code N, #1
Thread: Black
Rib: Gold and silver oval tinsel
Body: Back one-third is flat silver tinsel, the front two-thirds is orange Seal-Ex
Wing: Orange turkey tail fibers, tied Dee wing style
Hackle: Double dyed marabou, orange center with black tips, tied as a collar
Throat: Gadwall with a jungle cock drooping
Head: Thread
Fly Tier: Gary Grant

Orange Heron (Spey)

Hook: Gamakatsu T10-6H, #1/0
Thread: Orange
Tag: Small flat gold tinsel
Rib: Small flat gold tinsel
Body: Fluorescent orange floss (rear two thirds) and orange Seal-Ex (front one third)
Wing: Four fluorescent orange hackle feathers
Spey Hackle: Blue ear pheasant, palmered over the front body dubbing
Hackle: Light teal, tied as a throat
Head: Thread
Fly Tier: David Hunter

Orange Spey

Hook: TMC 7999, #3/0 - #6
Thread: Red
Rib: Gold oval tinsel
Body: First one-half is gold embossed tinsel; the second is orange yarn
Hackle: Amherst side tail, palmered as a spey body hackle
Hackle collar: Red over claret hackle, tied as an under collar
Hackle collar, top: Mallard flank dyed red, tied as an over collar
Head: Thread
Fly Tier: John Newbury

Orange Sunset Matuka

Hook: Partridge CS10/1, #2 - #8
Thread: Black
Tag: Small, silver oval tinsel
Rib: Small, silver oval tinsel
Body: Rear one-fourth is red floss and the front three-fourths is red angora goat dubbing
Wing: Two red hackle feathers under two yellow, tied matuka style
Hackle: Yellow and red, tied as a mixed color collar
Cheeks: Jungle cock nails
Head: Thread
Fly Tier: Mark Hoeser

Patricia

Hook: Alec Jackson Spey, #3 - #7
Thread: Claret
Tag: Flat silver tinsel
Tail: Claret hackle fibers
Rib: Flat silver tinsel
Body: Claret wool or seal substitute
Wing: White Arctic fox guard hairs or polar bear
Hackle: Claret, tied as a soft collar
Cheeks: Jungle cock, optional
Head: Thread
Fly Tier: Larry Nicholas

Peacock Herniator

Hook: TMC 200R, #4 - #10
Thread: Black
Rib: Optional oval silver tinsel
Body: Peacock Krystal Flash behind a peacock herl thorax
Wing: Four peacock herls under peacock Krystal Flash strands
Hackle: Spotted guinea hen, tied as a collar
Head: Thread
Fly Tier: Tim Paxton

Peacock Spider

Hook: TMC 7999, #2/0 - #2
Thread: Red
Body: Blue diamond braid
Hackle: Two peacock breast feathers, tied as a collar
Head: Thread
Fly Tier: John Newbury

Pete's Puppy

Hook: TMC 9394, #6 - #12
Thread: Black
Body: Flat, silver tinsel
Wing: Pheasant tail fibers, tied very sparse
Collar: Peacock herl
Head: Gold bead and thread
Fly Tier: Ilene Hirsh

Phoenix

Hook: Daiichi 2052, #4 - 310
Thread: Claret
Tail: Peacock sword herls
Rib: Oval silver tinsel over the front two-thirds of the body
Body: Back one-third is claret floss, the front two-thirds is peacock herl
Wing: Peacock body feather fibers over black bear, flanked by scarlet macaw tail fibers
Hackle: Red under claret hackle, tied as a collar
Head: Thread
Fly Tier: Gary Grant

Pink Mambou

Hook: Mustad 36890, #2 - #4
Thread: Red
Tail: Red hackle fibers
Body: Fluorescent pink and black chenille
Wing: Fluorescent pink calf tail hair
Hackle: Red saddle hackle, tied as a collar
Head: Thread
Fly Tier: Cliff Stringer

Purple Eagle

Hook: Partridge Code N, #1
Thread: Black
Rib: Gold and silver oval tinsel
Body: Back one-third is flat silver tinsel, the front two-thirds is purple Seal-Ex
Wing: Purple turkey tail fibers, tied Dee wing style
Hackle: Purple marabou, tied as a collar
Throat: Gadwall with a jungle cock drooping
Head: Thread
Fly Tier: Gary Grant

Purple Flame

Hook: Gamakatsu T10-3H, #2
Thread: Black
Tail: Flame-colored rabbit zonker strip
Body: Tail strip wrapped forward
Wing/Hackle: Purple marabou wrapped with the body material, two extra turns in front
Hackle: Teal flank feather, tied as a sparse collar
Head: Thread
Fly Tier: Jon Harrang

Purple Ghost

Hook: Partridge CS15, #4
Thread: Black
Body: Flat silver tinsel
Under Wing: Several strands of peacock herl
Wing: White sandwiched over purple Whiting Streamer Wings
Throat: Short red hackle fibers over long white over purple buck tail fibers
Cheeks: Jungle cock nail over teal flank feathers, tied to the sides
Head: Thread
Fly Tier: Thomas Leow

Purple Peacock Spey

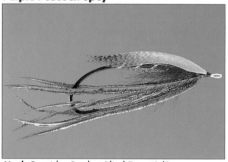

Hook: Partridge Bartleet Blind Eye, #1/0
Thread: Black
Rib: Oval silver tinsel
Body: Purple floss behind purple seal
Wing: Bronze mallard flank feather sections
Hackle: Peacock herl, tied as a beard
Head: Thread
Fly Tier: David Barlow

Purple Peril

Hook: Alec Jackson Spey, #3 - #7
Thread: Black
Tag: Flat silver tinsel
Tail: Purple hackle fibers
Rib: Oval silver tinsel, fine
Body: Purple wool
Wing: Pine marten guard hairs
Hackle: Purple, tied as a soft collar
Cheeks: Jungle cock, optional
Head: Thread
Fly Tier: Larry Nicholas

Purple Syntho

Hook: Mustad 36890, #1/0
Thread: Black
Tail: Purple SLF fibers
Rib: Gold oval tinsel
Body: Purple wool
Wing: Purple over orange over purple SLF fibers over orange Krystal Flash
Throat: Purple SLF fibers
Head: Thread
Fly Tier: Bill Chandler

Purple Tube Fly

Hook: Clear plastic tube, hook of choice
Thread: Black
Body: Embossed silver tinsel
Wing: Purple buck tail, tied sparse in the round
Head: Thread
Fly Tier: Kieran Frye

Rainlander

Hook: Mustad 80500BL, #2
Thread: Black
Tag: Flat gold tinsel
Butt: Orange floss
Tail: Grizzly dyed orange saddle hackle tips
Rib: Flat gold tinsel
Body: Black Chickabou, wrapped
Wing: Grizzly dyed orange saddle hackle tips
Hackle: Orange flank feather, palmered
Collar: Black flank feather
Head: Thread
Fly Tier: Henry Hoffman

Raspberry Flutter

Hook: Mustad 90240, #2 - #10
Thread: Black
Body: Fluorescent pink chenille
Wing: Raspberry Tie Well tinsel
Head: Thread
Fly Tier: Kieran Frye

Red Ant

Hook: Alec Jackson Spey, #3 - #7
Thread: Black
Tag: Flat silver tinsel
Tail: Red hackle fibers
Butt: Peacock herl
Body: Red wool
Wing: Pine marten guard hairs
Hackle: Brown, tied as a soft collar
Cheeks: Jungle cock, optional
Head: Thread
Fly Tier: Larry Nicholas

Red Beard

Hook: Mustad 36890, #2
Thread: Black
Tip: Flat gold tinsel
Tag: Yellow floss
Tail: Golden pheasant crest feather
Butt: Red ostrich herl
Rib: Flat gold tinsel
Body: Yellow floss
Wing: Gray squirrel tail fibers
Hackle: Red saddle hackle fiber, tied as a beard
Head: Thread
Fly Tier: Tom Broderidge

Red Butt Purple Skunk

Hook: TMC 7999, #2/0 - #2
Thread: Red
Tag: Red diamond braid
Body: Purple ice chenille
Wing: Cerise calf tail
Hackle: Purple, tied as a collar
Head: Thread
Fly Tier: John Newbury

Renegade Fox

Hook: Partridge CS10/1, #2 - #8
Thread: Black
Tag: Flat silver tinsel
Rear Hackle: Brown, tied directly in front of the tag
Body: Peacock herl, twisted and wrapped with the thread to improve durability
Wing: Fox squirrel tail fibers
Hackle: White, tied as a collar
Head: Thread
Fly Tier: Al Beatty

Renegade Rat

Hook: Partridge CS10/1, #3/0 - #10
Thread: Black
Tag: Flat silver tinsel
Tag Hackle: Four turns of brown
Rib: Flat silver tinsel
Body: Peacock herl, wrapped
Wing: Gray squirrel tail, tied low
Hackle: White, tied as a collar
Head: Thread
Fly Tier: Al Beatty

Rusty Rat

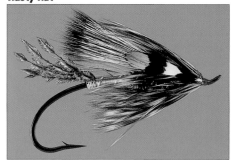

Hook: Alec Jackson Spey, #3 - #7   **Thread:** Red
Tag: Oval gold tinsel
Tail: Peacock sword herls
Rib: Oval gold tinsel
Veil: Rusty orange floss over the rear one third of the body
Body: One-third rusty orange floss behind two-thirds peacock herl, wrapped
Wing: Gray fox guard hairs
Hackle: Grizzly, tied as a soft collar
Cheeks: Jungle cock, optional
Head: Thread
Fly Tier: Larry Nicholas

Salmon River Spey

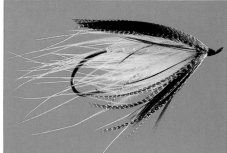

Hook: Partridge CS10/1, #1/0
Thread: Black
Tag: Fine oval silver tinsel
Rib: Medium oval silver tinsel
Body: Bright green floss
Wing: Bronze mallard
Under Hackle: Fluorescent green marabou, tied spey style
Hackle: Black schlappen under green dyed teal, tied as a collar
Head: Thread
Fly Tier: Bill Chandler

Shannan

Hook: Alec Jackson, #1/0
Thread: Black
Tail: Amherst/golden pheasant quill section flanked by slips of red goose shoulder
Rib: One each of flat and oval, silver tinsel
Body: Lavender silk
Wing: White goose shoulder slips flanked by Amherst pheasant
Hackle: Red, tied as a beard
Head: Thread
Fly Tier: David Barlow

Silver Hilton

Hook: Alec Jackson Spey, #3 - #7
Thread: Black
Tag: Flat silver tinsel
Tail: Pin tail fibers
Rib: Oval silver tinsel, fine
Body: Fine black chenille
Wing: Grizzly hackle tips, flared
Hackle: Grizzly, tied as a soft collar
Head: Thread
Fly Tier: Larry Nicholas

Silver Salmon Fly

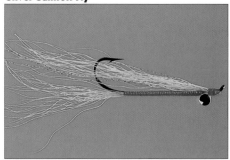

Hook: Mustad 9672, #1
Thread: Pink
Tail: Pink buck tail, twenty fibers
Body: Pink thread
Wing: Pink buck tail, twenty fibers & four strands of Krystal Flash
Eyes: Silver dumb bell, five-thirty seconds of an inch
Head: Thread
Fly Tier: Howard Patterson

Simple Alder Spey

Hook: Partridge CS10/1, #2 - #10
Thread: Black
Tag: Flat gold tinsel
Rib: Oval gold tinsel
Body: Peacock herl, wrapped
Under Wing: Fox squirrel tail fibers
Over Wing: Section of dark turkey tail, folded and tied tent style
Hackle: Blue eared pheasant, tied as a beard
Head: Thread coated with Aqua Flex
Fly Tier: Al Beatty

Skykomish Sunrise

Hook: Alec Jackson Spey, #3 - #7
Thread: Red
Tag: Flat silver tinsel
Tail: Red over yellow hackle fibers
Rib: Oval silver tinsel
Body: Fine red chenille
Wing: White Arctic fox guard hairs
Hackle: Red and yellow, tied as a soft collar
Cheeks: Jungle cock, optional
Head: Thread
Fly Tier: Larry Nicholas

Sockeye Salmon Fly

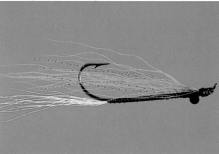

Hook: Mustad 9672, #1
Thread: Dark green
Tail: White buck tail, twenty fibers
Body: Tying thread
Wing: Green buck tail, twenty fibers & four strands of Krystal Flash
Eyes: Black dumb bell
Head: Thread
Fly Tier: Howard Patterson

Sol Duc Spey

Hook: Alec Jackson Spey, #3/0 - #2
Thread: Red
Tag: Flat silver tinsel
Rib: Oval silver tinsel, fine
Body: One-third orange floss behind two-thirds orange Angora goat dubbing, picked out
Wing: Four orange hackle tips, set low
Hackle: Yellow soft hackle, palmered over the front two-thirds of the body
Throat: Blue eared pheasant dyed black
Head: Thread
Fly Tier: Larry Nicholas

Solo's Orange Riffle

Hook: Atlantic salmon wet, #2 - #8
Thread: Black
Tag: Fine oval gold tinsel
Rib: Fine oval gold tinsel
Body: Black floss
Wing: Black bear (two-thirds) under gray squirrel (one-third)
Cheeks: Jungle cock (optional)
Hackle: Orange, tied as a throat
Head: Thread
Fly Tier: Farrow Allen

Sophie

Hook: Bartleet Blind Eye, #1/0   **Thread:** Primrose
Tag: Five turns of small gold tinsel, red floss
Butt: Black ostrich for both locations
Tail: Golden pheasant tippet feather
Rib: Flat and oval gold tinsel, wrapped on the back half of the body   **Body:** Red floss and yellow seal
Under Wing: Jungle cock feathers and nails
Wing: Built, red, yellow goose shoulder, Amherst/golden and bronzed mallard
Topping: Golden pheasant tippet
Hackle: Yellow, tied as a beard   **Head:** Thread
Fly Tier: David Barlow

Steelhead Ant

Hook: Alec Jackson Black, #1/0
Thread: Red
Tag: Small silver tinsel
Tail: Golden pheasant crest feather, dyed red
Butt: Peacock herl twisted with oval silver tinsel and wrapped
Body: Red floss
Wing: Fox squirrel tail hair
Hackle: Tragopan pheasant flank feather
Cheeks: Jungle cock nails, one per side
Head: Thread
Fly Tier: David Hunter

Ta

Hook: Partridge CS10/1, #2 - #10   **Thread:** White
Tip: Fine oval silver tinsel   **Tag:** Pale blue floss
Tail: Two golden pheasant crest feathers
Butt: Red wool
Rib: Medium oval silver tinsel
Body: Wine colored floss
Hackle: Blue, tied as a throat
Under Wing: Golden pheasant tippets, tied in strands
Over Wing: Married quill sections, white under wine goose shoulder under mottle peacock wing
Head: Red wool and red thread
Fly Tier: Ted Patlen

Tiger Paw

Hook: Alec Jackson Spey, #3 - #7
Thread: Black
Tag: Flat copper tinsel
Tail: Black hackle fibers
Rib: Flat copper tinsel
Body: Fine black chenille
Wing: Black Arctic fox guard hairs over five strands of peacock Krystal Flash
Hackle: Black, tied as a soft collar
Cheeks: Jungle cock, optional
Head: Thread
Fly Tier: Larry Nicholas

Tube Sunrise

Hook: Plastic tube, one inch long
Thread: Fluorescent orange
Tag: Oval silver tinsel
Rib: Oval silver tinsel
Body: Fluorescent orange chenille
Wing: White buck tail, tied "in the round"
Hackle: Grizzly dyed red under grizzly dyed yellow, tied as a collar
Head: Fluorescent orange BT's Tube Fly Head
Fly Tier: Al Beatty

U-B

Hook: TMC 7999, #2/0 - #2
Thread: Red
Tail: Peacock sword herls
Under Body: Flat silver tinsel
Body: Hot pink Edge Bright
Hackle: Two peacock breast feathers, tied as a collar
Head: Thread
Fly Tier: John Newbury

U-B #2

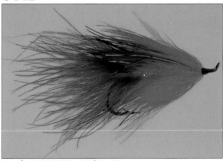

Hook: TMC 7999, #2/0 - #2
Thread: Black
Tail: Purple marabou
Body: Silver diamond braid
Wing: Purple Flashabou under purple marabou
Hackle: Cerise marabou, tied as a long collar
Head: Thread
Fly Tier: John Newbury

Velcro Skunk

Hook: Mustad 36890, #4 - #10
Thread: Black
Tail: Red hackle fibers
Rib: Flat, silver tinsel
Body: Black Velcro strip (non-hook part snags the fish's teeth to aid in hook penetration)
Wing: White buck tail or skunk hair
Hackle: Black, tied as a beard
Head: Thread
Fly Tier: Greg Peterka

Voodoo Bunny

Hook: Mustad 9672, #4 - #8
Thread: Tan
Body: Ginger rabbit zonker strip and orange crystal chenille wrapped together
Weight: Several turns of non-lead wire under the body material, optional
Head: Thread
Fly Tier: Ilene Hirsh

Woven Witch

Hook: Partridge CS10/1, #2 - #6   **Thread:** Black
Tag: Silver wire
Butt: White ostrich (one in the back and one in the middle)
Rib: Silver wire
Back Body: Black and white chenille, woven with the black on the top   **Front Body:** White chenille, wrapped
Under Hackle: White marabou, wrapped in a dubbing loop
Hackle: Natural guinea, tied as a collar
Head: Thread
Fly Tier: Gretchen Beatty

Wrinkles

Hook: Partridge CS10/1, #2 - #10   **Thread:** White
Tip: Fine oval silver tinsel   **Tag:** Yellow floss
Tail: Two golden pheasant crest feathers
Tail topping: Doubled kingfisher, tied flat
Rib: Medium oval silver tinsel
Body: Tied in four equal segments; yellow floss plus yellow, orange, and red mohair dubbing
Body Hackle: Yellow, palmered
Under Wing: Orange hen hackle feathers
Outer lower Wing: Three married quill sections; mottled peacock under yellow then red goose
Outer upper Wing: Three married quill sections; blue goose, mottled turkey, blue goose
Hackle: Bright red hackle, tied as a collar
Head: Black wool over black thread
Fly Tier: Ted Patlen

Yellow Eagle

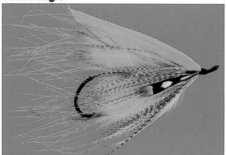

Hook: Partridge Code N, #1
Thread: Black
Rib: Gold and silver oval tinsel
Body: Back one-third is flat silver tinsel, the front two-thirds is yellow Seal-Ex
Wing: Yellow turkey tail fibers, tied Dee wing style
Hackle: Yellow marabou, tied as a collar
Throat: Gadwall with a jungle cock drooping
Head: Thread
Fly Tier: Gary Grant

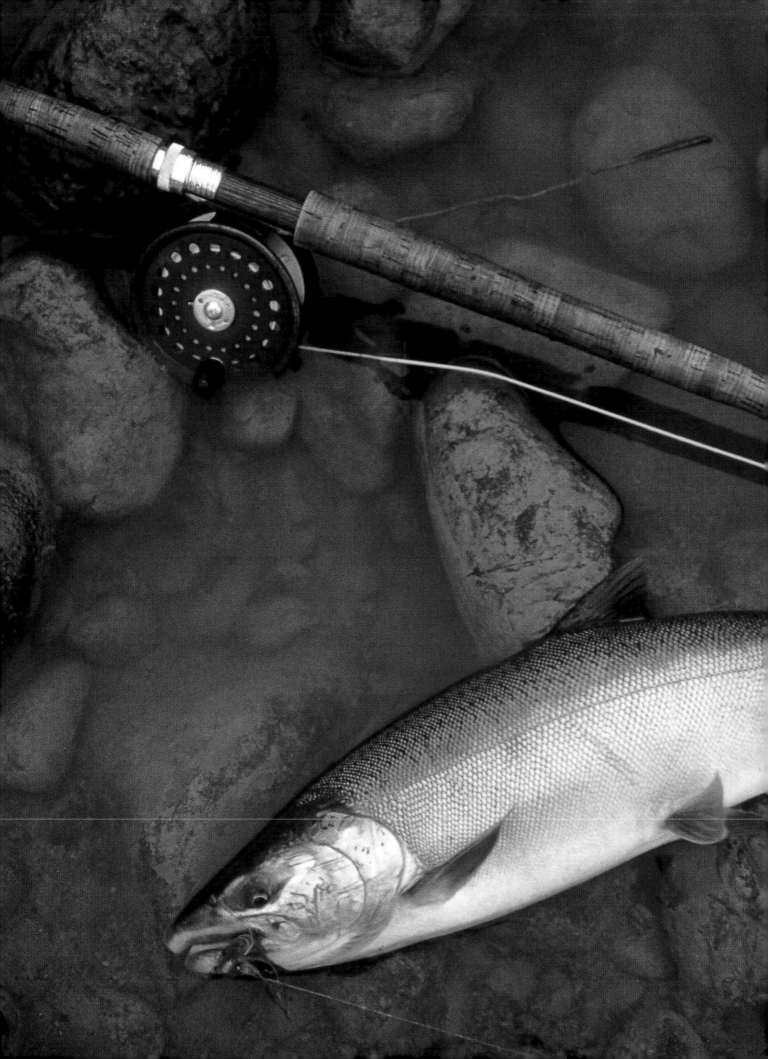

By Tom Broderidge

When I started fly fishing in 1961 it wasn't uncommon to approach warm water with a rather modest fly box. We might have carried a few cork poppers in panfish sizes and a few larger ones for bass. We also had a standard deer-hair bug or two. And then there was the ever-present Woolly Bugger and maybe a couple of feathered or bucktail streamers. With just a few basic flies we happily caught what we thought was our share of fish. How times have changed.

You only have to walk past the rows of fly tiers at any Federation of Fly Fishers Conclave to see that warmwater flies are now addressed as seriously and as imaginatively as flies for finicky salmon or selective trout. At the end of one row you might see a warmwater fly tier creating a chenille fly to which he adds rubber legs, carefully counting 44 — not 43 or 45, but exactly 44. Farther along the row, another tier has a small tank of water in which he demonstrates a minnow-like fly made to sink to a prescribed depth and then stay at that level as it maintains the upright orientation of a real baitfish.

Effective flies must resemble the natural foods they seek to imitate, and they must behave like natural foods as well. To those ends, warmwater tiers are continually investigating any new materials that might prove to be the cornerstone of a productive fly. They are also constantly experimenting with known patterns, varying design parameters such as a fly's balance point, its movement, or its color. In addition, they are always rigorously analyzing the successes of the best flies and the failures of those flies that do not work quite so well.

Warmwater fly boxes today still contain many classic patterns from the past, but those basic poppers, streamers, and deer-hair bugs are being joined by a growing number of new patterns, such as those described on the following pages. These new flies are innovative, well designed, and carefully crafted, and it would not be at all surprising if a few of them even became classic patterns themselves.

—Tom Broderidge
Havana, Florida

Baitfish and Panfish . . .

Angel Hair Perch Fry

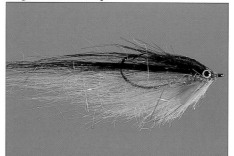

Hook: Keel hook, #2/0 - #1/0
Thread: White
Body/wings: Multiple applications of yellow and chartreuse Bestway Super Hair and Angel Hair
Over wing: Peacock Angle Hair, body/wings and over wing trimmed to shape
Eye: Stick on, white with black pupil
Pectoral fins: Orange hackles, trimmed to shape
Head: Thread
Coating: Aqua Flex or epoxy over the head and eyes
Fly Tier: Ted Patlen

Baby Bass Deep Minnow

Hook: Mustad 3366, #2 - #8 (the hook point rides up)
Thread: Brown
Wing: Brown Arctic fox
Throat: White Arctic fox, accented with green Krystal Flash and Flashabou
Eyes: Dumb bell, painted red with black pupils
Head: Thread
Fly Tier: Brian Shumaker

Baby Bluegill

Hook: TMC 9394, #10
Thread: Black
Tail: Four grizzly dyed olive saddle hackle feathers
Wing: Yellow dyed squirrel tail over yellow over white kit goat hair
Topping: Peacock Krystal Flash
Throat: White under red kid goat hair
Eyes: Stick on, silver with black pupils
Head: Epoxy coating over the thread and eyes
Fly Tier: David Hunter

Baby - S

Hook: Eagle Claw L787, #6
Thread: Clear mono
Under Body: Pearl Comes Alive
Wing: PolaFibre, olive, chartreuse, yellow, shrimp, and pink
Wing markings: Black felt tip marker
Throat: Hot orange PolaFibre
Eyes: Stick on doll eyes, silver with black pupils
Head: Thread
Fly Tier: Jerry Caruso

Barred Spider

Hook: Mustad 3399, #10 - #16
Thread: Black
Tail: Folded slip of barred wood duck feather
Rib: Gold wire
Body: Pale yellow SLF dubbing
Wing: Wood duck flank feather fibers
Hackle: Black hen, tied as a collar
Head: Thread
Fly Tier: Tom Logan

Bass Bunny

Hook: Daiichi 2461, #1/0 **Thread:** Egg shell
Tail: Chartreuse rabbit zonker strip **Rib:** Pearl braid
Weight: Several wraps of non-lead wire
Body: White SLF Dubbing
Wing: Chartreuse rabbit zonker strip, held in place with the rib
Throat: Yellow Lite Brite over olive Flashabou
Collar: Chartreuse and orange mixed deer hair
Head: White, chartreuse, and orange deer hair
Eyes: Three dimensional, orange with black pupils
Weed guard: Hard mono, optional
Fly Tier: Mark Hoeser

Beady Eye

Hook: Mustad 37187, #10
Thread: Fluorescent orange
Tail: Blue marabou, tied short and sparse
Body: Blue crystal chenille
Eyes: Dumb bell with stick on silver eyes with black pupils
Head: Thread
Fly Tier: Tommy Marks

Berry Duster

Hook: Mustad 3366, #1/0
Thread: Green
Body: Static duster fibers mixed with purple dyed deer hair, spun in a dubbing loop and trimmed
Hackle: Green dyed guinea
Head: Thread
Fly Tier: Gretchen Beatty

The Bird Fly

Hook: TMC 8089, #2
Thread: DaiRiki 5x tippet
Under body: Spun and trimmed deer hair
Body: Chickabou or marabou, color of choice
Wing and tail: Saddle hackle, any color
Legs: Rubber leg material
Hanger: Piano wire
Head: Spun and trimmed deer hair
Eyes: Green with black pupils
Application: Cut off the hook point and see how long the fish will hold the fly or return to recapture it
Fly Tier: Harry Smith

Black Baby

Hook: Mustad 3407, #2/0 - #4
Thread: Black
Tail: Two black Whiting American hen cape feathers
Body: Black chenille, tied in three segments separated by three sets of wings
Wings: Three sets of black American hen cape feathers, each set tied delta style
Head: Spun and trimmed deer hair
Fly Tier: Al Beatty

Blonde Stayner

Hook: Mustad 79580, #4 - #6
Thread: Black
Tail: Orange Krystal Flash
Body: Variegated olive/yellow chenille
Wing: Mallard flank dyed wood duck, tied flat on the top of the hook
Throat: Orange marabou
Head: Thread
Fly Tier: Cliff Stringer

Blue Pan Fish Nymph

Hook: Mustad 79580, #6 - #12
Thread: Black
Tail: Blue pheasant breast feather fibers
Rib: Fine copper wire
Body: Natural muskrat dubbing
Hackle: Partridge, tied as a collar
Head: Silver, black, or gold bead
Fly Tier: Hebert Carmen

Bozo

Hook: Mustad 36890, #8 - #12
Thread: Chartreuse
Tail: Natural deer hair, tied short
Body: Yellow deer, spun and trimmed
Wing: Green deer, flared and trimmed
Head: Chartreuse deer, spun and trimmed
Fly Tier: John Schaper

Braided Bream Fly

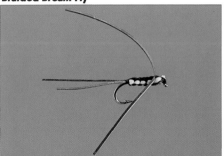

Hook: Mustad 3399, #12
Thread: Black
Tail: Black rubber leg material
Body: Black and yellow embroidery yarn, braided using the over hand knot method
Legs: Black rubber leg material, tied extra long
Head: Thread
Fly Tier: Tom Broderidge

Bully's Bluegill Spider

Hook: Mustad 94840, #10
Thread: Yellow or color to match the body
Body: Yellow chenille or color of choice
Legs: Yellow round rubber legs, four
Head: Thread
Fly Tier: Terry Wilson

Calf Tail Shiner

Hook: Mustad 3407, #1/0 - #8
Thread: White
Tail: Four white saddle hackles accented with pearl Flashabou
Body: Pearl diamond braid
Wing: Peacock over short white calf tail
Throat: Red over white calf tail
Eyes: Doll eyes, yellow with black movable pupils
Head: Thread coated with Aqua Flex
Fly Tier: Al Beatty

Chartreuse Bead Zonker

Hook: Daiichi 1720, #2 - #6
Thread: Chartreuse
Tail: Chartreuse zonker strip remaining from the wing
Body: Chartreuse Lite Brite dubbing
Wing: Chartreuse zonker strip
Thorax: Red Lite Brite behind a gold bead behind chartreuse Lite Brite
Head: Thread
Fly Tier: Bill Black, Spirit River Inc.

Chickatuka (Ginger)

Hook: Mustad 9672, #4 - #10
Thread: Black
Body: Flat, gold tinsel
Wing: Four ginger Soft Hackle feathers, tied divided and matuka style
Hackle: Ginger Chickabou, tied as a collar
Eyes: Gold bead chain
Head: Thread
Fly Tier: Dave Engerbretson

Crappie Bug

Hook: Mustad 3906B, #6 - #10
Thread: White
Tail: White marabou
Body: White crystal chenille
Eyes: Small silver or black dumb bell
Head: Red crystal chenille
Fly Tier: Kevin Cohenour

Crappie Fly

Hook: Mustad 9671, #8 - #12
Thread: Red
Tail: Three strands of peacock herl, trimmed to length
Rib: Oval silver tinsel and a single strand of peacock herl
Body: White Flex Floss
Wing: Grizzly hackle feather tips topped with two peacock herls
Hackle: White, tied as a short collar
Head: Thread
Fly Tier: Dick Steinhorst

Crystal Minnow

Hook: Mustad 9671, #6 - #12
Thread: Green
Tail: Several strands of Lumaflex with a few strands of pearl Flashabou
Body: Chartreuse crystal chenille
Body back: Excess strands from the tail, pulled over
Gills: Fluorescent orange thread
Eyes: Brass bead chain
Head: Thread
Fly Tier: Tommy Marks

Deer Hair Adam's Irresistible

Hook: Dry fly, #12
Thread: Black
Tail: Deer or moose
Body: Spun and trimmed deer hair
Hackle: Dyed brown and natural deer hair in a dubbing loop
Head: Thread
Fly Tier: Doug Christian

Double Sunny Bunny

Hook: Mustad 36890, #2
Thread: Olive
Back: Olive dyed zonker strip, laminate to the belly with contact cement
Belly: Cotton tail (dyed olive) zonker strip, laminated to the back with contact cement
Throat: Orange rabbit fur
Sides: Black prism tape
Eyes: Doll eyes, yellow with black pupils
Head: Thread
Fly Tier: Scott Sanchez

Double Up

Hook: Mustad 33957, #4 (bend to shape, the hook point rides up)
Thread: Clear mono
Tail fly: Peacock herl over brown and white buck tail mixed with gold Krystal Flash
Front fly: Peacock herl over brown and white buck tail mixed with gold Krystal Flash
Eyes: Stick on, yellow with black pupils
Heads: Aqua Flex coating over both heads and the eyes
Fly Tier: Al Beatty

Dun Irresistible

Hook: Mustad 80000, #12 - #18
Thread: Gray
Tail: Pheasant tail fibers
Body: Spun and trimmed deer hair
Hackle: Grizzly and barred ginger, mixed
Head: Thread
Fly Tier: Jack Pangburn

D. W. Special

Hook: Mustad 34011, #2 - #4 (bend back shape)
Thread: Clear nylon
Wing: White under orange poly material, topped with peacock Krystal Flash
Wing sides: Two grizzly feathers under wide holo graphic tinsel
Eyes: Silver stick on with black pupils
Head: Thread
Fly Tier: Tom Berry

Estaz Bug

Hook: Mustad 94840, #6
Thread: White
Tail: White marabou over pearl Comes Alive
Body: White Estaz, trimmed to a grub shape
Head: Thread
Fly Tier: Jerry Caruso

EZY Duster

Hook: Mustad 3366, #1/0
Thread: Pink
Tail: Static duster fibers accented with purple
   Flashabou
Body: Static duster fibers, wrapped
Wing: Static duster fibers accented with purple
   Flashabou
Throat: Static duster fibers accented with purple
   Flashabou
Eyes: EZY Eyes with stick on, gold with black pupils
Head: Thread and Aqua Flex coating
Fly Tier: Gretchen Beatty

Flashabou Minnow

Hook: Mustad 9671, #8 - #12
Thread: Black
Tail: Silver Flashabou
Body: Silver Flashabou, tied in two segments each
   with it's own wing
Wing: Two separate units of Flashabou, one from the
   center and the other from the hook eye
Gills: Several turns of red thread
Head: Thread tied large
Eyes: Painted white with black pupils (optional)
Fly Tier: Dick Steinhorst

Foam Cricket

Hook: TMC 200R, #8 - #14
Thread: Black
Rib: Black hackle trimmed short, palmered
Body: Thread under body and black closed cell foam
   as the over body
Legs: Knotted black hackle feathers
Wing: Ends of the leg feathers
Hackle: Black, tied as a collar
Head: Thread and foam
Fly Tier: Randy Inmon

Foam Damsel

Hook: TMC 200R, #8 - #14
Thread: Black
Rib: Black hackle trimmed short, palmered
Body: Blue closed cell foam
Wing: Thin, white packing foam, cut to shape
Hackle: Black, tied as a collar
Thorax: Blue foam
Head: Thread
Fly Tier: Randy Inmon

Foam Dragon

Hook: TMC 200R, #8 - #14
Thread: Black
Rib: Black hackle trimmed short, palmered
Body: Thread under body and black closed cell foam
   as the over body
Wing: Thin, white packing foam, cut to shape and
   colored with a felt tip marker
Hackle: Black, tied as a sparse collar
Head: Thread and black closed cell foam
Fly Tier: Randy Inmon

Golden Shiner

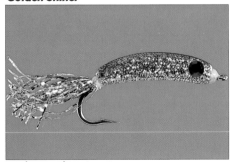

Hook: Mustad 34007, #1
Thread: Yellow
Tail: Gold braided mylar tubing, picked out
Under Body: Closed cell foam, cut to shape
Body: Gold braided mylar tubing, colored with felt tip
   markers
Eyes: Stick on, red with black pupils
Head: Thread
Fly Tier: Tom Broderidge

Green Fuzzy Wuzzy

Hook: Mustad 3906B, #8 - #14
Thread: Black
Tail: Black bear hair
Body: Green chenille, tied in two segments
Hackle: Black tied as two collars, one traditional and
   the other between the two body sections
Head: Thread
Fly Tier: Al Beatty

Grizzly Whistler

Hook: Gamakatsu SC15, #2/0
Thread: Red
Tail: Grizzly hen saddle feathers
Body: Red chenille
Hackle: Grizzly rooster saddle, tied as a collar
Eyes: Gold bead chain or dumb bell
Head: Thread
Fly Tier: Bernard Byng

G. W. Glory

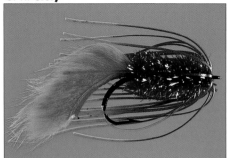

Hook: Mustad 3367, #2
Thread: Black
Tail: Pink zonker strip
Body: Purple ice chenille
Collar: Pink tipped purple Sili-legs
Weed guard: Stiff mono, thirty pound
Head: Thread
Fly Tier: Greg Weisgerber

Ice Spider

Hook: Mustad 94840, #8 - #14
Thread: Black
Tail: Silli-con leg material
Body: Black super fine chenille
Legs: Silli-con leg material
Head: Silver bead
Fly Tier: Paul Maurer

Indicator Shoe Fly

Hook: Mustad 94840, #8 - #12
Thread: Color to match the body
Shell back: Dark closed cell foam strip, tied pull over style
Body: Thin strip of furry foam under peacock herl
Legs: Two pairs of dark rubber legs (black or brown)
Indicator: Yellow tied on after the shell back is pulled over
Head: Trimmed foam remaining from the shell back
Fly Tier: Doug Christian

Jim's Flat Water Streamer

Hook: Mustad 36890, #4/0 - #1
Thread: Red
Weight: Soft stainless steel wire tied on the under side of the hook shank
Tag: Yellow floss   **Rib:** Yellow floss   **Body:** Red floss
Wing: Yellow marabou, tied in bunches around the hook shank
Topping: Several ostrich herls
Sides: Krystal Flash
Cheeks: Lacquered starling saddle feathers
Head: Yellow and black paint
Fly Tier: Jim Hoffman

Jointed Minnow

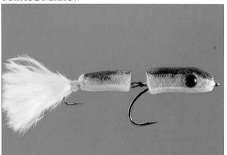

Hook: Two #10 hooks, TMC 9394 (rear section) and TMC 8089NP (front section)   **Thread:** White
Tail: White marabou, tied on the rear section
Body connector: Thirty-pound fire line   **Rear Body:** Pearl mylar tubing over white foam cylinder, coated with Softex or Aqua Flex   **Front Body:** Pearl mylar tubing over white foam cylinder, coated with Softex or Aqua Flex
Bodies: Both foam under bodies were shaped before applying the mylar tubing   **Body color:** Color bodies with felt tip markers prior to applying the coating
Eyes: Doll eyes, red with black pupils
Fly Tier: Lance Zook

J's Minnow

Hook: Mustad 9672, #6 - #12
Thread: Gray
Tail: Dun marabou
Over back: One or two strands of olive Brazilian Velour
Body: Silver tensile chenille
Gills: Red thread
Eyes: Stick on doll eyes, white with black pupils
Head: Thread
Fly Tier: Jerome Hebert

J. W. Minnow

Hook: Mustad 94840, #8 - #14
Thread: Black
Tail: Black marabou
Body: Purple fine chenille
Hackle: Very short grizzly, palmered
Head: Silver bead
Fly Tier: Paul Maurer

Laced Bass Buster

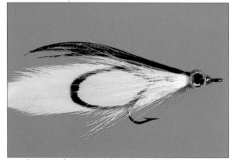

Hook: Mustad 3366, #1/0   **Thread:** Clear mono
Tail: White strung India neck hackle sandwiched under two American hen cape feathers
Tail flanking: Two laced American breast or saddle feather, tied on the sides
Body: Light tan Brazilian Velour
Wing: Peacock herl over white buck tail
Throat: White buck tail
Eyes: Fisker Design EZ-Eyes, stick on gold with black pupils
Head: Peacock (top) and red (bottom) craft paint coated with Aqua Flex
Fly Tier: Al Beatty

Miami Minnow (Perch)

Hook: Mustad 3366, #5/0 - #4
Thread: Green
Tail: Green over yellow Bailey's Wing Fiber
Body: Clumps of Bailey's Body Fur, colored with a felt tip marker and trimmed to shape
Eyes: Large doll eyes, white with black movable pupils
Head: Thread
Fly Tier: Paul Maurer

Misa's Williebugger

Hook: Mustad 9672, #8
Thread: Black
Tail: Purple marabou, accented with pearl Krystal Flash
Body: Purple marabou, twisted and wrapped
Hackle: Grizzly dyed hot orange, palmered
Head: Hot pink, ice chenille egg
Fly Tier: Misako Ishimura

M & M Candy

Hook: TMC 5263, #10 - #14
Thread: Fire orange
Wing: Cerise over white marabou accented with Krystal Flash, tied Clouser style
Eyes: Bead chain
Head: Thread
Fly Tier: Craig Riendeau

Mono Minnow

Hook: Mustad 9672, #10
Thread: Yellow
Tail: Marabou tip, tied short
Body: Body Basic Nymph Cord
Eyes: Melted mono
Head: Body Basic Body Braid
Fly Tier: Dustin Harris

Muskoka Muddler

Hook: Mustad 9672, #8
Thread: Black or brown
Tail: Hot orange Flurofibre
Body: Gold, flat tinsel
Wing: Peacock herl over gold Krystal Flash over brown marabou
Collar: Dyed brown deer hair, spun
Head: Dyed brown deer hair, spun and trimmed to shape
Fly Tier: Jerry Caruso

Mylar Minnow

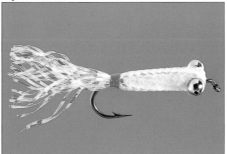

Hook: Mustad 9672, #8
Thread: Fluorescent pink
Tail: Picked out mylar tubing
Body: White ultra chenille
Over Body: Mylar pearl piping, small tied on the top and bottom
Eyes: Silver bead chain
Head: Thread
Fly Tier: Mike Hogue

The Natural

Hook: Mustad 3407, #2
Thread: Black
Tail: Brown buck tail, over pearl mylar tubing, picked out, and two barred ginger hackles
Body: Spun and trimmed deer hair
Eyes: Stick on, red with black pupils
Head: Thread
Fly Tier: Tom Broderidge

Needle Nose Minnow

Hook: Mustad 3407, #4
Thread: Yellow
Tail: White buck tail
Body: Thread
Wing: Chartreuse buck tail accented with pearl Krystal Flash, tied Clouser style
Gills: Red buck tail, tied short between the wing and tail
Eyes: Dumb bell, painted yellow with black pupils
Head: Thread
Fly Tier: Eric Wehnes

Northern Pike Rattler

Hook: Mustad 34007, #4/0 - #1/0
Thread: Green
Rattle: Glass rattle tied on the under side of the hook shank near the bend
Wing: White Fish Hair, colored with a felt tip marker
Topping: Several peacock herls
Eyes: White and red paint
Head: Painted green over the thread base
Fly Tier: Jim Hoffman

PB Minnow

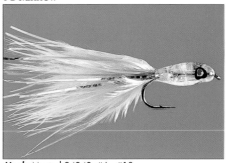

Hook: Mustad 94840, #6 - #10
Thread: White
Tail: White marabou accented with silver Flashabou
Body: Several glass beads coated with epoxy
Eyes: Stick on, black under yellow with red pupils
Head: Thread
Coating: Second layer of epoxy over the body, head, and eyes
Fly Tier: Paul Maurer

Pumpkin Trude

Hook: Mustad 94840, #12 - #16
Thread: Black
Tail: Golden pheasant crest feather fibers
Body: Pearl Flashabou and orange floss
Wing: Golden pheasant tippets, tied trude style
Beard: Pheasant tail fibers
Head: Thread
Fly Tier: Jack Pangburn

Randy's Bee

Hook: TMC 2487, #12
Thread: Black
Body: Foam cylinder punched from a black and white striped shower shoe
Wing: Grizzly hackle tips, trimmed to shape
Hackle: Grizzly, trimmed to shape
Head: Foam, thread
Fly Tier: Randy Inmon

Red Butt Big Eye

Hook: Mustad 79580, #4 - #10
Thread: Brown
Tail: Red yarn
Rib: Optional copper wire
Body: Dark olive chenille
Hackle: Furnace, palmered
Eyes: Dumb bell, tied on the under side of the shank
Head: Dark olive chenille, thread
Fly Tier: Herbert Carmen

Ribbon Shad

Hook: TMC 9394, #8
Thread: White
Tail: White Chickabou, topped with green ribbon floss
Body: Silver mylar tubing, topped with green ribbon floss
Hackle: White Soft Hackle, tied as a throat
Eyes: Stick on, gold with black pupils
Head: Thread coated with epoxy
Fly Tier: Henry Hoffman

Ruptured Duck

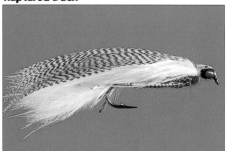

Hook: Mustad 79580, #6 - #10
Thread: White
Tail: White marabou, shank length
Body: Chenille under silver mylar tubing
Wing: White marabou under a mallard flank feather, tied flat
Throat: Small band of red dubbing
Eyes: Painted black with red pupil
Head: Thread
Fly Tier: Mike Jacobs

Shasta Shad

Hook: Mustad 37187, #2 - #6
Thread: White
Tail: White marabou, tied short and sparse
Body: Large pearl mylar tubing, shaped and coated with Aqua Flex or equivalent
Wing: Blue over white Fish Hair
Gills: Several wraps of red thread
Eyes: Painted yellow with black pupils
Weed guard: Mason mono, twenty-five pound test
Head: Thread
Fly Tier: Robert Meuschke

Shiny Shad

Hook: Mustad 3366, #2 - #10
Thread: Black
Tail: White over chartreuse marabou mixed with silver Flashabou
Body: Purple crystal chenille
Head: Thread
Fly Tier: Herbert Carman

Shoe Fly

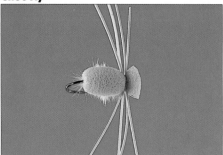

Hook: Mustad 94840, #8 - #12
Thread: Color to match the body
Shell back: Closed cell foam strip, tied pull over style
Body: Thin strip of furry foam under marabou twisted and wrapped
Legs: Two pairs of rubber legs
Head: Trimmed foam remaining from the shell back
Fly Tier: Doug Christian

SJB Shiner

Hook: Worm Hook, #1 (hook rides point up buried inside the body)
Thread: Clear mono
Tail: Pearl Comes Alive
Rattle: Tied on the hook at the eye, inside the body material
Body: Pearl E-Z Body Tubing, colored with felt tip markers
Eyes: Doll eyes, gold with black pupils
Coating: Five-minute epoxy, over the body and eyes
Fly Tier: Jerry Caruso

Smith's Shad

Hook: Mustad 3366, #2
Thread: Red
Tail: Pearl Krystal Flash
Body: White chenille
Wing/cheeks: Mallard flank feathers
Eyes: Stick on, red with black pupils
Head: Thread
Fly Tier: Mike Hogue

Spoon Fly

Hook: Mustad 94840, #6 - #12
Thread: Color to match the tail
Tail: Chartreuse marabou (or color of choice)
Body: Wire applied to the hook and bent to the "spoon shape"
Body fill: Five minute epoxy
Body color: Felt tip markers or glitter powder
Head: Thread
Fly Tier: Paul Maurer

Spruce Bend Back

Hook: Mustad 3366, #1/0 (bent to shape, the hook point rides up)   **Thread:** Black
Tail: Peacock Krystal Flash
Rib: Fine copper wire, optional
Body: Red floss and peacock herl
Wing: Four brown, black tipped Whiting American rooster hackle feathers
Hackle: Brown Whiting American, tied as a collar
Eyes: EZY Eyes with stick on, gold with black pupils
Head: Thread coated with Aqua Flex over the head and eyes
Fly Tier: Al Beatty

Squirrel Nymph)

Hook: TMC 5263, #2 - #12
Thread: Tan
Tail: Squirrel tan fibers
Rib: Pearl Flashabou
Body: Amber Antron dubbing
Thorax: Dark squirrel dubbing
Hackle: Ring neck pheasant body feather
Legs: Brown/black Silli-con leg material
Head: Brass bead
Fly Tier: Dave Whitlock

SRI Black Spider

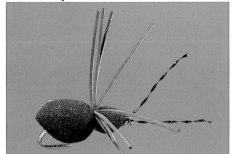

Hook: Daiichi 1100, #12 - #16
Thread: Black
Body: Black foam spider body
Legs: Black rubber leg material, three per side
Antenna: Black Crystal Splash
Head: Thread
Fly Tier: Bill Black, Spirit River Inc.

SRI Fire Beetle

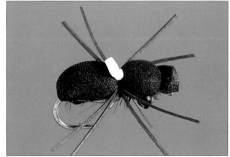

Hook: Daiichi 1100, #10 - #16
Thread: Black
Body: Red Lite Brite dubbing, tied in two segments
Over Body: Black closed cell foam strip, tied in two segments
Eyes: Black melted mono, placed in the front body segment
Legs: Black rubber leg material, four per side placed between the two body segments
Indicator: White closed cell foam
Head: Trimmed foam remaining from the over body
Fly Tier: Bill Black, Spirit River Inc.

SRI Yellow Spider

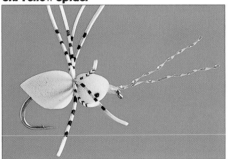

Hook: Daiichi 1100, #12 - #16
Thread: Yellow
Body: Yellow foam spider body
Legs: Yellow Micro Mini Round Rubber leg material, marked with a black felt tip
Antenna: Gold Crystal Splash
Eyes: Placed using a black felt tip marker
Head: Thread
Fly Tier: Bill Black, Spirit River Inc.

Stew's Killer Marabou

Hook: TMC 3761, #10
Thread: Black
Tail: Olive marabou
Rib: Optional copper wire
Body: Marabou remaining from the tail, wrapped
Wing: Olive marabou
Head: Peacock herl and thread
Fly Tier: Stew Stewart

Stubby Perch

Hook: Mustad 3366, #1/0
Thread: White
Tail: Short tuft of white calf tail fibers
Wing: Several tufts of white calf tail fibers, flanked with orange calf tail
Throat: White calf tail
Topping: Peacock herl
Eyes: Doll eyes, white with black pupils
Head: Colored with craft paint and coated with Aqua Flex
Fly Tier: Al Beatty

Suspended Minnow

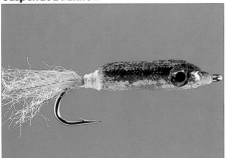

Hook: TMC 9394 NP, #2
Thread: White
Tail: Polar flash
Body: Quarter inch foam cylinder under mylar tubing, colored with felt tip markers
Eyes: Stick on with black pupils
Head: Thread
Coating: Aqua-Flex or Softex over the body, head, and eyes
Fly Tier: Tim Paxton

Swimming Boatman

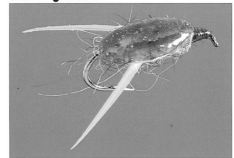

Hook: Mustad 9671, #10 - #14
Thread: Olive
Rib: Fine copper wire, optional
Body: Wapsi Sow Bug dubbing
Legs: Two yellow goose biots, tied in the middle of the body
Back: Artificial finger nail, cut to shape and colored with a brown felt tip marker
Coating: Crawfish color EZ Shape Sparkle Body and head cement
Head: Thread
Fly Tier: Tom Berry

Swimming Perch

Hook: Eagle Claw 214EL, #1/0
Thread: Clear mono
Tail: Pearl Comes Alive
Inner Body: White craft foam folded over a rattle
Over Body: Pearl E-Z Body Tubing, colored with felt tip markers
Front lip: Pearl E-Z Body Tubing, stiffen with epoxy
Eyes: Doll eyes, gold with black pupils
Coating: Epoxy over the body, eyes, and front lip
Fly Tier: Jerry Caruso

Tennessee Shad

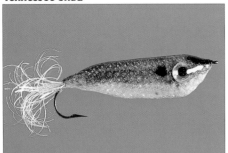

Hook: Eagle Claw 214EL, #1/0
Thread: Clear mono
Tail: Pearl Comes Alive
Inner Body: White craft foam folded over a rattle
Over Body: Pearl E-Z Body Tubing, colored with felt tip markers
Eyes: Doll eyes, silver with black pupils
Coating: Epoxy over the body and eyes
Fly Tier: Jerry Caruso

Terry's Ant

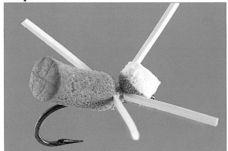

Hook: TMC 100, #12 - #14
Thread: Gray or black
Body: Foam cylinder punched from a multicolored shower shoe, tied McMurray ant style
Legs: White rubber leg material
Head: Foam remaining from the body
Fly Tier: Terry Alexander

Twitchy Richie

Hook: Mustad 94840, #6
Thread: Black
Rib: Thread wrapped body segments
Body: Black closed cell foam, tied in segments
Wing: Flashabou over white calf tail
Legs: Round rubber legs, assorted colors
Head: Thread anchoring a yellow foam diving collar
Fly Tier: Mike Telford

White River Demon

Hook: Mustad 94830, #10
Thread: Fluorescent orange
Tail: White rabbit fur
Weight: Ten wraps of non-lead wire
Body: Pearl plastic yarn
Hackle: White saddle, palmered
Head: Silver bead
Fly Tier: Jerry Caruso

Whit's Sculpin

Hook: TMC 200R, #2 - #10   **Thread:** Tan
Rib: Fine copper wire   **Body:** Tan rabbit dubbing,
Wing: Four grizzly dyed olive or brown, tied matuka style
Fins: Ring neck pheasant body feathers
Collar: Olive, black, brown, and tan deer hair, mixed and spun
Head: Olive, black, brown, and tan deer hair, spun and trimmed to shape
Eyes: Dolls eyes, green with black pupils
Weed guard: Hard mono, set in the trimmed head Crazy Glue
Fly Tier: Dave Whitlock

Yellow Fly

Hook: Mustad 3399, #10 - #16
Thread: Primrose
Tail: Wood duck flank feather fibers
Rib: Gold wire
Body: Bright yellow Antron dubbing
Wing: Wood duck flank feather fibers
Hackle: Black hen, tied as a collar
Head: Thread
Fly Tier: Tom Logan

Zeke's Fly

Hook: Mustad 37160, #10 - #14
Thread: Yellow
Tail: Short tuft of parachute cord, fuzzed apart
Rib: Color wire
Body: Yellow yarn
Back: Parachute cord, colored with a felt tip marker
Hackle: Grizzly, tied semi beard style
Eyes: Black glass bead on mono melted on the ends to anchor they eyes
Head: Thread
Fly Tier: Jim Hoffman

Crayfish and Leeches . . .

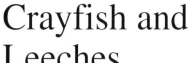

Already Crunched Crawdad

Hook: Mustad 9672, #6 - #10
Thread: Brown
Weight: Fifteen turns of non-lead wire
Tail: Tuft of white marabou under a tuft of orange marabou
Butt: Fluorescent orange crystal chenille
Body: Brown crystal chenille
Legs: Orange and white round rubber leg material
Head: Gold bead (optional), thread
Fly Tier: Deke Meyer

Batman

Hook: Mustad 34007, #1 - #2
Thread: Black
Tail/flash: Pearl Krystal Flash
Body: Black Ice Chenille
Eyes: Gold dumb bell
Claws: Black zonker strips, tied in front of the eye (also close to the hook bend)
Head: Thread
Fly Tier: Kevin Cohenour

BB Mini Leech

Hook: Daiichi 1100, #14 - #18
Thread: Purple
Tail: Purple marabou accented with purple Crystal Splash
Rib: Fine silver wire, optional
Body: Purple ostrich herl
Head: Black Brite Bead, thread
Fly Tier: Bill Black, Spirit River Inc.

BC Crayfish

Hook: TMC 200R, #2 - #10   **Thread:** White
Mouth parts: Pheasant breast feather fibers
Antenna: Pheasant tail fibers
Claws: Pheasant breast feather fibers
Rib: Thread
Body: White and orange chenille, white in the back and orange in the front
Legs: White hackle, palmered
Carapace: Tan Furry Foam, colored with a felt tip marker
Tail: Excess carapace material, extending in front of the hook eye
Fly Tier: Gale Doudy

Bead Eyes Leech

Hook: Mustad 9672, #6 - #10
Thread: Black
Tail: Black marabou
Rib: Two strands of peacock Krystal Flash
Body: Black leech yarn (picked out) over several turns of non-lead wire
Eyes: Silver bead chain
Head: Thread
Fly Tier: Mike Jacobs

Black Killer Leech

Hook: Daiichi 1100, #6 - #12
Thread: Black
Tail: Black marabou accented with black Crystal Splash
Body: Black ostrich herl
Head: Black Brite Bead, thread
Fly Tier: Bill Black, Spirit River Inc.

Bob's Crawdad

Hook: Mustad 79580, #6
Thread: Black
Mouth parts: Green Krystal Flash
Claws: Squirrel tail fibers, divided
Rib: Gold wire
Body: Olive/black variegated chenille
Back: Olive Furry Foam, mottled with a felt tip marker
Hackle: Grizzly dyed olive
Tail: Extension of the Furry Foam back, trimmed at the hook eye
Head: Thread
Fly Tier: Mike Hogue

BT's Bunny

Hook: Mustad 33957, #4 - #8   **Thread:** Brown
Mouth parts: Fox squirrel tail fibers
Antenna: Two strand of dark Krystal Flash
Eyes: Melted mono and black glass beads, coated
with black Aqua Head   **Rib:** Fine copper wire
Claws: Two brown zonker strips with the hair removed
from half of each   **Body:** Brown Brazilian Velour
Legs: Brown saddle hackle, palmered
Carapace: Chamois strip, colored with a brown felt
tip market
Tail: Remaining chamois from the carapace
Fly Tier: Al Beatty

Chamois Crayfish

Hook: Mustad 9672, #2 - 36   **Thread:** Black or brown
Mouth parts: Tuft of gold Krystal Flash
Eyes: Melted mono, coated with black Aqua Head,
tied extended
Claws: Tan chamois, natural or colored with a felt
tip marker
Body: Brown Brazilian Velour
Carapace and Tail: Tan chamois, natural or colored
with a felt tip marker
Weight: Dumb bell eyes, tied at hook eye under shank
Head: Thread
Fly Tier: Al Beatty

Clawless Crawdad

Hook: DaiRiki 700B, #4 - #10 (the hook point rides up)
Thread: Brown
Tail: Tan/black speckled Sili Legs mixed with black
Krystal Flash
Rib: Fine copper wire
Body: Tan chenille
Carapace and Tail: Chamois marked with a felt tip marker
Hackle: Brown hen saddle feather
Legs: Tan/black Sili Legs, three per side
Weight: Dumb bell, tied on top of the shank
Head: Thread
Fly Tier: Lance Zook

Crawdad Craig

Hook: Mustad 9671, #4 (bent to shape, the hook
point rides up)   **Thread:** Olive
Weight: Dumb bell eyes, tied at the hook eye
Antenna: Black Krystal Flash
Claws: Four dark green and black hackle feathers
Eyes: Melted mono
Rib: Olive dyed mono
Body: Olive chenille
Legs: Olive rubber leg material
Coating: Epoxy or Aqua Flex
Head: Thread
Fly Tier: Craig Riendeau

Crawling Crayfish

Hook: Mustad 3366, #1 (the hook point ride up)
Thread: Orange   **Tail:** Grizzly dyed orange Chickabou
Rear Hackle: Grizzly dyed orange Soft Hackle, tied
collar style   **Eyes:** Medium sized dumb bell, tied on
top of the shank (causes the point to ride up)
Body: Orange chenille, the top of the body is colored
with a brown felt tip marker
Front Hackle: Grizzly dyed orange Soft Hackle, tied
as a collar
Claws: Grizzly dyed orange hen saddles feathers,
trimmed at the tip   **Head:** Thread
Fly Tier: Tom Broderidge

Crawman

Hook: Mustad 34007, #1/0 - #2
Thread: Olive
Body: Pearl/olive Estaz
Eyes: Dumb bell, tied at the hook bend
Antenna: Peacock Krystal Flash, tied at the hook bend
Claws: Olive rabbit fur clumps, tied on the sides near
the hook bend
Head: Thread
Fly Tier: Dave Duffy

Creek Crawler

Hook: DaiRiki 710, #2 - #6   **Thread:** Brown
Mouth parts: Unstacked fox squirrel tail fiber and tuft
of squirrel dubbing
Eyes: Melted mono
Claws: Pheasant body feathers, trimmed to shape
Rib: Brown mono
Body: Tan Squirrel Bend dubbing
Carapace: Clear plastic strip
Legs: Pheasant body feather
Weight: Dumb bell eyes, tied at the hook eye
Head: Thread
Fly Tier: Duane Hada

Dr. T's Sqleech

Hook: TMC 300R, #12 - #16
Thread: Tan
Tail: Fox squirrel tail fibers, tied long and sparse
Weight: Fourteen turns of .015 non-lead wire
Rib: Copper wire, optional
Body: Brown squirrel dubbing, tied in a dubbing loop
and picked out
Head: Thread
Fly Tier: Terry Pfannenstiel

Easy Crayfish

Hook: Mustad 3906, #10
Thread: Tan
Mouth parts: Fox squirrel tail fibers
Body: Tan chenille
Eyes: Melded mono, painted with black Loon Hard
Head
Legs: Tan soft hackle, optional
Tail: Butt ends of the squirrel tail mouth parts
Head: Thread
Fly Tier: Jerry Smalley

Easy Rabbit Leech

Hook: Mustad 9672, #6
Thread: Black
Tail: Tuft of black rabbit fur
Wing and Body: Tufts of black rabbit fur tied staggered along the top and bottom of the hook
Head: Thread
Fly Tier: Jerry Smalley

Egg Sucking Leech

Hook: Mustad 36890, #4
Thread: Purple
Tail: Purple marabou
Body: Purple Body Basic Braid
Hackle: Purple saddle, palmered
Head: Salmon Body Basic Braid
Fly Tier: Dustin Harris

Eric's Killer Crayfish

Hook: Mustad 9674, #6
Thread: Olive
Claws: Olive buck tail accented with olive Krystal Flash, divided
Eyes: Silver dumb bell, tied at the hook bend
Rib: Thread
Body: Olive crystal chenille
Carapace: Olive Swiss straw
Tail: Excess Swiss straw from the carapace
Head: Thread
Fly Tier: Eric Wehnes

Extended Leech

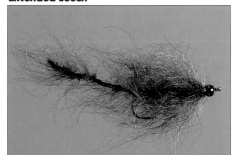

Hook: Daiichi 1750, #4
Thread: Clear mono
Tail: Furled leech yarn, extended body style
Body: Leech yarn, wrapped
Head: Black bead
Fly Tier: Shane Stalcup

Fighting Crayfish

Hook: Daiichi 1720, #2 - #8
Thread: Black
Antenna: Black rubber leg material, tied at the hook bend
Claws: Black zonker strips
Mouth parts: Brown tuft of marabou
Eyes: Melted mono
Rib: Fine copper wire
Body: Black Possum Plus dubbing
Carapace: Brown Body Stretch
Tail: Body Stretch trimmed just in front of the hook eye
Fly Tier: Bill Black, Spirit River Inc.

Gar Leech

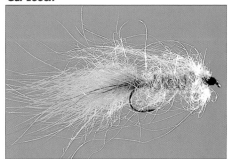

Hook: TMC 5263, #8 - #14
Thread: Black
Weight: Lead free wire along the entire hook shank
Tail: Tuft of red fox fur
Body: A blend of white and blue Polar Air, applied with a dubbing loop
Head: Thread
Fly Tier: Sodie Sodamann

Hank's Crayfish

Hook: Mustad 79580, #4 - #8   **Thread:** Olive
Tail: Grizzly dyed olive soft hackle, tied at the hook eye
Claws: Grizzly dyed olive schlepped tips
Weight: Strip of non-lead wire down each side of the hook
Rib: One pound mono
Body: Light olive chenille
Shell back: Grizzly dyed olive schlappen, ribbed in place
Hackle: Grizzly dyed olive schlappen, picked out from the shell back
Eyes: Artificial flower stamens
Head: Olive beaver dubbing to cover the thread wraps
Fly Tier: Henry Hoffman

Hot Glue Dad

Hook: TMC 205BL, #4 (straightened out)
Thread: Clear mono
Claws: Trimmed hackle feather or Fish Claws
Eyes: Orange accent eyes
Feelers: Grizzly dyed orange Chickabou
Body and back: Hot glue
Legs: Grizzly dyed orange Chickabou and terrestrial legs
Weight: Dumb bell eyes
Tail: Grizzly dyed orange Chickabou, tied at the hook eye
Fly Tier: Shane Stalcup

Leonard

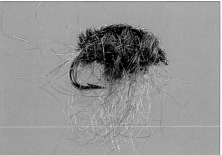

Hook: Mustad 3906, #10
Thread: Black
Rib: Copper wire
Body: Dark olive dubbing, applied full and picked out
Wing case: Peacock herl
Head: Thread
Fly Tier: Daniel Schapaugh

Medusa

Hook: Mustad 9672, #8
Thread: Fluorescent green
Tail: Olive ostrich herls
Body: Green Seal-EX
Wing: Three clumps of olive ostrich herls, spaced along the body
Head: Thread
Fly Tier: Tom Berry

Mini-Craw

Hook: Mustad 3906B, #10
Thread: Olive
Weight: Several turns of non-lead wire, optional
Tail/claws: Sili-con leg material, color to match the body
Body: Variegated chenille, color to match the natural crayfish
Head: Thread, tied large
Fly Tier: Tommy Marks

Mugger

Hook: Mustad 9672, #4
Thread: Black
Tail: Black marabou and peacock Krystal Flash
Weed guard: Hard mono
Body: Large dark olive crystal chenille
Hackle: Black saddle, palmered
Eyes: Dumb bell, optional
Head: Thread, tied large and coated with Aqua Flex or Flexament
Fly Tier: Bill Murdich

Muskrat Leech

Hook: Mustad 37187, #6
Thread: Black
Tail: Thin cross cut muskrat strip
Body: Muskrat strip, wrapped
Head: Thread
Fly Tier: Robert Meuschke

#22

Hook: Mustad 3906, #8 - #12
Thread: Black
Tail: Olive marabou, very sparse
Rib: Copper wire
Body: Dark olive muskrat dubbing
Wing case: Peacock herl
Head: Thread
Fly Tier: Daniel Schapaugh

Plastic Crawfish

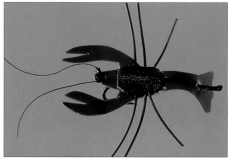

Hook: Mustad 80500BL, #4
Thread: Black
Body and claws: Cut to shape from plastic (old check book cover)
Antenna: Thin black mono, glued to the front of the body
Eyes: Drop of black lacquer
Back: Separate piece of plastic or leather
Legs: Rubber leg material, glued between the body and the back
Weight: Non-lead or copper wire
Fly Tier: Jack Pangburn

Ron's Flashy Leech

Hook: DaiRiki 700B, #2 - #12
Thread: Black
Tail: Black marabou
Body: Black crystal chenille, trimmed flat on the top and bottom
Head: Thread
Fly Tier: Paul Maurer

Salty Leech

Hook: Mustad 34011, #6 - #10
Thread: Brown
Tail: Long brown marabou, tied full
Body: Purple mohair yarn with Flashabou
Preparation: Mohair yarn is formed in a dubbing loop with the Flashabou, tied very full
Head: Thread
Fly Tier: Bob Lay

Sanchez Crawdaddy

Hook: DaiRiki 700, #4   **Thread:** Orange
Weight: Copper cone head
Claws: Brown rubber leg material and brown rabbit hair
Rib: Amber dyed mono
Body: Tan chenille
Carapace: Orange dyed rabbit strip, trimmed to shape and impaled on the hook
Tying the carapace: Impale on the hook, pull it over, and rib it into position
Legs: Three brown leg strands, threaded through the carapace and glued into position   **Head:** Thread
Fly Tier: Scott Sanchez

Schuylkill Punch

Hook: Daiichi 2461, #6
Thread: Copper
Weight: Silver dumb bell eyes
Mouth parts: Tan Flurofibre
Antenna: Black Kinky Hair
Claws, carapace, and Tail: Orange Flurofibre
Carapace Coating: Five minute epoxy
Body: Dark and copper thread
Head: Thread
Fly Tier: Jerry Caruso

S. E. Crawdad

Hook: Mustad 9672, #6 - #12   **Thread:** Tan
Mouth parts: Ginger hackle fibers
Antenna: Moose main fibers   **Eyes:** Melted mono
Claws: Pheasant hen body feather, trimmed to shape
Legs: Ginger hackle
Rib: Thread
Body: Dark tan dubbing
Carapace: Tan closed cell foam, colored with light
   brown wood stain and felt tip marker
Tail: Excess foam from the carapace
Head: Thread
Fly Tier: Jerome Hebert

Shaggy Leech

Hook: Mustad 9672, #8
Thread: Olive
Tail: Olive marabou
Body: Body Basic Blend
Hackle: Olive saddle, palmered
Head: Thread
Fly Tier: Dustin Harris

Simpleton

Hook: Mustad 3906B, #10 - #12
Thread: Yellow
Tail: Yellow marabou or color of choice
Rib: Fine silver tinsel
Body: Fine chenille, color to match the fly
Hackle: Marabou feathers tied as a collar, color to
   match the tail
Head: Thread
Fly Tier: Mike Jacobs

SRI Crayfish

Hook: Daiichi 1720, #2 - #8
Thread: Brown
Antenna: Brown rubber leg material
Mouth parts: Brown tuft of marabou
Eyes: Melted mono
Claws: Brown zonker strips
Rib: Fine copper wire
Body: Brown Possum Plus dubbing
Carapace: Brown Body Stretch
Tail: Body Stretch trimmed just in front of the hook eye
Fly Tier: Bill Black, Spirit River Inc.

Wilson's Craw Bully

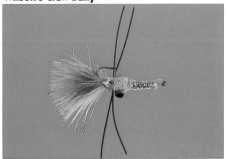

Hook: TMC 200R, #6 - #8
Thread: Brown
Tail: Copper Krystal Flash surrounded by ginger
   marabou topped with orange marabou
Under Body: Copper Krystal Flash, wrapped around
   the hook shank
Body: Clear Jelly Rope tipped with E-Z Shape Sparkle
   Body, sand color
Legs: Brown round rubber leg material
Eyes: Red dumb bell with black pupils
Head: E-Z Shape Sparkle Body, sand color
Fly Tier: Terry Wilson

Eels and Snakes . . .

Baby Garden Snake

Hook: Mustad 36890, #4
Thread: Olive
Tail: Olive zonker strip, tied long
Body: Olive zonker strip, wrapped
Eyes: Bead chain dyed black
Head: Rusty olive Body Basic Blend
Fly Tier: Dustin Harris

Big Eye Elver

Hook: Mustad 94720, #2
Thread: Hot orange
Tail: Black marabou, tied very long
Body: Variegated sparkle chenille, olive/black
Hackle: Black schlappen
Eyes: Doll eyes, gold with black pupils
Head: Black craft bead, coated with epoxy over
   thread, bead, and eyes
Fly Tier: Jerry Caruso

Black Magic

Hook: Mustad 34007, #4/0 (two)
Thread: Black
Trailing Hook: Steel shock tippet inside peacock braided tubing
Tail: Long black zonker strip, tied to trailing hook
Body: Black Spirit River Polar Aire, tied in clumps on the top and bottom of the hook shank
Wing: Long tuft of black Polar Aire
Eye: Stick on doll eyes, silver with black pupils
Head: Thread
Shock tippet: Black plastic coated steel cable
Fly Tier: Kim Jensen

Bonker Snake

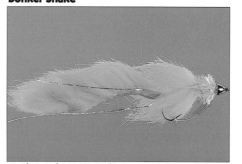

Hook: Daiichi 2722, #1/0
Thread: Chartreuse
Tail: Chartreuse zonker strip, accented with silver Fly Flash
Body: Chartreuse zonker strip wrapped collar style behind chartreuse ice chenille
Legs: Chartreuse rubber leg material
Head: Gold Spirit River Cone Head Bead
Fly Tier: Bill Black, Spirit River Inc.

Braided Eel

Hook: Herter's 81B, #4 jig hook
Thread: Chartreuse
Tail: Chartreuse Chickabou
Body: Chartreuse parachute cord
Hackle: Chartreuse Chickabou, tied to the sides
Eyes: Spirit River Real Eyes
Head: Thread coated with epoxy
Fly Tier: Henry Hoffman

Braided Snake

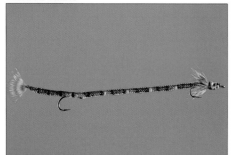

Hook: Daiichi #452 & #510, #4 (double hook)
Thread: Chartreuse
Tail: Chartreuse dyed grizzly Chickabou
Rib: Thread, tied in segments to bind the second hook and mono to the body
Body: Chartreuse parachute cord, colored with a brown and red felt tip marker
Hackle: Grizzly dyed chartreuse Chickabou, tied as a collar
Eyes: Stick on, silver with black pupils
Head: Thread coated with epoxy
Fly Tier: Henry Hoffman

Eel Bugger

Hook: Mustad 79580, #4 - #6
Thread: Black
Tail: Two grizzly dyed olive neck hackles, tied divided
Body: Dark olive chenille
Hackle: Grizzly dyed olive saddle hackle, palmered
Head: Thread
Fly Tier: Cliff Stringer

Evin's Eel

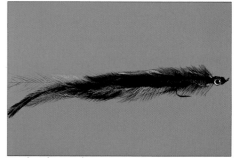

Hook: Salmon or bass stinger, #2
Thread: Black
Tail: Black emu feathers flanked by olive emu feathers
Body: Black chenille
Wing: Two olive under two black emu feathers
Eyes: Doll eyes, gold with black pupils
Head: Black chenille
Fly Tier: Bill Chandler

Fire Tiger

Hook: Mustad 94720, #2
Thread: Clear mono
Tail: Sili Legs (chartreuse, lime, & orange) over pearl Comes Alive
Inner Body: White craft foam strips
Outer Body: Pearl E-Z Body Tubing, colored with felt tip markers
Eyes: Doll eyes, silver with black pupils
Coating: Epoxy over the body and eyes
Fly Tier: Jerry Caruso

Floating Eel

Hook: Mustad 37187, #6
Thread: Orange
Tail: Orange rubber leg material tied to orange Antron yarn, braided
Under Body: Packing foam
Body: Orange Antron yarn
Weed guard: Hard Mason mono
Head: Thread
Fly Tier: Robert Meuschke

Foam Snake

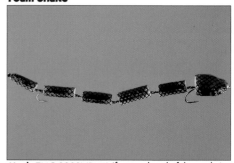

Hook: TMC 8090NP, #6 (front or head of the snake)
Body hooks: Five TMC 9394, #10 (tied as individual segments, all but one cut off)
Thread: White
Body: White foam cylinder covered with mylar tubing, coated with Softex, five sections
Head: White foam trimmed into a wedge shape, covered and coated same as the body
Body/head color: Colored with felt tip markers before coating with the Softex
Eyes: Doll eyes, red with black pupils
Fly Tier: Lance Zook

Lily Worm

Hook: Mustad 39189, #1/0 (the hook point rides up)
Thread: Yellow
Tail: Yellow zonker strip, tied hide side up when the hook is in the vise
Body Hackle: Yellow and black Soft Hackle, tied as alternating colored collars
Eyes: Dumb bell, painted green with black pupils (cause the hook point to ride up)
Head: Thread
Fly Tier: Chris Mihulka

Poly Eel

Hook: Eagle Claw L197G, #4/0
Thread: White
Tail: Long, natural Zonker strip, several wraps of the strip at the tie in point
Body: Gray macramé yarn, combed and trimmed wool head style
Eyes: Stick on doll eyes, white with black pupils
Head: Thread
Coating: Clear silicone over the top of the body, and the head and eyes
Fly Tier: Ron Winn

Red Head Streak

Hook: Mustad 3366, #1/0
Thread: Red
Tail: Peacock herl over brown over white buck tail, mixed with gold Krystal Flash
Eyes: Stick on over the head and under the Aqua Flex coating
Head and snout: Red speckled craft paint covered with Aqua Flex
Fly Tier: Al Beatty

Roger Rabbit

Hook: Mustad 3366, #1/0
Thread: Brown (or color to match the fly)
Tail: Brown (or color of choice) zonker strip, tied long
Hackle: Brown zonker strip, wrapped around the hook behind the head
Head: Brown Brazilian Velour
Fly Tier: Al Beatty

Sluggo Tube Fly

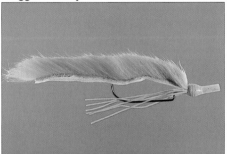

Hook: Use with a worm hook
Thread: Yellow
Body and Tail: Silicone coated zonker strip, additional glitter is optional
Legs: Round rubber legs, optional
Tube: chartreuse plastic or color of choice
Fly Tier: Scott Sanchez

Stalcup's Lizard

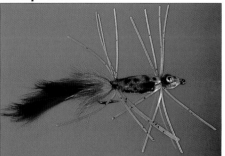

Hook: Daiichi 1750, #2
Thread: Clear mono
Tail: Olive zonker strip
Body: Closed cell foam, colored with felt tip markers
Body Coating: Softex mixed with glitter and fish scale powder
Legs: Olive Sili Legs, tied in two bunches of six legs
Eyes: Small doll eyes, green with black pupils
Head: Thread coated with Softex
Fly Tier: Shane Stalcup

Zonker Strip Worm

Hook: Mustad 37187, #2
Thread: Black
Tail: Zonker strip, purple or color of choice
Body: Purple crystal chenille or color of choice
Hackle: Grizzly, tied as a collar
Weed guard: Hard mono
Head: Orvis cone, large or medium
Fly Tier: Kevin Cohenour

Frogs, Poppers, Sliders, and Divers . . .

Baby Doll Muddler

Hook: Mustad 3366, #2 - #6
Thread: White
Tail: Black over white marabou accented with pearl Krystal Flash
Gills: Three turns of red chenille directly behind the hackle
Hackle: White deer hair, spun and trimmed as a collar
Head: White deer hair, spun and trimmed to shape
Eyes: Large doll eyes, white with black movable pupils
Weed guard: Hard mono, optional
Fly Tier: Mitch Whitney

Bare Bones Popper

Hook: Mustad 33903, #10
Thread: Red
Tail: Squirrel, dyed color of choice
Body/Head: Shower shoe cylinder, colors of choice
Fly Tier: Tommy Marks

Basic Bluegill Popper

Hook: Mustad 33903, #10
Thread: Black
Tail: Gray squirrel tail fibers
Body/Head: Shower shoe cylinder cut with the stripes around the section, colors of choice
Hackle: Grizzly, tied as a collar
Legs: White rubber leg material, laced through the head/body
Fly Tier: Tommy Marks

Bass Wog

Hook: Daiichi 2461, #1/0 (the hook point rides up)
Thread: Orange
Tail: Red Sili Leg material over silver Comes Alive
Tail covering: Orange marabou wrapped collar style
Head: Orange dyed deer hair, trimmed to shape
Eyes: Stick on doll eye, green with black pupils
Fly Tier: Jerry Caruso

Bleeding Blueback

Hook: Daiichi 2461, #1/0
Thread: Clear mono
Tail: Sili Legs over pearl Comes Alive
Inner Body: White craft foam folded over a rattle
Outer Body: Pearl E-Z Body Tubing, colored with felt tip markers
Eyes: Doll eyes, gold with black pupils
Coating: Epoxy over the body and eyes
Fly Tier: Jerry Caruso

B-2 Dragon Fly

Hook: TMC 8089, #10
Thread: Orange on the weed guard, black on the fly
Rib: Thread, tied as individual segments
Body: Blue closed cell foam, tied extended body and in segments
Wing: Four zing wings
Eyes: Plastic bead chain, black
Head: Foam and thread
Weed guard: Hard mono, optional
Fly Tier: Mike Telford

Bunny Diver

Hook: Daiichi 2722, #2 - #6   **Thread:** Chartreuse
Tail: Grizzly dyed chartreuse hackle feathers, divided delta style
Wing: Chartreuse zonker strip over Crystal Splash
Legs: Rubber leg material
Collar: Pearl Fly Flash over chartreuse dyed deer, spun as a collar
Weed guard: Hard mono
Head: Black and chartreuse dyed deer, spun and trimmed to shape
Eyes: Stick on doll eyes, white with black pupils
Fly Tier: Bill Black, Spirit River Inc.

Chug A Plug

Hook: Mustad 3366, #1/0 (in a tube fly)
Tube: Two inch brass tube
Thread: White
Tail: Dark over white buck tail, spun around the tube
Body: White chenille
Hackle: White, palmered
Head: White, round closed cell foam
Fly Tier: Al Beatty

Copco Perch

Hook: Mustad 3407, #1/0
Thread: Yellow
Tail: Yellow zonker strip with gold Flashabou
Gills: Red hackle fibers
Body: Yellow chenille
Wing: Yellow zonker strip under grizzly dyed yellow hackle feathers
Eyes: Stick on doll
Head: Large mylar tubing coated with Aqua Flex or equivalent
Fly Tier: Robert Meuschke

Crippled Baby Bass

Hook: TMC 511S, #1/0
Thread: Black
Tail: White over olive marabou
Body: Light flex cord braid colored with felt tip markers and coated with Softex
Body coloring: The coloring and eye placement float the fly on its side
Eyes: Doll eyes, white with black movable pupils, place on the side of the fly
Weed guard: Hard mono
Lip: Hard mono coated with Softex
Fly Tier: Mike Telford

Das Rat

Hook: Mustad 3366, #1/0 - #6
Thread: Black
Tail: White nylon cord
Weed guard: Hard mono
Body: Spun and trimmed deer hair
Head: Thread
Fly Tier: Ted Patlin

Deceiving Popping Spoon

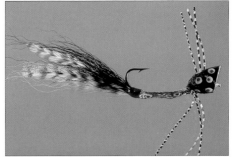

Hook: Mustad Keel Hook, #2/0 - #2 (hook point rides up)   **Thread:** Red
Tail: Black buck tail over green Krystal Flash flanked by two grizzly dyed yellow saddle hackles **Butt:** Red thread
Body: Gold mylar tubing, flattened with gold flake nail polish
Legs: Green/black Sili Leg material, three per side
Head: Cork or foam popper, painted green with a yellow mouth
Eyes: Yellow with red pupils over the under body and the popper head
Fly Tier: Tom Tripi

Deer Hair Bass Bug

Hook: Mustad 37189, #2 - #10
Thread: Yellow
Tail: Two long and two shorter grizzly dyed yellow hackle feathers, tied splayed
Hackle: Grizzly dyed yellow, tied as a collar behind the head
Head: Yellow and black deer hair, spun and trimmed to shape
Legs: Black rubber leg material
Weed guard: Hard mono, optional
Fly Tier: Mitch Whitney

Deer Hair Mouse

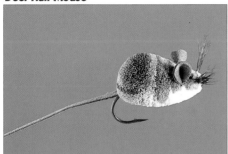

Hook: Partridge CS41, #3/0
Thread: Black
Tail and ears: Gray Ultra Suede
Body: Spun and trimmed natural deer hair
Belly: Spun and trimmed white deer hair
Whiskers: Moose hair
Eyes: Black plastic, glued in place
Head: Thread
Fly Tier: Chris Helm

Doug's Spider

Hook: Mustad 94831, #8 - #10
Thread: Black
Body: One fourth inch strip of black closed cell foam, tied in two folder over segments
Wing: Deer hair dyed chartreuse
Legs: Four pairs of rubber legs, color of choice
Head: Foam remaining from the body pulled over and tied wing case style
Fly Tier: Doug Christian

Floating Pumpkin

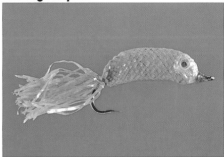

Hook: Mustad 34011, #1
Thread: Red
Tail: Orange braided plastic tubing, picked out
Under Body: Closed cell foam, trimmed to shape
Body: Orange braided plastic tubing
Eyes: Stick on, green with black pupils
Head: Thread
Fly Tier: Tom Broderidge

Fly By Night

Hook: Mustad 37187, #6
Thread: White
Tail: Black fox, under four strand of Flashabou, flanked by two scarlet hackle feathers
Head/collar: Black behind scarlet spun and trimmed deer hair
Fly Tier: Wayne Luallen

Foam Body Popper

Hook: Mustad 9672, #4 - #6
Thread: Black
Tail: Chartreuse marabou with a few strand of purple Flashabou
Hackle: Grizzly, tied as a collar behind the popper head
Head: Purple foam head, Crazy Glue into position
Eyes: White doll eyes, Crazy Glue on the side of the head
Legs: White round rubber, pulled through the body with a needle
Fly Tier: Cliff Stringer

Foam Diver

Hook: Daiichi 2720, #4
Thread: Clear mono
Tail: Grizzly dyed orange over chartreuse saddle hackles over orange marabou
Hackle: Grizzly dyed orange and chartreuse saddle hackle, tied as a collar
Legs: Mixed orange and chartreuse round rubber legs
Eyes: Doll eyes, green with black pupils
Head: Closed cell foam, colored with felt tip markers, coated with Softex
Fly Tier: Shane Stalcup

Foam Diver

Hook: Daiichi 2720, #2 - #6 **Thread:** Clear mono
Tail: Chartreuse, orange, and white marabou over
  pearl Krystal Flash
Tail flanking: Two white dyed chartreuse saddle hackle feathers
Hackle: Chartreuse saddle hackle, tied as a collar behind
  the head **Legs:** Orange rubber leg material, four per side
Head: Closed cell foam strip pulled over and tied into
  place anchoring the legs in the process
Head: Pearl and black fish scale powder mixed in epoxy
Eyes: Small doll eyes, gold with black pupils
Coating: Epoxy over the head and eyes
Fly Tier: Shane Stalcup

Foam Fry

Hook: Daiichi 2720, #2
Thread: Clear mono
Tail: Olive over white flanked by black marabou,
  mixed with Flashabou
Body: Closed cell foam covered with Softex, glitter,
  and pearl fish scale powder
Body color: Colored with felt tip markers prior to the
  application of Softex
Eyes: Stick on, yellow with black pupils
Head: Softex over the body, head, and eyes
Fly Tier: Shane Stalcup

Foam Slider

Hook: Mustad 33903, #2/0 - #6
Thread: Black
Tail: Squirrel tail under several long black saddle
  feathers accented with Flashabou
Weed guard: Hard mono, optional
Body/Head: Slider body shaped from a piece of
  shower shoe
Hackle: Wide, webby black hackle, tied as a
  skirt/collar
Legs: Black rubber leg material, laced through the
  body/head, four per side
Fly Tier: Tommy Marks

Frog Popper

Hook: Mustad 33903, #4 - #6
Thread: Olive
Tail: A few strands of green Krystal Flash over two
  grizzly dyed olive Soft Hackles
Hackle: Grizzly dyed olive Soft Hackle, tied as a collar
Legs: Yellow rubber leg material, three per side
Head: Cabela's Perfect Popper, painted olive/black
  on top and yellow on the bottom
Eyes: Doll eyes, white with black movable pupils
Fly Tier: Dave Engerbretson

Fun Foam Frog

Hook: Mustad 33903, #6 **Thread:** Yellow **Tail:** Yellow
marabou and Krystal Flash under two grizzly dyed
olive hackle feathers **Tail topping:** Olive dyed deer
hair, one-half the length of the tail
Hackle: Several turns of grizzly dyed olive hackle feathers
Head: Six sections of yellow fun foam, laminated with
  rubber cement
Shaping the Head: Use scissors and fine sand paper
Head topping: Felt tip markers to color and spot,
  cover with clear nail polish and glitter
Eyes: Doll eyes mounted with super glue gel
Fly Tier: Doug Christian

Fun Foam Popper

Hook: Eagle Claw 214EL, #1/0
Thread: White
Tail: White marabou over pearl Comes Alive
Body and Head: White fun foam
Hackle: Grizzly, wrapped in a tight palmer
Eyes: Optional, red and black fabric paint
Head: White fun foam circle
Fly Tier: Jerry Caruso

Fun Foam Popper

Hook: Mustad 33903, #8
Thread: Black
Tail: Tuft of tan rabbit topped with tan dyed deer hair
  flanked by two orange rubber legs
Hackle: Grizzly dyed brown, tied as a collar behind
  the body
Body: Five colored section of two millimeter fun foam,
  glued, cut, and sanded to shape
Eyes: Doll eyes, white with black movable pupils
Legs: Orange rubber leg material, inserted into the
  body with a needle
Fly Tier: Doug Christian

Goddard Bee

Hook: Mustad 94840, #10
Thread: Black
Body: Yellow and black deer hair, spun and trimmed
Hackle: Black, tied sparse
Head: Thread
Fly Tier: Mike Jacobs

Green Foam-Tec Slider

Hook: Daiichi 2722, #2 - #6
Thread: White
Tail: Yellow Crystal Splash under red Fly Flash
Wing: Four yellow hackle feathers, tied splayed
Hackle: Yellow, tied as a collar behind the head
Head: Green Foam-Tec popper head, tied on the
  shank backwards
Legs: Green and yellow rubber leg material, one of
  each per side, tied using a needle
Eyes: Doll Eyes, yellow with black pupils
Weed guard: Hard mono
Fly Tier: Bill Black, Spirit River Inc.

Hair Popper

Hook: Mustad 3399A, #1
Thread: Black
Tail: Two furnace hackles with several strands of Krystal Flash
Head: Gray, green, and orange deer hair, spun and trimmed to shape
Fly Tier: Cliff Stringer

Helm's Popper

Hook: Partridge GRSS4, #1 **Thread:** Black
Tail: Dyed yellow variant hackle feathers, paired
Tail accent: Black and yellow rubber leg material mixed with Tie Well pearl flash
Skirt: Four variant dyed yellow hackles, wrapped
Body: Natural, yellow, black, and white deer hair; spun and trimmed to shape
Legs: Black and yellow rubber leg material mixed with the spun deer hair
Eyes: Doll eyes, amber with black pupils
Head: Thread
Fly Tier: Chris Helm

Irresistible Diver

Hook: Daiichi 2546, #2/0 - #4
Thread: White
Tail: Two white under two grizzly dyed red hackle feathers over red Crystal Splash
Legs: Red and white rubber leg material, two per each color per side
Wing: White deer hair under pearl Fly Flash
Head: Red behind white spun and trimmed deer hair
Eyes: Stick on doll eyes, white with black pupils
Weed guard: Hard mono
Fly Tier: Bill Black, Spirit River Inc.

J. W. Popper

Hook: Mustad 3366, #4
Thread: Yellow
Tail: Two grizzly dyed yellow saddle hackles
Rib: Thread
Body: Yellow closed cell foam strip, tied in three segments
Wing: Deer hair
Head: Spun and trimmed deer hair, natural and white, Aqua Flex on the front
Fly Tier: Paul Maurer

Laced Diver

Hook: Mustad 3366, #1/0
Thread: Clear mono
Tail: White strung India hackle feathers inside two American hen cape hackles
Tail flanking: Laced American hen breast or saddle feathers
Wing: White buck tail fibers
Throat: White buck tail fibers
Collar: Spun deer hair, trimmed as part of the head
Head: Spun and trimmed deer hair
Eyes: Stick on, movable eyes, white with black pupils
Fly Tier: Al Beatty

Madam X Dragon Fly

Hook: DaiRiki 270, #4
Thread: Fluorescent red
Weed guard: Hard mono, optional
Body: Dyed dark elk hair, tied extended body style
Wing: Dark elk and root beer crystal flash
Head and collar: Dark elk, tied bullet head style
Legs: Brown and red rubber leg material
Fly Tier: Scott Sanchez

Megamoth

Hook: Mustad 37187, #1/0
Thread: White
Tail: Natural deer hair
Body: Spun and trimmed deer hair
Wing: Deer hair
Head: Trimmed deer hair
Fly Tier: Ron Graunke

Mike's Foam Popper

Hook: Mustad 3366, #2/0
Thread: Black
Tail: Lambs wool with Krystal Flash, colors of choice
Body: Orange closed cell foam, or colors of choice
Hackle: Grizzly dyed orange
Legs: Sili-con leg material, threaded through the body
Fly Tier: Mike Hogue

Mini Deer Hair Popper

Hook: Mustad 3905B, #8 - #12
Thread: Black
Tail: Deer hair and two strands of pearl Krystal Flash
Body: Spun and trimmed deer hair
Legs: White round rubber leg material
Head: Thread
Fly Tier: Kevin Cohenour

Mini Frog (Popper)

Hook: Mustad 3366, #6
Thread: Olive
Tail: Grizzly dyed olive Chickabou over gold/black Sili Leg material
Tail flanking: Grizzly dyed olive hen cape feathers, tied to the sides
Hackle: Grizzly dyed olive hen saddle hackle, tied as a collar
Eyes: Three dimensional, amber with black pupils
Head: Olive and yellow deer hair, spun and trimmed to shape
Fly Tier: Mark Hoeser

Mini Ultra Foam-Tec Popper

Hook: Daiichi 2546, #6 - #10   **Thread:** Black
Tail: Two red and two black hackle feathers accented with black Crystal Splash
Hackle: Red and black mixed, tied collar style behind the head
Head: Black/red hand painted Ultra Foam Popper Body, small size
Legs: Black and red rubber leg material, one of each color per side
Eyes: Stick on doll eyes, red with black pupils
Weed guard: Hard mono
Fly Tier: Bill Black, Spirit River Inc.

Not So Basic Popper (Bluegill)

Hook: Mustad 33903, #8
Thread: Red
Tail: Squirrel tail, under orange marabou between matched brown hackles as kickers
Body/Head: Foam shower show cut so the stripes are length wise on the section
Hackle: Grizzly dyed orange saddle hackle, tied as a collar
Legs: White rubber, laced through the body/head, three per side
Fly Tier: Tommy Marks

Olive Corulid

Hook: TMC 200R, #8 - #16
Thread: Olive
Tail: Barred ginger hackle fibers
Body: Dyed olive deer hair, spun and trimmed to shape
Eyes: Melted mono
Hackle and wings: Two barred ginger hackles, wrapped leaving the excess for wings
Fly Tier: Al Beatty

Olson's Deceiver

Hook: Mustad 34011, #1
Thread: Red
Tail: Silver Krystal Flash over white buck tail, flanked by two white saddle hackles
Body: Spun and trimmed deer hair in two segments, white and red
Hackle: Red saddle hackle, tied as a collar
Head: Thread
Fly Tier: Tom Broderidge

100 Eyed Popper

Hook: Mustad 33900, #1/0 - #8
Thread: Black
Tail: Chartreuse marabou and stretch floss (as legs) with a small tuft of red marabou
Tail flanking: Two black saddle hackles with painted eyes along the stems
Legs: Six green Sili Legs in front of the hackle
Hackle: Chartreuse saddle hackle, tied as a collar
Head: Cork or foam, painted green and covered with multiple eyes
Eyes: Painted yellow with red highlighted black pupils
Fly Tier: Tom Tripi

Orange Tiger

Hook: Daiichi 2461, #1/0
Thread: Clear mono
Tail: Sili Legs over pearl Comes Alive
Inner Body: White craft foam folder over a rattle
Outer Body: Pearl E-Z Body Tubing, slider style, colored with felt tip markers
Hackle: Black soft hackle, tied as a collar
Eyes: Doll eyes, gold with black pupils
Coating: Epoxy over the eyes and body
Fly Tier: Jerry Caruso

Polly Frog

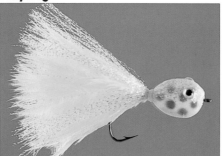

Hook: Mustad 37187, #4
Thread: Yellow
Tail: Yellow marabou and Krystal Flash
Body: Beau Mac Cheater, yellow with orange spots
Eyes: Stick on, yellow with black pupils
Head: Thread
Fly Tier: Dustin Harris

Prism Fire Tiger (Diver)

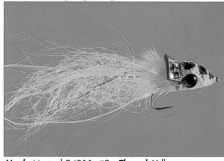

Hook: Mustad 34011, #2   **Thread:** Yellow
Tail: Chartreuse Bozo Hair, yellow rubber leg material, and prism Flashabou
Gills: Orange deer hair, spun and trimmed
Collar: Yellow deer hair, spun with part becoming a portion of the head
Diver collar: Thin piece of red foam covered with green Tiger Tape
Head: Yellow and green deer hair, spun, flared, and trimmed to shape
Eyes: Doll eyes, red with black pupils
Fly Tier: Scott Sanchez

Purple Foam-Tec Slider

Hook: Daiichi 2722, #2 - #6   **Thread:** Black
Tail: Red Fly Flash mixed with copper Crystal Splash
Wing: Two orange inside two Purple hackle feathers, tied splayed
Hackle: Orange and purple mixed, tied as a collar behind the head
Head: Purple Foam-Tec popper head, tied on the shank backwards
Legs: Purple and orange rubber leg material, one of each per side, tied using a needle
Eyes: Doll Eyes, red/black pupils **Weed guard:** Hard mono
Fly Tier: Bill Black, Spirit River Inc.

Rapala Diver

Hook: Mustad 34111, #1/0 - #4
Thread: Black
Tail: Green zonker strip with Krystal Flash, colors of choice
Body: White Estaz
Gills: Fine pink chenille
Wing: Rest of the zonker strip from the tail
Head & collar: Spun and trimmed deer hair, color to match the rest of the fly
Eyes: White and black post eye, glued into place
Fly Tier: Dave Duffy

Schnauzer, Dark

Hook: Mustad 37187, #2 - #10
Thread: Black
Tail: Black zonker strip, tied leather side up
Rib: Thread
Under Body: Yarn, tied larger at the hook eye
Body: Dark antelope hair, stacked and tied with the tips to the rear
Flanks: Two zonker strips, tied to the sides
Lip: Formed from the antelope hair butts and black silicone caulk
Head: Thread
Fly Tier: Harry Smith

Schnauzer, Light

Hook: Mustad 37187, #2 - #10
Thread: Black
Tail: Brown or tan zonker strip, tied leather side up
Rib: Thread
Under Body: Yarn, tied larger at the hook eye
Body: Light, natural antelope hair, stacked and tied with the tips to the rear
Flanks: Two light zonker strips, tied to the sides
Lip: Formed from the antelope hair and clear silicone caulk
Head: Thread
Fly Tier: Harry Smith

Scud Slider

Hook: Mustad 3906B, #6
Thread: Yellow
Tail: Grizzly dyed yellow hackle feathers, tied splayed
Collar: Yellow dyed deer hair, spun to shape
Head: Yellow dyed deer hair, spun and trimmed to shape
Fly Tier: Paul Maurer

Shoe Fly

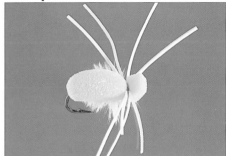

Hook: Mustad 94840, #8 - #12
Thread: Yellow or color to match the fly
Body: Yellow marabou (or color of choice), twisted into a rope and wrapped
Over Body: Strip of yellow closed cell foam (or color to match the body)
Legs: Four rubber legs, color to match the body
Head: Trimmed section of the over body
Fly Tier: Doug Christian

Shower Shoe Popper

Hook: Mustad 33903, #2/0 - #6
Thread: Yellow
Tail: Squirrel tail, tied short with flash material of choice, under two orange hackles as kickers
Body/Head: Foam block of shower shoe material, sanded to shape, split and glued on the hook
Hackle: Wide, webby saddle hackle, tied as a skirt/collar
Legs: Laced through the head/body, one towards the rear and the other towards the front
Fly Tier: Tommy Marks

Simple BB Popper

Hook: Daiichi 2722, #2 - #6
Thread: Black
Tail: Red tuft of marabou, tied short
Wing: Black marabou accented with pearl Fly Flash
Legs: White rubber leg material
Hackle: Black, tied as a collar behind the popper head
Head: Black Foam-Tec popper head
Eyes: Stick on doll eyes, yellow with black pupils
Weed guard: Hard mono
Fly Tier: Bill Black, Spirit River Inc.

Slider Frog

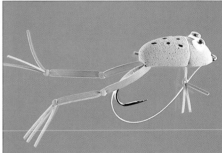

Hook: TMC 8089NP, #10
Thread: White
Weed guard: Hard mono, optional
Legs: Green rubber hackle, knotted
Body: Size four green foam spider body, painted spots yellow/green
Eyes: Small doll eyes, white with black movable pupils
Head: Thread
Fly Tier: Lance Zook

WARMWATER FLIES | 175

Sliding Shad

Hook: Daiichi 2720, #6
Thread: Clear mono
Tail: White zonker strip over four white saddle hackle feathers
Collar: Stacked deer hair
Body: T.C.S. popper body, colored with felt tip markers
Body Coating: Softex and glitter powder
Eyes: Small doll eyes, yellow with black pupils
Head: Thread
Fly Tier: Shane Stalcup

Soft Pop Frog

Hook: TMC 8089, #2 - #10   **Thread:** White
Tail: Chartreuse Super Floss & chartreuse dyed grizzly hen saddle feathers
Body: Foam cylinder or caulking rod, colored with felt tip markers
Hackle: Grizzly dyed chartreuse, tied as a collar
Legs: White rubber leg material, threaded through the body, three per side
Eyes: Doll eyes
Head: Thread
Coating: Aqua Flex or Softex over the body and eyes
Fly Tier: Tim Paxton

Soft Tiger Frog

Hook: TMC 8090, #4 - #6
Thread: Black
Tail: Two grizzly dyed olive hackles, tied flared to provide action
Hackle: Grizzly dyed olive, tied as a thick collar
Legs: Olive Super Floss, knotted
Head: One-eighth inch closed cell foam, laminated, olive or colors to match
Eyes: Doll eyes, olive with black pupils
Fly Tier: Chris Mihulka

Soft Tiger Popper

Hook: TMC 8090, #4 - #6
Thread: Black
Tail: Yellow marabou or color of choice
Body Hackle: Alternating collar of black and yellow hackle feathers
Legs: Black round rubber leg material, tied to the side just behind the head
Head: Laminated one-eighth inch pieces of closed cell foam, cut to shape
Eyes: Doll eyes, red with black pupils
Fly Tier: Chris Mihulka

Sparkle Popper (Black)

Hook: Mustad 33903, #4 - #6
Thread: Black
Tail: Pearl Krystal Flash between matched pairs of black Soft Hackle feathers
Hackle: Two black Soft Hackle feathers, tied as a collar
Head: Cabela's Perfect Popper, painted black
Eyes: Doll eyes, white with black movable pupils
Legs: Black rubber leg material, threaded through the head
Fly Tier: Dave Engerbretson

SRI Pencil Popper, Trout

Hook: Daiichi long shank, #2/0
Thread: White
Tail: White under pink under green under black Crystal Splash
Head: Spirit river Hard Foam Pencil Popper body, painted black, pink, and white
Weed guards: Hard mono, two strands parallel
Fly Tier: Bill Black, Spirit River Inc.

SRI Performance Popper

Hook: Daiichi 2722, #2
Thread: Gray
Tail: Amber under yellow buck tail, mixed with copper Krystal Flash
Legs: Hot orange rubber leg material
Head: Spirit River Hard Foam Popper Body, painted green/black (top) and orange (bottom)
Eyes: Stick on, gold with black pupils
Weed guards: Hard mono, two strands parallel
Fly Tier: Bill Black, Spirit River Inc.

Stalcup's Tadpole

Hook: Daiichi 2720, #4
Thread: Clear mono
Tail: Olive rabbit strip, tied fairly short
Throat: Tuft of olive rabbit fur
Legs: Olive Sili Legs, tied short and to the sides
Body: Closed cell foam covered with Softex, glitter, and pearl fish scale powder
Eyes: Small doll eyes, green with black pupils
Head: Thread
Fly Tier: Shane Stalcup

Stealth Muddler

Hook: Mustad 37187, #2 - #6   **Thread:** Black
Tail: Black over brown over olive over white buck tail, mixed with Flashabou
Tail flanking: Brown hackle feathers, tied on the sides
Body: Black crystal chenille
Wing: Peacock herl over moose mane, mixed with Flashabou
Collar: Black deer hair, spun and trimmed as part of head
Head: Black, olive, and white deer hair, spun and trimmed to shape
Eyes: Stick on doll eyes, yellow with black pupils
Fly Tier: Tom Tripi

Swimming Frog

Hook: Daiichi 2720, #4
Thread: Clear mono
Tail: Olive rabbit strip, split and tied divided
Legs: Olive Sili Legs, tied in two groups
Body: Contrasting colors of rabbit strip, coated with epoxy and pearl glitter
Body back color: Colored with felt tip markers
Belly: Epoxy and pearl glitter
Eyes: Yellow push pins with a black felt tip marker pupil
Head: Thread
Fly Tier: Shane Stalcup

Threadfin Shad (Mini Diver)

Hook: Mustad 3366, #6
Thread: Gray
Tail: Gray rabbit zonker strip over silver Krystal Flash flanked by two grizzly hen cape feathers
Hackle: Grizzly hen cape feather, tied as a collar
Collar: Deer hair, spun and trimmed as part of the head
Head: Spun and trimmed deer hair
Weed guard: Hard mono, optional
Fly Tier: Mark Hoeser

Tim's Twit

Hook: TMC 8089, #2 - #10
Thread: White
Tail: Grizzly dyed yellow saddle feather or color of choice
Body: Foam cylinder, colored with felt tip markers as desired
Legs: One-eight inch foam, tied loop style
Hackle: Grizzly dyed yellow or color of choice
Head: Thread
Fly Tier: Tim Paxton

Ty's Tantalizer

Hook: Mustad 80300BR, #2 - #10
Thread: Orange
Tail: Olive marabou over dyed orange and grizzly dyed olive hackle feathers, paired
Tail accent: Orange rubber leg material and Tie Well pearl flash
Body: Orange, olive and black dyed deer hair; spun, flared and trimmed to shape
Eyes: Doll eyes, amber with black pupils
Head: Thread
Fly Tier: Chris Helm

Ultra Foam-Tec Popper

Hook: Daiichi 2546, #1/0 - #4   **Thread:** White
Tail: Two grizzly under two chartreuse hackle feathers accented with pearl Crystal Splash
Hackle: Grizzly and grizzly dyed chartreuse, tied collar style behind the head
Head: Green/black hand painted Ultra Foam Popper Body, large size
Legs: Yellow rubber leg material, inserted with a needle, four per side
Eyes: Stick on doll eyes, yellow with black pupils
Weed guard: Hard mono
Fly Tier: Bill Black, Spirit River Inc.

Walt Popper, Bass

Hook: Mustad 33903, #4   **Thread:** White
Tail: Red and white calf mixed with silver Flashabou
Body coating: #872 Food Service foil applied with Barge Cement   **Scales:** Roll a socket wrench handle over the foil covered body   **Body paint:** Black and white
Eyes: Painted, yellow under orange with black pupils
Coating: Epoxy
Wing: Four grizzly hackles, tied splay style
Hackle: Grizzly, tied as a collar behind the head
Throat: Red marabou, tied sparse and encased in the coating   **Head:** Thread
Fly Tier: Walt Holman

Walt Popper, Gold

Hook: Mustad 33903, #4   **Thread:** White
Tail: Red calf mixed with red Krystal Flash
Body coating: #712 Reynolds silver foil applied with Barge Cement   **Scales:** Roll a socket wrench handle over the foil covered body   **Body paint:** Black and white
Eyes: Painted, yellow under orange with black pupils
Coating: Epoxy   **Wing:** Four grizzly dyed yellow hackles, tied splay style   **Hackle:** Grizzly dyed yellow, tied as a collar behind the head   **Throat:** Red marabou, tied sparse and encased in the coating
Head: Thread
Fly Tier: Walt Holman

Warped Frog

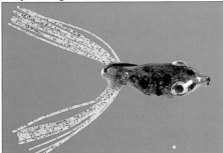

Hook: Daiichi 2461, #1/0
Thread: Clear mono
Legs: Chartreuse/green Sili Legs, divided by the end of the body
Inner Body: White craft foam folded over a rattle
Outer Body: Pearl E-Z Body Tubing, colored with felt tip markers
Eyes: Doll eye, gold with black pupils
Coating: Epoxy over the body and eyes
Fly Tier: Jerry Caruso

Water Dog

Hook: Mustad 36890, #2
Thread: Black
Tail: Black marabou tuft under two black hackles, tied divide
Body: Spun and trimmed black deer hair
Wing: Black marabou, tied to the sides
Head: Spun and trimmed black deer hair
Eyes: Stick on, red with a black pupil
Fly Tier: John Schaper

Wiggle Leg Frog

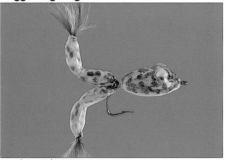

Hook: Daiichi 2720, #4
Thread: Clear mono
Legs: Closed cell foam threaded on a hook plus tuft of marabou on each
Body: Foam threaded on a hook
Coating and color: Colored with felt tip markers, and glitter mixed with epoxy
Eyes: Doll eyes, white with black pupils
Head: Thread
Fly Tier: Shane Stalcup

Wobbly Frog

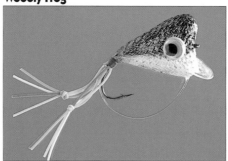

Hook: TMC 8089, #6
Thread: Orange
Legs: Multi-colored round rubber legs material, knotted
Body: Light flex cord braid, colored with felt tip markers and coated with Softex
Eyes: Doll eyes, white with black movable pupils
Weed guard: Hard mono
Lip: Hard mono coated with Softex
Fly Tier: Mike Telford

Jigs and Nymphs . . .

All Purpose Nymph

Hook: Daiichi 1750, #8
Thread: Clear mono
Tail: Short tuft of brown leech dubbing
Body and Wing: Multiple clumps of brown leech dubbing, tied along the shank
Head: Black bead
Fly Tier: Shane Stalcup

A. P. Olive Nymph

Hook: Mustad 3906B, #6 - #22
Thread: Olive
Tail: Moose body hair
Rib: Gold wire
Body: Olive dyed beaver dubbing
Wing case: Moose body hair remaining from the tail
Legs: Six strand of moose hair remaining from the wing case
Head: Beaver dubbing, thread
Fly Tier: Andre Puyans

A. P. Peacock & Pheasant

Hook: Mustad 3906B, #6 - #22
Thread: Black
Tail: Pheasant tail fibers
Rib: Copper wire
Body: Bronze peacock herl
Wing case: Pheasant tail fibers remaining from the tail
Legs: Six pheasant tail fiber remaining from the wing case
Head: Thread
Fly Tier: Andre Puyans

Baby Clouser Deceiver

Hook: Mustad 3407, #4 - #12
Thread: Black
Tail: Black saddle hackle feathers accented with black Krystal Flash
Body: Purple diamond braid
Wing: Peacock herl over black over purple buck tail
Throat: Black buck tail under a short tuft of red rabbit fur
Eyes: Heavy dumb bell, painted white with black pupils
Head: Thread coated with Aqua Flex
Fly Tier: Al Beatty

Bass Bully

Hook: Mustad 37187, #6
Thread: Purple
Tail: Twister tail, purple with blue flecks
Body: Purple crystal chenille
Legs: Sili-Legs, purple with blue flecks
Eyes: Red dumb bell with black pupils
Head: Salt water blue E-Z Shape Sparkle Body
Fly Tier: Terry Wilson

Black Bear Leech

Hook: Mustad 31753, #2/0 - #1/0
Thread: Black
Skirt: Natural black bear hair, tied completely around the hook shank
Head: Molded head painted black
Band: Mylar rainbow tinsel, wrapped as a band behind the head
Fly Tier: Reginald Denny

Black Tease

Hook: Daiichi 1720, #2 - #8
Thread: Black
Tail: Black marabou, tied long
Legs: Chartreuse rubber leg material, three per side
Body: Black zonker strip, wrapped around the hook shank
Head: Chartreuse Hot Bead, thread
Fly Tier: Bill Black, Spirit River Inc.

Bowen Damsel

Hook: Daiichi 1130, #10
Thread: Olive
Tail: Grizzly dyed olive marabou
Body: Olive pre-tape tied extended body style over the tail material
Thorax: Olive Spirit River Fine & Dry dubbing
Wing case: Brown Swiss straw
Eyes: Melted mono
Head: Thread
Fly Tier: Bill Black, Spirit River Inc.

Chartreuse Yummie

Hook: Mustad 9272, #2
Thread: Chartreuse
Tail: Chartreuse marabou
Rib: Tying Thread
Weight: Twenty wraps of .025 non-lead wire
Body: Chartreuse crystal chenille
Legs: Chartreuse round rubber leg material, tied as two double legs
Hackle: Chartreuse saddle hackle, palmered
Head: Thread
Fly Tier: Dave Duffy

Conehead Bass Bug

Hook: Mustad 79580, #2 - #4
Thread: Black
Tail: Chartreuse marabou with a few strands of Krystal Flash
Back Body: Chartreuse chenille with white hackle, palmered
Front Body: Black chenille with black hackle, palmered
Legs: White rubber, tied between the two body segments
Head: Silver cone
Fly Tier: Cliff Stringer

Cone Sucking Bunny Bugger

Hook: Daiichi 1720, #2 - #10
Thread: Black
Butt: Orange Lite Brite dubbing
Tail: Black zonker strip
Body: Black chenille
Body Hackle: Black, palmered
Wing: Black zonker strip
Head: Orange Hot Cone
Fly Tier: Bill Black, Spirit River Inc.

Crafty Clouser

Hook: Mustad 9672, #4 - #10 (the hook point rides up)
Thread: Brown
Tail: White craft fur
Body: Flat silver tinsel
Wing: Brown, copper Krystal Flash
Belly: White craft fur
Eyes: Dumb bell, painted white with black pupils
Head: Thread
Fly Tier: Duane Hada

Craig's Algae Fly

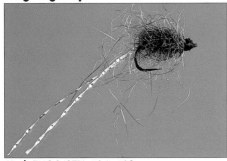

Hook: TMC 2487BL, #14 - #18
Thread: Black
Tail: Two strand of green Krystal Flash, tied long
Body: Dark green Awesome 'Possum dubbing, tied full and picked out
Head: Thread
Fly Tier: Craig Phillips

Cricket Nymph

Hook: Mustad 9672, #10
Thread: Black
Tail & antenna: Black fine rubber leg material
Rib: Fine copper wire
Body: Squirrel dubbing
Back & wing case: Dun Swiss straw
Legs: Black fine rubber leg material
Eyes: Black bead chain
Head: Thread
Fly Tier: Mike Hogue

Deadly Dragon

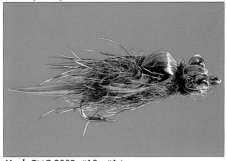

Hook: TMC 200R, #10 - #14
Thread: Brown
Tail: Two dyed gold goose biots
Body: Squirrel dubbing in a loop, tied full and picked out
Weight: Non lead wire or bead under the wing case
Wing case: Brown Swiss straw
Legs: Webby brown hackle, tied as a collar
Eyes: Melted mono
Head: Dubbing around the eyes
Fly Tier: Josh Thames

Dubbed Marabou Killer

Hook: Mustad 9671, #12
Thread: Olive
Tail: Olive marabou, tied short, flanked with gold Flashabou tied to the sides
Body: Olive marabou, dubbed using a dubbing loop
Eyes: Gold bead chain
Head: Thread
Fly Tier: Tom Broderidge

Duster Jig

Hook: Mustad 3366, #1/0
Thread: Pink
Tail: Static duster fibers
Rib: Silver tinsel, optional
Body: Static duster fibers, wrapped
Wing: Static duster fibers
Legs: Pink rubber leg material, five per side
Eyes: Large purple Razzle Eyes
Head: Thread and Aqua Flex
Fly Tier: Gretchen Beatty

Hare Dragon

Hook: Daiichi 2720, #4 (hook point rides up)
Thread: Clear mono
Tail: Olive zonker strip
Body: Zonker strip from the tail wrapped forward
Wing case: Medallion sheeting
Legs: Olive Sili Legs, spaced along the thorax
Thorax: Olive rabbit dubbing
Weight: Dumb bell with stick on eyes, white with black pupils
Head: Thread
Fly Tier: Shane Stalcup

Hot Cone Matuka Muddler

Hook: Daiichi 1720, #2 - #8
Thread: Black
Tail: Black zonker strip
Rib: Fine copper wire
Body: Black Lite Brite dubbing
Wing: Black zonker strip, accented with pearl Crystal Splash
Collar: Dyed black deer hair, spun and trimmed to shape
Head: Red Hot Cone
Fly Tier: Bill Black, Spirit River Inc.

Hot Head

Hook: Mustad 9672, #8
Thread: Fluorescent pink
Tail: Chartreuse ultra chenille
Tag: Thread
Body: Black chenille
Hackle: Black saddle, palmered
Head: Chartreuse plastic bead
Fly Tier: Mike Hogue

J's Hexagenia Nymph

Hook: Mustad 9672, #6 - #10   **Thread:** Black
Tail: Moose main fibers
Weight: Non-lead wire tied parallel under the hook shank
Gills: Pheasant after shaft feather, wrapped in the abdomen area
Abdomen: Black Brazilian Velour, tied on the top and bottom with gills to the sides
Legs: Black rubber leg material, tied between the two body segments
Thorax: Black and tan Brazilian Velour, woven
Head: Black bead
Fly Tier: Jerome Hebert

Jack's Black

Hook: Mustad 80250, #8 - #12
Thread: Black
Tail: Gold Krystal Flash, tied short
Body: Black chenille
Hackle: Black, palmered over the body
Back: Silver Krystal Flash, pulled over after wrapping the hackle
Head: Brass bead
Fly Tier: Dick Steinhorst

Jennifer's Pan Fish Shrimp

Hook: Mustad 37140, #2 - #14
Thread: Yellow
Feelers: Badger hackle tips
Eyes: Black glass bead secure by melted mono anchor
Rib: Copper wire
Body: Orange yarn
Back: Yellow closed cell foam, colored with a felt tip marker
Hackle: Ginger, palmered
Head: Trimmed foam and thread
Fly Tier: Jim Hoffman

Jig Crayfish

Hook: Eagle Claw 630, #6 - #8   **Weight:** 1/32 oz lead jig head, painted tan   **Thread:** Tan
Tail: Spare deer hair   **Antenna:** Pheasant tail fibers
Rib: Copper wire
Over body: One-half inch section of tan furry foam
Body: Tan furry foam, wrap two turns and attach the claws
Claws: Two rabbit fur clumps
Hackle: Ginger
Crayfish tail: Excess furry foam from the ribbed over body
Head: Thread
Fly Tier: Doug Christian

Jig Headed Chickabou

Hook: Mustad 9672, #6 - #8
Thread: Black
Tail: Black Chickabou
Rib: Fine gold wire
Body: Black and orange Chickabou, wrapped in three segments
Hackle: Black Soft Hackle
Eyes: Spirit River Real Eyes
Head: Black chenille
Fly Tier: Henry Hoffman

Jointed Sally

Hook: (front & back) Mustad 37187, #10, connected with heavy mono
Thread: Chartreuse
Tail: Twister tail, chartreuse with silver flecks
Body: Chartreuse crystal chenille
Legs: Double strand of chartreuse rubber leg material, knotted
Eyes: Yellow dumb bell with black pupils
Head: Chartreuse E-Z Shape Sparkle Body
Fly Tier: Terry Wilson

Krappie Killer

Hook: Mustad 9671, #10
Thread: Red
Tail: Fluorescent green marabou or color of choice
Body: Orange (top) and fluorescent green (bottom) chenille or colors of choice
Bead chain: Three set, two on the top and one on the bottom
Head: Thread
Fly Tier: Bill Chandler

Leech Jig

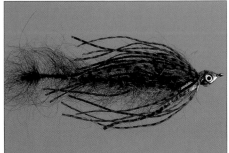

Hook: Daiichi 2720, #4
Thread: Clear mono
Tail: Purple leech yarn, furled into an extended body
Body: Leech yarn, wrapped
Legs: Purple Sili Legs, tied as a very long collar
Eyes: Dumb bell with stick on eyes, silver with black pupils
Head: Epoxy over the thread and eyes
Fly Tier: Shane Stalcup

L'il Blue Jig

Hook: Mustad 32756, #6 - #8
Thread: Blue
Tail: Golden pheasant crest feather
Body: Flat blue tinsel
Beard: Golden pheasant crest feather
Head: Molded, painted yellow with black pupils
Fly Tier: Reginald Denny

Marabou Jig

Hook: Mustad 79580, #4
Thread: Olive
Tail: Olive marabou with a few strand of Krystal Flash
Body: Root beer crystal chenille
Wing: Olive marabou
Eyes: Brass dumb bell, tied so the hook point rides up
Head: Thread
Fly Tier: Cliff Stringer

Melt Down Ant

Hook: Mustad 3906B, #10 - #12
Thread: Fluorescent orange & black
Body: Fluorescent orange back, black front, coat them with Aqua Flex or equivalent
Hackle: Black, tied sparse
Head: Thread
Fly Tier: Mike Jacobs

Monacacy Mauler

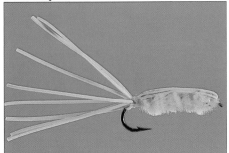

Hook: Mustad 9672, #8 - #10
Thread: Chartreuse
Tail: Chartreuse rubber leg material
Body: Chartreuse chenille, tied from the front to the back
Wing case: Chartreuse rubber leg material, tied in front and folded over
Head: Thread
Fly Tier: Terry Alexander

Mr. Right

Hook: TMC 205BL, #4 - #8 (the hook point rides up)
Thread: Black
Tail: Black marabou
Body: Black chenille
Hackle: Black saddle, palmered
Legs: Black round rubber leg material
Eyes: Dumb bell, painted yellow with black pupils (causes the hook point to ride up)
Head: Thread and black chenille
Fly Tier: Chris Mihulka

Mr. Rubber Legs

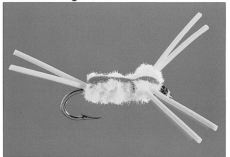

Hook: Mustad 9671, #10 - #12
Thread: Black
Tail: Yellow rubber leg material
Body: Chartreuse chenille
Over Body: Red floss
Legs: Yellow rubber leg material
Head: Thread
Fly Tier: Josh Hoeschen

Muskrat Dragon Nymph

Hook: Mustad 3906, #4
Thread: Black
Body: Muskrat strip, wrapped
Hackle: Teal flank feather, tied as a collar
Eyes: Melted mono
Head: Thread
Fly Tier: Robert Meuschke

Old Yeller Jig

Hook: Mustad 3366, #1/0 (the hook point rides up)
Thread: Yellow
Tail: Grizzly dyed yellow cape feathers, three pair
Body: Yellow chenille
Hackle: Grizzly dyed yellow, tied as a collar
Eyes: Silver dumb bell, (tied on top causing the hook point to ride up)
Head: Yellow chenille and thread
Fly Tier: Tom Broderidge

Orange Damsel

Hook: Mustad 33957, #14
Thread: Orange
Tail: Orange marabou tips, tied short and sparse
Rib: Strip of Flashabou
Body: Orange marabou
Thorax: Orange poly yarn
Legs: Orange hackle tips
Eyes: Melted mono
Head: Thread
Fly Tier: Jerry Smalley

Palmer Gnat

Hook: Scud, #10 - #12
Thread: Black
Tail: Several strands of fine white rubber leg material
Body: Black yarn
Hackle: Black, palmered
Head: Silver bead
Fly Tier: Tommy Marks

Purple Egg Sucking Dredger

Hook: Daiichi 1720, #2 - #10
Thread: Purple
Tail: Black marabou accented with pearl Fly Flash
Body: Thread
Wing: Purple marabou accented pearl Fly Flash
Throat: Black marabou
Legs: Purple rubber leg material, two per side
Eyes: Spirit River I-Balz dumb bell with stick on, pink with black pupils
Head: Purple marabou, wrapped with a red Hot Bead nose
Fly Tier: Bill Black, Spirit River Inc.

Red Egg Sucking Dredger

Hook: Daiichi 1720, #2 - #10
Thread: Red
Tail: Red marabou accented with pearl Fly Flash
Body: Thread
Wing: Pink marabou accented with pearl Fly Flash
Throat: Red marabou
Legs: Red rubber leg material, two per side
Eyes: Spirit River I-Balz dumb bell with stick on, pink with black pupils
Head: Red marabou, wrapped with a red Hot Bead nose
Fly Tier: Bill Black, Spirit River Inc.

Rick's Gill GRHE

Hook: TMC 5262, #8 - #14 (the hook point rides up)
Thread: Black
Tail: Wood chuck guard hairs
Rib: Fine copper wire
Body: Cream Super Fine dubbing
Thorax: Brown Awesome 'Possum dubbing
Eyes: Silver dumb bell, tied in the center of the thorax
Wing case: Pearl Krystal Flash
Head: Thread
Fly Tier: Craig Phillips

Rubber Rabbit

Hook: TMC 8089NP, #6 (the hook point rides up)
Thread: Purple
Tail: Purple zonker strip
Weed guard: Hard mono, optional
Body: Excess zonker strip from the tail, wrapped
Hackle: Purple speckled Sili Leg material, tied around the hook collar style
Head: Gold cone head, thread
Fly Tier: Lance Zook

Simple Shad Jig

Hook: Eagle Claw 570, #6 **Thread:** Black
Tail: Silver Krystal Flash sandwiched between red and white clumps of calf tail fibers
Body: 7/16 lead disc under a same sized disc of gold or silver holographic tape **Application:** Punch a hole through the lead/tape to accommodate the jig hook eye and fold the disc over the hook allowing the jig eye to extend up through the hole in the disc
Eyes: Painted, yellow with black pupils
Body paint: Painted black dot on each side of the body
Coating: Aqua Flex or Loon Soft Head
Fly Tier: Walt Holman

Sin City

Hook: TMC 900BL, #10
Thread: White
Tail: Light blue Krystal Flash
Body: Thread
Hackle: White, palmered over the body and in front of the wing
Wing: Light blue Krystal Flash
Head: Thread
Fly Tier: Craig Phillips

Sinking Spider

Hook: Mustad 3906B, #10 - #12
Thread: Color to match the body
Body: Chartreuse or hot pink yarn, wrapped in two segments
Legs: Rubber leg material tied between the two body segments
Head: Thread
Fly Tier: Tommy Marks

SRI Black Wooly Bomber

Hook: Daiichi 1720, #2 - #6
Thread: Black
Tail: Black marabou accented with pearl Fly Flash
Body: Black chenille accented with a pearl Fly Flash stripe on each side
Hackle: Black, palmered
Eyes: Real Eyes with stick on, gold with black pupils
Head: Black Lite Brite dubbing
Fly Tier: Bill Black, Spirit River Inc.

SRI Green Wooly Bomber

Hook: Daiichi 1720, #2 - #6
Thread: Green
Tail: Chartreuse marabou accented with pearl Fly Flash
Body: Chartreuse chenille accented with a pearl Fly Flash stripe on each side
Hackle: Black, palmered
Eyes: Real Eyes with stick on, gold with black pupils
Head: Chartreuse Lite Brite dubbing
Fly Tier: Bill Black, Spirit River Inc.

S. S. Damsel

Hook: TMC 200R, #10 - #14
Thread: Olive
Tail: Olive marabou, three to five tips
Rib: Clear Krystal Flash
Body: Closed cell foam under olive antron dubbing
Wing: Four strands of Krystal Flash, tied to the sides
Hackle: Partridge dyed olive
Head: Thread
Fly Tier: Jeffrey Hines

Steel Bugger

Hook: Mustad 33620, #4 - #8
Thread: Red
Tail: White marabou, tied very sparse
Body: Orange, chartreuse, and pink chenille
Hackle: White, palmered
Head: Brass bead
Fly Tier: Bill Chandler

Strip Tease

Hook: Daiichi 1720, #2 - #8
Thread: Purple
Tail: Purple zonker strip accented with pearl Crystal Splash
Legs: Chartreuse rubber leg material, three per side
Body: Purple zonker strip, wrapped around the hook shank
Head: Chartreuse Hot Bead, thread
Fly Tier: Bill Black, Spirit River Inc.

Terry's Nymph - Streamer

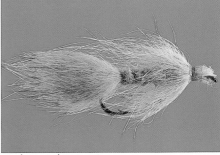

Hook: Mustad 9671, #8
Thread: Gray or color to match the body
Tail: Tuft of gray rabbit or color of choice
Weight: Several turns of non-lead wire, optional
Rib: Gold or copper wire
Body: Dubbed rabbit fur to match the tail
Head & collar: Rabbit fur tied back Thunder Creek style
Fly Tier: Terry Alexander

Velcro Bugger

Hook: Mustad 9672, #2 - #8
Thread: Black
Tail: Olive marabou or color of choice
Rib: Copper wire, optional
Body: Green Velcro strip (loop part of Velcro will snag the fishes teeth and aid in hooking)
Hackle: Large olive neck hackle or color of choice, palmered
Head: Thread
Fly Tier: Greg Peterka

Warmwater Coachman

Hook: Mustad 3906B, #8 - #14
Thread: Black
Tail: Short tuft of red marabou, tied sparse
Rib: Copper wire
Body: Peacock crystal chenille
Hackle: Brown hen hackle, tied as a collar
Head: Thread
Fly Tier: Terry Alexander

Who Bee

Hook: Jig hook, #6 - #12
Thread: Yellow
Tail: Chartreuse marabou, tied short and sparse
Body: Black/yellow variegated chenille
Head: Jig head painted yellow
Eyes: Black painted over the jig head
Fly Tier: Hebert Carmen

Woolly Jig

Hook: Small jig head, #12 - #14
Thread: Black
Tail: Black marabou
Body: Fine black chenille
Hackle: Grizzly, palmered
Head: Jig head, painted white
Fly Tier: Mike Jacobs

Wooly Bear

Hook: Mustad 9672, #6 - #10
Thread: Black
Body: Black and orange chenille, tied in three segments
Hackle: Light dun, palmered
Head: Thread
Fly Tier: Jack Pangburn

Chapter 6

SALTWATER FLIES

By Tom Tripi

Many fly tiers do not tie standard fly patterns in a strict sense of the word, i.e. they do not follow a specific recipe, but instead design a "new" fly by somewhat modifying the size, color, or shape of the original pattern. If the new fly is balanced, tied proportionately and swims right, we all know it will catch fish, especially saltwater fish. Now-a-days, a great majority of "new" saltwater flies are nothing more than modifications of older established patterns, i.e. the new red, white and blue Deceiver, represents a radical color change, but it's still a Deceiver. With all of the amateur fly tiers in the world working on new patterns and concepts, it's probably near impossible to claim that a new pattern is yours; surely someone has tied it in the past and just has not publicized their "secret".

I consider myself a fly designer. My commercial patterns are originals and I usually do not tie the so-called "standard" saltwater patterns. My fly tying studio is wide open, no materials are stored, and all are visible to me while I design and tie. One of my concerns relating to the designing of a new fly centers on its name. When it is named, I then tie a fly to match the name. Not many fly fishers have heard of a Muddled Deceiving spoon, or a Deceiving Popping Spoon (which are both for redfish), or an oldie but goody—the Circle Spoon (a 7/0 creation tied on a circle hook, and used for cobia). (And thanks to "FFFer" Jon Cave for conceiving the spoon fly!) The three preceding flies are examples of innovative stylizations to an older established pattern. The results are new or hybrid flies tied for different purposes. Although they are new flies, they certainly do not replace the base pattern. Included in this chapter are many patterns that represent the "state of the art" in current saltwater fly tying. They portray new, never-published patterns as well as clever innovations to the now-older "standards". The flies introduced signify the continuation of "adaptive reuse" of new, modern materials, many of which were never heard of years ago and were never intended for fly tying. They definitely expand upon an area in the modern art of tying that has the greatest artistic and design latitude—saltwater fly tying. Enjoy these pages, experiment with the patterns, and by all means, adapt and tie them for your own style of fly fishing.

—Tom Tripi
LaPlace, Louisiana

Atlantic, Gulf, and Pacific Coast Baitfish . . .

Albert Special

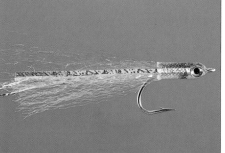

Hook: Eagle Claw 254, #1/0
Thread: Fine mono
Tail: White ultra hair
Body: Non-lead wire under silver body braid
Wing: Smoke ultra hair under silver metallic flash flanked by two strips of tinsel
Over Body: Pearl E-Z Body Tubing equal in length to the hook shank
Eyes: Stick on, silver with black pupils
Coating: Epoxy covering the over body, head, and eyes
Fly Tier: Gary Dubiel

All Purpose Deep Minnow (Clouser Style)

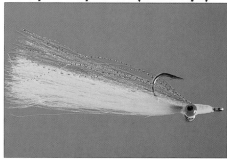

Hook: Mustad 34007, #1/0 - #10 (the hook point rides up)
Thread: Chartreuse
Eyes: Dumb bell, painted fluorescent pink with black pupils
Under Wing: Fluorescent green Fishair, tie on the top of the shank (under part of the fly's wing)
Wing: Silver Krystal Flash over pink Fishair over green Fishair (same color as the under wing)
Head: Thread
Fly Tier: Len Elzie

Atlantic Silver Side

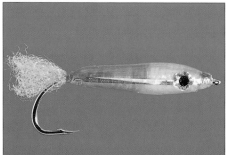

Hook: Mustad 34011, #2/0 - #2
Thread: White
Tail: Light tan macramé yarn, frayed and trimmed to shape
Body: Tan macramé yarn, wrapped to form a tapered body
Eyes: Stick on, silver with black pupils
Head: Thread
Coating: Epoxy or Aqua Flex over the whole body, eyes, and head
Fly Tier: Ron Winn

Autumn Ice

Hook: Mustad 3407, #2
Thread: Orange
Tail: Copper Krystal Flash over four dyed reddish-brown saddle hackle feathers
Hackles: Reddish-brown saddle hackle feathers tied fore and aft
Body: Orange Estaz
Head: Thread
Fly Tier: Tom Broderidge

Bead Head Candle Fish

Hook: Mustad 34007, #2 - #4
Thread: White
Wing: White under chartreuse buck tail with chartreuse Krystal Flash
Topping: Olive buck tail
Eyes: Molded green with black pupils
Head: Two silver lined crystal beads
Fly Tier: Roger Swengel

Bead Rattler

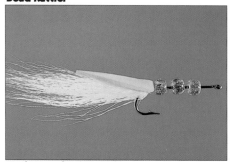

Hook: Mustad 34011, #1/0
Thread: White
Tail: Yellow closed cell foam over white buck tail, the foam is trimmed to an arrow head shape
Body: Three gold pony beads, the first is glued to the base of the tail, the others move freely
Head: Movable beads
Fly Tier: Tom Broderidge

Beaded Wobbler

Hook: Mustad 3407, #1
Thread: White
Tail: Silver Krystal Flash over a white zonker strip
Body: Four medium crystal beads and two large beads, strung and tied to the hook in three segments, the largest pair of beads are in the middle of the body
Body Coating: Loon Hard Head
Head: Thread
Fly Tier: Tom Broderidge

Belly Dancer (Clown)

Hook: Mustad 34007, #4/0 - #1/0 (hook point rides up)
Thread: Chartreuse
Body: Five extra large scarlet beads, tied on top of the hook (causes the point to ride up)
Under Body: Flat silver tinsel
Wing: Rainbow Krystal Flash over chartreuse over white buck tail, flanked by pearl Flashabou
Eyes: Molded eyes, white with black pupils
Head: Thread
Coating: Soft Body or Aqua Flex over the head and beads
Fly Tier: Joe Warren

Belly Dancer (Pearl Shad)

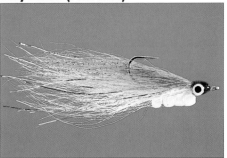

Hook: Mustad 34007, #4/0 - #1/0 (hook point rides up)
Thread: Black
Body: Four or five large pearl glass beads, tied on top of the hook (causes the point to ride up)
Wing: Gray over white buck tail, accented with Crystal Cloth and rainbow Krystal Flash
Eyes: Molded eyes, white with black pupils
Head: Thread
Coating: Soft Body or Aqua Flex over the head and beads
Fly Tier: Joe Warren

Belly Dancer (Silver Shad)

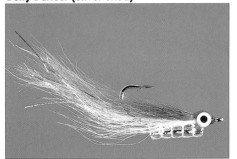

Hook: Mustad 34007, #4/0 - #1/0 (hook point rides up)
Thread: Black
Body: Five extra large glass beads, tied on top of the hook (causes the point to ride up)
Under Body: Flat silver tinsel
Wing: Dun over white buck tail, accented with Crystal Cloth and Polar Flash
Eyes: Molded eyes, white with black pupils
Head: Thread
Coating: Soft Body or Aqua Flex over the head and beads
Fly Tier: Joe Warren

Bendback Minnow

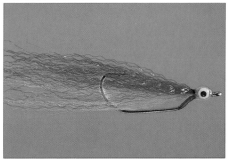

Hook: Mustad 34011, #2/0 - #2, bent to shape (the hook point rides up)
Thread: Orange
Wing: Purple over pink over white Super Hair
Throat: Red floss
Eyes: Stick on, yellow with black pupils
Head: Coated with epoxy or Aqua Flex
Fly Tier: Chris Mihulka

Big Eye Candle Fish

Hook: Mustad 34011, #4 - #10
Thread: White
Wing: White buck tail and silver Flashabou
Gills: Red tying thread
Topping: Rainbow Krystal Flash under olive buck tail
Eyes: Yellow dolls, four millimeter
Head: Epoxy between the eyes and over the head
Fly Tier: Roger Swengel

Big Skinny

Hook: Mustad 34011, #1/2
Thread: Clear mono
Tail: Dark blue over light blue over white Fishair, trimmed to shape
Body: Blue, plastic necklace tape
Collar: Blue in front of red chenille with a large craft bead centered over both
Eyes: Painted yellow with black pupils
Wing: Dark blue over white Fishair, tied sparse
Head: Thread
Fly Tier: Tom Berry

Black John

Hook: Mustad 34007, #2/0 - #8
Thread: Red
Tail: Black zonker strip flanked with a black marabou collar, mixed with pearl Krystal Flash
Rib: Silver wire
Body: Black chenille
Hackle: Black saddle hackle, palmered
Eyes: Black dumb bell
Head: Thread
Fly Tier: Len Elzie

Black Tip Hot Head

Hook: Eagle Claw, L193G #2/0 red
Thread: Red
Tail: White buck tail mixed with black Krystal Flash
Wing: Black Krystal Flash over olive over white buck tail
Wing flank: Whiting American Black Lace rooster feathers
Eyes: Stick on, gold with black pupils
Head: Thread coated with Aqua Flex
Fly Tier: Al Beatty

Blue Back Herring

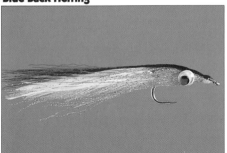

Hook: Mustad 3407, #1/0 - #4
Thread: White
Wing: Four white saddle hackles under pearl Flashabou and peacock Krystal Flash
Topping: Purple Flashabou
Belly: Light blue Krystal Flash
Eyes: Doll eyes, white with black movable pupils
Head: Thread
Coating: Aqua Flex or Soft Body over the head, eyes, and one-half of the wing
Fly Tier: Jack Pangburn

Blue Rip Tide

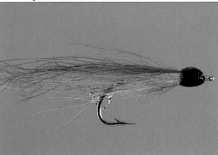

Hook: Mustad 34007, #3/0 - #1
Thread: Black
Tail: Picked out body material
Body: Silver mylar tinsel tubing
Wing: Dark blue over dyed turquoise polar bear hair
Belly: Dyed gray polar bear hair
Throat: Red polar bear hair
Head: Thread coated with epoxy
Fly Tier: Reginald Denny

Blue Royal (Mini Deceiver)

Hook: TMC 9394, #10
Thread: White
Tail: Two grizzly hackle tips with two white hackle tips over
Wing: Blue yak over white kid goat hair
Throat: White under red kid goat hair
Eyes: Stick on, white with black pupils
Head: Coated with epoxy over the thread and eyes
Fly Tier: David Hunter

Broadside Minnow

Hook: Mustad 3407, #4
Thread: White
Tail: White marabou under silver Flashabou flanked by two grizzly hackles
Throat: Red Krystal Flash
Body: White chenille under pearl mylar tubing
Wing: White marabou between two white hackle feathers
Eyes: Doll eyes
Head: Coated with clear Aqua Flex or equivalent and ultra fine pearl glitter
Fly Tier: Greg Weisgerber

Brooke Autumn Blonde

Hook: Eagle Claw 254NR, #2/0
Thread: Yellow
Tail: Red buck tail accented with gold Krystal Flash
Body: Gold diamond braid
Wing: Yellow buck tail accented with gold Krystal Flash
Eyes: Stick on, gold with black pupils
Head: Thread coated with Aqua Flex
Fly Tier: Gretchen Beatty

Brook's Blonde

Hook: Eagle Claw 254NR, #2/0
Thread: Olive
Tail: White buck tail
Body: Silver diamond braid
Wing: Olive buck tail
Eyes: Stick on, gold with black pupils
Head: Thread coated with Aqua Flex
Fly Tier: Gretchen Beatty

BT American (Bend Back)

Hook: Eagle Claw L143S, #1/0 - #2 (shaped bend back style, the hook point rides up)
Thread: White
Wing: Peacock herl over black buck tail over black Whiting American hackle feathers over white buck tail accented with gold Krystal Flash
Eyes: EZY Eyes with stick on, gold with black pupils
Head: Red Glitter Glue under an Aqua Flex coating, over the throat, eyes, and head
Fly Tier: Al Beatty

BT Bend Back

Hook: Eagle Claw L143S, #1/0 - #2 (shaped bend back style, the hook point rides up)
Thread: Black
Wing: Black over chartreuse over white buck tail accented with black Krystal Flash
Eyes: EZY Eyes with stick on, gold with black pupils
Head: Peacock Glitter Glue under an Aqua Flex coating, over the throat, eyes, and head
Fly Tier: Al Beatty

BT Clouser

Hook: Mustad 3407, #4 - #8 (the hook point rides up)
Thread: Hot orange (or color of choice)
Wing: Black over chartreuse over white buck tail accented with gold Krystal Flash
Eyes: EZY Eyes with stick on, gold with black pupils
Head: Thread and Aqua Flex, tied Clouser style
Fly Tier: Al Beatty

Bubble Dancer

Hook: Eagle Claw LO67, #4 (the hook point rides up)
Thread: Red
Tail: Pearl Krystal Flash and orange rubber leg material
Body: Chartreuse and orange marabou, tied in two segments, collar style
Eyes: Dumb bell, painted green with black pupils
Weed guard: Hard mono, optional
Head: Thread coated with epoxy or Aqua Flex
Fly Tier: Chris Mihulka

Charlotte (Tube Fly)

Hook: Two inch long tube, use with a Mustad 92553S or equivalent
Thread: Purple
Body: Pearl mylar tinsel
Wing: White over purple polar bear or equivalent, tied in the round
Head: Thread
Fly Tier: Reginald Denny

Chubbie

Hook: Mustad 3407, #2
Thread: Blue
Body and Tail: Light and dark blue yarn with silver braided mylar side strips
Tying instruction: All materials are tied at the hook eye, then folded back
Eyes: Doll eyes, white with black pupils
Head: Thread
Fly Tier: Tom Broderidge

Clouser Deceiver (Black)

Hook: Mustad 34007, #1/0 - #2
Thread: Black
Tail: Four black saddle hackles accented with black Krystal Flash
Body: Peacock diamond braid
Wing: Peacock herl over black buck tail, flanked with black Krystal Flash
Eyes: Heavy dumb bell, painted white with black pupils
Throat: Sparse black buck tail, tied to the end of the hook
Head: Thread coated with Aqua Flex
Fly Tier: Al Beatty

Clouser Deceiver (Blue)

Hook: Mustad 34007, #1/0 - #2
Thread: White
Tail: Four white saddle hackles accented with pearl Krystal Flash
Body: Pearl diamond braid
Wing: Peacock herl over blue buck tail, flanked with pearl Krystal Flash
Eyes: Heavy dumb bell, painted white with black pupils
Throat: Sparse white buck tail under a short tuft of red rabbit fur
Head: Thread coated with Aqua Flex
Fly Tier: Al Beatty

Clouser Deceiver (Pink)

Hook: Mustad 34007, #1/0 - #2
Thread: White
Tail: Four white saddle hackles accented with pearl Krystal Flash
Body: Pearl diamond braid
Wing: Purple over pink buck tail, flanked with pearl Krystal Flash
Eyes: Heavy dumb bell, painted white with black pupils
Throat: Sparse white buck tail under a short tuft of red rabbit fur
Head: Thread coated with Aqua Flex
Fly Tier: Al Beatty

Clouser Deceiver (Yellow)

Hook: Mustad 34007, #1/0 - #2
Thread: White
Tail: Four white saddle hackles accented with pearl Krystal Flash
Body: Pearl diamond braid
Wing: Peacock herl over yellow buck tail, flanked with pearl Krystal Flash
Eyes: Heavy dumb bell, painted white with black pupils
Throat: Sparse white buck tail under a short tuft of red rabbit fur
Head: Thread coated with Aqua Flex
Fly Tier: Al Beatty

Cocaho Seaducer

Hook: Mustad 34011, #2 - #6
Thread: Olive
Tail: Two pairs of olive grizzly saddle hackles, divided, with mixed strands of red, orange, and silver Krystal Flash
Body: Grizzly dyed olive saddle hackle, palmered and mixed with silver Flashabou
Eyes: Yellow and black paint
Head: Coated with red cement before placing the eyes, then coated with epoxy
Fly Tier: Dick Steinhorst

Cone Head Mullet

Hook: DaiRiki 930, #1/0 (bend back shape, the hook point rides up)
Thread: Red
Weight: Large silver cone head
Wing: Badger saddle hackles, silver Flashabou, and root beer Krystal Flash
Head: Pearl lure tape wrapped around the cone head and trimmed to shape
Eyes: Stick on, yellow with black pupils
Coating: Epoxy over the head and eyes
Fly Tier: Scott Sanchez

Croft's Articulated Candle Fish

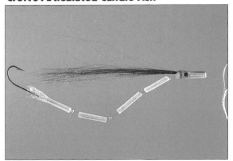

Hook: Mustad 34007, #4
Thread: Gudebrod tying mono
Body: One-eighth inch OD tube covered with braided mylar, super glued, & epoxied, cut into half inch sections; small hobby beads act as bearings between the tube sections
Wing: Moss green fish hair over olive fish hair, tied sparse
Head: Three wraps of red thread for the gills, epoxy coating after placing the eyes
Eyes: Silver stick on with black pupils
Fly Tier: Mike Croft

Dark Maine Deceiver

Hook: Mustad 34007, #2
Thread: Black
Tail: Four black saddle hackles accented with copper Krystal Flash
Body: Pearl mylar tubing
Wing: Peacock herl over black dyed buck tail
Throat: Short red tuft of Krystal Flash over black buck tail
Eyes: Painted, white with black pupil
Head: Thread coated with Aqua Flex
Fly Tier: Al Beatty

Dark Rip Tide

Hook: Mustad 34007, #3/0 - #1
Thread: Black
Tail: Picked out body material
Body: Silver mylar tinsel tubing
Wing: Black over purple dyed polar bear hair or equivalent
Belly: Dyed yellow polar bear hair
Throat: Red polar bear hair
Head: Thread coated with epoxy
Fly Tier: Reginald Denny

Deceiving Muddled Spoon Fly

Hook: Mustad 34011, #2/0 - #2 (hook point rides up)
Thread: Red
Tail: Flash mixed with chartreuse over white buck tail, flanked with grizzly dyed chartreuse saddles hackle
Tag: Red thread
Body: Gold mylar tube, flattened with clear finger nail polish into a spoon shaped body
Legs: Chartreuse/black Sili Leg material, four per side
Head and wings: Flared and trimmed chartreuse deer hair
Topping: Flashabou over the wings
Fly Tier: Tom Tripi

Dorado Fly

Hook: Mustad 9175, #3/0
Thread: White
Tail: Gold mylar braid, picked out
Wing: Green over chartreuse over white Fish Hair accented with Krystal Flash
Head: Epoxy mixed with green glitter on top
Eyes: Painted large, yellow with black pupils
Fly Tier: Chappy Chapman

Double G (Bend Back)

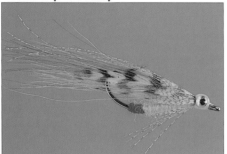

Hook: Mustad 34007, #2/0 - #8 (bent to shape, the hook rides up)   **Thread:** Fluorescent green
Butt: Fluorescent red wool   **Body:** Fluorescent green wool
Wing: Pearl Krystal Flash over green dyed goat hair and buck tail
Wing flank: Grizzly dyed chartreuse hackle feathers, one on each side
Throat: Pearl Krystal Flash, tied sparse
Cheeks: Mallard flank feather, one on each side
Eyes: Stick on, gold with black pupils
Head: Thread with epoxy over the head and eyes
Fly Tier: Len Elzie

Dr. Ed's Red Fish Special

Hook: Mustad 34011, #2 (the hook point rides up)
Thread: Black
Tail: Orange marabou
Body: Gold mylar tinsel under clear "V" Rib
Wing: Fox squirrel tail over gold Krystal Flash, flanked by two grizzly hackles
Eyes: Bead chain or dumb bell eyes
Head: Thread
Fly Tier: Ed Rizzolo

Eldridge Emu (Blue)

Hook: Mustad 34007, #1 - #6
Thread: White
Tail: White buck tail accented with pearl Krystal Flash
Body: Pearl diamond braid
Wing: Peacock herl over blue buck tail, flanked with two natural gray emu feathers
Throat: Long white buck tail accented with pearl Krystal Flash
Eyes: Doll eyes, white with black pupils
Head: Thread coated with Aqua Flex over the eyes and the first part of the wing/body
Fly Tier: Al Beatty

Eldridge Emu (Green)

Hook: Mustad 34007, #1 - #6
Thread: White
Tail: White buck tail accented with pearl Krystal Flash
Body: Pearl diamond braid
Wing: Peacock herl over green buck tail, flanked with two natural gray emu feathers
Throat: Long white buck tail accented with pearl Krystal Flash
Eyes: Doll eyes, pearl with black pupils
Head: Thread coated with Aqua Flex
Fly Tier: Al Beatty

Eldridge Emu (Orange)

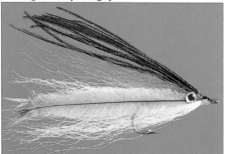

Hook: Mustad 34007, #1 - #6
Thread: White
Tail: White buck tail accented with pearl Krystal Flash
Body: Pearl diamond braid
Wing: Peacock herl over orange buck tail, flanked with two natural gray emu feathers
Throat: Long white buck tail accented with pearl Krystal Flash
Eyes: Doll eyes, white with black pupils
Head: Thread coated with Aqua Flex
Fly Tier: Al Beatty

E-Z Body Striper Fly

Hook: Eagle Claw 254, #6/0 – #1/0
Thread: White
Tail: Blue Super Hair topped with blue Flashabou
Body: Medium pearl E-Z Body Braid
Wing: Blue McFlylon
Throat: White McFlylon
Eyes: Three dimensional, silver with black pupils
Head: Thread, coated with Loon Hard Head Fly Finish
Fly Tier: Mark Hoeser

False Pilchard

Hook: Mustad 34007, #2/0 - #1
Thread: Gudebrod clear
Tail: Pearl Flashabou under six white hackles flanked by natural grizzly stripes
Hackle: Red, tied at the back of the body
Body: White crystal chenille
Eyes: Silver bead chain
Weed guards: Hard Mason mono
Head: Thread
Fly Tier: Len Roberts

Fat Head

Hook: Mustad 3407, #2
Thread: Yellow
Tail: Gold mylar tubing, sealed near the end with orange thread, tip is picked out
Wing: Red ostrich herl over four yellow saddle hackle feathers
Eyes: Doll eyes, white with black pupils
Head: Yellow chenille and thread, coated with Loon Hard Head
Fly Tier: Tom Broderidge

Flash Back

Hook: Mustad 34007, #2/0 and larger
Thread: Blue
Tail: Four white saddle hackle feathers over white buck tail
Wing: Blue Krystal Flash over white buck tail
Throat: Red marabou over white buck tail
Eyes: Doll eyes, white with black pupils
Head: Thread and epoxy over the head and eyes
Fly Tier: Tom Broderidge

Flasher

Hook: Mustad 34011, #1 (the hook point rides up)
Thread: Primrose
Tail: Clear mono and a gold Colorado spinner blade
Weight: Non-lead wire tied to the hook shank
Body: Gold embossed tinsel
Wing: Chartreuse Fishair over chartreuse wool
Eyes: Stick on, red with black pupils
Head: Thread and eyes coated with Loon hard Head or epoxy
Fly Tier: Tom Broderidge

Gary's Lil'haden

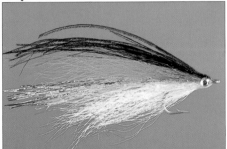

Hook: Eagle Claw 254, #2/0 - #1
Thread: Fine mono
Body: Non-lead wire covered with red body braid
Under Wing: White buck tail and pearl body braid, picked out
Wing: Peacock herl over olive buck tail over silver metallic flash
Eyes: Stick on, silver with black pupils
Head: Epoxy over the head and eyes
Fly Tier: Gary Dubiel

Goat Fish #1

Hook: Mustad 9175, #3/0
Thread: White
Tail: Gold mylar tubing, picked out
Wing: Black over red over white Fish Hair accented with the same color of Krystal Flash
Wing markings: Black bars placed using a felt tip marker
Gills: Fluorescent red single strand floss
Head: Epoxy mixed with glitter flakes on the top
Eyes: Painted large, yellow with black pupils
Fly Tier: Chappy Chapman

Goat Fish #2

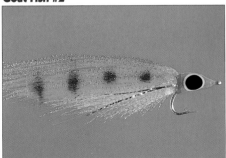

Hook: Mustad 9175, #3/0
Thread: White
Tail: Gold over pearl Krystal Flash
Wing: Pink over white Fish Hair accented with the same colors of Krystal Flash
Wing flank and marking: Flanked with silver Flashabou and marked with a felt tip marker
Head: Epoxy mixed with orange glitter
Eyes: Painted large, yellow with black pupils
Fly Tier: Chappy Chapman

Goat Fish #3

Hook: Mustad 9175, #3/0
Thread: White
Tail: Pearl Krystal Flash
Wing: Light blue over dark blue over green over pink Fish Hair accented with Krystal Flash
Gills: Fluorescent red single strand floss
Head: Epoxy mixed with green glitter on top
Eyes: Painted large, yellow with black pupils
Fly Tier: Chappy Chapman

Gold Fiber Minnow

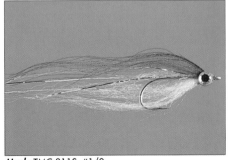

Hook: TMC 811S, #1/0
Thread: Fine mono
Wing: Black Flouro Fiber over white Flouro Fiber over gold metallic flash
Eyes: Stick on doll eyes, white with black pupils
Head: EZ Shape Sparkle Body material, olive on the top and red (gills) on the bottom
Fly Tier: Gary Dubiel

Golden Fleece

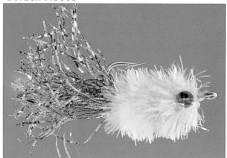

Hook: Mustad 3407, #2 (the hook point rides up)
Thread: Chartreuse
Tail: Gold braided mylar tubing, picked out
Body: Chartreuse ice chenille
Eyes: Dumb bell, painted hot orange with black pupils (causes the hook point to ride up)
Head: Thread
Fly Tier: Tom Broderidge

Greenling Minnow

Hook: TMC 9395, #2 **Thread:** Chartreuse **Tail:** Grizzly dyed olive Chickabou **Rib:** Medium copper wire
Body: Nylon parachute cord dyed Chartreuse
Wing: Four grizzly dyed olive hen saddle feathers, tied matuka style
Gills: Red Chickabou, tied on the sides before wrapping the hackle
Hackle: Grizzly dyed olive, tied as a collar
Eyes: Spirit River Real Eyes, white with black pupils
Head: Topped with green ribbon floss, topped with an epoxy coating
Fly Tier: Henry Hoffman

Gretchen's Candle

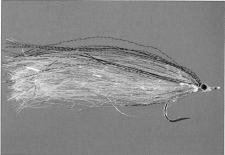

Hook: Eagle Claw 254NR, #1/0
Thread: Fluorescent lime
Body: Tiewell flash, wrapped
Wing: Tiewell flash, peacock over dark green over mixed pearl
Eyes: Fisker Design EZY-Eyes and stick on, gold with black pupils
Head: Thread and Aqua Flex
Fly Tier: Gretchen Beatty

Hopping John

Hook: Mustad 34007, #2/0 - #8
Thread: White
Tail: White zonker strip or white marabou, mixed with pearl Krystal Flash
Rib: Silver wire
Body: White chenille
Hackle: White saddle hackle, palmered
Eyes: Silver dumb bell
Head: Thread
Fly Tier: Len Elzie

Hot Head (Grizzly)

Hook: Eagle Claw L193G, #2/0 red
Thread: Red
Tail: White buck tail and black Krystal Flash
Wing: Olive over white buck tail, flanked by four grizzly hackle feathers
Eyes: Stick on, gold with black pupils
Head: Thread coated with Aqua Flex
Fly Tier: Gretchen Beatty

Ice Blue

Hook: Mustad 3407, #2
Thread: Blue
Tail: Blue Krystal Flash over four dyed blue saddle hackle feathers
Hackles: Blue saddle hackle feathers tied fore and aft
Body: Pearl Estaz
Head: Thread
Fly Tier: Tom Broderidge

Ice Royal

Hook: Mustad 3407, #2
Thread: Red
Tail: Gold Krystal Flash over four dyed red saddle hackle feathers
Hackles: Red saddle hackle feathers, tied fore and aft
Body: Yellow Estaz
Head: Thread
Fly Tier: Tom Broderidge

JP Sardina

Hook: Trey Combs Big Game, #3/0 - #1/0
Thread: Black
Wing: Olive over white buck tail accented with blue and pearl Flashabou
Belly: Pearl green Angle Hair
Eyes: Stick on, silver with black pupils
Head: Thread
Fly Tier: Jeff Priest

Juvenile Baitfish (Bend Back)

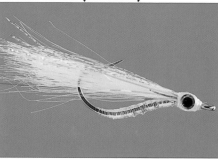

Hook: Mustad 34007, #2/0 - #8 (bent to shape, the hook rides up)
Thread: White
Weight: Several turns of non-lead wire
Body: Pearl, medium mylar tinsel
Wing: Pearl Krystal Flash over white Fishair flanked by pearl Flashabou on the sides
Eyes: Stick on, silver with black pupils
Head: Thread coated with epoxy over the eyes and head
Fly Tier: Len Elzie

Krystal Baby

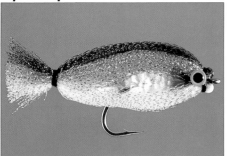

Hook: DaiRiki 930, #1/0
Thread: Black
Body: White chenille with red rabbit collar, tied as an under body
Wing: White under darker colors of Krystal Flash, tied pointing forward and pulled over
Fly Tail: Krystal Flash from the wing, tied together and trimmed to shape
Eyes: Doll eyes, blue with black pupils
Head: Thread
Fly Tier: Lance Zook

Lance's Sunshine Minnow

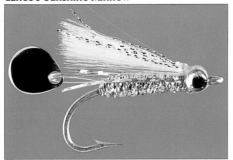

Hook: Mustad 34007, #2/0 - #6
Thread: White
Tail: Hard mono loop with Colorado spinner blade
Weight: Several turns of non-lead wire
Body: Pearl sparkle braid, wrapped
Wing: Pearl Krystal Flash over white Fishair flanked by pearl Flashabou on the sides
Eyes: Stick on, silver with black pupils
Head: Thread coated with epoxy over the eyes and the head
Fly Tier: Len Elzie

Lefty's Deceiver

Hook: Mustad 34007, #2/0 -#10
Thread: White
Tail: Eight white saddle hackle feathers
Body: Tying thread
Wing: Gray over white buck tail, several strands of Krystal Flash
Belly: White buck tail
Throat: Red Krystal Flash
Eyes: Silver stick on with black pupils
Head: Thread coat with epoxy
Fly Tier: Lefty Kreh

Light Maine Deceiver

Hook: Mustad 34007, #2
Thread: White
Tail: Four white saddle feathers accented with pearl Krystal Flash
Body: Pearl mylar tubing
Wing: Peacock herl over green dyed buck tail, flanked with grizzly dyed yellow feathers
Throat: Short red tuft of Krystal Flash over white buck tail
Eyes: Painted, white with black pupils
Head: Thread coated with Aqua Flex
Fly Tier: Al Beatty

Liljo

Hook: Mustad 34007, #2 - #4
Thread: White
Wing: White Arctic fox fur under pearl, olive, and dark green Polar Flash
Throat: Red yarn
Eyes: Spirit River 3-D Molded Eyes, silver 3.5
Head: Two large glass beads, clear/pearl color
Fly Tier: Roger Swengel

Lipstick Minnow

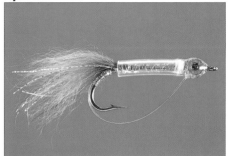

Hook: Mustad 34011, #2
Thread: Metallic sewing thread
Tail: Gray rabbit hair tuft with silver Krystal Flash
Under Body: Rainbow Krystal Flash
Over Body: Clear vinyl tubing
Eyes: Stick on, red with black pupils
Head: Thread with an epoxy coating over the eyes and head
Weed guard: Hard mono, optional
Fly Tier: Scott Sanchez

Lost Coast

Hook: TMC 911S, #1/0 - #2
Thread: Clear mono
Tail: Ten to twenty strand of pearl or silver Flashabou
Body and Wing: Frayed pearl Mylar Tubing with white Orvis' Widow's Web over
Application: Tied in three segments, collar style
Veiling: Metallic blue Flashabou under black Krystal Flash
Throat: Red Krystal Flash, tied sparse
Head: Thread
Eyes: Stick on, silver with black pupils coated with Loon Soft Head
Fly Tier: Mike McCarthy

Mac Pilchard

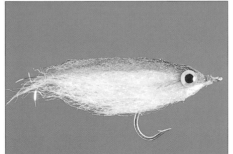

Hook: Mustad 34007, #2/0 - #2   **Thread:** White
Wing: Light color macramé cord (frayed), tied in three segments along the hook shank   **Belly:** One clump of the same color macramé cord as used for the wing
Shaping: Trim and tape both the belly and wings
Topping: Darker green macramé cord under green Krystal Flash
Lateral strip: Pearl Flashabou
Eyes: Stick on doll eyes, light green with black pupils
Coating: Epoxy or Aqua Flex over the front of the wings, head, and eyes   **Head:** Thread
Fly Tier: Ron Winn

Maybe Bunker

Hook: Mustad 94840, #1
Thread: White
Wing: Black over purple over white Polar Fibre with pearl Comes Alive mixed in
Eyes: Doll eyes, gold with black pupils
Throat: Red felt tip marker
Coating: Thinned clear silicone
Fly Tier: Jerry Caruso

Mihulka Surf Eel

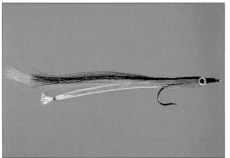

Hook: Mustad 34011, #2/0
Thread: Black
Body: Large pearl mylar tubing as an extended body, tied off with red thread and picked out
Wing: Black over chartreuse Super Hair
Eyes: Stick on, silver with black pupils
Coating: Epoxy or Aqua Flex over the body, eyes, and head area
Fly Tier: Chris Mihulka

Mylar Fishie

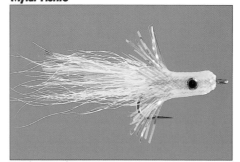

Hook: Mustad 34007, #4 - #10
Thread: White
Body and Wing: Pearl Flashabou over white buck tail
Head: Mylar tubing, reversed over the shank
Eyes: Stick on, white with black pupils
Coating: Aqua Flex or Softex over the head and eyes
Fly Tier: Ilene Hirsh

Nite Snooker

Hook: Eagle Claw 254, #2
Thread: Fine mono
Tail: Pearl Krystal Flash
Body: Pearl body braid
Wing: White Arctic fox hair
Head: Thread coated with pearl EZ Shape Sparkle Body
Fly Tier: Gary Dubiel

No MurSee Streamer

Hook: Mustad 3407, #2/0 - #1
Thread: Red
Body/Wing: White buck tail and silver Flashabou
Wing Topping: Twelve strands of peacock herl
Hackle: Red marabou, tied as a collar
Eyes: Painted, white with black pupils
Head: Thread
Fly Tier: Bill Murdich

Old Glory

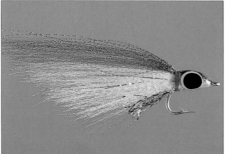

Hook: Mustad 9175, #3/0
Thread: White
Tail: Silver mylar tubing, picked out
Wing: Blue over white Krystal Flash mixed with blue and pearl Flashabou
Gills: Fluorescent red single strand floss
Head: Epoxy mixed with blue glitter on the top
Eyes: Painted large, yellow with black pupils
Fly Tier: Chappy Chapman

Pic's Special (Mohawk Spoon Fly)

Hook: Mustad 3407, #2/0 - #2 (hook point rides up)
Thread: Olive   **Tail:** Pearl Flashabou and two Reeves pheasant rump feathers, delta style
Eyes: Yellow dumb with a black pupil
Body: Gold mylar tube, tied part of the way around the hook bend to meet the eyes   **Body preparation:** Coat with nail polish and flatten into a spoon shaped body
Wing or body covering: Zonker strip over the spoon body
Legs: Eight green Sili Legs, tied at the eye
Weed guard: Mono loop, tied in at the eye, optional
Head: Thread
Fly Tier: Tom Tripi

Rabbit Shad

Hook: Mustad 3407, #1/0 - #2
Thread: White
Tail: White Zonker strip
Gills: Red hackle tied as a beard at the hook bend
Body: White yarn
Wing: Gray squirrel tail over a white Zonker strip
Head: Large mylar tubing
Eyes: Doll eyes, glued to the head
Coating: Aqua Flex or Softex over the head and eyes
Fly Tier: Robert Meuschke

Red Buster (Bendback)

Hook: TMC 411S, #1/0 (bent to shape, the hook point rides up)
Thread: Fine mono
Wing: Peacock herl over copper metallic flash over root beer dyed buck tail
Eyes: Stick on, yellow with black pupils
Head: Epoxy over the thread and eyes
Fly Tier: Gary Dubiel

Red Tailed Dart

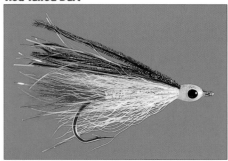

Hook: Mustad 34011, #2/0
Thread: White
Tail: Red buck tail, tied short and dense
Body: Silver braided mylar
Wing/collar: White buck tail with pearl Flashabou, tied around the hook as a collar
Topping: Eight strand of peacock herl
Eyes: Painted, white with black pupils
Head: Thread coated with epoxy
Fly Tier: Bill Murdich

Redfish Special

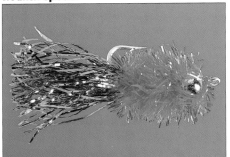

Hook: Mustad 3407, #2
Thread: Orange
Tail: Copper mylar tubing, picked out
Body: Hot orange ice chenille
Eyes: Silver dumb bell
Head: Thread
Fly Tier: Tom Broderidge

Sand Eel

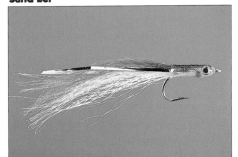

Hook: Eagle Claw 254, #1/0
Thread: Fine mono
Tail: White buck tail under pearl body braid (picked out) under pearl Krystal Flash
Body: Non-lead wire under pearl body braid
Wing: Olive buck tail flanked by two strip of silver tinsel
Over Body: Pearl E-Z Body Tubing equal in length to the hook shank
Eyes: Stick on, silver with black pupils
Coating: Epoxy over the body, head, and eyes.
Fly Tier: Gary Dubiel

Shad Bugger

Hook: TMC 5263, #6 - #12
Thread: Gray
Tail: White marabou accented with black Krystal Flash
Rib: Clear mono
Body: Pearl crystal chenille
Back: One strand of blue diamond braid
Hackle: Grizzly saddle, palmered
Head: Silver bead
Fly Tier: Bob Scheidt

Shad Fly

Hook: Mustad 34007, #6
Thread: White
Tail: Several strands of Krystal Flash, color of choice
Body: White chenille
Eyes: Dumb bell
Thorax/collar: Green Estaz or color of choice
Head: Thread
Fly Tier: Ted Patlin

Silver Side

Hook: Eagle Claw 254, #1/0
Thread: Fine mono
Tail: White buck tail under pearl body braid, picked out
Body: Non-lead wire under silver body braid
Wing: Peacock herl over green buck tail over silver and green metallic flash
Over Body: Natural E-Z Body Tubing equal in length to the hook shank
Eyes: Stick on, silver with black pupils
Covering: Double coat of epoxy covering the over body, head, and eyes
Fly Tier: Gary Dubiel

Simple Needlefish Fly

Hook: Mustad 34007, #3/0
Thread: Red single strand floss
Wing: White Fishair under pearl Krystal Flash under green Fishair under blue Krystal Flash under blue peacock Fishair
Eyes: Silver with black pupil, stick on style
Head: Epoxy over the head and eyes
Fly Tier: Steve Weinstein

Snook Bunny

Hook: Mustad 34007, #1
Thread: Orange
Tail: Rainbow Krystal Flash
Body: Zonker strip wrapped around the shank, color of choice
Hackle: One turn of a orange zonker strip
Eyes: Yellow and black fabric paint
Head: Orange thread and an epoxy coating
Fly Tier: Len Roberts

Spencer's Impostor

Hook: TMC 911S, #1/0 - #2
Thread: Clear mono
Tail: Ten to twenty strands of pearl and silver Flashabou
Body and Wing: Frayed pearl Mylar Tubing with black Orvis' Widow's Web over
Application: Tied in three segments, collar style
Veiling: Peacock Flashabou under black Krystal Flash
Throat: Pearl under red Krystal Flash
Head: Thread
Eyes: Stick on, silver with black pupils coated with Loon Soft Head
Fly Tier: Mike McCarthy

SRI Epoxy Cone Head

Hook: Daiichi 2546, #2 - #6
Thread: White
Tail: White buck tail under white, green, and black Crystal Splash, accented with pearl Fly Flash
Body: Pearl mylar over the wing and coated with five minute epoxy
Eyes: Stick on, silver with black pupils
Head: Silver Cone Head Bead, epoxy over the body, eyes, and head
Fly Tier: Bill Black, Spirit River Inc.

St. Marks Special

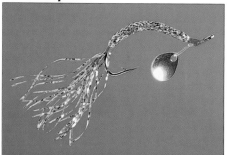

Hook: Mustad 37160S, #1
Thread: Hot orange
Tail: Gold braided mylar tubing, picked out
Body: Gold braided mylar tubing
Spinner blade: Size 99 gold Colorado blade held in place with clear mono
Head: Thread
Fly Tier: Tom Broderidge

Tarpon Treasure

Hook: Gamakatsu, #4/0
Thread: Yellow
Tail: Amherst pheasant tail feathers over rainbow Krystal Flash
Tail flanking: Two Mearns quail feathers, curved out, tied to the sides
Body: Silver fox zonker strip, two or three turns only
Hackle: Blue peacock breast feathers, tied as a collar
Eyes: Three dimensional, silver with black pupils
Head and snout: Thread coated with Loon Hard Head Fly Finish
Fly Tier: Mark Hoeser

Trout Buster (Bend Back)

Hook: TMC 411S, #1/0 (bent to shape, the hook point rides up)
Thread: Fine mono
Wing: Peacock herl over green buck tail over silver metallic flash
Wing flanks: Grizzly hackle feathers dyed green
Eyes: Stick on, yellow with black pupils
Head: Epoxy over the thread and eyes
Fly Tier: Gary Dubiel

TUMS

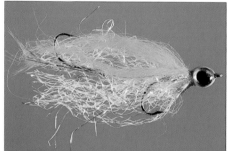

Stinger Hook: Mustad 92553S, #1/0
Front Hook: Mustad 34007
Thread: Gudebrod tying mono
Tail: Light blue dun, tip of feathers is trimmed to form the fish's tail
Connection: Heavy mono or wire core nylon
Belly: Three strands of braided mylar, unraveled
Wing: Olive Icelandic sheep, tied sparse
Gills: Tuff of red floss
Eyes: Gold stick on with a black pupil
Head: Covered with epoxy
Fly Tier: Mike Croft

Tuna Tamer

Hook: Mustad 34007, #2/0 - #2
Thread: Black
Tail: Black buck tail
Body: Thread
Wing: Black buck tail accented with pearl Krystal Flash, flanked with two red hackle feathers
Head: Thread
Eyes: Stick on doll eyes, silver with black pupils
Fly Tier: Michael Schweit

Two Streeter

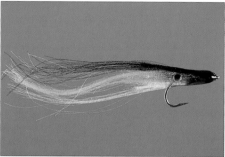

Hook: Gamakatsu, #4
Thread: White
Wing: Black over chartreuse over shrimp over white Fishair or equivalent fibers
Eyes: Stick on, silver with black pupils
Head: Five-minute epoxy over the head and eyes
Fly Tier: Jerry Caruso

Ultra Minnow

Hook: Mustad 34007, #1/0
Thread: Clear mono
Wing: Fluorescent green ultra hair, trimmed to shape and colored with a felt tip marker
Throat: Long white ultra hair under short red ultra hair
Eyes: Large doll eyes, white with black pupils
Head: Thread
Fly Tier: Bill Chandler

Wide Body Shad

Hook: Mustad 34011, #2
Thread: Black
Tail: Grizzly hen saddle hackle feathers
Body: Grizzly rooster saddle, palmered as a body
Cheeks: Spotted duck flank feathers
Eyes: Gold bead chain
Head: Black chenille and thread
Fly Tier: Bernard Byng

Wide Body Whistler, Olive

Hook: Gamakatsu SC15, #2/0
Thread: Green
Tail: Grizzly dyed olive hen saddle feathers
Body: Red chenille
Hackle: Grizzly dyed olive rooster cape feathers, tied as a collar
Eyes: Gold bead chain or dumb bell
Head: Thread
Fly Tier: Bernard Byng

Yellow Streaker

Hook: Mustad 3407, #2
Thread: Yellow
Tail: Pearl Krystal Flash over four yellow saddle hackle feathers
Weight: Several turn of non-lead wire
Hackle: Yellow marabou, tied as a collar
Eyes: Stick on, red with black pupils
Head: Thread
Fly Tier: Tom Broderidge

Zara Fly

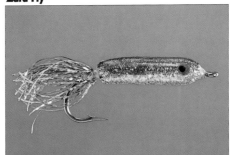

Hook: Mustad 34011, #1/0
Thread: Yellow
Tail: Gold mylar braid, picked out
Under Body: Foam popper body, trimmed to shape
Body: Gold mylar tubing, colored with felt tip markers
Eyes: Stick on, red with black pupils
Head: Thread
Fly Tier: Tom Broderidge

Bonefish, Crazy Charlie, and Epoxy Flies . . .

Baited Breath

Hook: Mustad 34007, #4 - #8 (the hook point rides up)
Thread: Black
Tail: Brown over ginger marabou fiber, tied sparse
Hackle: Cree or barred ginger, tied collar style at the hook bend
Body: Brown/ginger variegated chenille
Eyes: Black bead chain
Head: Thread
Fly Tier: Mitch Whitney

Beady Head Bone Fish

Hook: Mustad 34007, #4 - #8
Thread: White
Tail: Pink Krystal Flash
Body: Pink Krystal Flash, wrapped
Wing: White calf tail flanked with two grizzly hackle feathers
Under Head: Pink chenille
Head: Large pink glass bead, coated with epoxy
Fly Tier: Gale Doudy

Bird Shot Wobbler

Hook: Mustad 3407, #4 - #8   **Thread:** Red
Tail: Pearl Krystal Flash, tied long and sparse
Under Body: Trimmed rectangular milk carton plastic with split shot placed for eyes
Eyes: Split shot pressed into place on the under body and held in place with Zap-A-Gap
Body: Coated with blue Glitter Glue then coated with Aqua Flex   **Wing:** Two white Chickabou feathers
Hackle: Dyed red saddle feather, tied as a collar behind the body
Head: Thread
Fly Tier: Al Beatty

Black Shrimp

Hook: Mustad 3407, #6
Thread: Black
Body: Black crystal chenille
Eyes: Black plastic bead chain, tied near the hook bend
Wing: Black Krystal Flash over black Aqua Fibers over black calf tail
Legs: Black Sili Leg material
Head: Thread
Fly Tier: Ross Mueller

Buckshot Bonefish

Hook: Mustad 34007, #6 - #8
Thread: Orange
Tail: Orange marabou flanked with two grizzly dyed orange hackle feathers
Under Body: Clear hot glue
Eyes: Size six shot gun lead shot, hot glued to the sides of the under body
Head: Orange Krystal Flash, wrapped and coated with epoxy
Fly Tier: Gale Doudy

Bone Fish Wobbler

Hook: Mustad 3407, #4 - #8 (the hook point rides up)
Thread: Tan
Tail: Gold Krystal Flash, tied long and sparse
Body: Gold Krystal Flash, tied looped on the hook sides to form a base for the wobbler body
Wings: Four ginger Whiting American hackle feathers
Head: Thread coated with Aqua Flex
Fly Tier: Al Beatty

Capt. Len's Flats Shrimp

Hook: Mustad 34007, #4
Thread: Clear mono
Tail: Tan calf tail with rainbow #13 Krystal Flash
Hackle: Brown, palmered and trimmed on top
Eyes: Dumb bell marked with white fabric paint and black pupils
Weed guard: Hard Mason mono
Head: Five Minute Epoxy coating
Fly Tier: Len Roberts

Chick Pea

Hook: Eagle Claw 254NR, #1/0 - #8 (the hook point rides up)
Thread: Black
Body: Peacock glitter craft paint, coated with Aqua Flex
Wing: Peacock herl over white Chickabou
Eyes: Silver dumb bell with stick on, gold with black pupils
Head: Thread
Fly Tier: Al Beatty

Chum Charlie

Hook: Mustad 34007, #4 (the hook point rides up)
Thread: Chartreuse
Tail: Silver Polar Flash and white Arctic fox fur
Body: Thread
Wing: Chartreuse Poly Bear under Krystal Flash
Eyes: Spirit River Real Hot Eyes, chartreuse 7/32
Head: Thread
Fly Tier: Roger Swengel

Clouser Flash

Hook: Mustad 3407, #2 - #8
Thread: White
Tail: Pearl Flashabou
Body Pearl mylar tinsel, wrapped and epoxy coated
Collar: Red thread in the middle of the body
Eyes: Dumb bell, yellow with black pupils
Wing: Black buck tail
Head: Thread
Fly Tier: Bill Murdich

Copper Charlie

Hook: Daiichi X452, #4 - #8
Thread: Light brown
Body: Copper ribbon floss
Wing: Barred ginger Chickabou
Eyes: Spirit River Real Eyes, pink with black pupils
Head: Thread
Fly Tier: Henry Hoffman

Copper Cyclops

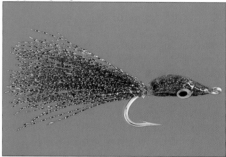

Hook: Mustad 3407, #2 - #8
Thread: Gold mylar
Tail: Copper Krystal Flash
Body: Copper Krystal Flash, coated with epoxy
Eyes: Stick on, yellow with black pupils
Head: Band of red thread coated with epoxy
Fly Tier: Tom Tripi

Dark Water

Hook: Mustad 3407, #4, bend back shape (the hook point rides up)
Thread: Gray
Body: Clear mono over gray thread
Wing: Short gray zonker strip
Eyes: Dumb bell
Head: Thread
Fly Tier: Tom Broderidge

DL's Crab

Hook: Mustad 34007, #4 - #8
Thread: Chartreuse
Tail: Pearl Flashabou, two brown hackle tips with two turns of brown hackle
Body: Tufts of tan and cream Aunt Lydia's carpet yarn, trimmed to shape
Weed guard: Hard mono
Eyes: Dumb bell, tied near the hook point
Head: Thread
Fly Tier: George Close

Duster Charlie

Hook: Mustad 3407, #4 - #8 (the hook point rides up)
Thread: Tan
Tail: Purple static duster fibers
Body: Purple static duster fibers
Under Wing: Purple static duster fibers
Wings: Four ginger Whiting American hackle feathers, tied modified Dee style
Hackle: Whiting American ginger hackle feather, tied as a collar
Head: Thread
Fly Tier: Gretchen Beatty

Epoxy Zonker

Hook: Mustad 3407, #4 - #8   **Thread:** Tan
Tail: Brown zonker strip
Under Body: Milk carton plastic, trimmed rectangular with split shot placed for eyes
Eyes: Spit shot pressed into place on the under body and held in place with Zap-A-Gap
Body: Coated with gold Glitter Glue then coated with Aqua Flex
Wing: Brown zonker strip, impaled on the hook and tied in place at the hook bend and eye
Head: Thread coated with Aqua Flex
Fly Tier: Al Beatty

EZY Charlie

Hook: Mustad 3407, #4 - #8 (the hook point rides up)
Thread: Black or white
Tail: Black Krystal Flash (or color of choice)
Body: Black Krystal Flash (or color of choice), wrapped
Under Wing: Black Krystal Flash
Wings: Grizzly Whiting American hackle feathers (or color of choice)
Eyes: EZY Eyes with stick on, gold with black pupils
Head: Thread and an Aqua Flex coating
Fly Tier: Al Beatty

EZY Duster Charlie

Hook: Mustad 3407, #4 - #8 (the hook point rides up)
Thread: Clear mono
Body: Pink and pearl crystal chenille
Under Wing: Purple static duster fibers mixed with purple Flashabou
Wing: Four white Whiting American hackle feathers, tied modified Dee style, under set of feathers are slightly longer than the over set
Eyes: EZY Eyes with stick on, gold with black pupils
Head: Thread and Aqua Flex
Fly Tier: Gretchen Beatty

Flashy Charlie

Hook: Mustad 3407, #4 - #8
Thread: Clear mono
Tail: Copper Krystal Flash
Body: Copper Krystal Flash
Wing: Mixed black and copper Krystal Flash, tied very sparse
Throat: Purple Flashabou, tied short and sparse
Eyes: Dumb bell with stick on, gold with black pupils
Head: Thread
Fly Tier: Al Beatty

Fox Flash

Hook: TMC 811S, #2 - #8
Thread: Tan
Tail: Tuft of red fox fur
Eyes: Gold dumb bell, tied near the hook bend
Body: Tan angora dubbing
Wing: Copper Krystal Flash
Head: Thread
Fly Tier: Sodie Sodamann

Gary's Bone Buster (Bend Back)

Hook: TMC 411S, #4
Thread: Fine mono
Wing: Pearl Krystal Flash over white calf tail flanked with grizzly hackle tips
Eyes: Stick on, silver with black pupils
Head: Epoxy over the head and eyes
Fly Tier: Gary Dubiel

Glass Sardine

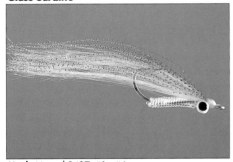

Hook: Mustad 3407, #1 - #6
Thread: White
Body: Clear mono, fifty-pound test
Wing: Very sparse layers of Krystal Flash (silver, pearl, chartreuse, and peacock) mixed with polar bear Fishair in alternating clumps
Eyes: Dumb bell, white with black pupils
Head: Thread
Fly Tier: Bill Murdich

Gold Chick

Hook: Eagle Claw 254NR, #1/0 - #8 (the hook point rides up)
Thread: Black
Body: Gold glitter craft paint, coated with Aqua Flex
Wing: White Chickabou
Eyes: Spirit River Real Eyes, yellow with black pupils
Head: Thread
Fly Tier: Al Beatty

Golden Badger

Hook: Mustad 3407, #1 - #4
Thread: Tan
Tail: Long, gold Krystal Flash
Body: Gold mylar tinsel
Wing: Badger fur, tied top and bottom Clouser style
Eyes: Dumb bell, yellow with black pupils
Head: Thread
Coating: Epoxy or Aqua Flex
Fly Tier: Bill Murdich

Golden Bone

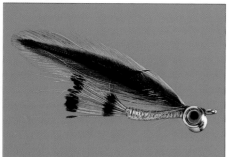

Hook: Mustad 34007, #4 - #10 (the hook point rides up)
Thread: Brown
Tail: Golden pheasant tippets
Rib: Clear mono
Body: Gold tinsel
Wing: Furnace hen feathers over a fox squirrel under wing
Eyes: Gold dumb bell with stick on eyes, orange with black pupils
Head: Thread
Fly Tier: Lance Zook

Insane Chuck

Hook: Mustad 3407, #6 - #10
Thread: Black
Tail: Two strands of copper Krystal Flash and peacock sword herls
Tag: Orange floss
Rib: Pearl Flashabou, wrapped under the body material
Body: Clear latex strip
Wing: Tan deer hair, spun and trimmed
Eyes: Small bead chain
Fly Tier: Tom Tripi

John's Critter, Pink

Hook: Daiichi 2546, #4 - #8
Thread: Pink
Tail: Pink marabou, tied sparse and accented with pink Crystal Splash
Eyes: Spirit River Real Eyes with stick on, gold with black pupils
Head: Pink Estaz
Fly Tier: Bill Black, Spirit River Inc.

John's Critter, White

Hook: Daiichi 2546, #4 - #8
Thread: White
Tail: White marabou, tied sparse and accented with pearl Crystal Splash
Eyes: Spirit River Real Eyes with stick on, gold with black pupils
Head: White Estaz
Fly Tier: Bill Black, Spirit River Inc.

Lenny's Blenny

Hook: Mustad 34007, #2 - #4
Thread: Gudebrod clear
Tail: Rainbow Krystal Flash under tan marabou
Body: Spun and trimmed deer hair
Hackle: Grizzly (dyed or natural), palmered through the deer hair
Weed guard: Hard Mason mono
Eyes: White and black fabric paint applied to small dumb bell eyes
Head: Epoxy coating
Fly Tier: Len Roberts

Len's Diamond Epoxy

Hook: Mustad 34007, #2 - #4
Thread: Gudebrod clear
Tail: Tan Fly Fur around rainbow Krystal Flash flanked by cree stripes
Hackle: Cree, tied as a collar behind the head
Weed guard: Hard Mason mono
Eyes: White and black fabric paint
Head: Five Minute Epoxy covering
Fly Tier: Len Roberts

Mihulka Special

Hook: Eagle Claw 1197N, #2 - #6 (the hook rides up)
Thread: Red
Tail: Orange marabou
Body: Gold or pearl mylar braid, squeezed flat and coated with epoxy
Legs: Orange rubber leg material
Wing: Orange calf tail fibers
Head: Thread coated with epoxy or Aqua Flex
Fly Tier: Chris Mihulka

Pearl Mini-Puff

Hook: Mustad 34007, #4 - #8
Thread: White
Body: Brown crystal chenille
Wing: Tan calf tail flanked by two grizzly saddle hackle tips
Eyes: Silver bead chain
Head: Thread
Fly Tier: Kevin Cohenour

Red Eye

Hook: Daiichi 2546, #4 - #8 (the hook point rides up)
Thread: mono   **Tail:** Short tuft of white marabou
Claws: Micro tubing with a white trimmed feather inside
Eyes: Melted mono accented with a red felt tip marker, one tied longer than the other
Body: Soft Body coating over the body and mono loops positioned on the back/belly
Wing: Mallard flank fibers over white marabou over pearl Krystal Flash
Eyes: Silver dumb bell eyes (cause the hook point to ride up)   **Head:** Thread
Fly Tier: Shane Stalcup

Ricky's Pink Charley

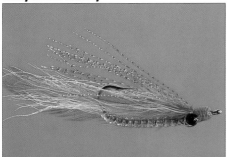

Hook: Mustad 34011, #2 - #4
Thread: Pink
Body: Pink thread base under Swannundaze 22
Wing: Pink buck tail under pink Krystal Flash flanked by two pink hackle feathers
Eyes: Black bead chain
Head: Thread
Fly Tier: Dick Steinhorst

Rocker

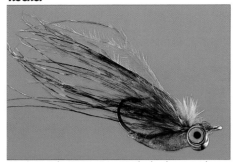

Hook: Daiichi 2546, #4 - #8 (the hook point rides up)
Thread: Clear mono
Eyes: Spirit River Real Eyes, tied at the hook eye
Rocking Body: Two mono loops from the bend to the eyes, slightly above the hook shank
Coating and color: Epoxy and glitter mix placed over the eyes, mono loops, and hook shank
Wing: Marabou, color of choice
Head: Thread and epoxy between the eyes and to the hook eye
Fly Tier: Shane Stalcup

Salt Shrimp

Hook: Daiichi 2546, #4 - #8 (the hook point rides up)
Thread: Clear mono **Mouth parts:** White Chickabou
Eyes: Accent Eyes, tied at hook bend extending to rear
Claws: Pink tubing with a trimmed feather inserted
Body: White Chickabou and pink Krystal Flash, coated with epoxy
Carapace: Clear Medallion Sheeting coated with epoxy, extended beyond the hook bend
Feelers and Legs: Excess Chickabou and Krystal Flash from the body **Weight:** Silver dumb bell eyes, tied near the hook eye **Head:** Thread
Fly Tier: Shane Stalcup

Salt Water Shad

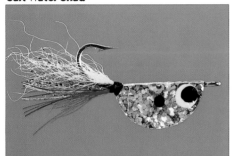

Hook: Mustad 34011, #4 (the hook point rides up)
Thread: Black
Tail: Green calf tail fibers over copper Krystal Flash over red calf tail
Body: 7/8 inch holographic discs glued to the same size lead sheet discs
Application: Folded over and glued to the hook
Eyes: Painted, yellow with black pupils
Body paint: Black dot on the sides of the body
Coating: Aqua Flex or Loon Soft Head
Fly Tier: Walt Holman

Shiny Streak

Hook: Mustad 34007, #4 - #10
Thread: White
Tail: Pink over white marabou, flanked with silver Flashabou
Body: Red crystal chenille
Head: Thread
Fly Tier: Hebert Carmen

Sim Ram

Hook: Mustad 34007, #4 - #8 (the hook point rides up)
Thread: Pink
Tail: Tan craft fur accented with pearl Krystal Flash
Body: Pearl diamond braid
Eyes: Silver dumb bell, tied on top of the shank to ride the hook point up
Wing: White rabbit fur clump
Head: Thread
Fly Tier: George Close

Snapping Shrimp

Hook: Mustad 3407, #6 - #8
Thread: Tan
Body: Tan chenille
Wing: Rainbow Krystal Flash under tan Fly Fur flanked with cree stripes
Weed guards: Hard Mason mono
Eyes: White and black fabric paint
Head: Five Minute Epoxy coating
Fly Tier: Len Roberts

Squirrel Charlie

Hook: Mustad 3407, #4 - #8 (the hook point rides up)
Thread: Black
Body: Peacock Tie well Maxi Braid
Wing: Squirrel tail fibers
Hackle: Brown Whiting American hackle feather, tied as a collar
Head: Thread coated with Aqua Flex
Fly Tier: Al Beatty

Sugar Shrimp

Hook: Mustad 34011, #1 **Thread:** Tan
Antenna: Six strands of long, root beer Krystal Flash
Eyes: Black plastic beads, mounted via melted mono
Mouth parts: Small bunch of root beer Krystal Flash
Rattle: Viper mini-glass rattle
Body & Legs: Large, pearl Cactus Chenille dyed tan or colored with a felt tip marker
Back & rostrum: Tan Ultra Hair treated with Aqua Flex or Flexament
Tail: Single, tan marabou feather tip, tied at the hook eye
Head: Thread
Fly Tier: Bill Murdich

Crab, Shrimp, Squid, and Worms . . .

Tail Bone

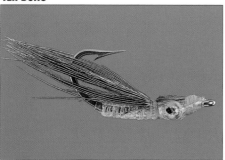

Hook: Mustad 3407, #4 - #8 (the hook point rides up)
Thread: White
Body: Clear plastic tubing over pearl Krystal Flash
Wing: Pheasant rump feather
Eyes: Clear plastic bead chain
Head: Thread
Fly Tier: Duane Hada

Baby Blue Swimming Crab

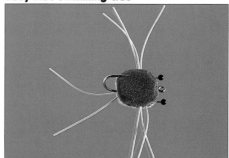

Hook: Mustad 34007, #2
Thread: White
Tail: White round rubber leg material
Weight: Two small dumb bell eyes tied in the body area
Legs: White round rubber leg material
Eyes: Black plastic tipped pins
Body: Top is cream fleece and the bottom is blue closed cell foam, hook rides point up
Head: Thread
Fly Tier: Deke Meyer

Brackish Water Shrimp

Hook: Mustad 3282, #6 bend back   **Thread:** Olive
Mouth parts: Badger hackle fibers
Body: Large gold bead and tan micro chenille
Wing: Partridge dyed olive, the ends trimmed and tied near the hook bend
Hackle: Olive Soft Hackle, tied collar style near the hook bend
Eyes: Melted mono, tied on the hook just behind the eye and extending past the hook bend
Tying note: The method for tying in the eyes also functions as a weed guard   **Head:** Thread
Fly Tier: Tom Berry

Capt. Len's Shrimp

Hook: Mustad 34011, #1/0
Thread: Clear mono
Tail: Tan Fly Fur, rainbow #13 Krystal Flash
Rib: Pearl Flashabou
Body: Tan Fly Fur dubbing
Hackle: Cree, grizzly, or barred ginger, palmered
Weed guard: Hard Mason, thirty pound
Eyes: Hard Mason, thirty pound, melted
Head: Shrimp's tail is Fly Fur coated with head cement
Fly Tier: Len Roberts

Cheryl's Brackish Water Shrimp

Hook: Mustad 3407, #3/0 - #2
Thread: Clear mono
Mouth parts: Tan marabou, pearl Flashabou, white craft hair, brown stretch floss
Flank: Two grizzly hackle feathers
Body: Silicone glue and tan Swiss straw over an under body from the mouth parts
Hackle: Grizzly, palmered
Tail: Tan Swiss straw, at the hook eye
Eyes: Flower stamens
Antenna: Horse tail fibers
Fly Tier: Tom Tripi

Chickabou Crab

Hook: Eagle Claw 413CAT, #1/0 - #6
Thread: Gray
Claws: Grizzly soft hackles, trimmed to shape, one each at the hook bend and eye
Eyes: Flower stamens, located in the center portion of the body
Body: Light and dark grizzly Chickabou, wrapped and trimmed to shape
Head: Thread
Fly Tier: Henry Hoffman

Chickabou Crab

Hook: Daiichi 2546, #4 - #8 (the hook point rides up)
Thread: Clear mono
Mouth parts: Pearl Krystal Flash
Eyes: Red Accent Eyes, tied extended behind the hook bend
Claws: Brown Fish Claws
Body: Ginger Chickabou
Back: Brown Soft Hackle feather, tied flat
Weight: Gold dumb bell eyes, tied at the hook eye
Head: Thread
Fly Tier: Shane Stalcup

Clear Braided Shrimp

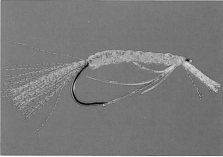

Hook: TMC 8089NP, #2
Thread: White
Mouth parts and Antenna: Pearl Krystal Flash, tied at the hook bend
Under Body: Pearl Krystal Flash
Body: Sparkle lace, braided using the over hand knot style
Legs: Ends of the body, tied under the hook
Head: Ends of the pearl Krystal Flash, coated with Loon Hard Head
Fly Tier: Tom Broderidge

Craft Fur Shrimp

Hook: Mustad 34007, #2 - #4 (the hook point rides up)
Thread: Tan
Tail: Tan craft fur marked with a felt tip marker
Tail accent: Gold or orange Krystal Flash
Body: Tan craft fur blended with gold or orange Lite Brite
Eyes: Gold dumb bell, tied on top to turn the hook point up
Hackle: Brown, palmered and trimmed on top
Weed guard: Hard mono, optional
Head: Thread
Fly Tier: George Close

Dubbing Brush Shrimp

Hook: Jardine F222, #6
Thread: Tan
Mouth parts: Grizzly hen hackle fibers
Antenna: Pheasant tail fibers
Eyes: Melted mono, colored with a black felt tip marker
Rib: Clear mono
Body: Natural squirrel dubbing brush
Hackle: Grizzly saddle, palmered
Shell back: Magic Shrimp Foil
Tail: Tan dubbing brush, coated with epoxy and shaped
Head: Thread
Fly Tier: Floyd Franke

Duct Tape Squid

Hook: DaiRiki 930, #3/0
Thread: White
Tentacles: Badger saddle hackle mixed with gray and purple rubber leg material
Eyes: Large, strung pearl beads with painted black pupils
Body: Pearl crystal chenille
Carapace: Silver duct tape, top and bottom pieces stuck together, trimmed to shape
Head: Thread
Fly Tier: Scott Sanchez

Everything Fly

Hook: Mustad 34011, #1/0 - #4
Thread: Gudebrod clear
Tail: Rainbow Krystal Flash surrounded with tan Fly Fur, cree side stripes
Hackle: Cree, palmered for the body
Weed guards: Hard Mason mono
Eyes: Dumb bell
Head: Thread
Fly Tier: Len Roberts

Farrow's Rag Head Crab

Hook: Mustad 3407, #2/0   **Thread:** Chartreuse
Weight: Dumb bell eyes, tied at the hook eye
Mouth: Krystal Flash with Aunt Lydia's rug yarn
Eyes: Melted mono, painted black, coated with epoxy
Under body: Aunt Lydia's rug yarn, x-wrapped
Legs: Rubber hackle or Silli-con, x-wrapped between the yarn strands   **Claws:** Olive grizzly hen saddle feathers, tips trimmed   **Back:** Finely chopped olive, brown, & tan rug yarn, mixed   **Belly:** Finely chopped tan rug yarn   **Body coating:** Barge Cement or Elmer's Squeez-N-Caulk
Fly Tier: Farrow Allen

Fiddler Crab

Hook: Mustad 3366, #4 - #8
Thread: Clear mono
Tail: Two short golden badger hackle feathers, tied splayed
Legs: Rubber band mottled with a felt tip marker
Eyes: Black seed bead
Body: Brown suede ribbon, hot glue and epoxy into position
Body color: Felt tip marker
Coating: Gold EZ Sparkle Body
Head: Thread
Fly Tier: Tom Berry

Fiery Brown Calamari

Hook: Mustad 34007, #1/0
Thread: White
Mouth parts: Three turns of cinnamon Estaz
Tail/Legs: Eight fiery brown saddle feather tied in separately around the hook shank
Eyes: Large glass, yellow with black pupils
Body: Cinnamon Estaz
Squid's flukes: White craft fur, tied to the sides just behind the hook eye
Head: Thread
Fly Tier: Ted Patlin

Foam Crab

Hook: Mustad 3407, #2 (the hook point rides up)
Thread: Gray
Body: Tan closed cell foam, colored on top with a felt tip marker
Legs: White rubber leg material, colored with a felt tip marker
Eyes: Dumb bell
Head: Thread
Fly Tier: Tom Broderidge

Full Belly Shrimp

Hook: Mustad 3407, #4
Thread: Pink
Body: Brown crystal chenille
Wing: Amber Krystal Flash over white Aqua Fibers over tan calf tail
Legs: Amber/gold Sili Leg material
Eyes: Bead chain or dumb bell eyes
Head: Thread
Fly Tier: Ross Mueller

Furry Crab

Hook: Mustad 34011, #2 (the hook point rides up)
Thread: Orange
Mouth parts: Krystal Flash under Whiting American Laced furnace feathers, tied divided
Eyes: Melted mono, tied long and divided
Body: Tan chenille
Carapace: Tan furry foam, tied in the back and pulled over the body
Legs: White rubber leg material
Weight: Dumb bell eyes, tied near the hook eye
Head: Thread
Fly Tier: Al Beatty

GD Flea

Hook: Mustad 34007, #4, hook point rides up
Thread: Orange
Tail: Gold Krystal Flash
Body: Tan in front of orange Estaz
Wing: Tan craft fur
Eyes: Small dumb bell, tied on top of the shank so the point rides up
Head: Thread
Fly Tier: Gary Dubiel

Gold Swimming Shrimp

Hook: Mustad 34007, #1/0
Thread: Tan
Antenna: Two long strands of Bestway Super Hair
Mouth parts: Tan Bestway Super Hair mixed with tan craft fur, trimmed to shape
Eyes: Melted fifty-pound mono, colored with a felt tip pen
Body: Dubbed tan craft fur, long section left at the hook eye to form the tail
Carapace: Gold Corsair tubing, trimmed to shape and set in place with epoxy
Head: Thread
Fly Tier: Ted Patlin

Green Thing

Hook: Mustad 3407, #2
Thread: Chartreuse
Tail: Red yarn
Body: Chartreuse Estaz
Eyes: Dumb bell, painted chartreuse with black pupils, tied at the hook bend
Head: Thread
Fly Tier: Tom Broderidge

Hair Crab

Hook: TMC 811S, #2 - #8
Thread: Black
Claws: Mottled hen hackle feathers with trimmed tips
Eyes: Gold dumb bell
Body: Deer hair, spun and trimmed to shape
Head: Thread
Fly Tier: Sodie Sodamann

Indian River Shrimp

Hook: Mustad 34007, #2 (bent near middle of hook)
Thread: Tan   **Mouth parts:** Tan calf tail fibers, tied short
Eyes: Black seed stems
Antenna: Brown or tan Silli-con leg material, tied near the hook bend
Body: Tan chenille marked with a brown felt tip marker
Hackle: Brown hackle, palmered
Shell back: Silicone sealant bead over copper Krystal Flash and Ultra Hair
Tail: Ultra Hair, tied at the hook eye
Head: Thread
Fly Tier: Ken Bay

Jack's Crystal Shrimp

Hook: Mustad 34011, #4
Thread: White
Tail/Antenna: Pearl Krystal Flash
Rostrum: Moose mane, peacock herl, and grizzly hackle tips
Body: Pearl Estaz
Eyes: Large black bead chain
Hackle: Grizzly, palmered and trimmed cone shaped tapering toward the hook eye
Wing/Legs: Yellow buck tail
Head: Thread
Fly Tier: Dick Steinhorst

Jazzey Crab

Hook: Mustad 3407, #2/0 - #2 (hook point rides up)
Thread: Olive   **Tail:** Four chartreuse stretch floss fibers, to form some of the legs at the hook bend
Body: Brown crystal chenille and palmered olive saddle hackle
Legs: Four chartreuse stretch floss fibers, to form the rest of the legs
Body Topping: Two pheasant "church window" feathers, tied delta style   **Eyes:** Silver dumb bell
Wing: Olive deer hair, flared and trimmed to shape
Head: Thread
Fly Tier: Tom Tripi

Jerry's Grass Shrimp

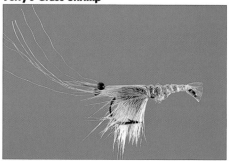

Hook: Mustad 9672, #6 - #12
Thread: White
Mouth parts: Dun hackle fibers
Antenna: Clear Ultra Hair, tied near the hook bend
Eyes: Melted mono
Rib: Thread
Body: Light gray muskrat dubbing
Carapace: Zip lock bag, cut to neck tie shape
Tail: Excess carapace material
Head: Thread
Fly Tier: Jerome Hebert

Keel Flats Shrimp

Hook: TMC 411S, #3/0 - #8
Thread: Pink
Tail: (mouth parts, antenna) pearl and pink Krystal Flash
Legs: Pink rabbit fur strip
Body: Pink Fly Foam, epoxy to the rabbit strip extended body style
Eyes: Melted mono, extending to the hook bend
Over Body: Pearl and pink Krystal Flash
Shrimp's Tail: Continuation of the over body, trimmed and epoxied
Head: Thread
Fly Tier: Deke Meyer

Leather Crab

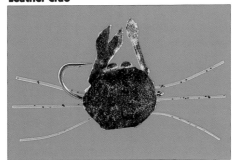

Hook: DaiRiki 930, #1/0 - #2
Thread: White
Weight: Non-lead tape under body
Claws: Cream ultra suede, trimmed and colored with felt tip markers
Legs: Tan/black speckled Sili Legs
Body: Cream ultra suede, trimmed and colored with felt tip markers
Eyes: Eyes on a plastic stick, green with black pupils
Head: Thread
Fly Tier: Lance Zook

Left Over Shrimp

Hook: Mustad 34007, #1/0 - #6
Thread: Clear mono
Mouth parts: White and natural buck tail, mixed and tied at the hook bend
Eyes: Melted mono and black beads, tied at hook bend
Hackle: White marabou under brown saddle, tied collar style near the hook bend
Rib: Clear mono
Body: Gold ice chenille
Carapace: Clear plastic bag material, cut to shape
Head: Thread
Fly Tier: Ron Winn

Len's Woolly Crab

Hook: Mustad 34007, #2 - #4
Thread: Gudebrod clear
Tail: Rainbow Krystal Flash under tan marabou flanked by cree side stripes
Body: Aunt Lydia's rug yarn dipped in rod wrapping color preserver, cut in half inch strips
Weed guards: Hard Mason mono
Eyes: Small dumb bell
Head: Thread
Fly Tier: Len Roberts

Mantis Shrimp

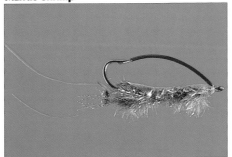

Hook: Mustad 34011, #2 - #6 (the hook point rides up)
Thread: White
Weight: Non-lead wire applied near the hook bend
Mouth parts: Green Krystal Flash
Antenna: Two green strands of fine rubber leg material
Eyes: Melted mono and black beads, tied near the hook bend, divided   **Rib:** Clear mono
Body: Olive ice chenille   **Carapace:** Clear poly bag material, trimmed to shape and tied on the shank bottom
Weed guard: Larva Lace just long enough to place the hook point inside the end   **Head:** Thread
Fly Tier: Ron Winn

Pearl Shrimp

Hook: Mustad 3407, #2 (the hook point rides up)
Thread: White
Tail: Pearl braided mylar tubing, picked out
Body: Large pearl Estaz
Eyes: Silver dumb bell, tied on top of the hook (causes the hook point to ride up)
Head: Thread
Fly Tier: Tom Broderidge

Pearl Thing

Hook: Mustad 3407, #2
Thread: Hot orange
Tail: Red yarn
Body: Pearl Estaz
Eyes: Dumb bell, painted hot orange with black pupils, tied at the hook bend
Head: Thread
Fly Tier: Tom Broderidge

Pheasant Under Grass

Hook: Mustad 34007, #2 - #6
Thread: Brown
Weed guard: Hard Mason mono
Eyes: Black dumb bell, tied at the hook bend
Mouth: Tan buck tail and copper Krystal Flash
Claws: Two grizzly dyed orange hackle feathers
Legs: Blue Sili-legs, sandwiched between the body parts
Body: Cream felt on the bottom and tan felt on the top,
Body Topping: Two pheasant body feathers, tied flat on top
Head: Thread
Fly Tier: Kevin Cohenour

Purple Fire Tail

Hook: Daiichi 2461, #1/0, hook ride point up
Thread: White
Tail: Hot pink Fishair
Extended Body: Braided purple Yak hair
Body: Purple Estaz
Wing: Red buck tail on top and white buck tail on the bottom
Eyes: Large with doll eyes glued on, chartreuse with black pupils
Head: Epoxy coating, thick
Fly Tier: Jerry Caruso

Quick Sinking Shrimp

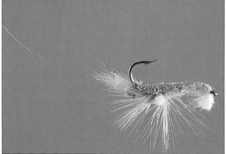

Hook: Mustad 34007 bent to keel hook shape, #1/0
Thread: Tan   **Antenna:** Two very long strands of Bestway Super Hair   **Mouth parts:** Tan Bestway Super Hair mixed with tan craft fur, trimmed to shape
Eyes: Melted fifty-pound mono, colored with a felt tip pen
Weight: Medium dumb bell eyes, painted tan
Legs: Tan hackle, dressed heavy
Body: Dubbed tan craft fur, long section left at the hook eye to form the tail
Carapace: Gold Corsair tubing, trimmed to shape and set in place with epoxy   **Head:** Thread
Fly Tier: Ted Patlin

Salty Shammy

Hook: Mustad 37160S, #3/0 (reshaped to flatten the fly body)   **Thread:** White   **Mouth parts:** Short tuft of elk hair topped with gold Krystal Flash
Antenna: Two strands of gold Krystal Flash
Rib: Copper wire
Eyes: Melted mono, painted black with Aqua Head
Body: Tan Brazilian Velour   **Carapace:** Natural chamois
Legs: Large white hackle
Weight: Dumb bell eyes, tied on the under side of the hook at the eye
Tail: Excess from the carapace, tied at the hook eye
Fly Tier: Al Beatty

Scott's Tubing Shrimp

Hook: DaiRiki 930, #4
Thread: Tan
Mouth parts: Tan marabou with root beer Krystal Flash
Antenna: Long strands of root beer Krystal Flash
Eyes: Melted mono or strung plastic beads
Rib: Heavy thread
Body: Tan crystal chenille
Carapace: Clear vinyl tubing, cut to shape
Weed guard: Hard mono, tied as a "V" near the hook eye
Head: Thread
Fly Tier: Scott Sanchez

Shammy Crab

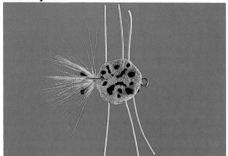

Hook: Eagle Claw 254NR, #2/0 (the hook point rides up)
Thread: White   **Mouth parts:** A tuft of gold Krystal Flash with white hackle around, tied collar style
Eyes: Melted mono colored with black Aqua Head, tied divided near the hook bend
Body: Tan chenille under body, covered with two circles of chamois
Body markings: Colored with a felt tip marker
Legs: White rubber leg material, three per side
Weight: Black bead chain, tied near the eye
Head: Thread
Fly Tier: Al Beatty

Shane's Mantis Shrimp

Hook: TMC 9394, #2   **Thread:** Clear mono
Tail: Green Z-Lon   **Rib:** Tying mono
Body: Green single strand floss
Gills: Fine tubing and Z-Lon
Legs: Z-Lon
Claws: Fish Claws
Wing case: Medallion Sheeting coated with epoxy or Aqua Flex
Eyes: Melted mono
Antenna: Small clump of Micro Fibetts
Head: Thread
Fly Tier: Shane Stalcup

Simple Salt Shrimp

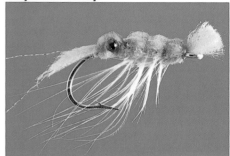

Hook: Eagle Claw 254NR, #1/0
Thread: Tan
Mouth parts: Tan BT's Dry Fly Poly Yarn
Antenna: Two strands of gold Krystal Flash
Eyes: Bronze Razzle Eyes
Rib: One strand of gold Krystal Flash
Body: Fluorescent orange chenille
Carapace: Tan BT's Dry Fly Poly Yarn
Tail: Excess fibers remaining from the carapace
Head: Thread
Fly Tier: Gretchen Beatty

Tape Crab

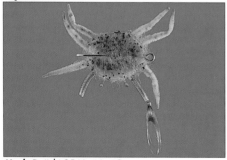

Hook: Daiichi 2546, #4 - #8
Thread: Clear mono
Legs: Ultra chenille, shaped on the end with a flame
Eyes: Melted mono, tied to the side of the hook shank
Claws: Grizzly Fish Claws
Weight: Non-lead disc under the body, epoxied into position
Body: Masking tape, coated with epoxy then covered with dubbing (color of choice)
Head: Thread
Fly Tier: Shane Stalcup

Vance's Grass Shrimp - Brown

Hook: Mustad 34011, #2 - #4
Thread: Brown
Tail: Gold Flashabou
Rib: Four, pound mono
Body: Small brown velour or chenille
Carapace: Copper or gold mylar tubing
Eyes: Black bead chain
Legs: Brown hackle, palmered
Beard: Fox squirrel tail
Head: Thread
Fly Tier: Dick Steinhorst

Offshore and Poppers . . .

Airhead

Hook: TMC 511S, #2/0 - #1/0
Thread: White
Tail: Mixed colors of Krystal Flash over silver tinsel over pearl Polar Flash
Tail flanking: Two grizzly dyed olive hackles
Over Body: Base ends of the tail flanking, glued to the top of the body with Softex
Body: Large E-Z Braid, coated with Softex, colored with felt tip markers
Eyes: Stick on, silver with black pupils
Fly Tier: John Ryzanych

Angel Hair Streamer

Hook: Eagle Claw 254NR, #2/0 - #4
Thread: White
Body/wings: Alternating clumps of Bestway Super Hair and Angle Hair, white on the bottom and silver gray on top
Throat: Red Flashabou
Eyes: Stick on, red with black pupils
Head: Thread
Coating: Epoxy over the head and eyes
Fly Tier: Ted Patlen

Auto Popper

Hook: Eagle Claw 254NR, #2/0
Thread: White
Tail: Dark green Flashabou over green buck tail over green dyed grizzly hackle feathers
Body: Green crystal chenille
Head: Round white foam covered with automotive flash tape
Eyes: Stick on, gold with black pupils
Fly Tier: Gretchen Beatty

Big Lipped Shrimp

Hook: Mustad 34011, #2   **Thread:** Pink
Mouth parts: Bailey's Float Vis, fluorescent pink and pink Flashabou and Krystal Flash
Antenna: Long strands of pink Krystal Flash
Eyes: Melted mono or fibers from a hair brush
Rib: Heavy tying thread
Body: Large pearl crystal chenille
Carapace: Thin, pink closed cell foam, cut to shape
Popping lip: Thin, pink closed cell foam, tied on top of the carapace
Head: Thread
Fly Tier: Scott Sanchez

Black & Green Minnow

Hook: TMC 511S, #2/0 - #2
Thread: Fluorescent orange
Tail and Wing: Excess pearl Flexicord from the head covering, picked out
Head covering: Pearl Flexicord over half the head, separated by the gills
Gills: Thread, excess Flexicord
Head: Balsa, shaped and painted green and black
Eyes: Painted large, yellow with black pupils
Coating: Epoxy
Fly Tier: Chappy Chapman

Black Squid

Hook: Mustad 3407, #7/0 - #2/0
Thread: Black - red
Tail: Black ostrich herl and ten black saddle hackles around a mixed Flashabou core
Saddle preparation: Black saddle feathers with painted white dots along the stem
Body: Black crystal chenille
Collar: Zonker strip, wrapped as a collar with the eyes in the middle
Eyes: Large pearl color plastic bead
Head: Black behind red thread, coated with epoxy
Fly Tier: Tom Tripi

Blue & White Minnow

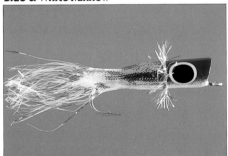

Hook: TMC 511S, #2/0 - #2
Thread: Fluorescent orange
Tail and Wing: Excess pearl Flexicord from the head covering, picked out
Head covering: Pearl Flexicord over half the head, separated by the gills
Gills: Thread, excess Flexicord
Head: Balsa, shaped and painted blue and white
Eyes: Painted large, yellow with black pupils
Coating: Epoxy
Fly Tier: Chappy Chapman

Blue Coho Trolling Fly

First Hook: Mustad 34007, #3/0 (cutting off hook point is optional)
Trailing Hook: Mustad 92553S, #2/0 - #1/0
Thread: Black
Trailer: Hook in a thirty-pound mono loop
Body: Silver mylar tubing
Wing: Turquoise under dark blue polar bear hair or equivalent
Belly: Gray polar bear hair or equivalent
Beard: Red polar bear hair or equivalent
Head: Thread coated with epoxy
Fly Tier: Reginald Denny

Blue Mackerel

Hook: Mustad 34011, #2
Thread: White
Tail: Light blue over white Crystal Splash, accented with pink Fly Flash
Body: Spirit River Saltwater Popper body, painted blue mottled over white
Side markings: Painted arrow-head, shaped black side markings
Eyes: Stick on, silver with black pupils
Head: Thread
Fly Tier: Bill Black, Spirit River Inc.

Blue Magic

Hook: Mustad 34007, #2
Thread: White
Wing: Silver mixed with blue rainbow Polar Flash, topped with green Flashabou
Throat: Red yarn
Head: Blue Dink Component #4, tied slider style
Fly Tier: Roger Swengel

Bunker Fly

Hook: Mustad 3407, #7/0
Thread: White
Tail: Four white saddle hackle feathers accented with pearl Flashabou
Wing: Peacock herl over purple buck tail over white buck tail
Wing flanking: Flanked with yellow buck tail on the sides
Throat: Red tuft of rabbit fur over white buck tail
Eyes: Doll eyes, yellow with movable black pupils
Head: Thread coated with Aqua Flex
Fly Tier: Al Beatty

Chartreuse Minnow

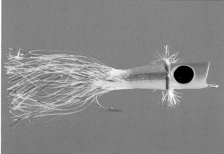

Hook: TMC 511S, #2/0 - #2
Thread: Fluorescent orange
Tail and Wing: Excess pearl Flexicord from the head covering, picked out
Head covering: Pearl Flexicord over half the head, separated by the gills
Gills: Thread, excess Flexicord
Head: Balsa, shaped and painted chartreuse
Eyes: Painted large, yellow with black pupils
Coating: Epoxy
Fly Tier: Chappy Chapman

Clark's Offshore Delight

Hook: Mustad Circle, #7/0 - #3/0
Thread: Red
Tail: Pink over yellow over chartreuse buck tail mixed with Krystal Flash and Flashabou
Flanking: Smaller red over yellow hackle feathers, tied on the sides of the tail
Body: Red thread
Hackle: Red, tied as a collar behind the eyes
Eyes: Large dumb bell
Wing: Pink buck tail
Head: Thread, tied as a beak
Fly Tier: Tom Tripi

Cobia Crab

Hook: Mustad Circle Hook, #7/0 (hook rides up)
Thread: Black
Tail: Red tinsel flash, olive marabou, red Sili Leg material, flanked with trimmed grizzly hackles
Eyes: Large dumb bell, tied at the hook bend
Body: Gold mylar tubing, tied flat with clear nail polish
Over Body: Fox zonker strip over the flatten mylar body
Wing: Olive marabou, red Sili Leg material, flanked with trimmed grizzly hackles
Head: Thread
Fly Tier: Tom Tripi

Cousin It

Hook: Eagle Claw 254NR, #5/0 - #4/0
Thread: White
Body/wings: White under chartreuse under blue Big Fly Fiber, strands of Krystal Flash mixed
Belly: Shorter curly Big Fly Fibers
Throat: Red Flashabou
Sides: One-half inch pearlescent ribbon, ends picked out
Eyes: Large stick on, white with black pupils
Head: Thread
Coating: Aqua Flex or epoxy over the head and eyes
Fly Tier: Ted Patlin

Curly

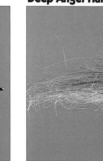

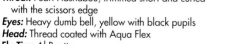

Hook: Mustad 34011, #4/0
Thread: Chartreuse
Tail: White buck tail over a mix of white and chartreuse schlappen feathers
Body: Thread
Wing: Chartreuse buck tail
Throat: Pearl Flashabou, trimmed short and curled with the scissors edge
Eyes: Heavy dumb bell, yellow with black pupils
Head: Thread coated with Aqua Flex
Fly Tier: Al Beatty

Deep Angel Hair Streamer

Hook: Eagle Claw 254NR, #2/0 - #4; hook ride point up
Thread: White
Body/wings: Alternating clumps of Bestway Super Hair and Angle Hair, white on the bottom and silver gray on top (hook ride point up)
Throat: Red Flashabou
Eyes: Spirit River dumb bell, red with black pupils
Head: Thread
Coating: Epoxy over the head and eyes
Fly Tier: Ted Patlen

Dick's Flash

Hook: Mustad 34011, #2
Thread: Yellow
Tail: Gold Flashabou, tied in the hook bend
Body: Gold Flashabou wrapped as an under body with Swannundaze over
Wing: Chartreuse buck tail under a green Flashabou topping
Hackle: Yellow
Eyes: Brass dumb bell
Head: Thread
Fly Tier: Dick Steinhorst

Dying Minnow

Hook: Mustad 34011, #1/0
Thread: Green
Body: Pearl Estaz
Under Wing: Pearl Krystal Flash over chartreuse Fishair
Wing flank: Grizzly over white hackle feathers, one set per side
Head: Edgewater Dink foam body component, #2 chartreuse
Head color: Red paint at the throat
Hackle: Red marabou, tied as a collar
Eyes: Stick on, gold with black pupils
Fly Tier: Len Elzie

Foil Popper

Hook: Mustad 32669, #1/0   **Thread:** White
Tail: Black, white, and red calf accented with silver and black Krystal Flash
Body coating: Thin silver foil applied with Barge Cement
Scales: Roll a socket wrench handle over the foil covered body
Body paint: Black and white
Eyes: Painted, yellow under orange with black pupils
Coating: Epoxy or Aqua Flex
Throat: Red marabou encased in the coating
Head: Thread
Fly Tier: Walt Holman

Glowing Needle

Hook: Mustad 94720, #2
Thread: Clear mono
Tail: Black/chartreuse Sili Legs over silver Comes Alive
Inner Body: White craft foam strips
Outer Body: White Corsair Tubing, coated with glow in the dark fabric paint
Body color: Felt tip markers
Eyes: Doll eyes, red with black pupils
Final Coating: Epoxy over the body and eyes
Fly Tier: Jerry Caruso

Gurgle Bug

Hook: Eagle Claw 254NR, #2/0
Thread: Yellow
Tail: Pearl Flashabou mixed with yellow buck tail, tied sparse
Body: Yellow floss
Hackle: Grizzly palmered and red tied as a throat
Over Body: Yellow closed cell foam, covered with pearl Flashabou
Head: Excess remaining from the over body, with pearl Flashabou
Fly Tier: Gretchen Beatty

Hot Tail Bunker, Purple

Hook: Daiichi 2546, #1/0
Thread: Purple
Tail: Purple zonker strip
Hot Tail: One half inch chartreuse zonker strip, glued to the end of the tail
Body: Purple zonker strip, wrapped collar style
Eyes: Large dumb bell with SRI 3-D glued on, yellow with black pupils
Legs: Rubber leg material
Head: Purple ice chenille
Fly Tier: Bill Black, Spirit River Inc.

Irresistible Bunny Diver

Hook: Daiichi 2546, #2 - #6
Thread: White
Tail: Grizzly, divided delta style
Wing: Black zonker strip over black Crystal Splash
Legs: Black rubber leg material
Collar: Peacock Fly Flash over dyed black deer, spun and trimmed
Head: Dyed black deer hair, spun and trimmed to shape
Eyes: Stick on doll eyes, white with black pupils
Weed guard: Hard mono
Fly Tier: Bill Black, Spirit River Inc.

Leftovers

Hook: Mustad 34011, #1
Thread: Green
Tail: Green buck tail accented with Tie Well and Krystal Flash
Hackle: White dyed green, tied as a collar
Body: Left over two-thirds of a #1 pencil popper body
Body color: Colored with multiple coatings of nail polish and glitter powder
Eyes: Stick on, fluorescent red with black pupils
Fly Tier: Len Elzie

Little Bunker

Hook: Mustad 3407, #5/0
Thread: White
Tail: Four white saddle feathers topped with copper Flashabou
Wing: Peacock herl over olive saddles feathers, flanked with natural emu feathers
Wing accent: Copper Flashabou
Throat: Red rabbit fur tuft over white buck tail
Eyes: Doll eyes, amber with black pupils
Head: Thread coated with Aqua Flex
Fly Tier: Al Beatty

Little Ray (Spoon)

Hook: Mustad 34011, #1/0
Thread: Clear mono
Tail: Purple Yak hair over white Fishair
Under Body: Sheet of closed cell foam, cut to shape and epoxied into place
Body cover: Pearl prism tape, cut to shape and epoxied into place
Under Body: White craft paint with glitter added
Eyes: Craft eyes, glued into place
Coating: Epoxy over the body and eyes
Fly Tier: Tom Berry

Mac Mullet

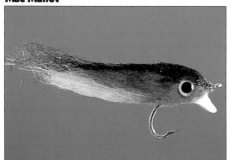

Hook: Eagle Claw DO67F, #2/0 - #2 **Thread:** White
Wing: Light, combed macramé yarn, trimmed to shape
Body: Light, combed macramé yarn, trimmed to shape
Body accent: Pearl Flashabou
Coating: Clear silicone
Wing topping: Dark, combed macramé yarn, trimmed to shape **Eyes:** Stick on, green with black pupils
Throat: Orange macramé yarn
Second coating: Clear silicone over the head, throat, topping and eyes
Head: Thread
Fly Tier: Ron Winn

Mangrove Cuckoo

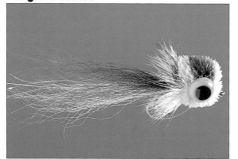

Hook: Mustad 34007, #1/0 - #2 **Thread:** White
Tail: Stacked buck tail, olive over blue over white accented with pearl Flashabou
Gills: Red hackle, tied as a collar near the hook bend, trimmed flat on the bottom
Hackle: White deer hair, spun to form a collar
Head: White spun with a clump of olive deer hair placed on the top, trimmed to shape
Eyes: Large doll eyes, yellow with black movable pupils
Weed guard: Hard mono, optional
Fly Tier: Mitch Whitney

Mega Popper

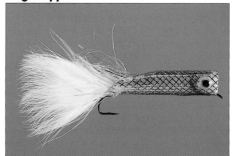

Hook: Partridge CS10, #2
Thread: White
Tail: White marabou
Body: White foam cylinder covered with mylar tubing, coated with Softex
Body color: Felt tip markers
Eyes: Doll eyes, yellow with black pupils
Head: Thread
Fly Tier: Lance Zook

Orange Minnow

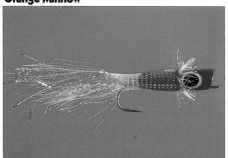

Hook: TMC 511S, #2/0 - #2
Thread: Fluorescent orange
Tail and Wing: Pink Krystal Flash under pearl Flexicord, picked out
Head covering: Pearl Flexicord over half the head, separated by the gills
Gills: Thread, excess Flexicord
Head: Balsa, shaped and painted fluorescent orange
Eyes: Painted large, yellow with black pupils
Fly Tier: Chappy Chapman

Pin Fish

Hook: Mustad 9175, #2/0
Thread: White
Body: Pearl Krystal Flash, wrapped with the wing segments
Wing: White, blue, olive, yellow, and gray Sea Fibres, tied Hi-Tie style in segments
Accent: Blue and yellow Krystal Flash mixed in the wing
Topping: Olive Krystal Flash
Belly: Gray Sea Fibres
Eyes: Dumb bell, painted red with black pupils
Head: Thread
Fly Tier: Ken Bay

Polgy

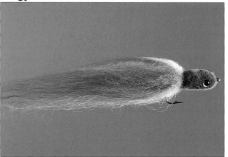

Hook: Mustad 34007, #2/0
Thread: Clear mono
Wing: Wool fibers, gray over blue over yellow over dark gray over white flanked by pink
Head: Brown and yellow wool, spun and trimmed to shape
Eyes: Doll eyes, yellow with black pupils
Fly Tier: Bill Chandler

Purple Coho Trolling Fly

First Hook: Mustad 34007, #3/0 (cutting off hook point is optional)
Trailing Hook: Mustad 92553S, #2/0 - #1/0
Thread: Black
Trailer: Hook in a thirty-pound mono loop
Body: Silver mylar tubing
Wing: Purple under black polar bear hair or equivalent
Belly: Yellow polar bear hair or equivalent
Beard: Red polar bear hair or equivalent
Head: Thread coated with epoxy
Fly Tier: Reginald Denny

Red & White Minnow

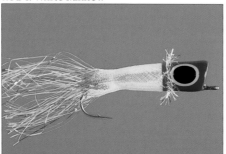

Hook: TMC 511S, #2/0 - #2
Thread: Fluorescent orange
Tail and Wing: Excess pearl Flexicord from the head covering, picked out
Head covering: Pearl Flexicord over half the head, separated by the gills
Gills: Thread, excess Flexicord
Head: Balsa, shaped and painted red and white
Eyes: Painted large, yellow with black pupils
Coating: Epoxy
Fly Tier: Chappy Chapman

Red Devil Popper

Hook: Mustad 3407, #2/0 - #2
Thread: Black
Tail: Gold sparkle flash flanked by four pheasant breast feathers
Accent: Ten orange stretch floss fibers, tied directly in front of the tail
Body: Black hackle, palmered
Legs: Black round rubber leg material, six legs
Head: Cork or foam, painted gold with multiple eyes
Eyes: Black with red highlighted yellow pupils
Fly Tier: Tom Tripi

Red Head & Pearl

Hook: Mustad 34011, #4/0
Thread: Fluorescent pink
Tail: Blue over white Fish Hair, tied with a slight up angle
Wing: Excess pearl Flexicord, picked out from the head covering
Head: Balsa, shaped and painted white and red
Gills: Thread, excess Flexicord
Head covering: Pearl Flexicord under an epoxy coating
Eyes: Painted large, yellow with black pupils
Fly Tier: Chappy Chapman

Red Slider

Hook: Daiichi 2546, #2 - #6   **Thread:** White
Tail: Mix of red Fly Flash and Red Crystal Splash
Wing: Two red inside two white hackle feathers, tied splayed
Hackle: Red and white mix, tied as a collar behind the head
Head: Foam-Tec popper head, attached to hook backwards
Eyes: Doll eyes, red with black pupils
Legs: White and red rubber leg material, one of each color per side placed using a needle
Weed guard: Hard mono
Fly Tier: Bill Black, Spirit River Inc.

Salt Water Boobie

Hook: Mustad 34011, #4
Thread: Fluorescent pink
Tail: Pink marabou, tied short
Body: Tying thread
Hackle: Pink turkey, palmered
Head: Round closed cell foam, covered with pink paint, coated with Loon Soft Head
Fly Tier: Tom Berry

Salt Water Soft Pop

Hook: TMC 511S, #2/0
Thread: White
Tail: Synthetic hair and Krystal Flash flanked by two white saddle feathers
Hackle: White, tied as a collar
Body: Five-eighths inch caulking rod, painted colors of choice, glitter on the belly
Eyes: Doll eyes
Head: Thread
Coating: Aqua Flex or Softex, over the body and eyes
Fly Tier: Tim Paxton

Silver Minnow Popper

Hook: Mustad 34011, #2
Thread: White
Tail: Black over white Crystal Splash, accented with pearl Fly Flash
Body: Spirit River Saltwater Popper body, painted black mottled over white
Eyes: Stick on, silver with black pupils
Head: Thread
Fly Tier: Bill Black, Spirit River Inc.

Squimp

Hook: Owner 5320, #5/0
Thread: Fluorescent pink
Tail: Pink Fish Hair accented with Krystal Flash, forty-five degree angle
Wing: Pearl Flexicord picked out from the head covering accented with Krystal Flash
Head: Balsa, shaped and painted fluorescent pink with large black eye
Head covering: Pearl Flexicord under an epoxy coating
Nose: Excess pearl Flexicord extending in front of the eye
Fly Tier: Chappy Chapman

Surface Slicer

Hook: Mustad 3407, #2
Thread: White
Tail: White saddle hackle feathers and silver Krystal Flash, super glued into the body
Body: Surf board foam, shaped and painted red
Eyes: Doll eyes, yellow with black pupils
Fly Tier: Tom Broderidge

Two Tube Fly

Back Hook: Eagle Claw 193G, 2/0 red (used with a two inch brass tube fly)
Thread: Red
Tail on the back fly: Dark and light buck tail tied to a brass tube fly
Body: (Back fly) white chenille
Hackle: White, palmered
Front Hook: Eagle Claw 254NR, #2/0 (the hook rides point up)
Tail on the front fly: (Tied on a one and one half inch brass tube) white buck tail
Body: White chenille, tied on one half of brass tube only

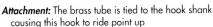

Attachment: The brass tube is tied to the hook shank causing this hook to ride point up
Wing: Three clumps of dark buck tail under black Krystal Flash
Throat: White buck tail
Eyes: Stick on, gold with black pupils
Head: Thread over the end of the tube and the hook, coated with Aqua Flex
First rigging: Fifty pound BT's Micro Backing, on the back hook through both tubes
Second rigging: Fifty pound BT's Micro Backing, nail/loop knot to the first hook eye
Connection: Both riggings pulled forward and connected with a double perfection loop
Fly Tier: Al Beatty

Tarpon and Barracuda Streamers . . .

Amherst Roach

Hook: Eagle Claw 254NR, #2/0 - 34
Thread: White
Tail: Four silver badger Coq de Leon cape feathers
Hackle: Amherst pheasant tippets, tied around the hook as a collar
Eyes: Stick on, gold with black pupils
Head and snout: Thread coated with Aqua Flex
Fly Tier: Gretchen Beatty

Baby Lobster

Hook: Mustad 3407, #2/0 - #2
Thread: Orange
Mouth parts: Fox squirrel dyed orange, tied short and sparse
Antenna: Stripped orange dyed saddle feather stems
Eyes: Melted mono and black beads, tied long with the mouth parts
Hackle: Two turns of natural guinea feather, tied collar style near the hook bend
Body: Orange ice chenille
Head: Thread
Fly Tier: Ron Winn

Blue Cockroach

Hook: Gamakatsu, #3/0 - #1
Thread: Black
Tail: Six black saddle hackles and blue Flashabou
Wing: Dyed blue squirrel with a tinsel topping, tied as an under collar
Hackle: Black saddle, tied as a collar
Head: Thread
Fly Tier: Kevin Cohenour

Boogie Bait (Clown)

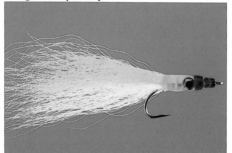

Hook: Mustad 34007, #4/0 - #1/0
Thread: Clear mono
Body and Head: Four or five large yellow glass beads, one extra large scarlet bead, and two large scarlet beads (coated later)
Tail: Pearl Krystal Flash over white buck tail
Wing: Yellow buck tail, anchored over the yellow glass beads
Eyes: Stick on, yellow with black pupils
Coating: Soft Body or Aqua Flex over the body and head
Fly Tier: Joe Warren

Boogie Bait (Electric Blue)

Hook: Mustad 34007, #4/0 - #1/0
Thread: Clear mono
Body and Head: Four or five aqua marine (sliver lined) glass bead, one extra large turquoise bead, and two large aqua marine beads (coated later)
Tail: Smoke Super Hair
Wing: Blue Crystal Cloth over dark blur Super Hair
Eyes: Stick on, silver with black pupils
Coating: Soft body or Aqua Flex over the body and head
Fly Tier: Joe Warren

Boogie Bait (Shad)

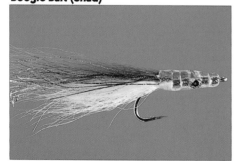

Hook: Mustad 34007, #4/0 - #1/0
Thread: Clear mono
Body and Head: Six large Killer Caddis glass beads (coated later)
Tail: White buck tail, rainbow Krystal Flash, and blue/sharkskin mixed Crystal Cloth
Wing: Dun gray buck tail, tied over the last two beads and secured with the tying thread
Eyes: Stick on, silver with black pupils
Coating: Soft Body or Aqua Flex over the body and head
Fly Tier: Joe Warren

Buchanan Bank Special

Hook: Mustad 7766, #3/0
Thread: Gudebrod G, both clear and orange
Tail: Deer hair tuft and orange SLF tuft between six grizzly hackles feathers, divided
Hackle: Orange and yellow dyed grizzly, tied as a collar
Stripe: Short natural grizzly, tied on each side
Head: Orange thread
Eyes: Yellow fabric paint with black pupil
Head: Five Minute Epoxy coating
Fly Tier: Len Roberts

Bunny Needlefish

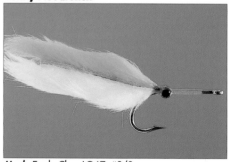

Hook: Eagle Claw LO67, #3/0
Thread: Chartreuse
Tail: Chartreuse and white zonker strips, glued together double bunny style (hide to hide)
Eyes: Doll eyes, red with black pupils
Head and snout: Thread coated with epoxy or Aqua Flex
Fly Tier: Chris Mihulka

Capt. Len's Black Dredge

Hook: Mustad 7766, #3/0
Thread: Clear mono
Tail: Several black saddle hackle feathers, pearl Krystal Flash
Hackle: Black, wrapped as a collar
Eyes: Black mono
Head: Epoxy over the head and eyes
Fly Tier: Len Roberts

Capt. Len's Everything Tarpon

Hook: Mustad 7766, #3/0
Thread: Black
Tail: Rainbow Krystal Flash under tan Fly Fur flanked by cree side stripes
Hackle: Grizzly, tied as a collar
Eyes: White and black fabric paint
Head: Thread with an epoxy coating
Fly Tier: Len Roberts

Cloudy Day

Hook: Mustad 34007, #3/0
Thread: Gray
Tail: Blue over purple over brown over black yarn, picked out
Hackle: Badger cape hackle, tied as a collar
Head and snout: Thread
Fly Tier: Tom Broderidge

Cone Head Bonker

Hook: Daiichi 2546, #1/0
Thread: White
Tail: White zonker strip
Body: White zonker strip wrapped collar style behind pearl ice chenille
Legs: White rubber leg material
Head: Gold SRI Cone Head Bead
Weed guard: Hard mono, two strands parallel
Fly Tier: Bill Black, Spirit River Inc.

Dare Devil Spoon

Hook: Eagle Claw L143, #2/0 - #2
Thread: Red
Tail: White Chickabou
Body: Red automotive flash tape
Eyes: Spirit River Real Eyes, red with black pupils
Head: Thread coated with Aqua Flex
Fly Tier: Al Beatty

Diving Tarpon Fly

Hook: Mustad 34011, #1/0
Thread: Clear mono
Tail: Bright pink over white craft fur
Hackle: Red and pink mixed, tied as a collar behind the head
Head: Plastic bead behind a snout of red micro chenille
Eyes: Stick on, yellow with black pupils
Coating: Soft Body or Aqua Flex
Fly Tier: Tom Berry

Furnace Glo

Hook: Mustad 3407, #1/0
Thread: Orange
Tail: Four Whiting American Laced furnace feathers, tied divided with Krystal Flash
Wing/collar: Fox squirrel tail, tied collar style
Eyes: Stick on, white with black pupils
Head and snout: Thread coated with Aqua Flex
Fly Tier: Al Beatty

Ginger Roach

Hook: Eagle Claw 254NR, #2/0 - #4
Thread: Black
Tail: Four ginger Whiting American cape feathers
Hackle: Golden pheasant body feathers, tied around the hook as a collar
Eyes: Stick on, gold with black pupils
Head and snout: Thread coated with Aqua Flex
Fly Tier: Gretchen Beatty

Golden Needle

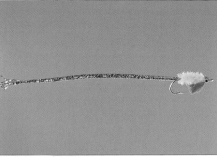

Hook: Mustad 3407, #1
Thread: Hot orange
Tail: Gold mylar tubing, sealed near the end with hot orange thread, picket out
Body: Yellow ice chenille
Beard: Red yarn, picked out
Eyes: Stick on, yellow with black pupils
Head: Thread with Loon Hard Head over the head and eyes
Fly Tier: Tom Broderidge

Golden Roach

Hook: Eagle Claw 254NR, #2/0 - #4
Thread: Yellow
Tail: Four brown Whiting American saddle hackles
Hackle: Golden pheasant tippet feathers, tied around the hook as a collar
Eyes: Stick on, yellow with black pupils
Head and snout: Thread coated with Aqua Flex
Fly Tier: Gretchen Beatty

Indestructible 'Cuda Fly

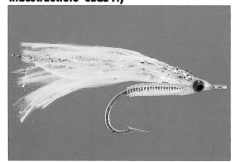

Hook: Mustad 3407, #2
Thread: White
Body: Flat silver tinsel under clear mono, tied nail knot style
Wing: Nylon craft cord with flash strands, combed out and trimmed to shape
Eyes: Stick on, red with black pupils
Head: Thread coated with Loon Hard Head
Fly Tier: Tom Broderidge

Jerry's Baby

Hook: Mustad 34007, #2
Thread: Orange
Tail: Four Whiting American Laced hen saddle feathers, tied divided
Hackle: Whiting American Laced hen saddle feather, tied as a collar
Head: Thread coated with Aqua Flex
Fly Tier: Al Beatty

Laced Apte Two (Red)

Hook: Mustad 3407, #1/0
Thread: Red
Tail: Four Whiting American Laced dyed red feathers, tied flat with Krystal Flash
Body: Thread
Wing/collar: Gray squirrel tail, tied collar style
Eyes: Stick on, white with black pupils
Head: Thread coated with Aqua Flex
Fly Tier: Al Beatty

Laced Captain

Hook: Mustad 3407, #1/0
Thread: Red
Tail: Four Whiting American Laced dyed pink feathers, divided and accented with Krystal Flash
Hackle: Whiting American Laced natural white/black, tied as a collar
Head: Thread
Fly Tier: Al Beatty

Laced Roach

Hook: Mustad 3407, #1/0
Thread: Black
Tail: Four Whiting American Laced dyed orange feathers, tied divided with Krystal Flash
Wing/collar: Gray squirrel tail, tied collar style
Eyes: Doll eyes, red with black pupils
Head: Thread coated with Aqua Flex, tied short
Fly Tier: Al Beatty

Len's Tarpon Ocean Runner

Hook: Mustad 7766, #3/0
Thread: Black
Tail: Bright orange SLF under six brown saddle hackle feathers
Hackle: Cream marabou, tied as a collar
Eyes: White and black fabric paint
Head: Thread and an epoxy coating
Fly Tier: Len Roberts

Mihulka Tube Fly

Hook: Eagle Claw LO67, #4/0 tied on to a fine cable "shock tippet"
Thread: Clear mono
Tying platform: A one-sixteenth tough plastic tube, tied tube fly style
Wing: Unraveled pearl mylar tube in the center surrounded by chartreuse Super Hair
Wing top and bottom: Red Super Hair, tied sparse on the top and bottom of the wing
Eyes: Large doll eyes, white with movable black pupils
Head: Thread coated with epoxy over the eyes and head
Fly Tier: Chris Mihulka

Pink Lady

Hook: Mustad 34011, #2/0
Thread: Black
Tail: Two black over two pink hackle feathers with red Krystal Flash
Body: Tying thread
Hackle: Pink behind red, tight palmer over the body
Eyes: Black strung beads with silver stick on with black pupils
Head: Black thread, tapered and coated with epoxy over the head & eyes
Fly Tier: Tom Berry

Red Death

Hook: Mustad 7766, #3/0 - #1
Thread: Black
Tail: Pearl Flashabou under six dyed black hackle, tied divided
Stripe: Natural grizzly, tied on each side
Hackle: Red, tied as a collar
Eyes: White fabric paint with black pupil
Head: Five Minute Epoxy coating
Fly Tier: Len Roberts

Red Tail

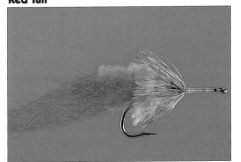

Hook: Mustad 34007, #2/0 and larger
Thread: Yellow
Tail: Red, orange, and yellow yarn, picked out and trimmed to shape
Hackle: Grizzly dyed yellow, tied as a collar
Head and snout: Thread
Fly Tier: Tom Broderidge

Red Wing Black Bird

Hook: Daiichi X452, #4/0
Thread: Black
Tail: Black Chickabou tuft under two black rooster tail feathers
Cheeks: Red Soft Hackle feather tips flanking the black tail feathers
Hackle: Soft Hackle/Chickabou, mixed and tied as a collar
Eyes: Stick on, silver with black pupils
Head and snout: Peacock ribbon floss, coated with epoxy or Aqua Flex
Fly Tier: Henry Hoffman

Spearing

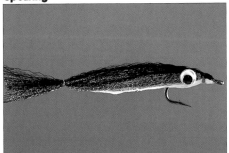

Hook: Mustad 3407, #1/0 - #4
Thread: White
Wing: Copper Krystal Flash under black Krystal Flash
Belly: White buck tail
Eyes: Doll eyes, white with black movable pupils
Head: Thread
Coating: Aqua Flex over the head, eyes, and wings
Tail: Wing tied off with copper wire to form the tail
Fly Tier: Jack Pangburn

Sue's Big Tuna

Hook: Mustad 3407, #7/0 - #2
Thread: Red
Tail: Red over orange over yellow buck tail mixed with Flashabou
Tail flanking: Smaller red over yellow hackle feathers
Body: Silver mylar tubing, open at both ends
Wing: Red over orange over yellow buck tail mixed with Flashabou
Wing flanking: Yellow hackle feathers, tied on the side
Throat: Fibers from the body, picked out and pulled back
Head: Thread
Fly Tier: Tom Tripi

Tarpon Deceiver

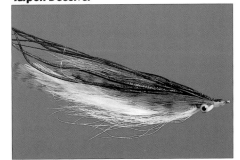

Hook: Mustad 34007, #2/0 - #4
Thread: White
Tail: Four white saddle feathers accented with pearl Flashabou
Body: Pearl diamond braid
Wing: Peacock herl over yellow/green mixed buck tail
Wing flank: Grizzly dyed insect green, tied on the sides
Throat: White buck tail
Eyes: Heavy dumb bell, painted white with black pupils
Head: Thread coated with Aqua Flex
Fly Tier: Al Beatty

Tarpon Ghost

Hook: DaiRiki 930, #3/0 - #1/0
Thread: White
Tail: Eight white neck hackles
Body/Hackle: Red body fur under gray body fur, both wrapped collar style in a dubbing loop
Eyes: Doll eyes, chartreuse with black pupils
Eye mounting: Eyes glued to a small strip of plastic bottle material and tied in with the head
Head: Thread coated with epoxy
Fly Tier: Lance Zook

Tarpon Shrimp

Hook: Mustad 7766, #3/0
Thread: Gudebrod clear
Tail: Rainbow Krystal Flash under six grizzly hackle feathers, divided
Collar: Light green Fish Hair
Head: Epoxy over green thread
Fly Tier: Len Roberts

Tarpon Tamer

Hook: Eagle Claw 254NR, #1/0
Thread: Fluorescent green
Tail: Tiewell green flash flanking chartreuse buck tail and dark green saddle hackles
Body Hackle: Chartreuse strung neck hackle, tied as a collar
Eyes: Fisker Design EZY-Eyes and stick on, gold with black pupils
Head and snout: Tying thread coated with Aqua Flex
Fly Tier: Gretchen Beatty

Tipped Tarpon, Bend Back

Hook: Eagle Claw L143S, #1/0 - #2, (shaped bend back style, the hook point rides up)
Thread: Fire orange
Wing: Four Whiting American white, black tip hackle feathers
Hackle: Three Whiting American grizzly hackles, tied dry fly style
Head: Thread coated with Aqua Flex
Fly Tier: Al Beatty

Triple Lace

Hook: Eagle Claw 254NR, #1/0
Thread: Fluorescent pink
Under Tail: Magenta Tiewell flash under pink and purple saddle hackle feathers
Tail flanking: Laced magenta American hen cape feathers, three per side
Body Hackle: American silver badger, tied as a collar
Head and snout: Tying thread coated with Aqua Flex
Fly Tier: Gretchen Beatty

Zonker Tail Cockroach

Hook: Gamakatsu, #3/0 - #1
Thread: Black
Tail: Tan zonker strip
Foul guard: Mono looped at the hook bend
Flash: Flashabou
Wing: Fox squirrel tail, tied as an under collar
Hackle: Grizzly, tied as a collar
Head: Thread
Fly Tier: Kevin Cohenour

Clifford Adams is from Eugene, Oregon where he has been a long-time supporter of the Federation of Fly Fishers. When a volunteer is needed for just about any project, Cliff will be one of those hard-working people who steps forward.

Terry Alexander, a native of Illinois, has lived in Frederick, Maryland for seventeen years. He is a research technician by trade, is married with two sons, and enjoys searching for new fishing locations with son, Ian.

Farrow Allen owned and operated a fly fishing shop in Burlington, Vermont for twelve years before selling it in 1988 and moving to New Hampshire to work with Dick Stewart on a five-book series of fly patterns. He is the former editor of Fly Tying Tips for *American Angler* and *Fly Tyer* magazines. He is currently the Fly Tying and Southeast Regional Editor at *Fly Fish America Magazine.* Farrow has been fly fishing and tying flies for thirty years and currently lives in Asheville, North Carolina with his wife Margret Kjartansson, two dogs, two cats, and a bird named Frances Fluffy Milhorn.

Jeff "Bear" Andrews is a well-recognized commercial tier and writer from Grand Ledge, Michigan. He is the recipient of the 1998 Bus Buszek Award. Jeff spends his time around the Tyathon (a fundraiser for conservation efforts) at all the national FFF Conclaves.

Jim Aubrey from Durango, Colorado has been tying flies for the past 60 years. He especially enjoys teaching children through the Bayfield County Middle School outdoor recreation class. Jim also teaches adult classes through the local community college.

Joe Ayre has graced this planet for more than 80 years. His home is in Pocatello, Idaho where he learned to tie flies at the young age of 70. Joe is a local fly tying celebrity and has drawn a large crowd at many fly tying demonstrations throughout the Rocky Mountain area.

Walter Babb is from Sweetwater, Tennessee where he works a full-time job, ties flies commercially, and guides in his spare time.

David Barlow is a native of England who is currently living in Salem, Oregon. He has tied for the past ten years and is primarily an Atlantic salmon fly tier.

Ken Bay from Holly Hill, Florida is an innovative fly tier with three published books to his credit: *Saltwater Flies, How To Tie Freshwater Flies,* and *American Fly Tiers Almanac.* Ken received the Buz Buszek Memorial Award in 1974 for fly tying excellence.

Gretchen & Al Beatty make their home in Delta, Colorado where they operate the family business (BT's Fly Fishing Products), write, and tie flies on a commercial basis. They are co-authors of this book and enjoy each other's company at the keyboard, the vise, and on the stream. Al is the Federation of Fly Fishers' 1999 Buz Buszek Memorial Award winner for fly tying excellence.

Tom Berry is an innovative fly tier from Bay St. Louis, Mississippi.

Bill Black is a very creative professional fly tier from Roseburg, Oregon. He is part owner of Spirit River, Inc., a company focused on supplying high-quality fly tying materials to fly tiers throughout the world.

Dave Borjas is from Dillon, Montana where he enjoys fishing his favorite bodies of water, the Beaverhead, Big Hole, and Ruby rivers.

James Bowen is a self-taught fly tier who has practiced the art for the past twenty-two years. He has six fly tying videos on the market with Bennett Watts Flytying Video Magazine. He often answers to "Mr. Realistic" due to the style of flies he ties. Jim is a commercial tier and guide from Idaho Falls, Idaho.

Tom Broderidge ties a wide range of flies for the varied waters near his home in Havana, Florida.

Jay Buchner is from Jackson, Wyoming where he has long been involved in the fly fishing business.

Kent R. Bulfinch from Yreka, California began tying flies in his native New Hampshire in 1925. He is the Federation of Fly Fishers' Buz Buszek Memorial Award winner for 1990 and is well known for his innovative, realistic patterns.

Mike Butler is from Jefferson City, Missouri.

Bernard Byng from Tracy, California has been tying flies and trout fly fishing for the past several years. Recently he discovered great striper and black bass fishing in his own backyard, the California Delta. When not fly fishing, Bernard enjoys helping his local FFF club, the Tracy Fly Fishers.

Herbert Carmon is from Pryor, Oklahoma where he enjoys pursuing all warmwater species.

Bill Carnazzo makes his home in Newcastle, California where he runs Spring Creek Fly Craft and Guide Service.

Jerry Caruso makes his home in Philadelphia, Pennsylvania where he has been fly fishing and tying flies for the last nine years. He ties very few traditional patterns, preferring to create or modify patterns to suit his needs.

Bill Chandler has been tying flies for both the angler and the collector for twenty years. He is an award-winning fly tier who has been featured in books and magazines. Bill demonstrates fly tying all over the eastern part of the country and loves to teach others the art and craft of fly tying.

George "Chappy" Chapman is from Woodland Hills, California where he enjoys retirement from a career in the United States Navy. He has tied flies for the past thirty years and demonstrated his skills at almost all of the Southwest Council Conclaves.

Jim Childers is retired from guiding and government work and lives in Lenoir, North Carolina. He enjoys hiking, fly fishing, mountain biking, fly tying, and bow hunting.

Doug Christian is a recently retired teacher who has been an avid fly tier for fifty years. He has been a featured demonstration fly tier at numerous local, regional, and national shows and felt honored to be named Southern Council Fly Tier of the Year in 1993. Doug's specialty is using crafts materials to construct warmwater flies.

Brett Clark is a young man from Sandy, Utah who is a commercial tier for Willow Creek Outfitters. He is an excellent innovator of some very successful tying techniques.

Lee Clark began using macramé yarn for fly tying in the early 1980s and finds its versatility accommodates many possible applications. He is a retired school teacher, lives in St. Helens, Oregon with his wife Betty, and is a contract tier for Umpqua Feather Merchants. Lee earned the Oregon Council's Fly Tier of the Year in 1989.

George Close, whose native waters are near his home in Kiel, Wisconsin, has fly fished from Nova Scotia to Montana and New Zealand. Now retired, he is focusing his fishing on still water and saltwater flats near his Florida winter home.

Kevin Cohenour is a Colorado native who first learned to tie flies in a Littleton, Colorado grade school. In a very short time he was producing serviceable fishing flies for his father and grand father. Currently he is a Chief Warrant Officer in the Navy and will soon retire to his native Colorado where he can catch up on his fly fishing.

Chuck Collins has been the owner of All Seasons Angler fly shop in Pocatello, Idaho for the past four years and a fly tier for the past forty years. He has demonstrated his tying skills at the regional and national levels.

LeRoy Cook makes his home in Idaho Falls, Idaho. As a teenager in the 1950s, he started bass and bluegill fly fishing in Missouri. From the farm pond in the Midwest to the West's big waters, he ties and fishes all kinds of flies.

Sister Carol Ann Corely is the fly fishing Catholic nun from Fort Smith, Arkansas. She creates, teaches, and demonstrates her techniques with a peppering of her keen wit and propensity for finding inexpensive fly tying materials.

Jim Cramer is a retired engineer living in Bodega Bay, California and has tied flies for over fifty years. He believes that flies do not have to be complicated to catch fish and enjoys the challenge of developing what he calls, "fast-tie patterns." Jim has authored articles for several national magazines.

Mike Croft lives in Tacoma, Washington with his wife Reba and sons, Patrick and Brendan. He fly fishes locally for salmon and sea-run cutthroat and has guided fly fishing trips into exotic tropical waters for sailfish, tuna, tarpon, and bonefish. Mike is the author of *Fish Bum's Guide to Catching Larger Trout* and teaches fly tying from Anchorage, Alaska to Nairobi, Kenya.

David Curneal started tying flies on his eighth birthday with a fly tying kit his father had given him. From that early beginning he has advanced to being co-owner of the Willow Creek Outfitters in Sandy, Utah.

Dan Curtis has been tying flies and fly fishing for the past twenty-two years. At one time he owned Curtis Hackle Co. with his father Bob Curtis. He sold the hackle company and started a guiding career focused on north Idaho streams. More recently in Dillon, Montana, Dan is guide and store manager for Dick Sharon Fishing Headquarters.

Royce Dam is a very talented fly tier skilled at all levels of tying from the very large to small. It is for this reason and many others he received the Federation of Fly Fishers' Buz Buszek Memorial Award for fly tying.

Reginald Denny is from Edmonton, Alberta, Canada where he operates Denny's Fly Tying Specialties. He is a highly skilled tier who ties a wide range of patterns.

Gale Doudy lives in Austin, Colorado on the banks of the Gunnison River where he has focused the last ten years guiding fly fishers. He is an avid fly tier, fly fisher, and member of TU and FFF. Gale is the current President of the Gunnison Gorge FFF/TU Club.

Gary Dubiel is a saltwater fly rod and light tackle guide in eastern North Carolina where he runs "Spec Fever" Guide Service. Captain Gary has fly fished the Eastern Seaboard, the Gulf of Mexico, and the Caribbean for numerous saltwater game fish. He has published his flies with the Fedération of Fly Fishers and with Lefty Kreh. Gary is an IGFA fly rod record holder.

Dave Duffy, a native of Butte, Montana, now makes his home in Spruce Pine, North Carolina where he fishes the Smoky Mountains for trout and smallmouth bass. He has tied flies for more than twenty years and caught the warmwater fishing bug while living in Minnesota.

Chuck Echer began his fly tying career in 1948. He has literally taught thousands of students the art of fly tying and fly fishing. He has demonstrated as a celebrity master fly tier since 1988, both at national and international major shows. He was the FFF 1993 Buz Buszek Memorial Award recipient.

Dean Elder, Jr. is from Marshalltown, Iowa where he is a member of the Hawkeye Fly Fishing Association.

Len Elzie is an economist by profession and a FFF member living in Tallahassee, Florida. He fishes the Florida Gulf Coast and enjoys developing and refining fly patterns for that area. Len teaches beginning and advanced fly tying, demonstrates at conclaves, and sometimes finds the time to tie a commercial fly order.

Dave Engerbretson from Moscow, Idaho is a well-known fly fishing personality. You can join him at his fly tying vise on PBS each Saturday morning to watch and learn. Dave is also on the Board of Governors for the Federation of Fly Fishers' fly-casting certification program.

Ed Engle is the author of *Fly Fishing the Tail Waters* and knows about flies that work. He started working as a guide in the 1970s and soon found he liked catching large fish on small flies.

Doug Farthing is from Camdenton, Missouri where he enjoys catching many warmwater species, especially catfish, on a fly.

Daniel J. Ferron from Green Bay, Wisconsin is a long-time supporter of the Federation of Fly Fishers. He has taught fly tying classes for the past thirteen years and enjoys fishing nearby waters as well as sampling those of Montana and Wyoming. Daniel is well known for the wooden framed landing nets, rods, and shadow boxes he manufactures.

Floyd Franke lives and works along the Beaverkill River in upstate New York. He operates his own guide service (Ephemera) and is an instructor at the Wulff School of Fly Fishing. His fly tying creations have appeared in such popular magazines as *Fly Fisherman, American Angler,* and *Flyfishing & Tying Journal.* Floyd is a life member of the Federation of Fly Fishers and a recipient of the NEC's Elsie and Harry Darbee Memorial Fly Tying Award.

Kieran C. Frye has been tying flies since 1982. He demonstrates and teaches fly tying to youth groups, clubs, and others across the United States and Europe. Kieran is a life member of both the Federation of Fly Fishers and Trout Unlimited.

Keith Fulsher originated the Thunder Creek Series of baitfish-imitating flies in 1962 and described his techniques for making them in his book *Tying and Fishing the Thunder Creek Series* published by Freshet Press in 1973. He also co-authored *Hair-Wing Atlantic Salmon Flies* with Charles Krom, published by Fly Tyer, Inc. in 1981. This was the first book to deal with hair-wing salmon flies on a comprehensive basis.

Barry Glickman is from San Rafael, California where he is a member of the Golden Gate Angling and Casting Club. Besides tying flies, he is also an artist specializing in fly print line art.

Buck Goodrich has been tying flies since 1947 and demonstrating fly tying since 1985. He is a fly tying instructor who specializes in flies that catch fish.

Gary Grant is the Secretary of the Federation of Fly Fishers and publisher of a quarterly journal on Atlantic salmon flies. When not found fishing the Henry's Fork or other waters in Idaho and Yellowstone Park, he can be found reading long-forgotten books on fly tying and fly fishing.

Ron Graunke is from Mount Airy, Maryland where he makes his living in the nursery and landscape business. He specializes in reforestation in his professional life and in catching fish in his private life. Ron is an active member of the Potomac Valley Fly Fishermen, is on the club's conservation committee, and is a regular demonstration fly tier.

Dana Griffin, III, has been on a fly fishing pilgrimage since the mid-40s, a journey that began on the San Juan River in northern New Mexico. In the late 60s he moved to Florida, began a fly tying course, and founded the North Florida Fly Fishers. Dana is the author of many articles on fly fishing and fly tying and is the on-camera tier in two videos.

Duane Hada from Yellville, Arkansas makes his living designing flies and guiding fly fishers for Ozark trout and smallmouth bass. He is a FFF Certified Casting Instructor.

Bruce Harang lives in Asheville, North Carolina at the junction of the Southern Appalachians, Smoky Mountains, and the Blue Ridge Mountains; an area containing over 4,000 miles of trout streams and four of the world's best tailwater trout fisheries. By profession a patent and trademark attorney, he is the Federation of Fly Fishers' trademark attorney. Bruce is a life member of the

FFF, the founder and president of the Smoky Mountain Fly Fishers, and co-founder and chairman of the Southern Appalachian Fly Tiers (the first overseas affiliate of the English Fly Dressers' Guild). He is also a fly fishing and fly tying bibliophile and fly fishing and fly tying history buff as well as an amateur aquatic entomologist.

George Harmeling is a life member of the Federation of Fly Fishers who began tying in 1973—almost six years before he finally finished his first fly. He enjoys tying all types of patterns without restricting himself to one particular style or technique; and classifies himself as a generalist.

Jon Harrang began tying flies in grade school and now, years later, specializes in tying steelhead and Atlantic salmon feather-wing patterns. He lives with his wife Shawn and daughter Rachael in Tillamook, Oregon.

Dustin Harris is from Monmouth, Oregon where he is owner and founder of Body Basics, a Northwest fly tying materials company.

Derek Harryman from Sandy, Utah is a commercial fly tier for Willow Creek Outfitters.

Jeff Hatton is a Colorado native who makes his home near Paonia. At the early age of six his father inflicted him with the fly fishing bug and he has pursued his passion ever since. Jeff guides, ties commercially, builds rods, and calls himself just another "trout bum."

Tom Hawley makes his home in Boulder, Colorado where pursues a career and ties flies commercially part time. He has been fly fishing and tying for the past six years.

Jerome Hebert is from Henderson, Louisiana where he operates A Bayou Runs Through It guide service.

Howard "Bud" Heintz has been a fly tier for over twenty-five years. He specializes in trout and bass flies and custom ties these patterns for Buz Buszek's Fly Shop. Bud is a Federation of Fly Fishers supporter, demonstration fly tier, and workshop presenter.

Christopher Helm from Toledo, Ohio has earned his reputation throughout the Federation of Fly Fishers for his incredible skill with deer hair, especially when spun on the hook. Besides keeping very busy tying spun-hair flies he also operates his business *Whitetail Fly Tieing Supplies*, distributes the Brassie® hair packer, and teaches fly tying clinics all over the world.

Jeffrey A. Hines is a past President of the Dallas Fly Fishers who makes his living practicing law in Plano, Texas whenever he is not fly fishing or fly tying. He is best known for tying soft-hackles, nymphs, and traditional wet flies which have appeared in the International Fly Tiers series of fly plates.

Ilene Hirsh is the sole proprietor of Flies By Ilene and has been tying flies on a commercial basis for over ten years. She specializes in Alaskan patterns and has a customer base throughout Alaska and the lower forty-eight states.

Mark Hoeser has been tying flies since 1987 and has been demonstrating fly tying at regional, international, and local shows near his home in Stockton, California since 1990. He enjoys all types of fly tying and is a recipient of over thirty national and international fly tying awards. Mark is also a Whiting Pro-Team demonstration fly tier.

Josh Hoeschen from Riegelsville, Pennsylvania is fourteen years old and has been tying flies for five years. He assisted with an entomology workshop at the Mid Atlantic Council youth camp, demonstrated fly tying at the New Jersey School of Conservation, and taught the beginning fly tying class at a recent MAC Conclave.

Henry Hoffman is from Warrenton, Oregon where he went from a part-time commercial fly tier to a full-time hackle raiser. In 1994 he received the FFF's Lee Wulff Award for developing the super-grade hackle. After selling his business Henry returned to tying and designing flies using rooster soft hackle, knee hackle, and chickabou.

Jim Hoffman from Lincoln, Nebraska started tying flies at the young age of eleven. Since that start he has enjoyed learning more about the sport and subsequently passing the knowledge along to his two children (both avid fly fishers). Jim particularly enjoys casting his three-weight rod rigged with a Blue Quill to fish on neighboring lakes and ponds.

Michael D. Hogue owns and manages Badger Creek Fly Tying. He demonstrates at local and international fly fishing shows. He developed Laura's Snowshoe Wulff while fishing the Hendrickson *invaria* hatch in southeast Minnesota. He uses it as a dry or emerger. One of his wife Laura's best days of dry-fly fishing occurred using this fly. It is her lucky fly.

Walt Holman lives in Madison, Alabama with his wife Gennie. They are both lifetime members of the Tennessee Valley Fly Fishers of the Southeastern Council of the Federation of Fly Fishers. Walt is a retired electronic engineer who has enjoyed tying and fishing his flies for the past fifty-three years.

Leonard Holt began fly fishing when he moved to Flagstaff, Arizona in late 1959. He regularly fished the local streams and lakes in southern Utah and southwestern Colorado. When he was enticed by Lee's Ferry tailwater at Glen Canyon Dam he discovered thousands of shrimp (scuds) in a low-water condition and a tier was born. He tied at his first conclave in 1984 and has continued ever since. He is past president of the Easter Rocky Mountain Council and is a founder of the Northern Arizona Fly Casters.

Craig Hull lives in Camp Hill, Pennsylvania. He has tied flies and fly fished since early childhood, which is now very near thirty-five years.

Joe Humphreys is an internationally known fly fisher and fly tier from Boalsburg, Pennsylvania. He has authored books, articles, and videos on a variety of techniques from night fishing for large brown trout to nymph-fishing tips.

David Hunter lives in Salem, Oregon where he enjoys fly fishing for wild trout in the rivers and streams of the Cascade Mountains. He also enjoys tying and fishing for steelhead and is an avid upland bird hunter.

Randy Inmon is an avid fly tier from Frederick, Maryland who works as a landscaper to support his fly fishing and tying addiction.

Misako Ishimura believes in the spiritual benefit of natural surroundings and is therefore active in many conservation projects in the USA and Japan. She currently serves as a director of the Theodore Gordon Fly Fishers, International Women Fly Fishers, and Juliana Berners Anglers. Misako's home waters are Willowemoc Creek and the Beaverkill River where she teaches casting clinics at her home in Roscoe, New York. In 1997, Misako won a NYCTU casting contest and participated as a Team-Japan angler in the 17th Annual World Fly Fishing Championship in Jackson Hole, Wyoming. Her many talents include poetry, nature notes, and painting.

Mike Jacobs has been a member of the Federation of Fly Fishers since 1977, and has been tying flies for over 30 years. He tied flies commercially for many years, but retired from commercial tying to devote more time to his fly tying materials business. Mike has also given free fly tying classes in east central Iowa for over 20 years, and in that time has instructed over 600 new fly tiers.

Gerald M. James began tying flies at the age of twelve in 1953 and began selling them commercially one year later. Professional fly tying was his prime interest for the next thirty-eight years. The last fifteen years he was sole fly tier for E.H. "Polly" Rosborough, originator of the fuzzy body nymph. Gerald ties presentation patterns and operates his fly fishing museum, "Ye Olde Fly Fishing Museum" in Grants Pass, Oregon.

Craig Janssen is from Bozeman, Montana where he makes his living tying flies commercially, guiding, and working in a fly shop.

Kim Jensen is owner and operator of Reel Bugs Custom Flies in South Weber, Utah. He has been tying flies for six year and has won local, national, and international fly tying contests. Kim is a member of the Whiting Farms Pro Team, FFF, and TU. He has tied at several regional and national FFF Conclaves.

John Kimura live in Alturas, California where he works for the California Department of Forestry and Fire protection as a Fire Crew Captain. He is a life member of the FFF who enjoys fishing for both fresh and saltwater species.

Bernard "Lefty" Kreh, very well known and recognized in the fly fishing and fly tying circles, lives in Hunt Valley, Maryland. He travels the world over spreading the fly fishing message. Lefty has published many books and developed even more fly patterns; the most famous of all is the Lefty's Deceiver.

Mel Krieger from San Francisco, California is a very well-known fly caster and the recognized father of the Federation of Fly Fishers' Casting Certification Program. He has published many books and videos about casting but few people realize he is also an accomplished fly tier.

Mike Latschar is a power plant mechanic in Farmington, New Mexico. He discovered fly fishing about six years ago and joined the local FFF Club, the San Juan Fly Fishing Federation, eventually becoming the president. Mike enjoys fishing for trout and warmwater species.

Bob Lay is a Montana fly tier with worldwide fly tying demonstration experience. He specializes in parachute patterns and is a long-time supporter of the Federation of Fly Fishers.

Judy Lehmberg from Dayton, Texas is the 1997 Buz Buszek Memorial Award winner. She ties Atlantic salmon flies for demonstrations and spring creek dries for her own fishing. Judy, an environmental science teacher at Lee College in Baytown, Texas, has held several positions with the FFF including Secretary and Vice President for Education.

B. J. Lester is a psychotherapist in the Boulder, Colorado area. She is a fly fishing guide, certified casting instructor, and fly fishing/fly tying teacher.

Tom H. Logan is from Tallahassee, Florida where he makes his living as a certified wildlife biologist. He likes to pursue warmwater fly fishing and enjoys tying classic trout patterns, which he uses to entice Smoky Mountain trout. Although Tom ties Atlantic salmon flies, his special interest is tying historic and modern soft-hackle patterns.

Ned Long from Tahoe City, California has been tying flies for over fifty years. He demonstrates and teaches his fly tying skills at all levels in the organization and is the recipient of the 1996 Buz Buszek Memorial Award.

Wayne Luallen is from Visalia, California where he has tied all manner of fly types since he began tying in 1974. He has taught fly tying classes in numerous locations around the world. Wayne especially enjoys teaching the "details" of fly tying. He received the Federation of Fly Fishers' Buz Buszek Memorial Fly Tying Award in 1991.

Ronn Lucas makes his home in Milwaukie, Oregon. He offers a unique line of fly tying products like Iridescent Dubbing, Flashback, Foamback, and Crystal Cloth.

Gordon Mankins has tied flies for over fifty years and is best known for his puff ants. He resides in Phoenix, Arizona where he teaches fly tying for local clubs and demonstrates fly tying at FFF Conclaves.

Vladimir Markov lives in Irkutsk, Russia where he enjoys tying and fishing with flies. His patterns are quite original and well worth special notice. Vladimir demonstrated his unusual flies for the first time in the US at the FFF Conclave in Idaho Falls in 1998.

Tommy Marks is from Mount Airy, Maryland where he spends much of his fly fishing time visiting local warmwater fisheries. His specialty is constructing popper and other warmwater type flies using shower shoes for the popper head.

Paul L. Maurer has been tying flies since the eighth grade. Tiers have noted him for using synthetic materials to produce realistic yet durable flies. Paul ties at FFF National and Regional Conclaves. He currently ties commercially and teaches float tube classes at Nicalet Technical College in Rhinelander, Wisconsin.

Mike McCarthy began fly tying and fly fishing at eleven years of age, 45 years ago. He is a Professor of Land Development and Environmental Planning at Texas A&M University near his home in Bastrop, Texas located along Texas' Colorado River.

Katie McEnerney from Bristol, Vermont is just sixteen years old and has already been tying flies for ten years having started at the age of six. Katie recently caught a ten-pound steelhead on a fly rod. When asked what she wanted for Christmas, this attractive young lady's first choice was neoprene waders! It sounds to the authors that this young lady certainly has her head on straight.

Kevin McEnerney lives on the New Haven River in Bristol, Vermont where he has been tying flies for the past thirty years. He has earned recognition around the world for his realistic patterns and artistic deer-hair flies. Kevin has had his work featured in the American Museum of Fly Fishing and in numerous books.

Deke Meyer is a full-time writer from Monmouth, Oregon where he resides with his fly fishing wife Barbara. He has written several hundred fly fishing articles and as of spring 1999 Deke has written nine books about fly tying and fly fishing. His latest book is *Fly Fishing Inflatables*. His next is about the latest in bass flies and tactics.

Robert Meuschke started tying flies after World War II and spent several summers working in Yellowstone Park. He owned the Woodlands Fly Shop in Mendocino, California for many years. Today he makes his home near Mount Shasta and enjoys demonstrating his fly tying skills at various FFF fly tying functions.

Chris Mihulka was born, and still lives, in Springfield, Oregon. In addition to designing fly patterns, he has published still photographs internationally and he is currently producing commercial videos.

L. K. "Buzz" Moss has only tied for a few years but in that time has progressed into a very talented fly tier. He is a contract fly tier for Willow Creek Outfitters in Sandy, Utah.

Chuck Moxley lives in Cortland, Ohio where he makes his living as a veterinarian. He has been a fly tier for twenty-five years and fishes mainly northwestern and central Pennsylvania.

Ross A. Mueller is from Appleton, Wisconsin and is the author of two Midwest fly fishing books, *Upper Midwest Flies That Catch Trout* and *Fly Fishing Midwestern Spring Creeks*. He spends his summers fishing spring creeks and his winters fishing salt water.

Bill Murdich resides in Tampa, Florida, where he designs, tests, and continuously refines fly patterns for fresh and salt water. Bill's background includes degrees in Environmental Conservation and Wildlife Ecology, and practical experience as a fisheries biologist. He has published articles in several magazines and has contributed to the FFF "International Fly Tiers Plate Series."

George Nelson has been fly fishing since the late 50's in the Smoky Mountains of Tennessee and has been fly tying since 1985. Friends and co-workers have discovered George's flies and he keeps busy filling their orders. George has demonstrated his skills for the last three years at the Fly Tying Exposition in Eugene, Oregon.

Larry Nicholas from Troutdale, Oregon is a member and founding president of the Northwest Flyfishers, an affiliate club of the Oregon Council of the Federation of Fly Fishers. He has been a hobby tier for the past fifty years and enjoys tying trout, steelhead, and Atlantic salmon flies. Larry is a career civil engineer who is currently serving as Director, Department of Environmental Services, Multnomah County, Oregon.

Marvin Nolte is a full-time professional fly tier specializing in classic Atlantic salmon flies. In 1995 he received the Federation of Fly Fishers' annual Buz Buszek Memorial Award for fly tying.

John Newbury lives in Chewelah, Washington where he raises exotic game birds. He specializes in tying patterns for stillwater trout and summer-run steelhead. John has been an FFF demonstration fly tier at many Conclaves and exhibitions.

Pat and Carol Oglesby live in Grand Junction, Colorado where they are fly fishing and tying partners as well as husband and wife. They are active in TU and the FFF. Both spend as much time as possible on their home waters, the Gunnison, Colorado, and Roaring Fork rivers.

John Oppenlander is a recreation forester in the Boulder, Colorado ranger district. He is a life-long fly fisher and fly tier.

Don Ordez is from Casper, Wyoming where he operates a highly successful business by day and a fly tying business (Fantasy Flies) by night. He has demonstrated at many regional and national FFF Conclaves and is known for his "extremes" in fly tying—very big flies like a 9/0 mouse and very small flies like a #32 Royal Wulff.

Matt Owens lives in Cedaredge, Colorado where he makes his living as a guide and commercial fly tier. Fly fishers long remember him for his quality trips on the Gunnison River.

Tony Pagliei is a warmwater guide from Lansing, Michigan where he owns and operates BC Outfitters. His fly fishing customers give him praise for his smallmouth bass and common carp guided trips.

Jack L. Pangburn is from Westbury, New York where he is an active member of the Federation of Fly Fishers, Trout Unlimited, United Fly Tyers, and Catskill Fly Tyers Guild. He has won several state, national, and international fly tying contests and has had his patterns published on several occasions. Jack is an Orvis fly tying instructor.

Ted Patlen is a husband, father, and teacher who does not remember not tying flies. He is a seven-time champion of international fly tying competitions and a former N.E.C. Fly Tyer of the Year. For a number of years Ted has demonstrated his ability at many fly fishing/tying functions from Calgary to the Netherlands.

Howard Patterson, age 74, is from Louisville, Kentucky and has fly fished all over the world. He teaches fly fishing for the adult education program in his area. Howard also builds fly rods and owns so many he has lost count and has used them to catch many different kinds of fish ranging in weight up to one-hundred pounds.

Tim Paxton from Eureka, California is a self-taught fly tier who has enjoyed the sport for the past thirty-five years. In 1980 he started Paxton's Buggy Nymph dubbing and this product began his adventures traveling to sporting shows, FFF Conclaves, and exotic fishing locations.

Bob Pelzl has tied flies over thirty years, and for the past twenty-five has conducted clinics and has taught fly fishing throughout the Southwest. He has demonstrated tying skills at Regional and International FFF Conclaves and taught for the Gary Borger Schools at Vermejo Park Ranch, New Mexico for fourteen years. Bob has published articles in *Fly Fishing the West* and *Fly Fisherman* magazines.

Greg Peterka is from Mount Vernon, Washington where he is past president of the Fidalgo Fly Fishers in Anacortes, Washington. He enjoys float tube fishing for trout and stream fishing for steelhead. Greg is a professional engineer for the local water utility and has been a fly fisher since 1988.

Terry Pfannenstiel from Manhattan, Kansas is a professional psychologist and the "mental health monitor" for his local Federation of Fly Fishers organization, the Flint Hills Fly Fishing Club. He is currently writing a book on the various fly fishing maladies that can befall a person—focused more toward the humorous side of the equation. Terry's fly fishing buddies often identify him as the "trout snob" .

Craig Phillips is a supervisory biologist at the Fort Riley military installation near his home in Manhattan, Kansas. A dedicated warmwater fly angler, he has recently focused his efforts on the Kansas tailwater grand slam—a carp, a gar, and a buffalo on the fly rod all in the same day. Craig also enjoys saltwater and trout fishing when he has the opportunity.

Jeff Priest has been fly fishing since a very young age but recently really caught the fly fishing "bug." He joined the Sierra Pacific Fly Fishers and recently became their head casting instructor. In Jeff's spare time you can find him fishing Santa Monica bay from one end to the other.

Andre Puyans is the 1977 recipient of the FFF's Buz Buszek Award for fly tying excellence. He is the innovator of the A.P. Nymph series and developed the loop-wing style. Andre is an author, fly tying authority, and fly fisher with over forty years experience.

Eric Pettine has been tying flies for forty years; the last twenty spent demonstrating at FFF, ISE, and club functions. He is a regular with the Speakers Bureau and is a news columnist and outdoor writer. Watch for two books by Eric due for publication in the near future.

Jeffrey Pierce from Auburn, New York has been fly fishing and tying flies for over fifteen years. He fly fishes for just about anything with fins but focuses most of his attention on trout, salmon, and pike. Jeffrey is the Sales Coordinator for O. Mustad & Son and the Partridge Company.

Ray Radley is from Arcata, California where he has been a fly tier for the past fifty years. His specialty is trout and steelhead flies.

Richard Raisler from Mount Vernon, Washington is president of the Fidalgo Fly Fishers and a director for the Washington State Council of the Federation of Fly Fishers. He enjoys angling for summer-run steelhead and Atlantic salmon using a floating line.

T. D. Relihan is an Orvis-endorsed fly fishing guide from Grand Junction, Colorado. He has been tying for eight years and focuses on patterns that catch fish based on his experience as a guide.

Don Richards makes his home in Helena, Montana where after retiring from the USPS he spends his time tying commercially and working in a fly shop. When not occupied in these two activities you will find him on the Missouri River working a caddis or Trico hatch.

Toby Richardson is from Tyrone, Pennsylvania where he makes his living tying flies and guiding through the Juniata Guide Service. He ties many Dette and other Eastern traditional patterns.

Rainy Riding resides in Logan, Utah where she makes her living running her highly successful fly fishing business, Rainey's Flies & Supplies. She has earned recognition for her innovative fly patterns and foam body material.

Craig Riendeau from Mundelein, Illinois is a fly fishing veteran of over thirty years. He enjoys warmwater species and is an active member of the Dupage River Fly Tyers (DRIFT), a Great River Council club.

Ed Rizzolo has tied flies for more than fifty-five years and has been Chairman of the Fly Tying Committee for the Texas Fly Fishers from Houston, Texas for the past twelve years. The Southern Council awarded him the Teacher of the Year in 1988. Ed enjoys fishing for redfish near his home and his patterns are a favorite of many area anglers

Len Roberts, age fifty-two, made a career change to guiding seven years ago as a matter of survival. He escaped the highly competitive television production industry (including two shows in New York City) to a more leisurely lifestyle in the Florida Keys. After fishing every day for a couple of years he started guiding and designing flies and has not looked back since. Today Len enjoys both guiding and teaching fly tying and fly fishing.

Michael Rogers is a native of Klamath Falls, Oregon where fifteen years ago he made the mistake of catching a North Umpqua summer-run steelhead. His friends and family claim he has not been the same since.

Ted Rogowski is a practicing attorney from Olympia, Washington. As a young fly tier and a member of the Angler's Club of New York he learned and helped develop patterns with fly tying notables such as Lee Wulff and Ernest Schwiebert. His patterns truly are a piece of history.

Ian Russel is from Edmonton, Alberta, Canada where he has enjoyed tying all types of dry and wet flies for the past twenty-eight years. Besides being a member of the FFF, Ian is also a member of the Fly Dresser's Guild and the Grayling Society.

John Ryzanych has spent the last twenty years fishing and instructional guiding the saltwaters of the Pacific Northwest, Mexico, and the South Pacific. As the owner of ICON Products (Softex), John has brought innovative products and fly patterns to the sport of fly fishing.

Scott Sanchez has tied flies for twenty-seven years and taught his first fly tying class at the age of fourteen. He has subsequently worked with Jack Dennis on books/videos. Scott is the star of the video *Understand Fly Tying Materials* and is one of the more innovative fly tiers.

Daniel Schapaugh lives in Manhattan, Kansas where he enjoys fishing for the many species the area has to offer. He also enjoys extended trips to other areas like Canada and the western United States.

John Schaper is a native of Minnesota who now makes his home in Grand Junction, Colorado where he works at Whiting Farms as a hackle grader. He is one of the better fly tiers and a definite expert on feather construction and quality.

Bob Scheidt from Fresno, California has been tying flies for the past twenty-five years but still has not learned to tie on a rotary vise. He prefers tying with natural materials, enjoys teaching others the art of fly tying, and is looking forward to tying nymphs with some of the "hot new products" on the market.

Jack Schlotter retired in 1994 after thirty-five years with the U.S. Forest Service. He is now enjoying life as a full-time fly fisher and fly tier. He is a fly designer for Umpqua Feather Merchants and teaches fly tying classes each winter through the McKenzie Outfitters in his hometown of Medford, Oregon. Jack is a regular participant at the FFF Fly Tying Exposition in Eugene, Oregon each spring.

Dave Schmezer from Latrobe in the Laurel Highlands of Pennsylvania has been tying flies for seven years. He has demonstrated his skills on a local basis, at FFF Conclaves since 1995, and in Volumes 5 and 6 of *Patterns of the Masters*.

Jim Schollmeyer is from Salem, Oregon where he makes his living as an author and photographer for fly fishing and fly tying books. You will note, from his patterns published here, Jim is also a highly skilled fly tier.

Eric Schubert is a retired Los Angeles police officer now making his home in Coeur d' Alene, Idaho where he spends his time fishing the area waters and teaching fly tying with his local FFF club, The North Idaho Fly Casters.

Michael Schweit from Northridge, California started fly fishing in salt water at the age of twelve when he caught his first albacore tuna. He is hooked and continues to enjoy saltwater fly fishing today some fifteen years later.

Jim Shearer is from Kennewick, Washington where he is a retired police officer currently making his living as a commercial fly tier. Jim has demonstrated his tying skills at several Council and National Conclaves.

Tak Shimizu resides in Edmonton, Alberta, Canada and has been tying flies for the past twenty-four years. His specialty for the last ten years has been classic Atlantic salmon flies.

Brian Shumaker is from New Cumberland, Pennsylvania where he is a fly fishing guide for smallmouth bass on the Susquehanna River. He was an exhibitor at the recent Mid Atlantic Council Conclave.

John Simonson started fly tying and fly fishing in the early 1990s. His move to Oregon opened the door for him to learn from fellow Federation of Fly Fishers club members.

Steve Skrubis is originally from Montreal, Quebec, Canada where he was a professional hockey player. He now makes his home in Rochester, New York with his wife Lisa and their new son, Chase. When Steve has time away from his duties as the Manager of Financial Marketing Solutions for Unisys Corporation, he chases big browns, cohos, steelhead, and chinook in nearby Lake Ontario tributaries.

Jerry L. Smalley is a longtime fly tying and casting instructor who lives in the Flathead Valley of Montana. He has been a demonstration fly tier at FFF Conclaves, is a FFF Certified Casting Instructor, and is an active outdoor writer.

Harry Smith is from Santa Ana, California where he has been an avid fly tier and fly fisher for more than fifty years. He has recently developed a style of fishing in which he does not have a hook on his fly; he encourages the fish to "grab and hold" for as long as it can. Around a campfire we often talk about "the one that got away." "All of mine do," says Harry. "It's payback time: I've been trying my whole life to get fish to take a fly, now I won't let them have it!"

Paul "Sodie" Sodamann is the Vice President for Conservation for the Southern Council of the FFF. Aside from being a seventh grade science teacher, Sodie teaches a one-hour fly fishing class for Kansas State University, and owns a small fly shop in St. George, Kansas.

Tony Spezio is from Flippin, Arkansas where he is well known for his custom-tied flies and rod-building/repair.

Shane Stalcup lives in Colorado and has been a commercial fly tier for the past eighteen years, a material manufacturer for the past seven, and has operated a mail order business for the past six years. He eats, sleeps, and thinks of nothing else but fly fishing. Shane enjoys the sport throughout the west with his Labrador buddies - Maggie and Yogi.

Bruce Staples is an international fly tier from Idaho Falls, Idaho. He has served as Conclave Fly Tying Chair and chair of the East Idaho Fly Tying Exposition on several occasions. Bruce is the author of several books.

Dick Steinhorst is a retired petroleum engineer from Lafayette, Louisiana; the heart of Acadiana. He was born in Oklahoma and started warmwater fishing over sixty years ago but did not really pursue the sport until after World War II. Dick started tying flies after moving to Louisiana because no one locally carried anything but popping bugs. He is the founder of the Acadiana Fly Rodders of Lafayette, Louisiana.

Stew Stewart is from Shingletown, California in the heart of the Sierra Nevada Mountain where he enjoys pursuing trout in the area waters. When not fly fishing he makes his living as the owner of the Shingletown Realty.

Paul Stimpson is from Ogden, Utah where he has enjoyed tying flies for the past fifteen years. He is currently tying flies commercially for Arrick's Fly Shop in West Yellowstone, Montana and Wild Country Outfitters in his hometown.

Randy Stonebraker began fly fishing at a young age with his grandfather and father. He enjoys sharing his fly tying skills with others by teaching fly tying classes for the local community college and demonstrating fly tying at local, regional, and FFF national events.

Cliff Stringer caught his first fish on a fly in 1938. He has been going steady ever since. He teaches classes for community schools. Cliff attended his first Conclave in 1973 in Sun Valley, Idaho and tied at his first in Jackson, Wyoming.

Gene Stutzman is from Lebanon, Oregon where he has been tying flies for over thirty-five years. Gene has tied professionally since 1968 and concentrates his fishing time, on the coastal lakes and streams near his home.

Steve Summerhill grew up fly fishing for salmon, trout, and steelhead in his native Alaska. He currently resides in southwest Montana where he is a fly fishing guide and commercial fly tier.

Roger Swengel is a retired dispensing optician living in Poulsbo, on the Olympic Peninsula in Washington State. He has been tying and teaching fly tying for about twenty years.

Mike Telford lives in Fresno, California where he enjoys a variety of cold- and warmwater fishing opportunities. He enjoys designing and tying flies for the varied types of fishing so readily available near his home.

Morgan Thalken is from Sacramento, California where he enjoys tying flies and saltwater fly fishing. He has demonstrated at regional and national FFF Conclaves.

Josh Thames from Mount Airy, Maryland has been tying flies for the past five years. He has been a regular demonstration fly tier at the last three regional Mid Atlantic Council Conclave, a major accomplishment for this fourteen year old.

Jerry Toft is Chief Financial Officer for Whiting Farms, producers of Hoffman & Whiting Hackles. He makes his home in Cedaredge, Colorado.

Adam Trina wetted his first fly at age 10 and was a professional tier by age 13. Since drifting west from Lake Placid to Missoula, Montana in 1991 he has been a professional guide and fly tier.

Tom Tripi has been involved in all aspects of fly fishing for over thirty years. He is a FFF master casting instructor, as well as a master-level fly dresser. Although a professional fly tier and fly designer, his expertise is in exact imitation insect and aquatic flies for exhibits and collectors. Tom is an avid collector and restorer of bamboo fly rods and is actively involved in seminar presentations, writing, wildlife illustration, and astronomy. The New Orleans Fly Fishers selected him as the 1998 Man of the Year.

Gene Trump has earned recognition as an outdoor writer, photographer, and cartoonist from Corvallis, Oregon. His work regularly appears in many fly fishing magazines.

Dan Turner has been tying flies since 1990 and fishing near his home in Thornton, Colorado. The Fryingpan River is his personal favorite. Dan was the Eastern Rocky Mountain Council President for four years and is currently enjoying his retirement.

Charles Vestal has been tying trout flies for nearly fifty years. He specializes in small patterns preferring size sixteen and smaller. Recently Charles has redirected his fly tying in another direction, classic Atlantic salmon flies.

Joe Warren is from Carson, Washington where he regularly fishes the Columbia River. He has authored *Tying Glass Bead Flies* and *Fly Tying with Poly Yarn* (Frank Amato Publications) and has published numerous fly fishing articles. Joe demonstrates his fly tying skills at the International Sportsmen's Expo in Portland, Oregon and at the Oregon Council FFF Northwest Fly Tyer's Expo in Eugene, Oregon.

Eric Wehnes from Jefferson City, Missouri is now fifteen years old and started tying flies five years ago. He is a member of the Capital City Fly Fishers (CCFF) and ties flies and fly fishes to fight boredom. Eric credits his father, Mark Van Patten, and Keith Bolten for his improved fly tying skills.

Steve Weinstein is a part-time outdoor writer and a full-time saltwater fly fishing fanatic. He serves on the Board of Directors for the Mid-Atlantic Council.

Greg Weisgerber is from Gresham, Oregon where he likes to design and tie flies using innovative techniques and materials. He recently demonstrated at the Northwest Fly Tyers Exposition in Eugene, Oregon.

Joyce Westphal is a CRNA (nurse anesthetist) by day and fishing/tying addict the rest of the time. She lives in Provo, Utah with great fishing available on the Provo River, even in the city limits, which makes it easy for her to indulge her favorite sport.

Dave and Emily Whitlock from Midway, Arkansas are very well known to their many fans from all corners of the world. They are long-time Federation members who have demonstrated their many talents at all levels in the organization. The Federation of Fly Fishers gave Dave the 1972 Buz Buszek Memorial Award for fly tying excellence.

Mitch Whitney is a very skilled spun-hair fly tier. He demonstrates fly tying at all levels across the country and at shows near his home in Houston, Texas.

Bob Williams, from Richmond Hill, Ontario, Canada, is an avid fly fisher and fly tier. When he is not going after Atlantic salmon in his native New Brunswick, he spends his time chasing Ontario's rainbow and brook trout.

Robert Williamson is a part-time professional fly tier and free lance writer. His articles have appeared in *Fly Tying*, *Flyfishing & Tying Journal*, and *Utah Fishing & Outdoors* magazines. Robert is the distributor for the O2 Body Material that allows fly tiers to create air-filled flies.

Terry Wilson is a fly fishing author whose articles have appeared in *Warmwater Fly Fishing, The Flyfisher, Bassmaster, Flyfishing & Tying Journal*, and other magazines. With his wife, Roxanne, he authored *Bluegill Fly Fishing and Flies*, released in March 1999 by Frank Amato Publishing, Inc. Terry is the creator of Bully's Bluegill Spider and other warmwater flies that he features in his articles.

Ron Winn is from Melbourne, Florida where he enjoys tying and fishing flies and making his living as a Certified Public Accountant.

Tim Witsman is from Grand Junction, Colorado where he teaches fly tying and operates his business, Bogus Bugs. His motto is quality flies for quality fish. He bases much of his fly tying on information he collects while seining local waters.

Carl E. Wolf is a semi-retired, ex-guide, lecturer, instructor, and workshop leader focusing on aquatic and terrestrial entomology, and fly fishing, tying, and casting. He has held various offices in TU and FFF and has participated in the founding of three fly fishing clubs. Carl is co-author of several books and numerous articles and is currently the Riparian Editor for *The Angler's Journal*. He resides where the Yellowstone and the Bighorn River meet in Montana.

Ralph Wood is a guide on the Yuba, Truckee, and Feather rivers in California's Sierra Nevada Mountains. He has written for *California Flyfisher* and three chapters for *Fly Fishing Northern California* by Seth Norman. Ralph bases his C&R Guide Service out of Grass Valley, California.

Rich Youngers is a professional fly fishing guide who owns Creekside Fly Fishing Shop in Salem, Oregon.

Kurt Zelazny lives in Montrose on the western slope of Colorado and has been a tying and fly fishing addict for years. He enjoys both moving and still water, but has a definite preference for rivers and streams.

Ruth Zinck has tied with the "Master" at eleven FFF Conclaves and served on the WRMC Board for ten years as the Senior VP for Canada. In 1998 she received the Fly Tier of the Year award from her Council. Ruth is a member of the Women's Fly Fishing Association of Alberta. She teaches fly tying at the Casting for Life Retreats organized by that organization. She created the Royal Lady especially for the breast cancer survivors who attend these weekends. The colors of this beginner's fly are significant; black to remember, pink for survival, and white for hope.

Lance Zook started tying flies with a couple of books from the library and a handful of improvised tools and materials. He joined the Hawkeye Fly Fishing Association in 1991 and eventually started writing a club newsletter column called "The Fly Line".

Pattern Index